PAPERS AND PROCEEDINGS

Transitions in Work and Learning

Implications for Assessment

Alan Lesgold, Michael J. Feuer, and Allison M. Black, Editors

Board on Testing and Assessment
Commission on Behavioral and Social Sciences and Education
National Research Council

NATIONAL ACADEMY PRESS
Washington, D.C.   1997

NATIONAL ACADEMY PRESS • 2101 Constitution Avenue, NW • Washington, DC 20418

NOTICE: The project that is the subject of this report was approved by the Governing Board of the National Research Council, whose members are drawn from the councils of the National Academy of Sciences, the National Academy of Engineering, and the Institute of Medicine. The members of the committee responsible for the report were chosen for their special competences and with regard for appropriate balance.

This report has been reviewed by a group other than the authors according to procedures approved by a Report Review Committee consisting of members of the National Academy of Sciences, the National Academy of Engineering, and the Institute of Medicine.

This study was supported by Grant No. K43173008060 between the National Academy of Sciences and the National Office of School-to-Work Opportunities, U.S. Department of Education. Any opinions, findings, conclusions, or recommendations expressed in this publication are those of the author(s) and do not necessarily reflect the view of the organizations or agencies that provided support for the project.

Library of Congress Cataloging-in-Publication Data

Transitions in work and learning : implications for assessment / Alan
    Lesgold, Michael J. Feuer, and Allison M. Black, editors.
        p.   cm.
    Papers presented at a conference in March 1996.
    "Board on Testing and Assessment, Commission on Behavioral and
Social Sciences and Education, National Research Council."
    Includes bibliographical references.
    ISBN 0-309-06365-5 (pbk).
    1. Vocational evaluation—United States. 2. School-to-work
transition—United States. 3. Vocational education—United States.
4. Occupational training—United States. 5. Labor market—United
States. I. Lesgold, Alan M. II. Feuer, Michael J. III. Black,
Allison M. IV. National Research Council (U.S.). Commission on
Behavioral and Social Sciences and Education. Board on Testing and
Assessment.
LC1048.V63.T73 1997
370.11′3′0973—dc21
                                                            97-21176
                                                            CIP

Additional copies of this report are available from the National Academy Press, 2101 Constitution Avenue, NW, Lock Box 285, Washington, DC 20055. (800) 624-6242 or (202) 334-3313 in the Washington Metropolitan Area. Internet, http://www.nap.edu

Printed in the United States of America

VOLUME CONTRIBUTORS

LARRY CUBAN, School of Education, Stanford University

MICHAEL J. FEUER, Board on Testing and Assessment, National Research Council

HARRY J. HOLZER, Department of Economics, Michigan State University

GLYNDA HULL, College Writing Programs, University of California, Berkeley

ALAN LESGOLD, Learning Research and Development Center, University of Pittsburgh

ROBERT J. MISLEVY, Educational Testing Service, Princeton, NJ

BONALYN NELSON, School of Industrial and Labor Relations, Cornell University

DENNIS PARKER, NAACP Legal Defense and Education Fund, New York, NY

KENNETH PEARLMAN, Lucent Technologies, Sarasota, FL

LAUREN B. RESNICK, Learning Research and Development Center, University of Pittsburgh

NEAL SCHMITT, School of Education, Michigan State University

RICHARD J. SHAVELSON, School of Education, Stanford University

ROBERT ZEMSKY, Institute for Research on Higher Education, University of Pennsylvania

HJH4@ GEORGETOWN. EDU

ACKNOWLEDGMENTS

Many members of the Board on Testing and Assessment helped in the design of the March 1996 conference and in the review of the papers included in this volume. We are especially grateful to Alan Lesgold, who chaired the conference and whose active involvement in all aspects of the board's work has been invaluable. In addition to chairing the conference, Alan contributed his own paper, which provides a particularly enriching blend of ideas about the current and future status of work and testing. Board members Lauri Bassi, Art Goldberger, Bob Linn, Carl Kaestle, Paul Sackett, Bill Taylor, and Jack Whalen played a major role in framing the conference, reading the papers, and offering invaluable commentary. Former board members James Outtz and Brigitte Jordan also provided important guidance and commentary. We are grateful to all these individuals for their tireless efforts on behalf of the board.

The board also asked an outside group of experts to serve on an ad hoc advisory committee. We thank Vicki Vanderveer, David Grissmer, and Anne Borthwick for their time, energy, and excellent contributions.

BOTA staff member Allison Black was primarily responsible for the difficult and complex tasks of managing the editorial and logistical aspects of the book. Karen Mitchell read early drafts and helped in numerous important ways.

Finally, we wish to acknowledge the National Office of School-to-Work Opportunities for its interest in and financial support of this project. In particular, Nevzer Stacey deserves special credit for her unflagging dedication to the principle that good human resources policy deserves (and requires) good science.

Richard J. Shavelson, *Chair*
Michael J. Feuer, *Director*
Board on Testing and Assessment

The National Academy of Sciences is a private, nonprofit, self-perpetuating society of distinguished scholars engaged in scientific and engineering research, dedicated to the furtherance of science and technology and to their use for the general welfare. Upon the authority of the charter granted to it by the Congress in 1863, the Academy has a mandate that requires it to advise the federal government on scientific and technical matters. Dr. Bruce M. Alberts is president of the National Academy of Sciences.

The National Academy of Engineering was established in 1964, under the charter of the National Academy of Sciences, as a parallel organization of outstanding engineers. It is autonomous in its administration and in the selection of its members, sharing with the National Academy of Sciences the responsibility for advising the federal government. The National Academy of Engineering also sponsors engineering programs aimed at meeting national needs, encourages education and research, and recognizes the superior achievements of engineers. Dr. William A. Wulf is president of the National Academy of Engineering.

The Institute of Medicine was established in 1970 by the National Academy of Sciences to secure the services of eminent members of appropriate professions in the examination of policy matters pertaining to the health of the public. The Institute acts under the responsibility given to the National Academy of Sciences by its congressional charter to be an adviser to the federal government and, upon its own initiative, to identify issues of medical care, research, and education. Dr. Kenneth I. Shine is president of the Institute of Medicine.

The National Research Council was organized by the National Academy of Sciences in 1916 to associate the broad community of science and technology with the Academy's purposes of furthering knowledge and advising the federal government. Functioning in accordance with general policies determined by the Academy, the Council has become the principal operating agency of both the National Academy of Sciences and the National Academy of Engineering in providing services to the government, the public, and the scientific and engineering communities. The Council is administered jointly by both Academies and the Institute of Medicine. Dr. Bruce M. Alberts and Dr. William A. Wulf are chairman and vice chairman, respectively, of the National Research Council.

Contents

Transitions in Work and Learning

1

Introduction

Michael J. Feuer and Richard J. Shavelson

The American labor market is experiencing a dramatic transition. Between 1970 and 1993 the proportion of all U.S. workers employed in manufacturing fell by 41 percent, from 27 percent of total employed to 16 percent. In one year alone, 1992-1993, 40 million new jobs were created in the nonfarm sector, while some 238,000 manufacturing jobs were lost. The shift has clearly been in the direction of employment that relies on a different mix of skills. For example, as reported by the Bureau of Labor Statistics (U.S. Department of Commerce,1994), the fastest-growing occupations include home health aides, physical therapy aides, computer engineers, and scientists; the fastest-declining occupations are frame wirers, signal or track switch maintainers, and central office operators.

At the same time, the distribution of earnings among U.S. workers has shifted dramatically. On average, male high school graduates aged 25-34 earned 15 percent less in 1989 than in 1979 (Levy and Murnane, 1992). And the gap between the earnings of high school and college graduates grew from 13 to 43 percent between 1982 and 1992.

These shifts have contributed to a growing sense of alarm about the capacity of the nation's schools to supply adequately skilled graduates to the work force. Indeed, concern with long-term productivity and competitiveness has been a principal force behind the wave of education reform efforts that began in the mid-1980s. But the role that schools can or should play in preparing people to enter the world of work is hotly debated. Business leaders tend to lament the low skill

This chapter draws on the published conference summary, *Transitions in Work and Learning: Implications for Assessment* (Washington, DC: National Academy Press, 1996).

levels of entry-level workers but are often unclear about exactly what skills are most important; educators tend to challenge the notion that their principal objective should be to supply skilled laborers, even as many of them recognize the public's historical faith in schools as the gateway to good jobs and a high standard of living. With nearly constant reminders of the economic revolution affecting all industrial societies, questions about how to define and measure workplace competencies, how to establish skill requirements, and how to create incentives for teaching and learning in schools and work establishments have again risen to the fore. The central questions are often posed with deceiving simplicity:

- How is work changing?
- What skills are required to perform productive work?
- What methods are needed to provide accurate information about the supply of skills and employers' demands?
- What are the effects of using tests and other indicators of performance on efficient and equitable functioning of labor markets?

To help nurture the important and ongoing national dialogue on these issues, the National Research Council's Board on Testing and Assessment convened a two-day conference in March 1996, at which a group of researchers and policy makers engaged in an interdisciplinary review and discussion of available data and implications for assessment policy. This activity reflects on one of the board's principal mandates: to foster high-level scientific deliberations on public policy issues that involve the design, uses, and effects of testing and assessment technologies.

The board commissioned a set of papers for the conference that, together, offer a uniquely cross-cutting view of the evolving role of assessment in fostering both improved learning and clearer signaling of individuals' skills. The authors were asked to draw on their own research expertise and to consider the implications of their work for the more general questions surrounding education, training, and school-to-work policies.

The papers in this volume are grouped into five parts, following the format of the conference. Part I consists of two papers that raise the fundamental underlying question: Does empirical evidence support the claim of a skills mismatch in the U.S. economy? Expressed differently, are changes in the organization and output of work in the U.S. economy creating a demand for skills that are not adequately provided by the existing education system?

In his paper, Harry Holzer reports that economic returns to education have risen dramatically in recent years and argues that the supply of skilled workers has not kept pace with the shifting labor market demand for higher levels of educational attainment. Although this short-run imbalance could theoretically be overcome in the long term if employers and workers invest in appropriate education and training, Holzer cautions against overreliance on the market's capacity for self-correction. Among the policies that he urges exploration of are those that can improve the quality and flow of information between the education and work sectors, which suggests the need for test-based data that signal the skills that young workers should acquire and that provide employers with reliable information about workers' likely future productivity.

In Chapter 2, Robert Zemsky offers a different perspective on the skills gap hypothesis. He argues that most employers do not believe that schools can fulfill their needs, no longer look to the schools as a fertile ground for future employees, and would prefer to rely on an older cohort of workers with labor market experience. Taking issue with those who point to a lack of communication between schools and workplaces as the principal explanation of weaknesses in the American school-to-work transition system, Zemsky argues that employers are typically unable to articulate what skills they need, so that even if better communication links were established the content of the communications would still be inadequate. In his view, employers resort to a "trial-and-error" hiring strategy, reserving the best jobs for those with significant prior experience. Zemsky claims this is a contributing factor to the phenomenon of labor market "churning" wherein young workers spend many years after formal schooling moving into and out of various jobs.

Part II of the volume moves the discussion from the macroperspective of aggregate economic and survey data into a detailed microlevel exploration of the changing nature of jobs in specific workplaces. The papers by Bonalyn Nelsen and Glynda Hull represent the increasingly important ethnographic perspective on labor markets, which adds richness and texture to discussions about the skill demands of employers, the organization of education and training, and the possible effects of alternative assessment and credentialing strategies. Nelsen reports on her research on automobile repair technicians and offers evidence that on-the-job learning is a necessary step in becoming a top-level repair technician and that such learning builds on social skills as well as more traditional academic skills. Her paper underscores the importance of including measures of "social capital"—skills and knowledge required to evaluate and respond to situational demands in social settings—in studies of changing skill demands and the educational implications.

Similarly, Hull focuses on a particular type of workplace—electronics factories in Silicon Valley. Her main argument is that literacy skills are critical in the definition of high-performance workplaces. For example, reorganization of the electronics factory into a high-performance workplace with work teams had an enormous effect on the literacy requirements of front-line workers engaging in circuit assembly. Especially in multilingual workplaces, Hull argues, "a literate identity is an important aspect of a worker's sense of [self]." Based on her ethnographic study, she concludes that requirements for formal, informal, written, and oral communications are changing significantly as companies become high-performance work organizations. Her suggestion that workers with limited English language skills can develop compensatory mechanisms for effective com-

munication with co-workers and supervisors points to the need for careful definition of "literacy" in the context of workplace performance and productivity.

Part III addresses the implications of changing workplaces for the assessment and measurement of skills. Robert Mislevy's principal suggestion is that
assessment tools need to be developed that more accurately reflect real-world
situations in which learning takes place. Mislevy argues that increasing heteroge-
neity in the workplace demands that assessment tools provide fair and accurate
information on a wide range of skills and abilities and that tests alone cannot
measure abilities independent of cultural and other factors that influence the
effectiveness of learning environments.

Kenneth Pearlman concentrates on the manager's perspective of screening
and selection decisions and on the importance of "cross-functional skills," such
as organizing, planning, decision making, negotiating, and teamwork, in the
evolving high-performance workplace. Pearlman suggests that assessment and
learning need to be tightly integrated activities and argues for the creation of
"programs that integrate, motivate, and reward development of [cross-functional]
skills in K-12 education."

How will changing definitions and requirements of work, coupled with new
approaches to selection, screening, and assessment, be constrained by the legal
and social environment? This was the basic question posed in the fourth session
of the conference, which included papers by Dennis Parker and Neil Schmitt.
Parker calls attention to the purpose of the School-to-Work Opportunities Act—
to improve the school-to-work transitions of *all* students. The goal of greater
inclusion holds important implications for testing and assessment. On the one
hand, linking schools and workplaces more tightly suggests a significant role for
testing as a means of evaluating the extent to which young people have acquired
the requisite skills; but as Parker notes, schools and school districts must be
aware of the legal and social issues that surround the use of tests as gatekeepers
for employment opportunity.

In his paper, Schmitt discusses the formidable challenge of using valid assessments to achieve a capable and diverse work force within the constraints of
the 1991 Civil Rights Act. His paper offers five approaches to meeting the
challenge: (1) include additional measures of job-related constructs that have
little or no adverse impact; (2) change the format of questions or the types of
responses required; (3) use computer or video technology to present test items;
(4) employ procedures currently used in education, such as portfolios and "authentic" assessments; and (5) change the way scores are used and interpreted and
consider the use of "bands" rather than cut scores and rankings. Schmitt is
guardedly optimistic about the combined effects of these strategies but argues for
continued exploration of new assessment methods well suited to the changing
demands of work and learning.

Part V of this volume offers three overarching perspectives on the evolving
literature and policy debate over school-to-work transitions and the roles of as-

sessment. Larry Cuban urges greater consideration of the historical and political contexts of the policy debate. Lauren Resnick advocates the possibility of strengthening human intellectual capacity by employing an effort-based school-to-work system. Alan Lesgold offers the perspective of a cognitive psychologist and provides a provocative set of suggestions stemming from research on the types of knowledge necessary and useful in various work contexts.

Among Cuban's key suggestions is that the role of teachers be kept in sharp focus: to argue that schools must change, he notes, means that teachers must "alter [their] behavior in ways to make learning better for students." But, he warns, if one accepts the basic premise that schools are responsible for young people's transitions to work, it follows that those who have caused the existing problem (teachers) are also the ones expected to bring about the solution.

Resnick suggests an alternative effort-based approach to our nation's present system of education and its accompanying modes of entry into the work force, which, according to her, is designed around the belief that talent and ability are largely inherited and fixed. Resnick posits that it is our current approach to educational practice and not our teachers that is the cause of existing problems. Implementation of the effort-based system Resnick describes would provide some remedy for what she views as a two-tiered education system driven by our perceptions of students' talent and ability.

Lesgold, too, draws attention to the conflicting and potentially incompatible demands placed on schools and teachers. He notes, for example, that while teamwork and quick thinking are often cited as critical parts of modern work, these are not necessarily the kinds of skills and abilities that schools are expected to emphasize: indeed, whether teamwork and quick thinking can be made compatible with other goals of education—individual and independent thinking, careful (often necessarily slow) experimentation with new ideas—raises a serious issue for policy makers aiming for better links between the worlds of formal schooling and postsecondary learning and work environments.

The papers in this volume make a significant contribution to our understanding of the complex and interlocking issues of changing work, learning, and assessment. They provide the conceptual frameworks and empirical bases necessary for inquiry into the pressing issues surrounding transitions into and between learning and work environments. The Board on Testing and Assessment plans to continue to serve as a focal point for these issues.

REFERENCES

U.S. Department of Commerce
    1994   *Statistical Abstract of the United States: The National Data Book.* Washington, DC: U.S. Department of Commerce.
Levy, F., and R.J. Murnane
    1992   U.S. earnings levels and earnings inequality: A review of recent trends and proposed explanations. *Journal of Economic Literature* 30:1333-1381.

2

Is There a Gap Between Employer Skill Needs and the Skills of the Work Force?

Harry J. Holzer

INTRODUCTION

Discussions in the popular press and in the policy-making community frequently imply that there is a "skills gap" in the U.S. economy—a gap between the skills needed by employers and the skills of workers in the labor force. Because of this alleged gap, a wide range of policies involving education and job training are frequently advocated by various groups and individuals. But what is the evidence that such a gap truly exists? And if it does, what skills are in particularly short supply in the work force? The latter question has been especially difficult to answer, at least partly because of a lack of available quantitative data on employers and their needs.

"SKILLS GAPS" IN THE WORK FORCE: CONCEPTUAL ISSUES

If a gap truly exists between the skills that employers need and those held by the work force, can this be inferred? What would be the likely economic effects of such a gap? Why might the choices of employers and employees with respect to skill acquisition still result in such a gap?

Mismatches in the Short and the Long Run

In recent years there has been much discussion among various social scientists of a skills mismatch in the work force, with the implication that this helps to account for the low employment rates of such groups as inner-city minorities (Wilson, 1987; Kasarda, 1995). Indeed, *mismatch* is another term for what economists have often called structural unemployment, a situation in which jobs are actually available but unemployed workers cannot be hired because they lack the necessary skills, reside in the wrong area, and the like. (For a very recent description of "structural unemployment" in an introductory text, see Case and Fair, 1996.)

But unemployment is not the only possible result of such a situation. To an economist, mismatch suggests a gap between the demand and supply sides of the labor market—that is, between employers and prospective employees—terms of some particular characteristic. Thus, a skills mismatch might arise because the demand for workers with certain skills (such as higher education) has increased more rapidly than the supply of such workers.

Figure 2.1A illustrates the results of such a shift in demand from less educated workers to more educated ones. As the figure shows, the demand shift should result in both lower wages and lower employment among the less educated in the short run (and the opposite for the more educated), with the exact effects depending on the elasticity of the labor supply—that is, the responsiveness of the supply of workers to wage levels.[1] The lower this is the smaller will be the loss of employment and the greater the loss of wages for this group.[2]

Thus, widening wage and/or employment gaps between education groups could be interpreted as a sign that relative demands have shifted between them and that some degree of mismatch exists. Widening gaps in earnings or employment between specific demographic groups with more or less education (such as blacks and whites) could also result, and, even within a group whose members have comparable amounts of education, widening gaps for other dimensions of skills (such as those measured by test scores) could also indicate relative shifts in labor demand.

This analysis is strictly short run in nature. The new and higher wage gap between education groups would imply a higher return to investment in that particular skill, which should lead to greater enrollment in higher education (Becker, 1975). In the long run the relative supply of educated workers should gradually shift out while the relative supply of less educated workers should diminish (Figure 2.1B). This will, in turn, reduce the wage gaps between the two groups.

---

[1]This analysis assumes that the market was in equilibrium to begin with and that it will be so after the demand shifts occur. If wages are rigid, especially in the downward direction for less educated workers, the result would be somewhat less reduction in wages and somewhat more loss of employment (and a rise in unemployment) among less educated workers, but the overall implications of the analysis still hold.

[2]The elasticity of the labor supply is reflected in the shape of the labor supply curve; the steeper the curve, the lower this elasticity is. A low elasticity implies that people will choose to work regardless of the wage level, while a higher elasticity implies that people will choose not to work at low wage levels.

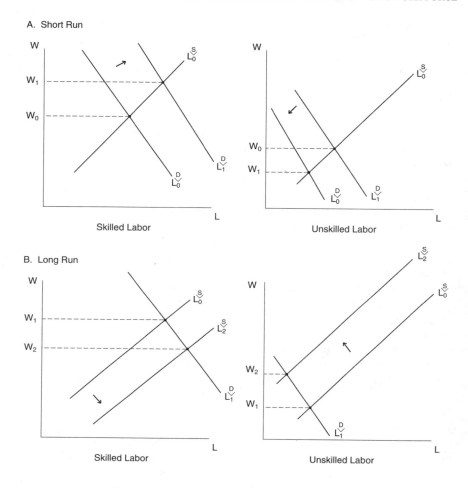

Note: W = wages. L^S = labor supply. L^D = labor demand.

FIGURE 2-1 Shifts in demand for skills and supply adjustments in the labor market.

The adjustment process could continue until the gap in earnings between the two groups is restored to its initial level. Alternatively, the initial gap might not be reached if (1) the demand for skills continues to increase and to outpace supply adjustments or (2) there are barriers or costs that limit the magnitudes of the supply adjustments. The second situation might, for instance, occur if too few students who graduate from high school have academic backgrounds that are strong enough for them to consider enrolling in college. Furthermore, the rising costs of attending college, combined with cuts in financial assistance for lower-

and middle-income families, could limit enrollments of students from such families (Kane, 1995).

Other imperfections in capital and labor markets might tend to reinforce these factors, leading to investments in higher education that are too small to restore earlier differentials between groups.[3] In this case the wage and employment effects of mismatch will persist, even in the long run.

Finally, higher unemployment (as opposed to just lower employment) can also result from labor market mismatch.[4] This will occur if (1) there are rigidities (such as minimum-wage laws) that keep wages among the less educated from fully adjusting to the lower equilibrium levels shown in Figure 2.1A or (2) the less educated prefer to keep searching for better jobs, rather than accepting jobs with lower wages.[5] In both cases, one would expect to find the coexistence of (1) higher job vacancy rates for at least some firms and (2) higher unemployment rates for workers.[6]

Employer Choices: Hiring, Training, and Other Options

At least in theory, employers' skill needs are not fixed or absolute, and employers have a greater degree of choice over what they need than they might acknowledge. In the long run, employers choose among different levels of capital and technology that imply varying needs for skilled versus unskilled labor. For instance, a decision to replace production workers with some type of capital

---

[3]These other market imperfections include liquidity constraints on individuals (so that people are unable to borrow for college education today against their expected future earnings), planning horizons that are too short, and inaccurate expectations of future wages that understate returns to education. Of course, a different set of inaccurate expectations could just as easily lead to *over*investment in education (relative to what is "socially optimal"), as could a variety of other circumstances in which education merely serves as a sorting or signaling device rather than as a productivity-raising investment. For a recent statement of the latter arguments, see Weiss (1995).

[4]Lower employment could exist without higher unemployment if those without work withdraw from the labor force altogether. The issue of whether the distinction between being in and being out of the labor force makes sense for all those without work has been debated by economists in recent years (e.g., Clark and Summers, 1982; Flinn and Heckman, 1993).

[5]The issue of whether or not minimum wages contribute to unemployment among low-wage workers continues to be debated among economists (e.g., Card and Krueger, 1994; Neumark and Wascher, 1995). If their higher unemployment is due to longer periods of job search, this might be attributable to higher *reservation* (or minimally acceptable) wages among workers rather than government barriers in the labor market (e.g., Feldstein and Poterba, 1984).

[6]A skills mismatch would certainly result in high vacancy rates for jobs requiring more skills; if less skilled workers then refuse to accept lower-wage jobs, vacancy rates would rise for jobs requiring fewer skills as well. While there have been some analyses of job vacancy rates over time or across areas and job categories in the United States (e.g., Abraham, 1983; Holzer, 1989, 1994), such data are not routinely collected by the U.S. government; therefore such analyses are quite rare.

equipment will change employers' relative demands across skill categories. Workplace organization and job descriptions are clearly malleable over a long-term time horizon, and employers frequently make choices about whether or not to upgrade hiring requirements along educational or experience dimensions (e.g., Levy and Murnane, 1995).

Even in the short run, with a given set of jobs, employers face a variety of choices regarding needed skills. For instance, employers who have difficulty filling vacant jobs could attract more (and presumably better-qualified) applicants by choosing to pay higher wages.[7] Alternatively, firms could invest more in recruiting, through advertising or the use of employment agencies (Holzer, 1987).

Finally, employers could generate more highly skilled employees by training the workers they hire, rather than demanding applicants who have certain skills ex ante. Clearly, the strategies of increasing wage levels or recruitment might only redistribute a fixed number of skilled workers among employers; the strategy of training workers would help to generate a higher overall level of skill in the work force.

Firms can choose how much training to invest in employees on the basis of prospective market returns for such training through, for example, higher employee productivity. If the skills employers hope to generate are completely *general*—that is, can be used in many types of work settings—they will generally choose not to bear the costs of such training since employee turnover may cause them to lose their investments. In this case, employers will provide such training only if they can transfer the costs to employees (by paying them lower wages) or can reduce turnover (through apprenticeships, etc.). As the skills needed become more *specific* to an industry, an occupation, and, especially, an individual firm, employers should be more willing to share in these costs (Becker, 1975).

But a firm's willingness to make these investments might be limited by a variety of market imperfections, such as wage rigidities, financial constraints, and short-term planning horizons.[8] Furthermore, the provision of training might actually cause employers to *raise,* rather than lower, their ex ante skill requirements if they view certain personal skills as being *complements* to, rather than *substitutes* for, the ones they hope to provide through training. (See, e.g., Lynch, 1992, and Cappelli, 1996, for some mixed evidence on this issue.)

The training choices of firms might therefore reinforce gaps or mismatches

---

[7]The notion that it might be cost effective for firms to pay wages above the market level has been emphasized in the economics literature on "efficiency wages" (e.g., Katz, 1986) and in the human resources literature. But for many firms a low-wage/high-turnover policy might still be the most efficient strategy.

[8]For instance, minimum-wage laws may prevent firms from paying lower wages to employees while they are training them, which may make firms reluctant to invest in such training at all. Liquidity constraints on a firm (from limitations on its ability to borrow) or pressure from stockholders to stress short-term profitability rather than long-term growth might similarly reduce a firm's training investments. See Lynch (1993).

between their own skill needs and those of less educated workers, instead of helping to mitigate those gaps.

Inferring Applicants' Skills

Employers might have a clear sense of what tasks need to be performed on their jobs and what skills and personal characteristics are necessary for performing those tasks. But those skills are often not directly *observable* to an employer at the time of hiring. In other words, the employer will often not know very much about an applicant's prospective ability to perform well on the job. Therefore, employers look for a variety of personal credentials, such as level of education, previous job training or work experience, and references. During interviews, they also look for a variety of personal characteristics, such as social and verbal skills and attitude. Other screens, such as tests (either of cognitive abilities or specific job tasks), are sometimes used as well.

An applicant's personal characteristics or test results are used as *signals* or predictors of future productivity on the job, rather than considered to be indicators per se of the skills required for job performance. Of course, the ability of these credentials and characteristics to actually predict job performance may be quite limited (Bishop, 1993). Employers' perceptions of some of them, especially attitudes, are inherently subjective and could lead to discriminatory hiring outcomes as well. Indeed, at least some firms are aware of potential legal constraints on their ability to use certain screens that they cannot tie directly to job performance.[9]

More generally, the costs to employers of obtaining various kinds of information (such as school grades, transcripts, and criminal background checks) might outweigh the information's potential usefulness, thereby discouraging employers from seeking information that would better enable them to judge worker quality.[10] Thus, mismatches between jobs and workers could result from employers' lacking *information* that would enable them to identify skilled applicants as well

---

[9]These constraints arise out of the 1971 U.S. Supreme Court decision in *Griggs v. Duke Power* (401 U.S. 424, 1971), which established that hiring procedures that have "disparate impacts" on the employment of whites and minorities create a prima facie case for discrimination and require the employer to establish some link between these procedures and employee performance on the job. These principles were reaffirmed in the Civil Rights Act of 1992. Of course, firms differ greatly in the extent to which they think they are subject to such legal constraints; for instance, large firms appear much more concerned than smaller firms (Holzer, 1996).

[10]Bishop (1989) has argued that employers would use academic grades to evaluate applicants (and students would have more incentive to perform better in high school) if transcripts were more easily attainable from high schools. Bushway (1995) also argues that the costs of doing checks on criminal backgrounds dissuade many employers from doing so and may actually hurt the wages of young black males, who are often generally suspected of having criminal records.

as from low overall *skill* levels among applicants.[11] Both of these problems can stem from "market failures" in private-sector labor markets, and a variety of policy interventions may be appropriate if evidence of these problems is found in labor market data.

GENERAL ECONOMIC EVIDENCE

The above discussion suggests that, when the demand for certain skills grows relative to their supply in the labor market, those skills will generate higher returns (at least in the short run). Therefore, one way of making inferences about "skill gaps" is to review the general empirical evidence on labor market returns to various skills and how they have changed over time.

Returns to Education

The simplest and most easily observable measure of labor market skill is the number of years of schooling and educational degrees that an individual has obtained. On this dimension the evidence is strong and very clear: the returns to education have risen quite dramatically in recent years. For instance, in 1979 the average weekly earnings for young college graduates were about 45 percent of those for high school graduates; by the late 1980s the ratio had risen to about 85 percent (Katz and Murphy, 1992).

This rising gap in earnings between more and less educated workers has coincided with a dramatic decline in the real hourly earnings of less educated males, especially among the young. Thus, the real wages of male high school graduates between the ages of 25 and 34 declined by over 20 percent from the late 1970s to the late 1980s (Katz and Murphy, 1992); the declines for male high school dropouts were even larger. In contrast, real wages rose modestly for young males with college or higher degrees and rose substantially for college-educated young females (Bound and Holzer, 1995). (The gender gap in earnings declined at all levels of education during the 1980s, even while inequality was growing across other dimensions. See Blau and Kahn, 1994, for explanations of why this might have occurred.)

These changes in relative and real wages across groups parallel the changes that have occurred in employment rates (or annual hours worked). Basically, employment and labor force participation rates have risen for young females, especially the more educated, while they have declined quite substantially for male high school dropouts and blacks (Juhn, 1992; Bound and Holzer, 1995). The falling employment rates for young and less educated black males have also

---

[11]These microlevel mismatches because of poor information could also result in higher vacancy rates in skilled job categories or high turnover rates, where the latter occur as employers (or employees) realize they made "errors" in the hiring process.

coincided with a rapid rise in criminal activity and incarceration rates for them, especially relating to the drug trade (Freeman, 1994; Piehl, 1995).

Overall, this pattern of falling employment and wages for the less educated and rising employment and wages for the more educated strongly suggests that employers' demands have shifted toward workers with higher education more rapidly than the relative supplies of the two groups have been able to adjust. Indeed, relative increases in the supply of college graduates actually slowed during the late 1970s and early 1980s, reflecting an earlier drop in college enrollment rates as well as the declining number of young people in the "baby bust" cohort. These enrollment drops appear to have contributed to the market premiums that college graduates have enjoyed (Katz and Murphy, 1992). More recent evidence suggests that enrollment rates have recovered somewhat since then (in response to the rising returns for education) and are likely to continue to rise (Mincer, 1994). But few observers expect these increases to be sufficient to fully reverse the recent increases in earnings gaps between education groups, especially since the relative demand for college-educated workers will continue to grow (Bishop, 1995).

Why does the demand for workers with higher education continue to rise? Growing international competition and the exodus of manufacturing plants from the United States to lower-wage areas are frequently mentioned as major reasons for these changes. But these labor market changes have occurred in nonmanufacturing (or nontraded goods and services) as well as manufacturing industries; even among the latter, most of the changes have occurred *within* particularized manufacturing industries rather than *between* industries whose relative employment levels are affected by trade (Berman et al., 1994; Freeman, 1995a).

The most likely suspect for this shift in employer demand is a rapid increase in the pace at which employers have implemented various *technological changes*. Computer-related technologies (such as CAD-CAM and robotics) have clearly transformed many manufacturing processes. At the individual level, computer use is clearly correlated with higher educational attainment or wage levels among workers (Krueger, 1993), and at the industry level, industries in which technological changes have been most rapid have also experienced the largest declines in employment among less educated production workers (Berman et al., 1994).

Of course, technological change need not always be "biased" toward more highly educated workers (Goldin and Katz, 1995), and examples can certainly be found of computers leading to lower rather than higher skill requirements for workers. But, on average, rising capital intensity and technological improvement seem more likely to be associated with higher demand for educated labor in the United States (Bartel and Lichtenberg, 1987; Hamermesh, 1993). Changes in the organization of production that at least some firms have chosen to undertake, such as total quality management and other "high-performance" workplace activities, might also increase employers' demand for education (e.g., Ichniowski et al., 1995; Cappelli, 1995b, 1996). A variety of industry case studies seem to corroborate that this occurs with technological change and/or workplace reorganization (e.g., Bureau of Labor Statistics, 1984, 1986; Bailey, 1990; Levy and Murnane, 1995).

Thus, the data strongly suggest that employer demand for more educated workers has risen relative to their supplies in recent years. The case for a skills gap or mismatch in education levels can therefore be made. This is true even though overall unemployment levels in the United States are not high, especially relative to European countries. Apparently, the relative demand shifts in this country have largely resulted in low wages for the less educated (except among high school dropouts and young blacks, as noted above), while in Europe they have mostly resulted in lower employment rates (e.g., Freeman and Katz, 1994).[12]

Finally, there appears to have been no strong trend toward greater or lesser overall job stability in recent years, as measured by turnover rates or job tenure (i.e., time with a single employer). However, average tenure has declined somewhat among the lowest-wage employees. Whatever the causes of these trends, they certainly do not imply a greater willingness among employers to invest in job training for their low-tenure employees.[13]

A variety of caveats might be mentioned here. For one thing, although not all young college graduates will easily find employment, especially at relatively high wages (Hecker, 1992), they are, on average, a good deal more likely to do so than are those without college degrees, and the gaps between the abilities of these two groups to do so have certainly risen in the past 10 to 15 years (Bishop, 1995; Murnane, 1995). Furthermore, the rising relative demand for college-educated workers is not the only reason for the declining wages of the less educated. Falling rates of union membership, falling real minimum wage levels, and rising immigration all appear to have contributed to this development (e.g., Freeman, 1995c; Dinardo et al., 1995; Jaeger, 1995). Furthermore, the rise in labor market inequality has occurred even *within* education groups as well as within every other observable demographic category, and these increases remain not well understood (Levy and Murnane, 1992).

Finally, the falling wages of less educated workers in the United States reflect

---

[12]On the other hand, Freeman (1995b) notes that if employment and unemployment rates in the United States for the least educated males are adjusted so that those incarcerated are included among the nonemployed, U.S. employment numbers become much more comparable to those of Europe.

[13]See, for instance, Swinnerton and Wial (1995, 1996), Diebold et al. (1996), and Farber (1994). The wave of firm restructuring in the early to mid-1990s may not yet be reflected in these data, though there has been some recent evidence of stagnating earnings among older college-educated males who may be experiencing declines in job tenure (Murnane, 1995). The apparent inconsistency between the rising skill and training needs of employers and their possibly declining commitment to long-tenure jobs is stressed by Cappelli (1996).

the recent decline in overall earnings and productivity growth as well as a widening of wage inequality—that is, a stagnating mean (or median) level of earnings along with growing variance around that mean. The explanations for this overall stagnation are not widely understood, nor is there much consensus regarding future trends in this area. (For a very readable summary of trends and the historical perspective on this question, see Madrick, 1995.)

Despite these questions and caveats, the evidence strongly suggests that a rise in the demand for educated workers relative to their supply has widened the gaps in relative earnings and employment rates between more and less educated workers, consistent with a "skills gap."

Test Scores

The fact that earnings inequality has risen even within educational categories raises the question of whether employer demand for skills measured along other dimensions has risen as well (e.g., Juhn et al., 1993).

One measure of individual abilities that varies within educational categories can be found in scores on tests of cognitive ability. A long and sometimes controversial literature has appeared over several decades on the extent to which test scores actually measure cognitive abilities, on their environmental versus hereditary determinants, and on their correlations with earnings (e.g., Jencks, 1972; Herrnstein and Murray, 1994; Goldberger and Manski, 1995; Hauser and Carter, 1995). But some important new evidence on the labor market effects of test scores has emerged in the past few years. For one thing, Murnane et al. (1995) have found that the returns to test scores (especially for math) rose significantly during the 1980s. Indeed, they found that the entire increase in returns to college education for females can be accounted for by the increased return to test scores during that period. Murnane et al. also found that wage returns to test scores rose with the number of years of labor market experience. This reflects the fact that test scores (and cognitive abilities more generally) are not observable by employers at the time of hiring. But the rising returns to these scores with experience indicate that they may well be correlated with subsequent labor market performance, which employers can more easily observe over time.[14]

Other studies (e.g., O'Neill, 1990; Ferguson, 1993; Neal and Johnson, 1995) have also found that differences in hourly earnings between whites and blacks (after educational differences have been controlled for) can be accounted for largely by differences in the scores of the two groups on armed forces qualifying tests. Effects of test scores on the relative employment rates of whites and blacks have also been found (e.g., Rivera-Batiz, 1992), though a substantial racial differ-

---

[14]Hunt (1995) reviews the psychometric literature on the measurement of IQ and its links to actual work performance. Bishop (1989, 1995) provides some economic evidence that links test scores to work performance on a variety of tasks as well as earnings.

ence remains here even after these differences are controlled for. While the test scores of blacks have risen in recent years relative to those of whites (Grissmer et al., 1994), the economic returns to test scores appear to have risen even more rapidly, thus preventing any relative improvement in black-white wage rates (Bound and Freeman, 1992).

A similar story can be told about overall test scores in the population: they rebounded somewhat from their lows in the 1970s (Bishop, 1992), especially among the lowest-scoring groups. But this did not occur rapidly enough to offset the rising returns and resulting increases in inequality associated with these differences. Summary data on the National Assessment of Educational Progress test scores still indicate large fractions of the population scoring at very low levels of reading or mathematical competence (Barton and Kirsch, 1990). The lower means and higher variances in test scores among less educated workers in the United States than in several other industrial countries have also been linked to the greater relative declines in earnings that have occurred here in recent years (Bishop, 1989; Nickell, 1997) as U.S. workers have appeared to have more difficulty adjusting to recent shifts in labor demands.

A few caveats are in order here. The magnitudes of estimated relationships between test scores and earnings or job performance are not enormous—test scores generally account for little more than 10 to 20 percent of the variance in earnings or job performance (Bishop, 1995; Hunt, 1995). Some questions remain as to what the scores really measure and whether their correlations with measured job performance are real or spurious. For blacks these questions are even greater than for whites.[15]

Nevertheless, employer demand for cognitive abilities seems to be growing even within educational categories and is apparently growing more quickly than the supply of these skills can respond. Thus, the economic returns to these abilities appear to be rising as well.

EMPLOYERS' SKILL DEMANDS: SURVEY EVIDENCE

The Multi-City Employer Survey

While the evidence cited above clearly indicates that relative employer demand has shifted to workers with more education and better cognitive abilities, many questions remain unanswered. Exactly what skills do employers currently need among their less educated (i.e., noncollege) workers? How do employers seek these skills—that is, how do they screen for them, and what observable credentials and characteristics do they regard as signals of potential

---

[15]Hunt (1995) notes that test scores generally have even less predictive power with regard to job performance for blacks than for whites, while Rodgers and Spriggs (1995) argue that test scores are rewarded quite differently in the labor market for blacks than they are for whites.

ability?   What are the consequences for workers who cannot provide these signals?

To help provide answers to these questions, I recently administered a new survey to some 3,200 employers in four large metropolitan areas: Atlanta, Boston, Detroit, and Los Angeles.   (This survey is part of a larger Multi-City Study of Urban Inequality [MCSUI], funded by the Ford and Russell Sage foundations in these four metropolitan areas.)   The survey was administered over the phone between June 1992 and May 1994 to individuals in the establishments who were identified as being responsible for the hiring of noncollege workers in general or workers in specific occupations.   The sampling process used here generated a stratified random sample of employers who are distributed across establishment size categories in roughly the same proportions as the overall labor force.[16]   Because of this sampling property, the characteristics of a sample of newly filled jobs at these firms can be considered, which should fairly well represent the jobs that are now being filled by employers and which new job seekers will currently face in the labor market.

Survey respondents were asked a variety of questions about all currently filled or vacant jobs at the firm as well as the last job that they filled and the last worker hired into this job, including the skills needed, recruitment and screening methods used, and demographic characteristics of hired workers.   Data regarding the latter are analyzed below.[17]

Table 2-1 presents data on the cognitive and social tasks that need to be performed daily on these jobs and the personal skill credentials required of people who are hired.   The tasks are measured as responses to questions of how frequently each task in the list had to be performed (i.e., daily, at least once a week, once a month, or never).   The credentials are based on a question of whether or not each is "absolutely necessary," "strongly preferred," etc.   (The credentials are counted as "required" if they are listed as "absolutely necessary" or "strongly preferred.")   These results are presented for all jobs together and separately for jobs that do and

---

[16]Roughly 30 percent of respondents were drawn from the names of employers generated by respondents to the MCSUI household surveys in these four areas; by definition, the employers in this part of the sample are weighted in proportion to where people actually work. The remainder of the sample was drawn from lists of employers generated by Survey Sampling, Inc. These lists were random samples within employer size categories, drawn to approximate the distribution of workers across these categories in the work force. The overall response rate among firms that passed the screening was 67 percent. The analysis of response rates across size categories shows little evidence of selection bias along these dimensions, thus suggesting that the ex ante sampling criteria are largely reflected in the data. See Holzer (1996).

[17]An employee-weighted sample of the most recently filled job at each firm will, over a reasonable period of time, also include those that were vacant for a lengthy time period. The sample will underrepresent new hires at high-turnover firms, though they will accurately measure the number of actual jobs that are filled by these many new hires. New hires at firms experiencing net employment growth will also be underrepresented here.

TABLE 2-1   Skills and Credentials Required for New Jobs (percentage)

	All Jobs	College Required	No College Required	
			White-Collar	Blue-Collar/ Service
Daily task performance				
Customer contact	73%	82%	82%	51%
Reading or writing paragraphs	68	91	67	51
Arithmetic	68	77	70	56
Computer	56	74	70	20
Required credentials				
High school diploma	78	100	82	54
GED accepted	—	—	66	44
GED not accepted	—	—	16	10
General work experience	70	75	72	62
Specific work experience	64	74	64	56
Previous training or certification	43	56	39	37

NOTE: All results are sample weighted.

do not require college degrees. The latter category is also divided by occupational category: white-collar versus blue-collar and service jobs.[18]

The results show that credentials requirements and task performance on newly filled jobs are extensive. Almost three-fourths of these jobs involve daily customer contact (either in person or on the phone); over two-thirds require daily reading or writing of paragraph-length material and the use of arithmetic; and well over half involve the use of computers.[19] Furthermore, almost two-thirds require not only general work experience but also specific experience related to the particular type of work, and over 40 percent require some type of certification of previous training.

These requirements vary with the educational requirements of the job and by occupation. Thus, jobs that require a college education generally require a higher degree of daily task performance and more experience or training than jobs that do not require college; among the latter, white-collar jobs require more than blue-collar and service jobs. But even for blue-collar and service jobs, requirements are quite extensive. Over half of these jobs require daily customer contact, reading and writing, arithmetic, general work experience, or specific work experience. Indeed, only about 5 percent of all jobs in central-city areas require none of these tasks, and the percentage requiring none of these credentials is the same (Holzer,

---

[18]Jobs are categorized as white collar if they are professional, managerial, technical, clerical, or sales jobs. Blue-collar jobs include the skilled crafts as well as machine operators and laborers. The service jobs include such categories as food service (i.e., waiters, waitresses), cleaning occupations (e.g., janitors), and various nontechnical health aides (such as orderlies or nurses' assistants).

[19]There were separate questions in the survey on reading and writing of paragraph-length material. Jobs requiring writing almost always require reading as well, though the converse is not true.

1996). Comparable statistics for suburban areas are just a few percentage points higher.

Of course, some questions remain about whether or not the requirements are hard and fast—in other words, whether employers really do as they say. But no such questions even seem relevant for the task performance data, which report current employee activities, and the responses to questions on hiring requirements are largely confirmed by information, where it is available, on the characteristics of the workers actually hired for these jobs.[20]

Thus, these data cast considerable doubt on whether there are enough jobs available with very low skill requirements to absorb all potential workers with very low skills, especially if welfare recipients are soon required to seek work in large numbers (Holzer, 1996).[21]

As argued above, the tasks represent some of the actual skills needed for job performance, while the credentials are signals of a candidate's potential ability to perform a job. But employers appear to use a wide range of other screens as well to gauge these signals, and they also use a variety of attitudes about various personal characteristics in making their hiring decisions.

Table 2-2 provides data on these other screens and attitudes. It shows that written applications, personal interviews, and requests for references are almost universally used, even though there are some major doubts about their predictive power or objectivity (Karren, 1980). Nonphysical tests are now used in 29 percent of all cases, and work samples are reviewed in 21 percent; over 40 percent use at least one or the other.[22] On the other hand, checks on educational or criminal backgrounds are made less than one-third of the time.

The data presented here on employer attitudes toward various personal characteristics are striking. For noncollege positions (the only ones for which these questions were asked), employers would not hire people who had been unemployed for over a year in about 30 percent of the cases; they would not hire anyone with only short-term or part-time work experience in about 50 percent of the cases; and they would not hire anyone with a criminal record almost 70 percent of the time.

The aversion of employers to hiring those with spotty work histories has been noted by Ballen and Freeman (1986), who argue that previous employment

---

[20]For instance, the fraction of workers hired with educational attainments less than the stated requirements was very small (i.e., under 10 percent). Of course, the tendency of firms to hire such workers should vary with the degree of tightness in the labor market and the nature of the skill or credential in question.

[21]This potential imbalance is suggested by the fact that over half of long-term welfare recipients (who are those most likely to be affected by time limits or other work requirements) are high school dropouts; most can report no recent work experience, and most score in the bottom quintile of the population in tests for cognitive ability (Burtless, 1995). These women also constitute roughly 10 to 15 percent of the household heads in major central cities, and most will probably seek employment in central-city areas (owing to transportation or informational limitations).

[22]Roughly one-fifth of the jobs that require either a test or a work sample require both, though there is some possibility that these categories are picking up the same activity.

TABLE 2-2   Other Screens and Employer Attitudes for New Jobs
(percentage)

	All Jobs	College Required	No College Required	
			White-Collar	Blue-Collar/ Service
Other screens:				
Written application	82%	86%	83%	80%
Interview	88	91	89	85
References	76	86	75	69
Test (not physical)	29	25	34	25
Work sample	21	29	16	21
Education check	30	42	30	23
Criminal record check	32	34	33	29
Would hire applicant with				
Unemployment for entire past				
year	—	—	70	72
Short-term or part-time				
work experience only	—	—	50	49
Criminal record	—	—	31	34

instability sends a very negative signal to employers. Evidence on the possible "scarring" effects of early unemployment more generally is mixed and is consistent with the smaller negative effects this trait has on hiring. (See Ellwood, 1982, and Meyer and Wise, 1982, for earlier analyses of this issue and Rich, 1994, for a more recent analysis.)

The large fraction of employers who will not hire people with criminal records stands in sharp contrast to the much smaller fraction who actually check criminal records. As noted above, the costs of checking criminal records are quite high in many places, and therefore many employers forgo this information. Unfortunately, some probably infer such activity from the race, age, and gender of job applicants; and, given the high rates of crime among less-educated and unemployed black males, many employers will likely be especially suspicious of young black males who lack employment for significant periods of time (Bushway, 1995). Thus, developing more effective ways of signaling one's work-related experiences could be especially important for youth in these situations.

Table 2-3 provides information on how many of these firms have actually experienced rising skill needs in the past 5 to 10 years and which skill needs have risen. The data indicate that 42 percent of establishments report rising skill needs, with somewhat higher rates in the jobs requiring college and somewhat lower ones in blue-collar and service jobs. These data may well understate the extent that skill needs have increased in this period.[23]

---

[23]The data do not include establishments and firms that went out of business during this period or those that began operation very recently. These omissions probably bias the results on skill changes downward.

TABLE 2-3   Increases in Skills Needed for New Jobs in Past 5 to 10 Years (percentage

			No College Required	
	All Jobs	College Required	White-Collar	Blue-Collar/Service
Skill needs higher				
Yes	42%	50%	43%	32%
No	58	50	57	68
Of those with increases, primarily which skills?				
Read/write/arithmetic	33	26	33	42
Social/verbal	36	44	34	30
Computer	31	30	33	28

The data also indicate that the demands for basic numeracy/literacy, social/verbal, and computer skills have risen more or less equally, even across educational and occupational categories. Interestingly, the rising need for basic skills has been highest among noncollege blue-collar and service jobs, where they have always been in relatively less demand; this confirms the earlier finding that even within these categories fewer jobs are available that do not involve substantial need for basic cognitive functions. On the other hand, the need for social and verbal skills has risen the most for jobs requiring a college education.

Do any of these skill needs and employer attitudes affect who actually gets hired, especially once obvious characteristics such as educational attainment are controlled for? Table 2-4 presents data that speak to this issue. Percentages are given for newly hired workers in these jobs who are either black or Hispanic. This is done for all job categories as well as for subsets of jobs in which each cognitive or social task or each credential is either required or not required.

The results clearly indicate that blacks and Hispanics are hired less frequently for jobs for which any of these tasks or credentials is required. In percentage terms the differences are not small. For example, the gap of 12 percentage points between those hired into jobs that require computer use and those hired into jobs that do not constitutes a difference of 32 percent (with the second group used as the base).

In separating blacks and Hispanics, some interesting differences emerge. Basically, Hispanics are more disadvantaged by requirements for high school diplomas and direct customer contact, while blacks are more disadvantaged by previous experience and training requirements (Holzer, 1996).[24]

Separating by gender also indicates that black and Hispanic *males* are the

---

[24]Since Hispanics are less likely to graduate from high school than blacks (see, e.g., Hauser and Phang, 1993), they are relatively more disadvantaged in jobs for which a high school diploma is required. But blacks seem to have more difficulty obtaining the necessary work experience or training in the market to make jobs with these requirements attainable.

TABLE 2-4   Blacks and Hispanics Hired Into New Jobs by Skills and
Credentials Required (percentage)

			No College Required	
			/hite-:ollar	Blue-Collar/ Service
All jol	PW: Baldwin 1		8%	44%
Jobs r				
perfor				
Cus			.7	41
Rea			:5	45
Ari			!4	39
Cor			!6	42
Jobs i	Workforce			
Hig			26	39
GE			26	39
No			24	38
Ge			24	44
Sp			25	44
Pr			24	42
Jobs				
perfc				
Cu			34	48
Re			35	44
Arithmetic	43	ɔι	39	52
Computers	38	09	35	45
Jobs not requiring credentials				
High school diploma	47	—	41	51
GED	—	—	42	55
No GED	—	—	35	38
General work experience	38	14	39	45
Specific work experience	37	24	35	46
Previous training	33	17	31	46

groups most limited by these requirements. In fact, the rising skill needs of
employers might well account for most or all of the relative deterioration in
wages as well as employment that these groups have experienced in the past 10 to
20 years (Holzer, 1996).

Of course, these results do not prove that the real skills gap between whites
and minorities drives the observed employer behavior; instead, discriminatory
perceptions of ability could result in these outcomes as well. But given the gaps
that have been documented between average black and white education and
experience levels, test scores, and so forth, it seems likely that at least part of the
observed results are based on real differences in average skills.[25]

---

[25]For educational attainment the tendency of a hired worker to not meet the stated requirement was actually higher among blacks and Hispanics than whites, especially at firms practicing
affirmative action in hiring.

Other Recent Survey Evidence

In addition to the employer survey in the MCSUI project reviewed above, a number of other surveys of employers have been administered in the past 5 to 10 years that focus on many of these issues. (Descriptive and qualitative data on employers' skill needs can be found in the report of the Secretary's Commission on Achieving Necessary Skills [SCANS], as described in Packer and Wirt, 1992, and also in Carnevale et al., 1990.) Among the best known of these are (1) a survey of over 3,000 employers in 1994 designed by the National Center on the Educational Quality of the Workforce (EQW), administered by the U.S. Bureau of the Census and funded by the U.S. Department of Education; (2) a mail survey of over 2,500 employers administered by the National Federation of Independent Businesses in 1987; and (3) local surveys administered in New York City in late 1993 by the city's Department of Employment and in Milwaukee in October 1993 and 1994 by the Employment and Training Institute of the University of Wisconsin-Milwaukee. Other surveys of employers include an update of the Employment Opportunity Pilot Project of firms by Barron et al. (1994) and a variety of surveys discussed by Kling (1995). The focus here is on those that deal primarily with hiring requirements and methods.

Also, some much more qualitative and in-depth surveys of smaller samples of employers have been administered in Chicago, Detroit, Atlanta, and Los Angeles (Kirschenman and Neckerman, 1991; Moss and Tilly, 1995; Kirschenman et al., 1995). These surveys generally provide little quantitative information but generate interesting descriptive material that would be hard to generate in the less personal formats (i.e., phone and mail surveys) used in the large-sample studies.

Among the many issues that have been addressed in these surveys (and in reports based on them) are (1) the frequency with which certain skills and personal characteristics are considered important by employers for job performance, (2) the weights placed by employers on a variety of screens and hiring requirements as well as their perceptions of applicants they hire, (3) more objective measures of how these skills and screens contribute to worker or firm performance, (4) the extent to which various skill needs are rising, and (5) the ability of employers to hire employees with the relevant skills. Of course, the responses to at least some of these questions will be subjective and hard to interpret clearly. But they still provide some interesting descriptive data on how employers view their skill needs and hiring.

Employers consistently report that basic literacy and numeracy skills are very important for virtually all jobs. In the New York City survey these skills are heavily weighted in every job category, though again somewhat less in the blue-collar and service jobs than in the white-collar ones.[26] Listening and speaking

---

[26]On a scale of 0 to 100 for measuring the "importance" of each skill, reading and writing and math skills were ranked 92 to 99 for managerial jobs, 89 to 99 for professional jobs, 77 to 86 for technical and skilled jobs, 81 to 97 for clerical and sales jobs, 55 to 81 for service jobs, and 50 to 79 for semiskilled and unskilled (blue-collar) jobs. See New York City Department of Employment (1995). The survey gauged the importance of the lists of skills used in the SCANS report.

skills are also considered important in white-collar and service jobs but less so in blue-collar jobs.

A variety of personal qualities, such as responsibility, integrity, and self-management, are considered almost as important as the basic skills described above, and in blue-collar and service jobs they are even more important.[27] These results are consistent with those of Moss and Tilly (1995), who stress the importance of what they refer to as "soft skills"—that is, communication skills and attitudes/motivation. (See also Cappelli, 1995a.) In addition, the New York City survey found that thinking skills, such as decision making, reasoning, problem solving, interpersonal skills, and working with technology are all relatively important in white-collar jobs and (in some cases) in service jobs as well.[28]

These results are consistent with the notion that growing numbers of companies are reorganizing jobs and work in ways that require more problem-solving ability on the part of employees, though this is not true universally. For instance, in the EQW survey 37 percent of establishments use some type of total quality management, which usually requires workers to have a higher degree of analytical ability; fewer establishments use a variety of other high-performance organizational strategies, such as teams (used by just 12 percent). (See National Center on the Educational Quality of the Workforce, 1995.)

As for screens and hiring requirements, both the New York City and the EQW surveys found that employers rank attitudes and communication skills as the most important characteristics they look for when screening candidates. Interviews are also given a lot of weight, despite the findings (noted above) from the human resources literature that question the objectivity and predictive power of information gained in interviews.[29] Somewhat more objective measures of skill, such as previous experience and work history, are given almost as much weight in these studies as the attitude and communication measures. References and recommendations score highly as well, as do industry-based credentials in the EQW and previous training for some occupations in the New York City survey.[30]

The evidence on measures of academic background is somewhat more mixed. On the one hand, educational requirements do exist on most jobs. For instance,

---

[27]The mean scores for personal qualities were 84 for service workers and 82 for blue-collar workers, compared with 79 and 68, respectively, on all basic skill categories. Personal qualities had mean rankings of 74 to 93 in the various white-collar occupations, whereas basic skills averaged 81 to 96.

[28]The "thinking skills," which cover a broad range of skills, have mean scores of 87 and 91 in the managerial and professional categories, 72 in the technical jobs, 73 in sales and clerical jobs, 67 in the service occupations, and 62 in blue-collar jobs.

[29]Moss and Tilly (1995) quote a few employers who claim that they just try to get a "feel" for the candidate in interviews and put a lot of weight on this subjective impression.

[30]For instance, the mean scores on these responses in the EQW survey (on a scale of 1 to 5) are as follows: attitude, 4.6; communication skills, 4.2; previous work experience, 4.0; recommendations from current or previous employers, 3.4; and industry-based credentials, 3.2. See Black and Lynch (1995).

the Milwaukee survey shows that only 23 percent of full-time jobs do not require high school or more education, as well as training and/or experience.[31] On the other hand, in both the New York City and the EQW surveys, years of schooling gets only a moderate weight in subjective rankings of importance in all except professional and managerial jobs (where college is required). In the EQW survey, academic performance is given even less weight than the number of years of schooling.[32]

But these results must be interpreted with some caution. For one thing, the vast majority of job applicants today have at least a high school diploma; therefore, this credential alone signals little about potential ability to an employer. On the other hand, failure to hold a diploma sends a much more negative signal to employers, which may be only partly offset by a GED (Cameron and Heckman, 1993). Thus, a high school diploma is necessary but not sufficient as a signal of academic quality. Furthermore, most employers do not use transcripts or other indicators of academic performance since they are so hard to obtain (Bishop, 1989); in other words, it is because of the high cost of using them, rather than their low benefit, that employers generally do not weight this information highly.

The relative importance of education levels and academic performance to job outcomes has been established in a few statistical studies of these relationships. For instance, Black and Lynch (1995) have shown that the average educational attainment of employees contributes positively and significantly to the value of output at the establishment level, as does the use of academic grades in hiring in nonmanufacturing establishments. Bishop (1993), in analyzing the National Federation of Independent Businesses data, also found that employer perceptions of academic skills contribute somewhat to their evaluations of worker performance. Bishop found that occupational skills, the ability to learn new things, and leadership also contribute to worker performance in most occupational categories and that basic work habits contribute significantly in the blue-collar categories.

Some consensus is found across these studies in terms of the growth of skill needs. The EQW survey reports growing needs for skills in 56 percent of establishments, which seems relatively consistent with findings in the New York City survey and the Moss-Tilly interviews. The area of highest growth in the need for skills is in computers, especially in white-collar jobs; 30 to 50 percent of these

---

[31]These data suggest a somewhat greater availability of jobs with no requirements than did the numbers from my own survey mentioned above. This might partly reflect a longer set of requirements listed in my questions and Milwaukee's very tight labor market (in which employers are likely to loosen some requirements in order to be able to attract workers).

[32]In the New York City survey, the receipt of a high school diploma or equivalent is given a score of only 37 in semiskilled or unskilled blue-collar jobs and 52 in service jobs, whereas attitudes and work habits score 90 and above. In the EQW survey, years of schooling completed is ranked 2.9, academic performance 2.5, reputation of school 2.4, and teacher recommendations 2.1. See Black and Lynch (1995).

jobs in the New York City survey show growing computer needs, with somewhat smaller rates of growth in the other job categories and other skill areas.

Finally, employers report difficulty in obtaining employees with the necessary skills for a variety of reasons. For instance, the Milwaukee survey (especially in 1994) was administered during a very tight labor market (with local unemployment of just 4.0 percent). Thus, roughly 60 percent of employers report some difficulty in filling jobs and give somewhat higher rates for jobs that have lower educational or experience requirements. But in other surveys employers generally report that it is the relative quality of applicants, rather than their numbers, that generates their hiring difficulties. For instance, roughly 30 percent of applicants in the New York City survey were judged deficient in a variety of skill categories by employers; even among those hired, deficiencies in basic skills were reported in 10 percent of the cases and in higher numbers of cases on other skill categories.[33] Respondents to the EQW survey report similar numbers.

Bishop (1993), using the National Federation of Independent Business survey, focuses on a somewhat different problem: the inability of employers to gauge whether an applicant possesses the necessary skills and personal characteristics given the limited information they have at the time of hiring. Bishop reports that employers have somewhat greater difficulty in judging such characteristics as the ability to learn new skills, work habits and attitudes, and leadership than basic skills or previous job skills acquired. He also found consistent evidence of large performance "surprises," measured as the differences between expected performance at the time of hiring and performance measured later. Bishop therefore argues for a variety of ways in which matches between jobs and employees might be improved through better provision of information to employers.

CONCLUSION

The market rates of return for education and test scores have been rising since the late 1970s. This is consistent with the idea of a skills gap or mismatch, in the sense that the demands for schooling and cognitive abilities in the labor market rose more rapidly than did their supplies. Real wages have declined substantially for less educated (i.e., noncollege-educated) males, and employment has declined, especially among blacks and high school dropouts (who are increasingly substituting illegal for legal modes of work).

My survey data indicate that employer demands for basic cognitive and social skills as well as for various credentials (such as high school diplomas, specific experience, and previous training) are extensive; indeed, very few new jobs are available for workers without these skills and credentials. The skill needs of employers are generally rising. Employer attitudes also indicate a great deal of

---

[33]In the New York City survey, the greatest deficiencies among those hired are reported in the areas of thinking skills (39.5 percent) and technological/computer skills (26 to 28 percent).

skepticism about workers with unstable employment histories and those suspected of having criminal records. Many of these hiring requirements and employer attitudes seem to limit the employment options available for less educated and especially minority workers.

Other recent employer surveys mostly confirm these findings. While basic skills are required by employers in almost all jobs, so are a variety of communication skills and personal qualities (such as motivation and good work habits). Analytical skills (such as problem-solving abilities) are mostly valued in white-collar jobs or in other jobs where firms are using so-called high-performance work practices. When hiring, employers heavily weight impressions from their personal interviews as well as previous experience, training, and work history. Applicants' educational histories (e.g., whether they graduated from high school, what grades they achieved) get somewhat less weight in the employers' mind, though clearly not zero, and when educational attainment is considered in hiring, it does seem to contribute to worker performance. Some educational attainment is thus clearly *necessary* for workers to be hired and to perform well, even if it is not *sufficient*. Finally, there is some evidence that employers have relatively little information that truly enables them to distinguish strong job candidates from weak ones (in terms of prospective job performance).

On-the-job training for employees might be another way for employers to meet their skill needs, and evidence from the EQW survey shows a moderate increase in the proportion of firms providing such training (National Center on the Educational Quality of the Workforce, 1995). But the provision of such training is likely to be limited by a variety of market imperfections, and the training is unlikely to benefit employees who (owing to the rising skill needs of employers) have difficulty being hired in the first place or who are not likely to remain with a single employer for very long.

Overall, then, a labor market is found in which disadvantaged workers (especially minorities and high school dropouts) often appear to have difficulty meeting the basic skill requirements necessary for employment, while high school graduates generally gain employment more easily but primarily at low wages. Improving the educational levels and cognitive abilities of these groups would certainly help to narrow the growing gaps in employment and earnings between them and the more skilled workers and might even contribute to improved economic performance and productivity growth for the economy as a whole. (For a recent discussion of the relationship between educational attainment and productivity growth, see Griliches, 1996.)

Making information about prospective worker skills more available to employers and improving its quality should enable employers to use such information more frequently in their hiring decisions. This, in turn, might improve the incentives for academic performance among high school students, an area that now appears to be quite weak. With more highly skilled workers and better matches between worker skills and job requirements, employers might also become more willing to invest in job training and longer-term commitments to their employees.

REFERENCES

Abraham, Katherine
1983   Structural-frictional v. demand-deficient unemployment. *American Economic Review* 73(4):708-724.
Bailey, Thomas
1990   *Changes in the Nature and Structure of Work: Implications for Skill Requirements and Skill Formation.* Berkeley: National Center for Research on Vocational Education, University of California.
Ballen, John, and Richard Freeman
1986   Transitions between employment and nonemployment. Pp. 75-114 in *The Black Youth Employment Crisis*, R. Freeman and H. Holzer, eds. Chicago: University of Chicago Press.
Barron, John, Mark Berger, and Dan Black
1994   Employer Search, Training, and Vacancy Duration. Mimeo, University of Kentucky, Lexington.
Bartel, Ann, and Frank Lichtenberg
1987   The comparative advantage of educated workers in implementing new technology. *Review of Economics and Statistics* 69(1):1-11.
Barton, Paul, and Irwin Kirsch
1990   *Workplace Competencies: The Need to Improve Literacy and Employment Readiness.* Washington, DC: Office of Educational Research and Improvement, U.S. Department of Education.
Becker, Gary
1975   *Human Capital.* Cambridge, MA: National Bureau of Economic Research.
Berman, Eli, John Bound, and Zvi Griliches
1994   Changes in the demand for skilled labor within U.S. manufacturing: Evidence from the annual survey of manufacturers. *Quarterly Journal of Economics* 109:367-97.
Bishop, John
1989   Incentives for learning: Why American high school students compare so poorly to their overseas counterparts. Pp. 17-52 in *Labor Economics and Public Policy*, Research in Labor Economics, Vol. 11, L.J. Bassi and D.L. Crawford, eds. Greenwich CT: JAI Press.
1992   The Impact of Academic Competencies on Wages, Unemployment, and Job Performance. Carnegie-Rochester Conference Series on Public Policy 37:127-194.
1993   Improving job matches in the U.S. labor market. Pp. 335-400 in *Microeconomics*, Vol. I, Brookings Papers on Economic Activity. Washington, DC: Brookings Institution.
1995   Is the Market for College Graduates Headed for a Bust? Demand and Supply Responses to Rising College Wage Premiums. Working paper, Cornell University, Ithaca, NY.
Black, Sandra, and Lisa Lynch
1995   Human Capital Investments and Productivity. Mimeo, Harvard University, Cambridge, MA.
Blau, Francine, and Lawrence Kahn
1994   Rising wage inequality and the U.S. gender gap. *American Economic Review* 84: 23-28.
Bound, John, and Richard Freeman
1992   What went wrong? The erosion of relative earnings and employment among young black men in the 1980's. *Quarterly Journal of Economics* 107:201-232.

Bound, John, and Harry Holzer
  1995   Demand Shifts, Labor Market Outcomes, and Population Adjustments: 1980-1990. Mimeo, Michigan State University, East Lansing.
Bureau of Labor Statistics
  1984   *The Impact of Technology on Labor in Four Industries: Hosiery/Folding Paperboard Boxes/Metal Cans/Laundry and Cleaning.* Bulletin 2182. Washington, DC: U.S. Department of Labor.
  1986   *Technology and Its Impact on Labor in Four Industries: Tires/Aluminum/Aerospace/Banking.* Bulletin 2242. Washington, DC: U.S. Department of Labor.
Burtless, Gary
  1995   The employment prospects of welfare recipients. Pp. 71-106 in *The Work Alternative,* D. Nightingale and R. Haveman, eds. Washington, DC: Urban Institute Press.
Bushway, Shawn
  1995   Labor Market Effects of Permitting Employer Access to Criminal History Records. Mimeo, Carnegie-Mellon University, Pittsburgh, PA.
Cameron, Steven, and James Heckman
  1993   The nonequivalence of high school equivalents. *Journal of Labor Economics* 11(1, Part 1):1-47.
Cappelli, Peter
  1995a Is the "skills gap" really about attitudes? *California Management Review* 37(4):108-124.
  1995b Technology and skill requirements: Implications for establishment wage structures. *New England Economic Review* (May-June):139-154.
  1996   Rethinking Employment. *British Journal of Industrial Relations* 33:563-602.
Card, David, and Alan Krueger
  1994   Minimum wages and employment: A case study of the fast-food industry in New Jersey and Pennsylvania. *American Economic Review* 84:772-793.
Carnevale, Anthony, Leila Gainer, and Ann Meltzer
  1990   *Workplace Basics: The Essential Skills Employers Want.* New York: Jossey-Bass.
Case, Karl, and Ray Fair
  1996   *Principles of Macroeconomics,* 4th ed. Englewood Cliffs, NJ: Prentice-Hall.
Clark, Kim, and Lawrence Summers
  1982   The dynamics of youth unemployment. Pp. 199-234 in *The Youth Labor Market Problem: Its Nature, Causes and Consequences,* R. Freeman and D. Wise, eds. Chicago: University of Chicago Press.
Diebold, Francis, David Neumark, and Daniel Polsky
  1996   Comment on Kenneth Swinnerton and Howard Wial, "Is job stability declining in the U.S. economy?" *Industrial and Labor Relations Review* 49:348-352.
Dinardo, John, Nicole Fortin, and Thomas Lemieux
  1995   Labor Market Institutions and the Distribution of Wages, 1973-1992: A Semiparametric Approach. Working paper, National Bureau of Economic Research, Cambridge, MA.
Ellwood, David
  1982   Teenage unemployment: Permanent scars or temporary blemishes? Pp. 349-390 in *The Youth Labor Market Problems: Its Nature, Causes and Consequences,* R. Freeman and D. Wise, eds. Chicago: University of Chicago Press.
Employment and Training Institute
  1994   Survey of Job Openings in the Milwaukee Metropolitan Area: Week of October 24, 1994. Milwaukee: University of Wisconsin.
Farber, Henry
  1994   Are Lifetime Jobs Disappearing? Job Duration in the United States, 1973-93. Mimeo, Princeton University, Princeton, NJ.

Feldstein, Martin, and James Poterba
  1984   Unemployment insurance and reservation wages. *Journal of Public Economics* 23(1-2):141-167.
Ferguson, Ronald
  1993   New Evidence on the Growing Value of Skill and Consequences for Racial Disparity and Returns to Schooling. Mimeo, Harvard University, Cambridge, MA.
Flinn, Christopher, and James Heckman
  1993   Are unemployment and out of the labor force behaviorally distinct states? *Journal of Labor Economics* 1(1):28-42.
Freeman, Richard
  1994   Crime and the Job Market. Working paper, National Bureau of Economic Research, Cambridge, MA.
  1995a   Are your wages set in Beijing? *Journal of Economic Perspectives* 9(3):15-32.
  1995b   Incarceration v. the Dole: U.S. and European Modes of Dealing with Unskilled Men. Mimeo, Harvard University, Cambridge, MA.
  1995c   Labor Market Institutions and Earnings Inequality. Mimeo, Harvard University, Cambridge, MA.
Freeman, Richard, and Lawrence Katz
  1994   Rising wage inequality: The U.S. v. other industrial countries. Pp. 29-62 in *Working Under Different Rules*, R. Freeman, ed. New York: Russell Sage Foundation.
Goldberger, Arthur, and Charles Manski
  1995   The bell curve: A perspective from economics. *Focus* (Fall/Winter): 23-24.
Goldin, Claudia, and Lawrence Katz
  1995   *The Decline of Non-Competing Groups: Changes in the Premium to Education, 1890-1940.* Working paper, National Bureau of Economic Research, Cambridge, MA.
Griliches, Zvi
  1996   *Education, Human Capital, and Growth: A Personal Perspective.* Working paper, National Bureau of Economic Research, Cambridge, MA.
Grissmer, David, Sheila Kirby, Mark Berends, and Stephanie Williamson
  1994   *Student Achievement and the Changing American Family.* Santa Monica, CA: RAND Corporation.
Hamermesh, Daniel
  1993   *Labor Demand.* Princeton, NJ: Princeton University Press.
Hauser, Robert, and Wendy Carter
  1995   The bell curve: A perspective from sociology. *Focus* (Fall/Winter): 25-27.
Hauser, Robert, and Hanam Samuel Phang
  1993   *Trends in High School Dropout Among White, Black and Hispanic Youth: 1973 to 1989.* Discussion paper, Institute for Research on Poverty, University of Wisconsin, Madison.
Hecker, Daniel
  1992   Reconciling conflicting data on jobs for college graduates. *Monthly Labor Review* 115(7):3-12.
Herrnstein, Richard, and Charles Murray
  1994   *The Bell Curve.* New York: Basic Books.
Holzer, Harry
  1987   Hiring procedures in the firm: Their economic determinants and consequences. Pp. 243-274 in *Human Resources and the Performance of the Firm*, M. Kleiner, R. Block, M. Roomkin, and S. Salsburg, eds. Madison, WI: Industrial Relations Research Association.
  1989   *Unemployment, Vacancies, and Local Labor Markets.* Kalamazoo, MI: Upjohn Institute for Employment Research.

1994   Job vacancy rates in the firm: An empirical analysis. *Economica* 61(241):17-36.
1996   *What Employers Want: Job Prospects for Less-Educated Workers.* New York: Russell Sage Foundation.

Hunt, Earl
1995   *Will We Be Smart Enough?* New York: Russell Sage Foundation.

Ichniowski, Casey, Kathryn Shaw, and Giovanni Prennushi
1995   *The Effect of Human Resource Management Practices on Productivity.* Working paper, National Bureau of Economic Research, Cambridge, MA.

Jaeger, David
1995   Skill Differences and the Effects of Immigrants on the Wages of Natives. Mimeo, University of Michigan, Ann Arbor.

Jencks, Christopher
1972   *Inequality.* New York: Basic Books.

Juhn, Chinhui
1992   Decline of male labor market participation: The role of declining labor market opportunities. *Quarterly Journal of Economics* 107:79-121.

Juhn, Chinhui, Kevin Murphy, and Brooks Pierce
1993   Wage inequality and the rise in the returns to skill. *Journal of Political Economy* 101:410-442.

Kane, Thomas
1995   *Rising Public College Tuition and College Entry: How Well Do Public Subsidies Promote Access to College?* Working paper no. 5164, National Bureau of Economic Research, Cambridge, MA.

Karren, Robert
1980   *The Selection Interview: A Review of the Literature.* Washington, DC: Office of Personnel Management.

Kasarda, John
1995   Industrial restructuring and the changing location of jobs. Pp. 215-167 in *State of the Union*, Vol. I, R. Farley, ed. New York: Russell Sage Foundation.

Katz, Lawrence
1986   Efficiency wages: A partial evaluation. *NBER Macroeconomics Annual.* National Bureau of Economic Research, Cambridge, MA.

Katz, Lawrence, and Kevin Murphy
1992   Changes in relative wages, 1963-87: Supply and demand factors. *Quarterly Journal of Economics* 107:35-78.

Kirschenman, Joleen, and Katherine Neckerman
1991   We'd love to hire them but. . . . Pp. 203-232 in *The Urban Underclass*, C. Jencks and P. Peterson, eds. Washington, DC: Brookings Institution.

Kirschenman, Joleen, Philip Moss, and Chris Tilly
1995   Employer Screening Methods and Racial Exclusion: Evidence from New In-Depth Interviews with Employers. Mimeo, Russell Sage Foundation, New York.

Kling, Jeffrey
1995   High performance work systems and firm performance. *Monthly Labor Review* 118:29-36.

Krueger, Alan
1993   How computers have changed the wage structure: Evidence from microdata, 1984-89. *Quarterly Journal of Economics* 108:33-60.

Levy, Frank, and Richard Murnane
1992   U.S. earnings levels and earnings inequality: A review of recent trends and proposed explanations. *Journal of Economic Literature* 30(3):1333-1381.

1995   With What Skills Are Computers a Complement? Mimeo, Massachusetts Institute of Technology, Cambridge, MA.

Lynch, Lisa
    1992   Private sector training and the earnings of young workers. *American Economic Review* 82:299-312.
    1993   The economics of youth training in the United States. *Economic Journal* 103:1292-1302.

Madrick, Jeffrey
    1995   *The End of Affluence*. New York: Random House.

Meyer, Robert, and David Wise
    1982   High school preparation and early labor market experience. Pp. 27-348 in *The Youth Labor Market Problem: Its Nature, Causes and Consequences*, R. Freeman and D. Wise, eds. Chicago: University of Chicago Press.

Mincer, Jacob
    1994   *Investment in U.S. Education and Training*. Working paper no. 4844, National Bureau of Economic Research, Cambridge, MA.

Moss, Philip, and Chris Tilly
    1995   *Soft Skills and Race: An Investigation of Black Men's Employment Problems*. Working paper, Russell Sage Foundation, New York.

Murnane, Richard
    1995   Is the Market for College Graduates Headed for a Bust? Demand and Supply Responses to Rising College Wage Premiums. Mimeo, Harvard University, Cambridge, MA.

Murnane, Richard, John Willett, and Frank Levy
    1995   The Growing Importance of Cognitive Skills in Wage Determination. *Review of Economics and Statistics* 77:251-266 .

National Center on the Educational Quality of the Workforce
    1995   *First Findings from the EQW National Employer Survey*. University of Pennsylvania, Philadelphia, PA

Neal, Derek, and William Johnson
    1995   *The Role of Pre-market Factors in Black-White Wage Differences*. Working paper no. 5124, National Bureau of Economic Research, Cambridge, MA.

Neumark, David, and William Wascher
    1995   Minimum-wage effects on school and work transitions of teenagers. *American Economic Review* 85(2):244-249.

New York City Department of Employment
    1995   New York City Employer Survey: What Employers Require for Employment. Research report no. 1, New York City Department of Employment.

Nickell, Steven
    1997   The collapse in demand for the unskilled: What can be done? In *Demand-Side Strategies for Low-Wage Labor Markets*, R. Freeman and P. Gottschalk, eds. New York: Russell Sage Foundation, forthcoming.

O'Neill, June
    1990   The role of human capital in earnings differences between black and white men. *Journal of Economic Perspectives* 4(4):25-45.

Packer, Arnold, and John Wirt
    1992   Changing skills of the U.S. workforce: Trends of supply and demand. Pp. 31-80 in *Urban Labor Markets and Job Opportunities*, G. Peterson and W. Vroman, eds. Washington, DC: Urban Institute Press.

Piehl, Anne
  1995   Earnings Inequality and Incarceration over the 1980's. Mimeo, Harvard University, Cambridge, MA.
Rich, Lauren
  1994   The Long-Run Impact of Early Nonemployment: A Reexamination. Mimeo, University of Michigan, Ann Arbor.
Rivera-Batiz, Francisco
  1992   Quantitative literacy and the likelihood of employment among young adults in the United States. *Journal of Human Resources* 27(2):313-328.
Rodgers, William, and William Spriggs
  1995   What Does the AFQT Really Measure? Race, Wages, Schooling and the AFQT Score. Unpublished paper, The College of William and Mary, Williamsburg, VA.
Swinnerton, Kenneth, and Howard Wial
  1995   Is job stability declining in the U.S. economy? *Industrial and Labor Relations Review* 48(2):293-304.
  1996   Is job stability declining in the U.S. economy? Reply to Diebold, Neumark and Polsky. *Industrial and Labor Relations Review* 49(2):352-355.
Weiss, Andrew
  1995   Human capital v. signalling explanations of wages. *Journal of Economic Perspectives* 9(4):133-154.
Wilson, William
  1987   *The Truly Disadvantaged.* Chicago: University of Chicago Press.

3

Skills and the Economy: An Employer Context for Understanding the School-to-Work Transition

Robert Zemsky

INTRODUCTION

Today, two linked propositions frame many of the policies and much of the analyses focusing on the school-to-work transition: young workers need to possess more of the skills employers seek; and, if employers would only inform educators of the specific nature of those skills, schools could provide the requisite training and education. The role of public policy thus becomes one of convincing schools to listen to employers—to negotiate with them, really—and to persuade employers that the resulting improvement in young people's job readiness would be worth the additional taxes (Reich, 1991; National Center on Education and the Economy, 1990).

Over the last five years the work of my colleagues and I at the National Center on the Educational Quality of the Workforce (EQW) has persuaded us that this scenario—for all its symmetry and appeal to the ideal of a better-educated work force—does not correspond to the conditions we found as we worked with and surveyed employers on issues regarding the school-to-work transition. Much of the experience with school-business partnerships, for example, testifies to just how difficult it is for employers to articulate what skills they will require in the future, much less for schools to see employers as customers (Miller, 1988, 1991; McDermott, 1989; Rachlin and Shapiro, 1989; Spring, 1987). And most of the statistical evidence suggests that what today's young workers face is job rationing and declining real wages either because there are insufficient opportunities to absorb the skills they bring with them to the labor market or because employers do not want to hire them.[1]

---

[1] The most successful presenters of this argument have been Robert Reich (1991) and the authors of *America's Choice: High Skills or Low Wages* (National Center on Education and the Economy, 1990).

The principal advantage enjoyed by young workers today is that there are fewer of them. At the beginning of the 1980s, there were more than 27 million young people aged 16 to 26 who were not enrolled in school and who either had or were seeking full-time employment. Ten years later that same youth cohort (16 to 26) numbered just 22 million. With fewer young people competing for jobs, their participation in the labor force actually increased slightly, from 69 percent in 1981 to 70 percent in 1991, while the proportion of those working full time increased from 75 to 79 percent over the same decade. (The discussion of youth labor market characteristics presented in this and succeeding paragraphs is drawn from an analysis of the Current Population Survey contained in *Making Good Jobs for Young People a National Priority*, a publication of the National Advisory Board of the National Center on the Educational Quality of the Workforce, 1995a).

Offsetting this slight increase in employment, however, are three significant losses that substantially disadvantage this and succeeding generations of young people. In 1981, 19 percent of young workers in the United States were employed in full-time jobs in the manufacturing sector. Ten years later only 15 percent of youth worked full time in the same sector—a net loss of 1.65 million manufacturing jobs for young workers. At the same time, the proportion of full-time manufacturing jobs held by workers aged 16 to 26 fell from 23 percent in 1981 to 16 percent in 1991.

Changes in the armed services tell much the same story. In 1987 the armed services enlisted almost 300,000 new recruits—for the most part, young people with high school degrees but little subsequent postsecondary education. By 1993, these annual accessions to the military had been reduced by one-third, which meant 100,000 fewer recruits each year. The number is expected to drop even further as the military continues to downsize. What will be lost by the end of the decade are almost 1 million good jobs for young people: jobs with good pay, excellent benefits, opportunities to acquire technical skills, and further educational benefits after service (Barley, 1994; Laurence, 1994).

Not surprisingly, this decline in good jobs for young people has been accompanied by a general and persistent decline in the wages paid to them. Compared with their counterparts of a decade ago, young workers in the United States are more likely to have jobs for which they are paid less. When education, gender, race or ethnicity, and industry of employment are taken into account, young workers today earn, on average, more than 10 percent less in constant dollars than their counterparts a decade ago. For disadvantaged youth and those without high school credentials, the decline has been even more dramatic.

The strategy of schools' negotiating with employers to yield more work-relevant courses of study, resulting in the production of more work-ready young graduates, has proven to be difficult to implement. It is the dream of every school reformer committed to devising more work-relevant and/or work-based curricula to sit across the table from a group of employers who are ready and willing to tell the schools what they need. Much of the initial logic behind the current concern with the school-to-work transition derives from this promise: "If only concerned employers will tell us what they need, we can make sure that our schools deliver." Skeptics have suggested that schools do not work that way—that they are not customer centered, that they are more likely to draw on their own sense of what constitutes a good education than to ask what businesses need. Even more difficult, however, would be getting employers to the table, in part because they have given up on schools and in part because most employers do not know how to answer the question of what skills will they need in the future (Bailey, 1993; Doolittle and Ivry, 1993; Kazis, 1993b; Levy and Murnane, 1993; Osterman and Iannozzi, 1993; Stern, 1993).

The idea of a negotiated compact between schools and employers has its roots in the school reform movement of the late 1970s and early 1980s. Reformers wanted schools to gain a better sense of their customers and wanted those customers to help spur the reform movement itself. Initially, it was an idea that was pitched almost exclusively to the nation's major employers, those with sufficient corporate clout to make schools pay attention. Most major cities developed business-school partnerships of one form or another, each designed to enable schools and teachers to gain a better understanding of what the business community needed and for what it was willing to pay.[2]

In practice, however, many of the business men and women brought to the table by these partnerships had little firsthand knowledge of the skills their enterprises needed and whether, in fact, their businesses were having trouble finding qualified young workers. Most of the business seats at the "bargaining table"

---

[2]The causes underlying the declining fortunes of young workers are now the subject of a lively debate in the United States. On one side are those who argue that the problem lies with the preparation of young people for work—with their schooling and their antipathy to the discipline of work itself. These scholars and commentators would increase opportunities for young people largely through an aggressive agenda of school reform. Increase the skills and improve the attitudes young people bring with them to the labor market, they argue, and employment will follow. Within this agenda, probably the most radical proposal would have established a German-style apprenticeship system in the United States.

Those of us who hold the alternative view argue that—whatever the problems inherent in the skills and attitudes of young people—the larger problem is one of demand, not supply. As the American economy has undergone restructuring and its firms have reengineered their enterprises, employers have learned to thrive with fewer of the kind of entry-level positions historically filled by young workers.

The debate has, on occasion, become confounded with a more technical discussion of a secular shift in labor demand. The general consensus is that those with more skills have found it easier to find jobs paying higher wages than those with fewer skills. I have no quarrel with this consensus, except to note, as the text indicates, that on average all young people have lost ground in the pursuit of higher wages—those who have more skills have lost less ground than those who have fewer skills. This is also the point Sam Stringfield makes in a provocative analysis of schooling programs that enhance skills (Stringfield, 1995). For other research that parallels EQW's, see Mishel and Teixeira (1991).

were occupied by chief executive officers, business's "first citizens" long since removed from the hurly-burly of meeting production schedules and hiring and training new workers. Their notions of education were more general than specific, more likely to stress broad academic competencies than narrow technical skills. What the schools derived from these partnerships was not information but help—help in setting higher standards for graduation, in taking on the tough tasks of school restructuring, and in making the case for increased public support.

The downsizing of corporate America has been accompanied by an understandable lessening of business interest in the process, if not the progress, of school reform. There is less concern over the supply of future workers; there are also fewer of the professional staff members in large corporations who once regularly contributed to the operation of business-school partnerships. Yet identifying where and when these partnerships have persisted is an instructive exercise. As a general category, the most active partnerships today are in the form of private industry councils, established as part of the Jobs Training Partnership Act. When they work, they do so because employers are seen as customers with immediate needs for workers who know how to find and keep a job (Filipczak, 1993; National Commission for Employment Policy, 1993; DiMase and Boyle, 1991; Ketcham, 1990). Private industry councils have learned the tough lesson that the skills most needed concern comportment and the capacity to sell oneself in a buyer's market.

Though on a substantially smaller scale, business-school partnerships have also come to play an important role in the establishment of charter schools— educational institutions that are publicly funded but operate as quasi-independent schools responsible to a local board. Some of the most successful charter schools have been those driven by business-dominated boards assembled to make sure that the schools serve local employers as well as students. The board does not negotiate curricula on behalf of the business community, but rather insists that those responsible for the curricula are "out in the community" learning what employers want—that is, performing the kind of market research on which most successful enterprises depend (Lynn and Wills, 1994; Bailey and Merrit, 1993; Finegold, 1993; Hamilton and Hamilton, 1993; Kazis, 1993a; William T. Grant Foundation, 1992; Glennan, 1991; Barton, 1990; Carnevale et al., 1990; Education Writers Association, 1990; Glover, 1983).

It is important to note, however, that charter schools are the exception and not the rule. The reality that faces most young people, as well as most schools, is increasingly uncertain. The time between the conclusion of schooling and the securing of a permanent job is getting longer. The link between formal schooling and settled work is becoming more tenuous, while the possession of postsecondary credentials is becoming more essential.[3]

---

[3]In their analysis of job churning, Diebold et al. (1994) concluded that jobs in the 1990s were neither more nor less stable than during earlier decades—except for young workers, who experienced increased churning.

What schools are now discovering is that somehow they have come to matter less in the nation's economic calculus. They are more badgered than supported and are more likely to be blamed for what has gone wrong than to be assisted in implementing what might make it right. They are told that the students they graduate have not mastered basic problem-solving competencies, that too often they know little or nothing about the world of work, and that all too often they appear, particularly to would-be employers, as undisciplined and disinterested in work itself (Zemsky, 1994). Schools know they are being discounted, disconnected, and finally dismissed by more and more employers.[4] What they sense, as well, is that the link between education and the nation's productivity is itself at risk, to the detriment of both school and community (Shanker, 1995).

THE EQW NATIONAL EMPLOYER SURVEY

In the spring of 1995 the EQW reported the results of the first analysis of the its National Employer Survey—findings that documented just how much employers discounted information about a job applicant's schooling when making hiring decisions. The survey was designed by EQW, a joint venture of the University of Pennsylvania's Institute for Research on Higher Education and the Wharton School. This first nationally representative survey to test the link between employers and schools queried the managers and owners of just over 4,000 establishments employing 20 workers or more about their employment, training, and hiring practices. To capture the underlying factors that yield increases in productivity, respondents were also asked about the basic nature of their businesses: annual sales, principal products and services, investments in new equipment and new facilities, costs of materials used in production, and the average wages and levels of education of their workers (Lynch and Black, 1996a, 1996b; National Center on the Educational Quality of the Workforce, 1996).[5]

The EQW survey represents the culmination of 5 years of research that asked one of the basic questions motivating the National Research Council Board on

---

[4]EQW has received a great deal of correspondence from teachers, school administrators, and education officials expressing the difficulties in establishing successful links between education and the workplace. Two such letters stand out, sent by Alex May, technology supervisor for the Millville Public Schools in Millville, NJ, and by Edward Roeber, director of Student Assessment Programs for the Council of Chief State School Officers. EQW has also received correspondence from employers engaged in implementation of state and local school-to-work initiatives; one such employer is C. Arnold Decker, executive vice-president of the Sumter Cabinet Company in South Carolina, who has sought advice on facilitating partnerships with local schools. These three letters were received in response to EQW's policy statement, *On Connecting School and Work* (National Advisory Board of the National Center on the Educational Quality of the Workforce, 1995b), which discusses the discounting of schools by employers referenced here.

[5]These and related EQW materials are available free of charge from the National Center on the Educational Quality of the Workforce (EQW, University of Pennsylvania, 4200 Pine St., 5A, Philadelphia, PA 19104-4090; 1-800-437-9799; e-mail: eqw-requests@irhe.upenn.edu).

Testing and Assessment's interest in the school-to-work transition: What is it that employers want? In designing the research agenda, EQW assumed that the term "labor market" was more than a convenient metaphor wrapped in economic jargon—that there were in fact buyers and sellers in the form of employers, on the one hand, and schools and their graduates on the other. Having conceived of the school-to-work transition as the sum of a set of employee-seeking and job-finding transactions, we at EQW saw our task as essentially one of market research that could tell us what the employer/consumer was looking for and what schools as suppliers might best do with that information. In other words, we wanted to identify how schools might change what they do in order to make employers more informed—and, in that sense, more reliable customers.

Our focus was on the establishment rather than the firm because that is where most decisions to hire new workers occur. We wanted to know how hiring decisions were made, what type of information proved to be helpful, what skills as well as credentials employers considered to be important, and what kinds of training they provided for their employees. We wanted to know whether the most productive establishments within any given industry either hired or trained their workers differently than less productive competitors. Finally, to construct the necessary survey instruments and interview protocols, we wanted to know something about the attitudes employers had toward youth employment and the school-to-work transition. Our answers to these questions came in three basic bundles.

HOW EMPLOYERS TALK

We began our investigation with focus groups of employers in seven cities across the United States: Portland and Eugene, Oregon; Phoenix, Arizona; Indianapolis, Indiana; Cleveland, Ohio; Atlanta, Georgia; and Ithaca, New York. Whenever possible, we conducted two sessions per city—one drawing together human resource professionals from larger firms and the other consisting of small-business owners. The discussions themselves were remarkably similar across the focus groups, and the problem on which each focus group stumbled was the same: employers acknowledged that they ought to, but simply did not, see themselves as benefiting from their community's investments in work-related education (Zemsky, 1994).

The most discouraging discussions occurred when we asked about the employability of young people. In part, employers' laments incorporated the perennial concerns of older people about a generation that must inevitably replace them: young people lack discipline; they expect to be catered to; they don't want to do the dirty jobs; they don't respect authority. To these more or less traditional concerns were added worries about the quality of educational attainment: young people lack communication skills; they are neither numerate nor literate; they can't make change; they don't understand the importance of providing customer service (Zemsky, 1994).

These complaints were more than a fashionable echoing of the media's current fascination with educational deficiencies. Almost everyone had a story to tell—dealing with honors students who couldn't spell; sifting through hundreds of job applications and résumés in search of potential candidates capable of making a reasonably neat and complete presentation of their skills and aptitudes; firing one young worker after another who did not measure up on the job. The owner of one fast-food franchise reported that the average tenure of a first-time young worker was less than 2 weeks; often the owner would make up to eight hires before finding a new worker who could last longer.

This sense of "trial-and-error" hiring, rather than the successful screening of job applicants based on educational attainment, came to dominate the discussions. Most employers no longer expected high schools to supply their future workers. With the exception of fast-food franchises, businesses were finding the most likely pool of youth labor not among high school students but among college students, even college graduates. Put off by the young and saddened by their local high schools but without any interest in changing them, most employers with whom we talked had simply shifted their attention to the next age cohort, focusing on those in their mid-twenties or older. Given the surplus of younger people looking for work, employers had little trouble finding "older" young employees, frequently with 2 or more years of college. These individuals were depicted as the survivors—those with sufficient discipline, experience, skills, and motivation to be worth hiring.

ESTABLISHING A BASELINE

The EQW National Employer Survey documented what the focus groups reported. The survey was designed by Lisa Lynch, who is currently chief economist with the U.S. Department of Labor, in collaboration with EQW co-directors Peter Cappelli and Robert Zemsky. It was administered by the U.S. Bureau of the Census as a telephone survey in the late summer and early fall of 1994. The survey's sampling frame was the Census Bureau's Standard Statistical Establishment List, one of the most comprehensive and up-to-date listings of establishments in the United States. The EQW National Employer Survey oversampled establishments in the manufacturing sector and those with more than 100 employees. Public-sector employers, not-for-profit institutions, and corporate headquarters were excluded from the sample. The survey also excluded establishments with less than 20 employees, largely because of the difficulties inherent in drawing a reliable sample of small establishments. While these employers represent 85 percent of all establishments, they employ less than 25 percent of all workers (Lynch and Black, 1996a).

In all, 4,633 eligible establishments were contacted, of which 3,358 agreed to participate—a 72.5 percent response rate. Most refusals stemmed from the employer's reluctance to participate in a voluntary survey and to spend the requisite amount of time. There was no significant pattern to the refusals, except for manufacturing establishments with more than 1,000 employees.

The target respondent in manufacturing establishments was the plant manager and in nonmanufacturing establishments the local site manager. Multiple respondents were allowed for each establishment, typically because the interviewer was told that information such as annual sales or investments in physical capital could be better obtained from another manager or office within the same establishment. Just over 12 percent of the surveys were not included in the analysis, principally because the Census Bureau was not able to complete the interviews prior to October 1, the cutoff date designated in the survey design. The completed survey rate was thus 64 percent, and the survey results reported below are based on weighted results drawn from the complete responses.

It was intended that the EQW survey would provide a baseline for comparing employer attitudes, their estimation of employees' skills and proficiencies, investments in both formal and informal employee training, the type of information for which they looked when hiring new employees, and the collective as well as individual contributions that these characteristics appeared to make to an establishment's productivity. What we sought was a reality check—a counterbalance to the anecdotes that have become the almost exclusive source for estimates of how and when employers invest in the skills of their employees, the kinds of skills that will be required in the future, and the extent to which employers are likely to rely on schools to supply those skills.

We begin by noting that the restructuring of the American economy has not led to a deskilling of work. Quite the contrary, as Table 3-1 shows, only 5 percent of the establishments reported any reduction in the skill requirements of their jobs, while 56 percent reported increased skill requirements.

Employers' assessment of employee proficiency was more mixed. On average, establishments reported that just over 80 percent of their workers were fully proficient in their current jobs. That means that one out of every five workers was judged as being not fully proficient (see Table 3-2). Despite the richness of the data supplied by the EQW National Employer Survey, we were unable to construct a satisfactory model for identifying those attributes that either contributed to or sub-

TABLE 3-1   Percentage of Establishments That Have Increased, Decreased, or Not Changed Their Skill Requirements

Change in Skill Requirements	% Establishments
Increased	57
Decreased	5
Remained the same	39

NOTE: Data derived from Question 14 on the EQW National Employer Survey: "In the last three years, have the skills required to perform production or support jobs (primary or frontline services or support jobs) at an acceptable level increased, decreased, or remained the same in your establishment?"

TABLE 3-2   Percentage of Employees Proficient at Their Jobs

Proficient Employees[a]	% Establishments
< 75%	32
> 75% and < 85%	21
> 85% and < 95%	27
> 95%	19

[a]Mean employee proficiency across establishments = 80%
NOTE: Data derived from Question 37 on the EQW National Employer Survey: "What percentage of your workers would you regard as being fully proficient at their current jobs?

tracted from employer-supplied estimates of worker proficiency. We suspect that part of the answer lies in the high rates of turnover during the first year of employment reported by some firms. Another part of the answer may lie in the fact that the skill requirements for many current jobs are actually increasing—that workers were being required to "catch up" by acquiring new skills.

The EQW survey provides two additional benchmarks for gauging employers' current estimates of the skills and capacities of their employees. Almost universally, employers reported that they invested in employee training—informally through on-the-job training or its equivalent (97 percent) and formally through structured training programs (81 percent). As expected, large establishments were more likely to provide formal training than smaller ones, but even then, three out of four of the smallest establishments (20 to 49 employees) reported that they provided some formal training (see Table 3-3).

At the same time, there is little evidence that establishments were finding it necessary to make significant investments in either remedial or basic education—that employers either were having to fix what schools had gotten wrong or had to spend time or money bringing employees up to minimum skill standards (see Table 3-4). Indeed, we interpret the substantial investment that establishments were making in employee training to mean these employers had confidence in both the skills and the trainability of their work force.

The general conclusions drawn from the EQW National Employer Survey were that work and the organization of work are becoming more complex, that most establishments report their jobs require increased skills, and that most employers are investing in the skills of their workers partly to make them proficient in their current jobs but not to provide remedial training or education.

EDUCATION'S CONTRIBUTION TO ESTABLISHMENT PRODUCTIVITY

Another way to ask the "skills question" is to determine to what extent, if any, education contributes to establishment productivity. Here, I draw directly on the work of Lynch and Black (1996a), who used data from the EQW National

TABLE 3-3   Establishments Offering Formal and Informal Training by Establishment Size

No. of Employees	% Firms Providing Formal Training	% Firms Providing Informal Training
All	81	97
20 to 49	75	96
50 to 99	82	99
100 to 249	90	98
250 to 999	90	99
More than 1,000	99	98

NOTE: Information on formal training derived from Question 18 of the EQW National Employer Survey: "Does your establishment pay for or provide any structured or formal training either on the job (by supervisors or outside contractors) or at a school or technical institute?" Information on informal training derived from Questions 19 and 32b of the EQW National Employer Survey. Question 19 (for establishments that do not provide formal training) is "Unstructured or informal training includes situations in which employees learn by observing others doing a job in an informal one-on-one situation. Does your establishment provide informal (in-plant) instruction by supervisors or co-workers?" Question 32b (for establishments that provide formal training) is "Unstructured or informal training includes situations in which employees learn by observing others doing the job or are shown how to do a job in an informal one-on-one situation. In addition to your formal training program, does your establishment provide informal (in-plant) instruction by supervisors and co-workers?"

Employer Survey to estimate a standard Cobb Douglas production function. The output variable takes as its proxy the log of sales for calendar year 1993. The input variables/proxies are the 1993 book value of the capital stock; the total cost of goods and services used in the production of 1993 sales, including energy; total labor hours for 1993; and the average educational level of workers. The results of this unrestricted Cobb Douglas production function are reported separately for manufacturing and nonmanufacturing establishments in columns 1 and 3 of Table 3-5 (Lynch and Black, 1996a).

TABLE 3-4   Relative Ranking of Amount of Time Establishments Spend on Various Types of Training

Type of Training	Rank[a]
Training on the safe use of equipment and tools	1.7
Improving teamwork or problem-solving skills	1.5
Training in sales and customer service	1.5
Training to use computers and other new equipment	1.4
Remedial skills in literacy and arithmetic	0.4

[a]0 = none; 1 = little; 2 = some; 3 = most.
NOTE: Data derived from Question 28 on the EQW National Employer Survey: "Regarding your nonmanagerial and nonsupervisory employees, how much of their time in formal training is spent performing activities in the following categories?"

TABLE 3-5   Restricted and Unrestricted Cobb Douglas Production Function

Explanatory Variables	Dependent Variables			
	Manufacturing		Nonmanufacturing	
	Log (S)[a]	Log (S/hours*ED)[b]	Log (S)	Log (S/hours*ED)
Constant	0.341	1.06[d]	−1.252	0.946[d]
	(0.317)	(7.335)	(−0.659)	(2.717)
Log capital	0.25[d]	—	0.36[d]	—
	(11.304)		(9.957)	
Log (K/hours*ED)[c]	—	0.25[d]	—	0.35[d]
		(11.311)		(9.959)
Log materials	0.26[d]	—	0.06[d]	—
	(11.812)		(2.958)	
Log (materials/hours*ED)	—	0.26[d]	—	0.06[d]
		(11.84)		(2.971)
Log hours	0.47[d]	—	0.628[e]	—
	(12.45)		(10.948)	
Multiestablishment firm	0.13[d]	0.12[d]	−0.05	−0.02
	(2.257)	(2.183)	(−0.382)	(−0.163)
% Equipment < 1 year old	−0.003	−0.003	0.005	0.005
	(−1.331)	(−1.288)	(1.249)	(1.327)
% Equipment 1-4 years old	0.003[d]	0.003[d]	−0.0003	−0.0004
	(2.153)	(2.178)	(−0.155)	(−0.181)
Log average education	0.86[d]	—	1.29[e]	—
	(2.028)		(1.793)	
Log trained 1993	−0.12	−0.12	0.08	0.07
	(−1.294)	(−1.356)	(0.39)	(0.355)
Log trained 1990	0.09	0.09	−0.11	−0.09
	(0.994)	(1.030)	(−0.515)	(−0.425)
% workers < 1 year	−0.003	−0.003[e]	−0.008[d]	−0.009[d]
	(−1.61)	(−1.692)	(−2.692)	(−2.875)
Unionized	−0.05	−0.06	0.35[d]	0.38[d]
	(−0.793)	(−0.952)	(2.494)	(2.722)
Total quality management	−0.02	−0.03	−0.01	−0.001
	(−0.347)	(−0.483)	(−0.121)	(−0.012)
Benchmark	0.03	0.032	0.08	0.09
	(0.539)	(0.558)	(0.621)	(0.721)
Above capacity	0.218[d]	0.21[d]	0.37[e]	0.36[e]
	(2.114)	(2.063)	(1.816)	(1.796)
Below capacity	−0.005	0.001	0.005	−0.009
	(−0.10)	(−0.011)	(0.047)	(−0.076)
Export	0.10[e]	0.10[e]	−0.05	−0.0
	(1.845)	(1.796)	(−0.338)	(−0.157)
R & D Center	−0.01	−0.01	−0.05	−0.04
	(−0.200)	(−0.133)	(−0.334)	(−0.265)
Birth year of establishment	0.001	0.001	0.0004	0.0002
	(1.26)	(1.428)	(0.164)	(0.087)

TABLE 3-5   Continued

Explanatory Variables	Dependent Variables			
	Manufacturing		Nonmanufacturing	
	Log (S)[a]	Log (S/hours*ED)[b]	Log (S)	Log (S/hours*ED)
Industry controls	yes	yes	yes	yes
Summary statistics:				
N	821	821	525	525
Adjusted squared multiple correlation (R^2)	0.8387	0.4331	0.6512	0.3814

[a]S = sales
[b]ED = average educational level of workers
[c]K = capital stock
[d]$p \leq .05$.
[e]$p \leq .1$.
NOTE: t tests are given in parentheses.

Lynch and Black also estimated a restricted Cobb Douglas production function in which the proxy for the quality of labor is rewritten as the product of labor hours times average education. The results for the restricted estimation are presented in Table 3-5, column 2 for manufacturing and column 4 for nonmanufacturing establishments.

Two sets of findings emerge from this analysis. The first is that education matters—indeed, substantially. In the restricted model the implied coefficient on education suggests that a 10 percent increase in the average education of an establishment's work force raises productivity by 4.9 percent in the manufacturing sector and 5.9 percent in nonmanufacturing. Second, training—that is, further job-related education—also has an impact on productivity. For manufacturing establishments the greater the time spent in formal, off-the-job training, the higher the establishment's productivity. For nonmanufacturing employers the content of training has a similar impact on an establishment's productivity. Computer skills development, even when the results are controlled for industry, has a positive impact on productivity, leading Lynch and Black (1996a:25) to conclude that "it is not so much whether you train your workers but rather in what you train them that affects establishment productivity."

What Lynch and Black's analysis clearly suggests is that the underlying fundamentals of the system are sound: workers acquire skills in which employers invest through further training and education because to do so increases establishment productivity.

The problem, then, lies elsewhere, not in the current functioning of the system but in the likelihood that it will not be able to sustain itself. As documented through our focus groups and reported in the EQW National Employer Survey, employers have little or no faith in the capacity of schools to either provide or certify the skills on which the productivity of their enterprises depend. The EQW survey question that best highlights this disconnection between schools and employers asked employers how important the following attributes are in the decision to hire a new nonsupervisory or production worker: applicant's previous work experience, previous employer's recommendation, years of schooling, grades, teacher's recommendations, current employer's recommendation, reputation of applicant's school, applicant's attitude, applicant's communication skills, score on an employer-administered test, and industry-based credentials. Respondents ranked each attribute on a scale of 1 (not important) to 5 (very important). Four of the five bottom-rated attributes related to schools and schooling. Teacher recommendations came in dead last, and the fifth attribute of this set—industry-based credentials—may also reflect a bias against schools, since they are often the ones to provide both the training and the tests for these credentials (see Table 3-6).

It is the sense that "school doesn't matter" that bothers educators concerned with the contribution that education ought to make to the quality of the work force. Tell young people that school doesn't matter—and it won't! Expect, as a result, the conclusion that Albert Shanker, president of the American Federation of Teachers, drew when commenting on the findings presented in the EQW National Employer Survey: "It's obvious that the less attention employers pay to school performance, the less incentive kids have to achieve and the more poorly prepared they will be" (Shanker, 1995:E9). This self-fulfilling prophecy both disenfranchises the nation's noncollege-bound students and threatens to undermine education's contribution to productivity in the economy—unless other means are found to teach skills and instill discipline.

Intrigued by these results and troubled by their implications, the National

TABLE 3-6   Relative Ranking of Factors in Making Hiring Decisions

Applicant's Characteristics	Rank[a]
Attitude	4.6
Communication skills	4.2
Previous work experience	4.0
Recommendations from current employer	3.4
Previous employer recommendation	3.4
Industry-based credentials (certifying applicant's skills)	3.2
Years of schooling	2.9
Score on tests administered as part of the interview	2.5
Academic performance (grades)	2.5
Experience or reputation of applicant's school	2.4
Teacher recommendations	2.1

[a] 1 = not important or considered; 5 = very important.

NOTE: Data derived from Question 57 on the EQW National Employers Survey: "When you consider hiring a new nonsupervisory or production worker (frontline worker), how important are the following in your decision to hire?"

School-to-Work Office asked whether the EQW National Employer Survey could similarly document other opportunities and/or costs associated with employers' decisions to use—or not use—school measurements to screen job applicants. Do employers who use grades and school reputations when screening applicants or have students on their work sites incur lower recruiting costs? Are these employers more likely to invest in the training of these first-time workers during their first year of employment?

The answer to the first question turns out to be "no." If anything, the relatively small proportion of employers who use school measures when deciding whom to hire spend a higher proportion of their annual labor costs on the recruitment and selection of new employees—in retrospect, not an altogether unexpected finding. Using information from our focus groups with employers, however, we altered course. Many of these employers reported that they did not screen new hires, but instead "tried them out"—often resulting in a series of hires and fires until both employer and employee found a suitable match. What this trial-and-error approach to hiring suggests is that both direct and indirect recruiting costs are incurred by employers who do not use school measures to screen new hires—and that higher turnover rates for new frontline employees during their first year of employment might serve as one measure of indirect recruitment costs.

To test this hypothesis, we developed a logit model using as its dependent variable a Boolean value that split the sample into two categories: establishments with 10 percent or more of their work force with less than 1 year of tenure and establishments with less than 10 percent of their work force with less than 1 year of tenure. We controlled for the effect of both upsizing and downsizing, as well as for the size of the establishment and its industry using two-digit standard industrial classification codes. We also combined employers' ratings of the three schooling-based screens—grades, school reputation, and teachers' recommendations—into a single schooling-measures index (Zemsky et al., 1996).

The logit analysis yielded compelling results for both the manufacturing and nonmanufacturing sectors (see Tables 3-7 and 3-8). The models identify a significant negative relationship between school screening variables and low job tenure. Both manufacturing and nonmanufacturing establishments that use school measures as important criteria when screening and hiring new workers report, on average, fewer workers with 1 year or less of tenure. In addition, both manufacturing and nonmanufacturing establishments that offer tuition reimbursement have higher tenure.

We used the same statistical strategy to explore whether employers who use school measures when screening and hiring frontline workers are more likely to invest in the training of these new workers. In the logit models for formal training, the dependent variable was whether or not an establishment spends more or less than the median on training new nonsupervisory workers. We included as independent variables remedial skills training, tuition reimburse-

TABLE 3-7 Logistic Analysis Predicting Whether More Than 10 Percent of an Establishment's Employees Have 1 Year or Less of Tenure for the Manufacturing Sector

Variable	Parameter Estimate	Standard Error	Wald Chi Square	Pr > Chi Square	Standardized Estimate	Odds Ratio
Intercept	1.6164	1.5695	1.0606	0.3031	—	—
20 to 49 employees	-0.0034	0.3739	0.0001	0.9927	-0.000656	0.997
50 to 99 employees	0.0630	0.3230	0.0380	0.8454	0.013273	1.065
100 to 249 employees	0.4012	0.3007	1.7798	0.1822	0.084350	1.494
250 to 1,000 employees	0.4177	0.2528	2.7315	0.0984	0.106726	1.519
Establishment type	-0.2202	0.1900	1.3423	0.2466	-0.057864	0.802
Textile/apparel	-0.0218	0.3706	0.0035	0.9532	-0.003386	0.978
Lumber/paper	-0.3379	0.3480	0.9426	0.3316	-0.060383	0.713
Printing/publishing	-0.0682	0.3755	0.0330	0.8558	-0.011213	0.934
Chemicals/petroleum	-0.6990	0.4168	2.8121	0.0936	-0.106078	0.497
Primary metals	-0.7487	0.3662	4.1803	0.0409	-0.129211	0.473
Fabricated metals	-1.0912	0.3850	8.0329	0.0046	-0.182131	0.336
Machinery/electrical	-0.9958	0.3976	6.2723	0.0123	-0.173410	0.369
Transportation equipment	-0.6046	0.3930	2.3660	0.1240	-0.091745	0.546
Miscellaneous manufacturing	-0.0973	0.3399	0.0819	0.7747	-0.017527	0.907
Sizing	0.0407	0.00524	60.1946	0.0001	0.925540	1.042

Computer use	-0.00425	0.00310	1.8788	0.1705	-0.071664	0.996
Technical workers	-0.00858	0.0137	0.3901	0.5322	-0.047454	0.991
Clerical workers	-0.00878	0.0119	0.5472	0.4595	-0.054991	0.991
Frontline workers	-0.00131	0.00824	0.0253	0.8736	-0.015239	0.999
Change in skill requirements	-0.1298	0.1874	0.4796	0.4886	-0.034756	0.878
Remedial skills training	0.00079	0.1119	0.0000	0.9944	0.000348	1.001
New-hire orientation	0.5730	0.2373	5.8282	0.0158	0.124324	1.774
Tuition reimbursement	-0.8046	0.2237	12.9407	0.0003	-0.184538	0.447
Education, technical	-0.0402	0.0364	1.2145	0.2704	-0.059376	0.961
Education, frontline	-0.00032	0.0985	0.0000	0.9974	-0.000158	1.000
Education, clerical	0.00638	0.0688	0.0086	0.9260	0.004334	1.006
Recruitment costs	0.0520	0.0197	6.9436	0.0084	0.141137	1.053
Internship programs	0.1034	0.1961	0.2779	0.5981	0.028497	1.109
Cooperative hiring	0.3709	0.1995	3.4565	0.0630	0.087171	1.449
School screening	-0.1125	0.0276	16.5661	0.0001	-0.213766	0.894
Job experience screening	-0.0132	0.0380	0.1208	0.7281	-0.016303	0.987

Association of Predicted Probabilities and Observed Responses:

Concordant = 79.8%	Somers' D = 0.599
Discordant = 20.0%	Gamma = 0.600
Tied = 0.2%	Tau-a = 0.278
(176,726 pairs)	c = 0.799

TABLE 3-8 Logistic Analysis Predicting Whether More Than 10 Percent of an Establishment's Employees Have 1 Year or Less of Tenure for the Nonmanufacturing Sector

Variable	Parameter Estimate	Standard Error	Wald Chi Square	Pr > Chi Square	Standardized Estimate	Odds Ratio
Intercept	1.8240	1.2538	2.1166	0.1457	—	—
20 to 49 employees	-0.2440	0.3688	0.4377	0.5083	-0.061503	0.784
50 to 99 employees	-0.0930	0.3739	0.0618	0.8036	-0.021399	0.911
100 to 249 employees	-0.00884	0.3601	0.0006	0.9804	-0.001982	0.991
250 to 1,000 employees	0.3107	0.3700	0.7050	0.4011	0.064797	1.364
Multiestablishment	0.4307	0.2085	4.2684	0.0388	0.113243	1.538
Construction	-0.5302	0.4002	1.7553	0.1852	-0.099443	0.588
Transportation	-0.8187	0.4315	3.5999	0.0578	-0.129863	0.441
Communication	-0.4768	0.5079	0.8811	0.3479	-0.058952	0.621
Utilities	-2.1287	0.5308	16.0833	0.0001	-0.307912	0.119
Wholesale trade	-0.9016	0.4122	4.7846	0.0287	-0.168295	0.406
Retail trade	0.2463	0.4583	0.2888	0.5910	0.040215	1.279
Finance	-0.7068	0.4752	2.2120	0.1369	-0.103188	0.493
Insurance	-0.4836	0.4725	1.0473	0.3061	-0.069284	0.617
Hotels	0.4525	0.4393	1.0609	0.3030	0.075399	1.572
Business services	-0.2541	0.4443	0.3272	0.5673	-0.040610	0.776

Sizing	0.0207	0.00471	19.3501	0.0001	0.284879	1.021
Computer use	-0.00311	0.00285	1.1840	0.2765	-0.067406	0.997
Technical workers	0.00122	0.00712	0.0292	0.8644	0.013453	1.001
Clerical workers	0.00461	0.00816	0.3193	0.5720	0.046073	1.005
Frontline workers	0.00790	0.00569	1.9312	0.1646	0.137609	1.008
Change in skill requirements	-0.0998	0.2003	0.2485	0.6181	-0.026322	0.905
Remedial skills training	-0.1786	0.1328	1.8073	0.1788	-0.072714	0.836
New-hire orientation	0.5025	0.2431	4.2719	0.0387	0.113631	1.653
Tuition reimbursement	-0.6155	0.2195	7.8629	0.0050	-0.165248	0.540
Education, technical	-0.0460	0.0358	1.6476	0.1993	-0.074757	0.955
Education, frontline	0.00400	0.0503	0.0063	0.9366	0.004200	1.004
Education, clerical	-0.0666	0.0689	0.9350	0.3336	-0.052236	0.936
Recruitment costs	0.0615	0.0165	13.9786	0.0002	0.238934	1.063
Internship programs	0.3043	0.2119	2.0628	0.1509	0.083635	1.356
Cooperative hiring	-0.1232	0.2250	0.2997	0.5841	-0.029995	0.884
School screening	-0.0596	0.0311	3.6684	0.0555	-0.113788	0.942
Job experience screening	-0.0335	0.0424	0.6219	0.4303	-0.043169	0.967

Association of Predicted Probabilities and Observed Responses:

Concordant = 77.1%	Somers' D = 0.545
Discordant = 22.7%	Gamma = 0.545
Tied = 0.2%	Tau-a = 0.272
(108,800 pairs)	c = 0.772

ment, and new-hire orientation in order to control for any effects on the outcome variable produced by these activities. Our interest was to examine whether using schooling criteria to screen potential employees is related to the employer's investment in substantive add-on training for new hires during their first year of employment—not training that initiates new employees, remedies deficits in basic skills, or reflects an employee's decision to continue his or her formal, school-based education.

The logit model for the manufacturing sector indicates that establishments scoring high on the school-measures variable spend more on the training of new nonsupervisory workers (see Table 3-9). However, in the logistic model for the nonmanufacturing sector, the relationship between the school-measures index and training investment in new workers is positive but not significant. (See Table 3-10.) In addition, if the skill requirements to perform production and support jobs at an acceptable level have increased, these establishments also invest more in new-worker training. As in the manufacturing sector, establishments that offer more formal training on remedial skills and offer new-hire orientation also invest more in new-worker training.

Taken in conjunction with earlier findings derived from the EQW National Employer Survey, the results of our analysis for the National School-to-Work Office suggest the existence of a kind of education and training nexus. That is, by and large it is the same set of establishments that use school measures to screen job applicants, that invest in the initial training of new employees, that provide tuition benefits so employees can enroll in work-related courses outside the firm, that report increased skill requirements for their jobs, and that are more likely to have nonmanagers and nonsupervisors using computers.

MAKING SENSE OF THE JUMBLE

What these results also suggest is that schools and the skills they teach are important—that for some employers a reliance on schools to train and certify skilled workers creates a competitive advantage—but that most employers now seek skilled workers elsewhere. Two stories from our focus groups and interviews with employers bracket the issue. Not surprisingly, during these sessions, school systems in general and high schools in particular were subject to the same kind of battering that youth received. There were stories of high schools that could not or would not respond to employers, that did not know how to work with businesses, that were dismissive of students who did not want to go to college, that used their vocational programs as dumping grounds, and that misled their students by not stressing that holding on to a job was serious business. When hiring a young worker, most employers did not bother asking for a high school transcript, simply because they "wouldn't believe what the school was telling us." After more than 20 minutes of this sustained bashing, the human resources manager of a middle-sized manufacturing concern called the conversation to a halt, observing: "I am not a great fan of our local high schools. But what I want in a new worker no high school can supply—a 26 year old with three previous employers."

In interviews with employers we frequently ask: "Exactly what do you want schools and colleges to produce? What are the critical skills you want them to have?" For the most part these are questions that employers cannot answer, queries that somehow seem wholly disconnected from the reality of running a business and hiring a work force. We are met with either a kind of embarrassed silence or a short awkward speech about the importance of standards as well as skills. However, one manager of a service bureau in which most workers were required to master computerized systems knew what he was looking for: someone who could read a manual and get started; someone who would not bluff, who would not be afraid to ask a question when he or she should; and, finally, someone with sufficient communication skills and respect for his or her elders to be able to go down the hall "and ask old John how it's done."

What these anecdotes and data from the EQW National Employer Survey suggest is that the skills most employers want are the ability to complete tasks, to get the job done, and to be both self-motivated and trainable—in sum, to be a truly good learner. A minority of establishments still believe success in school certifies the presence of such skills. Most employers, not sharing this faith, would rather trust trial-and-error hiring of the young, reserving their best jobs for those who have successfully held a series of positions. School credentials are not important, but evidence that an applicant has successfully acquired job survival skills is.

When the members of EQW's National Advisory Board—all of whom have been chief executive officers of large enterprises—reviewed the evidence presented here, they recalled an earlier EQW study conducted by Joan Wills of the Institute for Educational Leadership and Irene Lynn of the U.S. Department of Labor (Lynn and Wills, 1994). Their study included a survey of firms that participated in work-based learning programs, such as apprenticeships and internships. Among employers participating in these programs there was a wellspring of support for both the initiatives and the quality of the young workers they attracted. Most participating firms found their students to be productive and contributing employees. Although they often echoed the complaints of other employers about the high schools with which they worked—citing that too often the participating schools were not sufficiently organized or did not attach high priority to the program—a clear majority of employers also reported that they would take additional students later and would recommend the programs to other small-business owners.

Such internships—whether for pay or credit—bring students into the world of work and into the kinds of plants, offices, stores, and service agencies where they are likely to spend their working lives. Internships have the added advantage of creating an informal effective communication channel through which

TABLE 3-9 Logistic Analysis Predicting Whether an Establishment Spends More Than the Median on Training New Nonsupervisory Workers Relative to Total Labor Costs for the Manufacturing Sector

Variable	Parameter Estimate	Standard Error	Wald Chi Square	Pr > Chi Square	Standardized Estimate	Odds Ratio
Intercept	−3.7098	1.4975	6.1374	0.0132	.	.
20 to 49 employees	0.1978	0.3456	0.3277	0.5670	0.038095	1.219
50 to 99 employees	0.4063	0.2957	1.8877	0.1695	0.085646	1.501
100 to 249 employees	0.2478	0.2730	0.8239	0.3640	0.052102	1.281
250 to 1,000 employees	0.1358	0.2200	0.3812	0.5370	0.034702	1.145
Multiestablishment	0.3367	0.1791	3.5345	0.0601	0.088488	1.400
Textile/apparel	−0.8948	0.3748	5.6998	0.0170	−0.139153	0.409
Lumber/paper	−0.5958	0.3451	2.9808	0.0843	−0.106474	0.551
Printing/publishing	−0.6487	0.3746	2.9986	0.0833	−0.106641	0.523
Chemicals/petroleum	−0.5500	0.3933	1.9559	0.1620	−0.083470	0.577
Primary metals	−0.6686	0.3539	3.5691	0.0589	−0.115396	0.512
Fabricated metals	−0.9934	0.3658	7.3751	0.0066	−0.165810	0.370
Machinery/electrical	−0.7835	0.3583	4.7818	0.0288	−0.136437	0.457
Transportation equipment	−0.8531	0.3813	5.0058	0.0253	−0.129461	0.426
Miscellaneous manufacturing	−0.7927	0.3447	5.2875	0.0215	−0.142828	0.453
Sizing	−0.00036	0.00216	0.0284	0.8661	−0.008284	1.000
Computer use	0.00597	0.00281	4.5171	0.0336	0.100600	1.006

Technical workers	0.0109	0.0116	0.8816	0.3478	0.060148	1.011
Clerical workers	0.00799	0.0110	0.5305	0.4664	0.050078	1.008
Frontline workers	0.0153	0.00745	4.2098	0.0402	0.177468	1.015
Change in skill requirements	0.0455	0.1754	0.0673	0.7953	0.012185	1.047
Remedial skills training	0.3292	0.1010	10.6160	0.0011	0.144788	1.390
New-hire orientation	0.9433	0.2347	16.1567	0.0001	0.204661	2.568
Tuition reimbursement	0.7016	0.2235	9.8562	0.0017	0.160894	2.017
Education, technical	0.0309	0.0349	0.7875	0.3749	0.045744	1.031
Education, frontline	−0.0533	0.0929	0.3284	0.5666	−0.026183	0.948
Education, clerical	0.0437	0.0650	0.4526	0.5011	0.029685	1.045
Employed < 1 year	0.00298	0.00658	0.2055	0.6503	0.021926	1.003
Recruitment costs	0.0942	0.0229	16.9471	0.0001	0.255527	1.099
Internship programs	−0.3051	0.1822	2.8033	0.0941	−0.084080	0.737
Cooperative hiring	0.4340	0.1823	5.6667	0.0173	0.101989	1.543
School screening	0.0714	0.0258	7.6277	0.0057	0.135674	1.074
Job experience screening	−0.0358	0.0360	0.9867	0.3205	−0.044199	0.965

Association of Predicted Probabilities and Observed Responses:

Concordant = 74.2%   Somers' D = 0.487

Discordant = 25.5%   Gamma = 0.488

Tied = 0.2%   Tau-a = 0.243

(189,476 pairs) c = 0.744

TABLE 3-10 Logistic Analysis Predicting Whether an Establishment Spends More Than the Median on Training New Nonsupervisory Workers Relative to Total Labor Costs for the Nonmanufacturing Sector

Variable	Parameter Estimate	Standard Error	Wald Chi Square	Pr > Chi Square	Standardized Estimate	Odds Ratio
Intercept	-0.4188	1.3192	0.1008	0.7509	—	—
20 to 49 employees	0.3741	0.3731	1.0052	0.3161	0.094301	1.454
50 to 99 employees	0.7644	0.3807	4.0310	0.0447	0.175903	2.148
100 to 249 employees	0.6063	0.3639	2.7765	0.0957	0.136044	1.834
250 to 1,000 employees	0.8106	0.3677	4.8599	0.0275	0.169062	2.249
Multiestablishment	0.1763	0.2127	0.6867	0.4073	0.046340	1.193
Construction	-0.4781	0.4173	1.3122	0.2520	-0.089668	0.620
Transportation	0.5683	0.4480	1.6097	0.2045	0.090149	1.765
Communication	1.4174	0.5577	6.4586	0.0110	0.175257	4.127
Utilities	0.7605	0.4705	2.6123	0.1060	0.110002	2.139
Wholesale trade	0.3749	0.4237	0.7830	0.3762	0.069975	1.455
Retail trade	0.00211	0.4626	0.0000	0.9964	0.000345	1.002
Finance	1.4017	0.5146	7.4203	0.0064	0.204649	4.062
Insurance	0.9170	0.4929	3.4615	0.0628	0.131389	2.502
Hotels	0.5889	0.4436	1.7626	0.1843	0.098136	1.802
Business services	0.3444	0.4598	0.5609	0.4539	0.055028	1.411
Sizing	0.00302	0.00401	0.5685	0.4509	0.041544	1.003
Computer use	0.00168	0.00287	0.3426	0.5583	0.036435	1.002

Technical workers	0.00635	0.00737	0.7425	0.3889	0.070201	1.006
Clerical workers	-0.0159	0.00837	3.6252	0.0569	-0.159249	0.984
Frontline workers	-0.00575	0.00590	0.9504	0.3296	-0.100072	0.994
Change in skill requirements	0.3615	0.2012	3.2300	0.0723	0.095327	1.436
Remedial skills training	0.6998	0.1487	22.1425	0.0001	0.284943	2.013
New-hire orientation	1.1836	0.2613	20.5152	0.0001	0.267675	3.266
Tuition reimbursement	0.1638	0.2263	0.5238	0.4692	0.043962	1.178
Education, technical	-0.0554	0.0376	2.1765	0.1401	-0.090042	0.946
Education, frontline	-0.0796	0.0532	2.2336	0.1350	-0.083573	0.924
Education, clerical	-0.00690	0.0702	0.0097	0.9217	-0.005412	0.993
Employed < 1 year	0.0130	0.00575	5.1294	0.0235	0.136349	1.013
Recruitment costs	0.0697	0.0202	11.9192	0.0006	0.270817	1.072
Internship programs	-0.0260	0.2134	0.0148	0.9032	-0.007134	0.974
Cooperative hiring	-0.0215	0.2247	0.0091	0.9239	-0.005226	0.979
School screening	0.0460	0.0317	2.0971	0.1476	0.087812	1.047
Job experience screening	-0.0916	0.0437	4.3926	0.0361	-0.118112	0.912

Association of Predicted Probabilities and Observed Responses:

Concordant = 80.1% Somers' D = 0.603
Discordant = 19.8% Gamma = 0.604
Tied = 0.1% Tau-a = 0.301
(108,500 pairs) c = 0.801

employers learn about schools and their students and through which schools learn about the needs and practices of employers.

Adopting the employer's perspective, I would refocus the Board on Testing and Assessment's interest in "The Knowledge Gap: Rhetoric vs. Evidence" (the title of a session at the board's March 1996 conference where this paper was first presented). I would expect the research community to certify that skills matter, principally by citing both the growing gap in wages between educated and uneducated workers and the contribution that years of schooling make to establishment productivity. I would then call attention to a different kind of "knowledge gap," the one that too often leads schools to claim that they "know best" and employers to discount what schools can in fact supply.

The conclusion that the EQW National Advisory Board reached was that, more important than further research on the functioning of the youth labor market, there is a need for increased contact between schools and employers—the kind of contact that only effective internship programs can supply. What employers need to know is which schools are the best suppliers of good workers. What schools need to know is what kinds of experiences their graduates are having in the workplace. In moving regularly between school and work, successful interns provide practical answers to both sets of questions.

What is envisioned is not so much a formal finding about whether or not a skills gap exists but rather a mechanism—a feedback loop, really—that allows both schools and employers to adjust continuously to the changing demand for skills in an increasingly complex and competitive economic environment.

ACKNOWLEDGMENTS

As is so often the case, I owe a special debt to Maria Iannozzi and my colleagues at the National Center on the Educational Quality of the Workforce. The particular focus of the center's research on the school-to-work transition owes much to the energy, persistence, and insight of Nevzer Stacey.

The work reported here was supported by the Educational Research and Development Center program, under agreement number R117Q00011-91, CFDA 84.117Q, as administered by the Office of Educational Research and Improvement, U.S. Department of Education. The findings and opinions expressed here do not necessarily reflect the position or policies of the Office of Educational Research and Improvement or the U.S. Department of Education.

REFERENCES

Bailey, Thomas
    1993   The School-to-Work Transition Process. Unpublished paper presented at the Youth Em-
            ployment Policy Seminar, March 3-4. (For a summary, see pp. 14-16 in Paul Osterman
            and Maria Iannozzi, *Youth Apprenticeships and School-to-Work Transition: Current
            Knowledge and Legislative Strategy*, EQW Working Paper WP14, National Center on the
            Educational Quality of the Workforce, Philadelphia, PA.)
Bailey, Thomas, and Donna Merrit
    1993   *The School-to-Work Transition and Youth Apprenticeship: Lessons from the U.S. Experi-
            ence.* New York: Manpower Demonstration Research Corp.
Barley, Stephen
    1994   *Will Military Reductions Create Shortages of Trained Personnel and Harm the Career
            Prospects of American Youth?* EQW Working Paper WP26. Philadelphia: National
            Center on the Educational Quality of the Workforce.
Barton, Paul
    1990   *Skills Employers Need—Time to Measure Them?* Policy information proposal. Prince-
            ton, NJ: Policy Information Center, Educational Testing Service.
Carnevale, Anthony, Leila Gainer, and Ann Meltzer
    1990   *Workplace Basics: The Essential Skills Employers Want.* San Francisco: Jossey-Bass.
Diebold, Francis, David Neumark, and Daniel Polsky
    1994   *Job Stability in the United States.* EQW Working Paper WP30. Philadelphia: National
            Center on the Educational Quality of the Workforce.
DiMase, Richard, and Elizabeth Boyle
    1991   Eastland invests in untapped resources. *Personnel Journal* 70(4):53-54.
Doolittle, Fred, and Robert Ivry
    1993   Programs for Out-of-School and Disadvantaged Youth. Unpublished paper presented at
            the Youth Employment Policy Seminar, March 3-4. (For a summary, see pp. 20-24 in
            Paul Osterman and Maria Iannozzi, *Youth Apprenticeships and School-to-Work Transi-
            tion: Current Knowledge and Legislative Strategy*, EQW Working Paper WP14, Na-
            tional Center on the Educational Quality of the Workforce, Philadelphia, PA.)
Education Writers Association
    1990   *Training for Work: What the U.S. Can Learn from Europe.* Washington, DC: Education
            Writers Association.
Filipczak, Bob
    1993   Bridging the gap between school and work. *Training* 30(12):44-47.
Finegold, David
    1993   *Making Apprenticeships Work.* RAND Corporation Issue Paper. Washington, DC: Insti-
            tute on Education and Training.
Glennan, Thomas, with Lin Lui
    1991   *Collaborating to Improve Work-Related Education: Preliminary Lessons from the Field.*
            Working draft, RAND Corporation. Washington, DC: Office of Educational Research
            and Improvement, U.S. Department of Education.
Glover, Robert
    1983   Collaboration in apprentice programs: Experience with in-school apprenticeship.
            Pp. 141-149 in *1984 Yearbook.* American Vocational Association, Alexandria, VA.
Hamilton, Stephen, and Mary Agnes Hamilton
    1993   *Toward a Youth Apprenticeship System: A Progress Report from the Youth Apprentice-
            ship Demonstration Project in Broome County, New York.* Ithaca, NY: Cornell Youth
            and Work Program, Cornell University.

Kazis, Richard
   1993a   *Improving the Transition from School to Work in the United States.* Washington, DC:
           American Youth Policy Forum, Competitiveness Policy Council, Jobs for the Future.
   1993b   School-Based Policies. Unpublished paper presented at the Youth Employment Policy
           Seminar, March 3-4. (For a summary see pp. 16-20 in Paul Osterman and Maria Iannozzi,
           *Youth Apprenticeships and School-to-Work Transition: Current Knowledge and Legisla-
           tive Strategy,* EQW Working Paper WP14, National Center on the Educational Quality of
           the Workforce, Philadelphia.)
Ketcham, Allen
   1990   Entrepreneurial training for the disadvantaged. *Training and Development Journal*
           44(11):61-63.
Laurence, Janice
   1994   *The Military: Purveyor of Fine Skills and Comportment for a Few Good Men.* EQW
           Working Paper WP25. Philadelphia: National Center on the Educational Quality of the
           Workforce.
Levy, Frank, and Richard Murnane
   1993   The Demand for Youth Labor. Unpublished paper presented at the Youth Employment
           Policy Seminar, March 3-4. (For a summary see pp. 11-13 in Paul Osterman and Maria
           Iannozzi, *Youth Apprenticeships and School-to-Work Transition: Current Knowledge
           and Legislative Strategy,* EQW Working Paper WP14, National Center on the Educa-
           tional Quality of the Workforce, Philadelphia.)
Lynch, Lisa, and Sandra Black
   1996a   *Beyond the Incidence of Training: Evidence from a National Employer Survey.* EQW
           Working Paper WP35. Philadelphia: National Center on the Educational Quality of the
           Workforce.
   1996b   *Employer-Provided Training in the Manufacturing Sector: First Results from the United
           States.* EQW Working Paper WP34. Philadelphia: National Center on the Educational
           Quality of the Workforce.
Lynn, Irene, and Joan Wills
   1994   *School Lessons, Work Lessons: Recruiting and Sustaining Employer Involvement in
           School-to-Work Programs.* EQW Working Paper WP28. Philadelphia: National Center
           on the Educational Quality of the Workforce.
McDermott, Kevin
   1989   U.S. business goes back to school. *D&B Reports* 37(3):26-29.
Miller, William
   1988   Employers wrestle with "dumb" kids. *Industry Week* 237(1):47-52.
   1991   The education of business. *Industry Week* 240(17):20-26.
Mishel, Lawrence, and Ruy A. Teixeira
   1991   *The Myth of the Coming Labor Shortage: Jobs, Skills, and Incomes of America's Work-
           force 2000.* Washington, DC: Economic Policy Institute.
National Advisory Board of the National Center on the Educational Quality of the Workforce
   1995a   *Making Good Jobs for Young People a National Priority.* EQW Policy Statement PS01.
           Philadelphia: National Center on the Educational Quality of the Workforce.
   1995b   *On Connecting School and Work.* EQW Policy Statement PS02. Philadelphia: National
           Center on the Educational Quality of the Workforce.
   1996   *Survey Instrument for the EQW National Employer Survey, Phase 1.* EQW Databook
           DB03. Philadelphia: National Center on the Educational Quality of the Workforce.
National Center on Education and the Economy, Commission on the Skills of the American Work-
           force
   1990   *America's Choice: High Skills or Low Wages!* Rochester, NY: National Center on
           Education and the Economy.

National Commission for Employment Policy
1993   *Private Industry Councils: Examining Their Mission Under the Job Training Partner-
        ship Act.* Washington, DC: National Commission for Employment Policy.
Osterman, Paul, and Maria Iannozzi
1993   *Youth Apprenticeships and School-to-Work Transition: Current Knowledge and Legisla-
        tive Strategy.* EQW Working Paper WP14. Philadelphia: National Center on the Educa-
        tional Quality of the Workforce.
Rachlin, Jill, and Joseph Shapiro
1989   No pass, no drive. *U.S. News and World Report* 106(June 5):49-51.
Reich, Robert
1991   *The Work of Nations: Preparing Ourselves for 21st-Century Capitalism.* New York:
        Knopf.
Shanker, Albert
1995   Where we stand: Linking school and work (paid advertisement, National Federation of
        Teachers). *New York Times* April 23:E9.
Spring, William
1987   Youth unemployment and the transition from school to work: Programs in Boston, Frank-
        furt, and London. *New England Economic Review* (March/April):3-16.
Stern, David
1993   The Gains from Working While in School. Unpublished paper presented at the Youth
        Employment Policy Seminar, March 3-4. (For a summary, see pp. 13-14 in Paul Osterman
        and Maria Iannozzi, *Youth Apprenticeships and School-to-Work Transition: Current
        Knowledge and Legislative Strategy,* EQW Working Paper WP14, National Center on the
        Educational Quality of the Workforce, Philadelphia.)
Stringfield, Sam
1995   Attempting to enhance students' learning through innovative programs: The case for
        schools evolving into high reliability organizations. *School Effectiveness and School
        Improvement* 6(1):67-96.
William T. Grant Foundation
1992   *Youth Apprenticeship in America: Guidelines for Building an Effective System.* Wash-
        ington, DC: William T. Grant Foundation Commission on Work, Family, and Citizen-
        ship.
Zemsky, Robert
1994   *What Employers Want: Employer Perspectives on Youth, the Youth Labor Market, and
        Prospects for a National System of Youth Apprenticeships.* EQW Working Paper WP22.
        Philadelphia: National Center on the Educational Quality of the Workforce.
Zemsky, Robert, Daniel Shapiro, Barbara Gelhard, and Maria Iannozzi
1996   *The Education and Training Nexus: Employers' Use of Academic Screens and the Provi-
        sion of New-Hire Training.* EQW Working Paper WP38. Philadelphia: National Center
        on the Educational Quality of the Workforce.

4
Should Social Skills Be in the Vocational Curriculum? Evidence from the Automotive Repair Field

Bonalyn Nelsen

INTRODUCTION

At the turn of the century it was common for wealthy families to enroll their daughters in institutions known as finishing schools. Although these institutions were far from progressive or enlightened by today's standards, they served what was then a socially valued purpose: imparting the social skills that would ease a young woman's entry into the adult role she would soon occupy. Of course, the roles of women in such families were quite different from women's roles today; apart from managing household servants, the chief occupation of such women consisted of entertaining and being entertained. Therefore, students were drilled in etiquette, connoisseurship, voice and music, the art of making lively and entertaining conversation, and other skills required by female members of genteel society. Through concerted practice in realistic settings, students gradually acquired the ability to adapt their behavior to various social settings and to project the image of grace and poise that was the hallmark of an accomplished wife and hostess (McBride, 1992).

Today, finishing schools and their unique brand of training are found only in the pages of history books. Two factors contributed to their demise. First, the roles for which they prepared young women no longer exist. It is now customary to prepare all young people for active, productive roles in the work force without regard to gender, race, or social class. Second, society's views on the importance of social skills and knowledge have undergone considerable revision. Although few parents and teachers would discount these skills entirely, the social capital imparted by finishing schools is generally considered to be far less important than the intellectual capital imparted by schools—basic literacy, numeracy, writing skills, and the like. When the perceived importance of role-specific social skills diminished, the need for structured opportunities devoted to imparting these skills evaporated, and the finishing schools disappeared.

But it may be time to reconsider the importance of social capital in general and social training in particular. Since the 1980s, researchers have penned countless reports and articles bemoaning the poor performance of recent high school graduates in the workplace (e.g., see National Commission for Excellence in Education, 1983; Gorman, 1988; Carnevale et al., 1988; Aerospace Education Foundation, 1989). Although the problem is commonly attributed to a lack of academic skills, recent evidence suggests it may be at least partly social in nature. Employers surveyed about their hiring preferences consistently rank a good attitude and the ability to adapt to work environments as more important than educational credentials (Barton, 1990). Many also report difficulty in finding young people who exhibit a desirable mix of behaviors and attitudes (Barton, 1990; Committee for Economic Development, 1984). It is hardly surprising, then, that employers are far more likely to dismiss employees for difficulties in adapting to the work environment than for failure to learn job skills (National Association of Manufacturers, 1990; Committee for Economic Development, 1991; Cappelli, 1995). This evidence has prompted at least one researcher to ask if the so-called skills gap is due to a deficit of prosocial attitudes and behaviors (see Cappelli, 1995).

It is important to consider this possibility, for if the skills gap can be partly attributed to a lack of social skills, simply reinforcing basic literacy and numeracy will be insufficient to improve the work performance of high school graduates. This essay takes up the idea that the poor performance of recent high school graduates may indeed be partly social in nature. However, I argue that the problem is rooted not only in a lack of generally useful attitudes and behaviors like responsibility and punctuality, as Cappelli (1995) suggests, but also in a deficit of the occupationally specific social skills and knowledge needed to thrive in today's workplace—precisely the type of social capital once imparted by finishing schools. But what is social capital, and why is it in short supply?

ROLE OF SOCIAL CAPITAL IN THE WORKPLACE

All social groups possess a set of cultural rules and norms that guide the behavior of members. Persons who aspire to membership must learn to identify and comply with those rules (Gerholm, 1990). Social capital consists of the skills and knowledge required to evaluate and respond to situational demands in social settings. It provides individuals with the ability to "fit in" or gain acceptance to social groups over time by appreciating the cultural rules and norms governing any given situation and adapting their behavior to comply with those rules. This ability is critical because individuals who experience difficulty in perceiving and adapting to cultural rules risk being labeled outsiders. As a rule, those who hold this marginal status receive fewer benefits. In work groups, benefits consist of favors, indulgence, offers of assistance, and, perhaps most important, access to the informal knowledge required for practice.

Broadly speaking, two types of knowledge are applied in work activities: formal and informal. Formal knowledge consists of facts, principles, theories, algorithms, and other abstract systematic forms of knowledge. It is usually explicit and decontextualized—characteristics that render this knowledge easily codifiable (Brown and Duguid, 1991). Hence, formal knowledge is found in manuals, protocols, computer programs, and various textual resources present in the workplace. Informal knowledge consists of heuristics, work styles, and other situated understandings about materials, tools, and techniques (Barley, 1985; Barley and Nelsen, 1995). It is largely tacit, embedded in activity, and tied to the particulars of work in a given setting. Because informal knowledge is seldom articulated and somewhat variable, it is rarely written down. Instead, the understandings that make up informal knowledge are lodged in the collective memory and work practices of the local community of practice.

The skills and knowledge required to obtain informal knowledge will be very different from those used to gain formal knowledge. To access formal knowledge, one has but to obtain the manual or program in which the knowledge is stored and find the needed information within. These resources are typically an "unrestricted good" provided by the employer and freely available to all employees. Indeed, newly hired workers can expect to receive numerous policy manuals and handbooks upon arrival at their new jobs. Manuals and textbooks are on hand for all who need them. Software is installed in workstations frequented by many employees. Thus, any worker with the ability to read and open a computer icon can acquire formal knowledge on the job. But informal knowledge is not an unrestricted good possessed by the employer and freely shared with all. Rather, it is the intellectual property of the community of practice in a given work setting. To access this information, new hires must successfully insert themselves into the community of practice and become an accepted member.

Social capital is vital on both accounts. Individuals with a deficit of social skills may never have the opportunity to acquire informal knowledge, for some degree of cultural proficiency is necessary to be hired in the first place. Social competence is often taken as an indicator of intellectual competence and technical ability (Gerholm, 1990). If job candidates behave awkwardly or inappropriately during an interview, employers may interpret their behavior as a sign of general incompetence. Thus, even talented, well-trained students can experience difficulty in the job market if they are unable to demonstrate a reasonable amount of social acuity during a job interview (Sternberg, 1993).

Social capital is just as important after a neophyte's arrival on the job. In fact, the quality of a new hire's informal education depends largely on his or her ability to create an impression suggestive of competency and sociability. Most informal knowledge is transmitted spontaneously, usually as relevant problems are encountered in the course of work activities, and is passed among workers in the form of bits of advice, stories, demonstrations, and brief instances of guided practice (e.g., see Barley and Bechky, 1994). One must be an "insider" to be actively included in such exchanges. Moreover, frequent contact between neophytes and experienced workers increases the likelihood that informal understandings will be passed (Gerholm, 1990). Communities of practice are inherently practical; members are less likely to invest time and effort in tutoring neophytes who appear to be technically or socially inept. Thus, neophytes who display considerable social prowess are more likely to enjoy the company of peers and, consequently, to receive more opportunities for informal instruction than those perceived as social misfits.

A lack of social acuity would not be problematic but for the fact that successful work practice hinges on mastery of informal knowledge. Although so-called unskilled and semiskilled workers have always relied almost exclusively on such knowledge (Kusterer, 1978), workers with considerable formal training also make extensive use of informal understandings. For example, technicians and technologists employed in fields where postsecondary education is either mandatory or customary claim that formal knowledge is far less important than the informal knowledge gained through experience and participation in the local community of practice (Barley, 1985; Barley and Nelsen, 1995). Professionals also report that much, if not most, of the learning central to their work took place after they completed formal studies and immersed themselves in work activities (Schon, 1983; Wagner, 1987; Wagner and Sternberg, 1985). In short, it appears that social capital and the ability to fit in are crucial to any young person's success on the job.

Developing Social Acuity for Work

Unfortunately, most students have few opportunities to develop this ability before being thrust into situations where they are expected to exhibit it. Schools do a fair job of inculcating reading skills, mathematical knowledge, and other forms of intellectual capital, but they can be poor places in which to become socially adept. This is because schools may fail to replicate the social environment found in the workplace, to impart social capital useful in the workplace, and to provide structured opportunities for learning and practicing social skills.

Replication of the Work Environment

Developing social capital requires familiarity with the social dynamics extant in the workplace. To impart such knowledge, schools must faithfully replicate the social environment found in work settings by creating situations that mimic those found in the workplace and populating them with actors found in such situations. Interaction with experienced practitioners, employers, consumers, suppliers, and other parties should take place under conditions similar to those found in the workplace and engender similar consequences. Students should be placed in a role like the one they will assume on the job and should have occasion to sample both the freedoms and the limitations inherent in that position.

Most schools and vocational training programs fail to provide these conditions. Because few consumers, employers, or other parties encountered in the workplace frequent schools with regularity, students have limited opportunities for interaction. The pressures and consequences of the interaction they do experience in school environments may be quite different from those found in work environments. Teachers and classmates may, for example, be far more tolerant of social nonconformity than employers and experienced workers. Aberrant behavior that garners a reprimand from a teacher or a trip to the principal's office can be grounds for immediate dismissal in work settings. And the role students occupy in the classroom may be quite unlike those in the workplace, although these may overlap for a short time. As a result, schools often do a poor job of providing the cultural backdrop against which social capital is acquired.

Congruence of Social Capital

The deficit of occupationally specific capital can be traced to another characteristic of school environments. Simply put, schools frequently pursue their own agendas by imparting social skills useful in schools—not the workplace. In his seminal study of socialization in the classroom, Philip Jackson (1968) noted that students are subjected to a "hidden curriculum" that implicitly inculcates social skills that make them more manageable in the classroom. Through judicious distribution of rewards and punishments, teachers encourage students to be patient and submissive, passive and quiet, and not to come readily to the aid of peers as such activity is labeled "cheating."

Although this sort of social capital undoubtedly makes students more tractable, it may do little to improve their chances of learning on the job. In fact, studies of socialization and learning in the workplace suggest that the social capital acquired in schools may actually hinder informal learning on the job. Both Becker (1972) and Kusterer (1978) noted that employers seldom assign formal responsibility for teaching newcomers how to perform their duties. Consequently, apprentices and new hires must assume responsibility for their own informal education by continually seeking opportunities for learning on the job. Individuals who are passive and submissive risk being overlooked or perpetually stuck with menial, unpleasant chores that offer few opportunities for acquiring new skills and knowledge (Barley and Nelsen, 1995). Even assertive newcomers will probably enjoy limited tutoring if they ignore norms of reciprocity governing exchanges of assistance and information for long.

Structured Opportunities for Learning and Practice

A few learning environments do meet the requirements outlined above. Craft apprenticeships, residencies in teaching hospitals, and the training of doctoral candidates in academic departments expose students to the social dynamics of the workplace, mainly because the learning and work environments are one and the same. However, even students in these exemplary settings may fail to acquire social capital if no deliberate efforts are made to impart it. For example, Gerholm (1990:263) has noted that academic departments make little deliberate effort to teach graduate students "the rules of the game" or to impress upon them the importance of learning cultural rules and norms, despite the fact that such knowledge profoundly affects the quality of their education and, eventually, their careers (see also Sternberg, 1993). Instead, students must pick up these implicit understandings on their own through interactions with teachers, peers, and staff members. This process becomes an informal sorting mechanism in academic departments: students who catch on readily become ensconced in the departmental community and enjoy enhanced opportunities for learning while those exhibiting less social acuity are branded outsiders and consequently enjoy fewer opportunities.

Although this Darwinian logic effectively selects out students who innately lack social ability (and who are consequently poor candidates for membership in the academic community), it may also have the unfortunate effect of excluding those who suffer a surmountable handicap in this area. One can reasonably expect students whose racial, ethnic, or class backgrounds or other characteristics differ from those predominating in the departmental community (and, by extension, the workplace) to experience some difficulty in picking up the cultural rules and norms that guide behavior in school and work settings. However, in the absence of explicit attempts to inculcate social capital to all, the cultural playing field may not be level.

The Importance of Social Capital

In sum, the idea of providing students with structured opportunities for acquiring occupationally specific social capital retains considerable merit even in today's more enlightened and productive age. These understandings are at least as important to success on the job as basic and technical skills. Yet most schools offer few opportunities to acquire them. Quite simply, schools are not workplaces. Hence, most are either unwilling or unable to provide the situations and settings that students will experience upon entering the work force. Even schools that faithfully replicate actual work settings seldom make deliberate attempts to impart these understandings. This implies that opportunities for acquiring social capital are haphazard at best and nonexistent at worst. It is little wonder, then, that employers are increasingly dissatisfied with the quality of social skills possessed by recent high school graduates.

An Alternative Model of Social Education

Obviously, reversing the deficit of social skills will require a search for alternatives to existing models of social education in the classroom. The finishing school represents one such model. These were institutions devoted to imparting the social capital required to ease young people into adult roles and help them become productive members of society. Because they were boarding schools, students were immersed in the social settings and roles they would soon occupy. Students were swept up in a dizzying round of balls, dinners, parties, and outings, all of which provided occasions for experiencing social dynamics in realistic settings. These activities were supplemented with formal instruction in social skills and structured opportunities for practice. Parlors and gardens became laboratories in which young women honed the social skills they would need for public life. Needless to say, because the schools existed expressly for imparting social capital, the skills and knowledge taught were congruent with those needed in the "workplace." These features made finishing schools highly effective vehicles for imparting the unique type of social capital required by the social elite.

I believe that today's students could benefit greatly from the type of instruction formerly provided by these schools. Of course, the modern-day "finishing school" would bear little resemblance to its forerunner in either form or content. For example, to maximize efficiency and comply with modern educational practices, instruction would take place within existing vocational training programs rather than boarding schools devoted solely to that purpose. "Laboratories" would consist of offices, sales counters, examination rooms, and shop floors rather than dress balls and tea parties. And the curricula would include strategies for handling difficult customers, reporting problems to the boss, or seeking the advice of experienced peers rather than being a gracious hostess. However, the purpose of the lessons would remain essentially the same: first, and perhaps most importantly, to sensitize students to the importance of social dynamics in the workplace; second, to make them familiar with the cultural rules of the occupation for which they are preparing; third, to note how these rules may vary across work settings; fourth, to acquaint students with the occupational roles they will soon occupy; and, finally, to tutor them in a variety of appropriate responses to social situations they will soon experience and to provide opportunities for practice.

None of these lessons are possible without a detailed knowledge of the cultural rules and norms observed in the occupation in question. Finishing schools owed their success largely to an impressive understanding of the social capital needed by women in upper-class households. This knowledge allowed the institutions to create a representative sample of social settings in which to learn and practice. In fact, the facilities themselves were carefully designed to create a physical and social atmosphere that faithfully mimicked those the students would enjoy upon graduation (McBride, 1992). Similarly, any discussion of modern-day "finishing schools" or formal social instruction must start with the development of a detailed understanding of the social capital needed by newcomers in a given occupational milieu. To this end, I will consider the example of automotive repair.

By drawing on data from an ethnographic study of auto repair, I will examine the sort of social capital required by workers in actual work settings. Auto repair is a field not renowned for social aplomb; automotive technicians would seem to be unlikely candidates for finishing schools. Yet, as I will show, social skills are of vital importance to the success of practitioners in this occupation. These data will be used to fashion a typology of social skills and knowledge required to ease entry-level automotive technicians into full-fledged occupational roles. Although by no means exhaustive, this typology offers a representative description of the types of social capital useful for gaining acceptance in work settings. The essay will conclude with a discussion of how this knowledge could be used to create opportunities for acquiring social capital useful in this occupational milieu.

DATA AND METHODS

Automotive repair is a field that offers a wide variety of services and service delivery formats.[1] To develop a more comprehensive understanding of these formats and their social dynamics, I chose to study two firms featuring highly contrasting models of service delivery.

The first firm was an independently owned dealership that sold and serviced the full line of vehicles produced by a U.S. automotive manufacturer. This was a high-volume shop offering a full range of maintenance and repair services. Most of the repair shop's business consisted of routine maintenance and warranty repair work on the product line featured by the dealership, although other work was willingly accepted. The shop's 16 technicians were assigned to one or more technical specialties (e.g., brakes, transmissions, tune-ups, and electrical system). Two of these technicians had been in the field for less than 2 years and, hence, held an apprentice-like status in the local community of practice. One other technician had worked in the field for less than 3 years. The remainder of the technical staff had considerable tenure, with the most senior employee logging 24 years with the dealership. In addition, the shop employed four predelivery inspection attendants to vacuum, clean, and prepare vehicles for delivery to clients; a parts-room attendant responsible for ordering and maintaining stock; five service advisers who handled customer service duties and paperwork; and three clerical employees. Managerial responsibilities were divided between two positions: a shop manager, who took responsibility for technician's work, and a service manager, who supervised the remaining staff and overall service operations.

---

[1] A service format represents an organizational template for service delivery in the after-market automotive repair industry (Mateyka et al., 1988). Five formats are dominant: speciality repair, mass merchandisers, independent repair shops, full-service gas stations, and new car dealerships.

The second research setting was a small, independently owned repair shop. Unlike the dealership, this shop provided only automotive maintenance and repair services. The owner was a technician who worked alongside the two technicians he employed in the shop's three service bays. Although he had been in the industry for 18 years and had owned his own shop for 6, his employees had only 3 and 5 years of experience, respectively. Both had been employed at the shop for approximately 3 years. The owner's spouse handled most of the clerical and administrative duties. The owner and his technicians were "bumper-to-bumper mechanics," who prided themselves on their general knowledge of automotive technology and ability to tackle most repairs. Most repair work was performed on site, although work requiring tools not owned by the shop, such as precision welding or grinding, was dispatched to various specialty shops in the vicinity.

My methods of data collection were identical for both research sites. I moved freely about the shop, spending much time observing how the technicians worked and interacted with others in their work area. I also observed activities in other areas, such as the detailing area, vehicle drop-off area, parts room, customer waiting areas, and parking lots. In each location, both workers and customers were encouraged to speak freely about their past and present activities and interactions. I observed activity at the dealership for 5 days per week for 6 to 10 hours a day. Observations at the independent shop were more sporadic, consisting of 4- to 8-hour periods once or twice each week. In total I logged 100 and 75 hours of observation, respectively, at the dealership and the independent shop. I jotted down field notes throughout the day and expanded them off site each evening while memories were still fresh.

These observations provided an invaluable opportunity to witness firsthand the social dynamics of the workplace: the exchange of information and assistance, the socialization of employees, the forging of alliances, the enactment and violation of cultural rules and norms. These observations were supplemented by detailed taped interviews conducted with 18 technicians, shop owners, and service managers employed in other auto repair shops. In addition to other topics, technicians were encouraged to offer detailed accounts of their early experiences on the job. Particular attention was paid to instances in which technicians had committed social gaffes and the lessons they learned as a result. Questioning also focused on strategies they successfully employed to win the acceptance of peers and avoid attributions of incompetence (namely, "looking stupid"). Shop owners and service managers were encouraged to describe their expectations for entry-level automotive technicians and to recount examples of behavior that met, exceeded, or fell short of their expectations.

These data were analyzed with an iterative process of coding and hypothesis formation. The first wave of coding identified various types of social capital used in the workplace: knowledge useful for exchanges of assistance; for accessing, disseminating, and evaluating informal knowledge; and so on. Subsequent analysis was devoted to elaborating these categories to fashion a typology of social capital useful to entry-level automotive technicians. It is to this typology that I now turn.

FITTING IN AND GETTING BY: SOCIAL CAPITAL IN AUTO REPAIR

Although repair shop owners, service managers, and technicians expressed slightly different opinions about what skills and abilities were required by entry-level automotive technicians, all agreed that two types of competencies are indispensable. The first consists of basic and technical skills. Entry-level technicians should have the ability to read, write, and perform basic arithmetic and should have a firm grasp of relevant technical skills: a knowledge of safety and tool use; a basic understanding of the function of automotive systems, their components, and repair procedures; the ability to perform visual inspections; and a familiarity with manual usage. The second type of competency is social. This is manifest in the ability to fit into the shop surroundings: to get along with co-workers and management, to communicate effectively, to impress clients with their competent and professional manner.

Neophytes could ill afford a serious deficiency in either area. Entry-level automotive technicians were subjected to close scrutiny before and after their arrival on the job. Opinions about the new hires' technical and social competency were quickly formed in the workplace and, once made, were not easily shifted. It is customary for all new hires to serve a 60- or 90-day probationary period. However, informants reported that dismissal within a week or two of hiring was common if new hires showed signs of faltering.[2] Although these practices may seem slightly Draconian, informants offered numerous justifications for their actions. Owners and service managers noted that botched repairs could result in thousands of dollars' worth of damage and life-threatening hazards—liabilities that no shop could afford. Disrespectful or curt treatment could produce a disgruntled customer and result in lost profits as surely as technical mishaps. Also, skilled technicians were highly sought after and, once found, were enticed to remain. Thus, many shops featured close-knit groups of technicians of long tenure. If new hires appeared unwilling or unable to adapt their behavior to the shop's existing social structure, they would quickly be shown the door. Finally, some shops invest considerable funds in training their technicians; shop owners and managers want to expend these funds wisely by

---

[2]The use of assistants or teams was more prevalent in speciality repair shops, such as those that provided precision grinding and machining services or that rebuilt transmissions. In such shops, assistants would be employed to remove and install engines and transmissions, while technicians were charged with diagnosing and repairing the units. Dealerships also made occasional use of apprentices or assistants in this way. But for the most part, technicians work on a wholly independent basis.

retaining only those candidates who seem to be good prospects for long-term employment.

The opinions rendered by experienced technicians could be just as swift and final. Experienced technicians realized that virtually all entry-level technicians would require a good deal of assistance and guidance to succeed on the job. However, they saw little point in investing time and effort in cultivating neophytes who showed scant promise, particularly when they knew such workers seldom stay long. Hence, individuals whose work or behavior displayed disregard for either technical standards or the rules and norms valued by practitioners were soon identified, avoided, and left to fend for themselves. "There are a lot of fish in the sea," noted one technician, "but only a few are keepers. As far as I'm concerned, the rest can work somewhere else." The implications of these views are clear—entry-level automotive technicians can greatly enhance their success on the job by understanding and exhibiting social capital. An informed and realistic view of expectations regarding their performance allows neophytes to more easily meet the behavioral requirements of the workplace. It also allows them to identify social pitfalls before they succumb. Both are central to avoiding attributions of incompetence and to winning acceptance among employers, managers, and fellow workers. The salient types of social capital are discussed below.

Displaying a "Proper" Attitude

The acceptance of an entry-level technician hinges largely on the ability to display an attitude that simultaneously projects an air of confidence and one of humility (Nelsen and Barley, 1994). Entry-level technicians must convince clients of their ability, persuade superiors of their worth as an employee, and assure experienced peers that they are worthy of help and instruction. Evincing an air of aplomb is necessary on all accounts. In interactions with customers, confidence is reflected in how technicians present themselves and their work:

> It's important that the technician projects a certain confidence in his abilities. That means not guessing, not going before the customer and saying, "Well, I'm not sure what it could be . . . could be this or could be this . . ." Instead, he should say, "We're going to find out what we need to fix. This is what I'm going to do to find that out." You have to understand that diagnosing some of these problems today can take up to 2 hours, and that's a lot for the customer to pay for. So they want to know that the technician knows what he's looking for, that he knows what he's doing. (*service manager, dealership*)

In the shop, confidence is manifested in a willingness to tackle unfamiliar, unusual, and, eventually, complex tasks. Although entry-level technicians were expected to display a certain amount of hesitation or self-doubt, this behavior was expected to be quickly replaced with an air of determination and poise as experience grew. Trepidation expressed at confronting a task for the first time was indulged, particularly if the repair was particularly complex or unusual. But neophytes were expected to overcome their reluctance after their second or third encounter. The abilities of those who disregarded this norm by continually expressing self-doubt became suspect.

Humility is also necessary for successful role performance; this attitudinal characteristic is evident in a willingness to admit mistakes or puzzlement, to ask questions, and to seek the counsel of knowledgeable peers and managers. In a purely instrumental sense, these behaviors are necessary to signal a need for help and advice and to avoid attributions of incompetence. Experienced technicians and managers agreed that failure to make inquiries and to seek second opinions about diagnoses and procedures was a significant source of error and led to the formation of negative perceptions about neophytes' promise:

> New guys get themselves into trouble because they don't ask. There are always different ways of doing things, so test the waters by asking the boss. Let me make the decision. For example, if a customer asks for something that doesn't sound right, like they don't want to authorize work needed for safety reasons . . . that's a potential liability to the shop. Well, let me decide how to handle the situation; don't take on too much authority. (*owner, independent shop*)

As the foregoing quotation suggests, humble behavior did more than signal a need for help and information. Expressions of humility signaled acknowledgment of an employer's authority and experienced peers' superior expertise and status in the community of practice. Thus, neophytes who failed to admit their ignorance or who failed to occasionally ask for assistance not only gave the impression that they were more expert than they really were, but also tacitly denigrated the accumulated skills and knowledge of experienced peers. As one subject noted, this was an impression that an entry-level automotive technician could ill afford:

> Car people like to tell you how much they know. "Oh, yeah, I know that; I've done that." And that's the absolute worst thing [entry-level technicians] can do. . . . If a new guy walks into a shop and tells [experienced technicians] how much he knows, who's gonna be there to help him when he really needs help? Most of the technicians I've known have always been happy to help a new guy as long as the attitude was right. But as soon as you start tellin' an old-timer how much you know, they're gonna turn you off like a radio and just let you sink or swim. (*technician, independent shop*)

Adherence to a Work Style

Adherence to a work style entails adopting a style of practice deemed crucial for avoiding the types of trouble that occur in a particular work context. A work style does not specify what procedures must be done but rather how procedures should be carried out. In auto repair it represents a collection of preemptive strategies and behaviors useful for outwitting the foibles of automotive technology and for being efficient in a demanding, pressure-filled work environment. As automotive technology has become complex, diagnosis and repair are more difficult and time consuming. Yet, as competitive pressures and the cost of parts and labor increase, technicians are pressed to work faster and more efficiently. The competing demands of complex technology and efficiency increase the probability that misdiagnosis and error will occur. Neophytes can greatly enhance their reputations among employers and peers by learning and demonstrating various behavioral strategies to cope with these pressures.

Improvisation is one such strategy. Technicians were expected to become quite flexible and resourceful in adapting their practice to meet the exigencies of technology and time. Workers prided themselves on their innovation in the area of tool use, for example. A variety of household objects were substituted for costly tools and supplies—common petroleum jelly for white automotive grease; nail polish for marking paint; a humble paper clip for jumper wires; or, in cars featuring built-in diagnostic displays, a digital diagnostic scanner. Some problems can be diagnosed only by recreating the physical states of operation under which they appear. For instance, when a thermistor or temperature-sensitive sensor is tested, the engine must be hot. Technicians regularly experimented with ways to fool the vehicle or component into activity without actually spending the time necessary to recreate physical states. Hence, rather than allowing an engine to idle for extended periods or taking a test drive, technicians would use a portable hair dryer to trigger a thermistor.

Tight tolerances and complex designs make modern automotive technologies far less tolerant of contamination than those of the past. Contamination includes not only dirt and other contaminants accumulated during normal use but also matter introduced by the technician during repair procedures. The presence of even minute quantities of extraneous material can cause a component to fail. For instance, a stray metal filing trapped in a combustion chamber during reassembly will quickly pit and score the surface of pistons and cylinder walls. And lint from a shop rag used to clean parts of an automatic transmission prior to reassembly will block check valves and subsequently cause shifting problems. Cleanliness is therefore an important part of the technician's work style. Technicians took pains to carefully remove any foreign matter that might impede the vehicle's operation and employed work practices known to reduce contamination, such as using compressed air rather than a shop rag to dry parts of an automatic transmission. Cleaning habits demonstrated a concern for efficiency as well. When disassembling brakes, workers would place springs, calipers, and other components on shop rags and slide these beneath the vehicle before turning the rotors. Not only did this practice keep components free of dirt and stray metal filings, it also eliminated the need to wipe down each component separately before reassembly.

Technicians saved both time and trouble by adopting an organized methodical approach to their work. This was demonstrated in an exacting attention to detail. In one shop such concern was witnessed whenever an engine was prepared for removal from a vehicle. Before removing the engine, the technician dabbed the connections of vacuum hoses with nail polish of various colors and labeled wiring connectors with masking tape. Marking existing connections not only made the process of reconnecting hoses and wires much more efficient, it also decreased the frustrating possibility of making improper connections. A methodical approach was also manifest in a general concern for being organized and efficient. Technicians recommended placing the tools most frequently used on a small cart that could be wheeled from car to car as they worked, thus sparing them the trouble of making multiple trips to the tool box or searching about for tools. Parts were also kept organized and accounted for by storing them in labeled boxes prior to reassembly.

Finally, the technicians' preferred work style includes the ability to work independently and engage in self-directed practice. Automotive technicians seldom work as teams. Even very complex jobs, such as removing and rebuilding an engine, are accomplished by a single technician in most shops.[3] From their first day on the job, entry-level technicians also have a set of assigned tasks they are expected to accomplish independently of others. This was somewhat challenging for neophytes, of course; their lack of experience and informal knowledge made frequent requests for help and guidance a practical necessity. However, once advice or instruction was given, neophytes were expected to "run with it," or apply it on their own, and gradually wean themselves from their peers' assistance.

Knowledge of Occupational Image

All neophytes must develop an intuitive sense of the identity of their occupation and its relations with other occupations (Gerholm, 1990) as well as an understanding of how one should project and modify that image in various social situations. For entry-level automotive technicians, this required a general understanding of norms governing demeanor, communication, and the manipulation of symbols.

Demeanor

A technician's demeanor is reflected in bearing or conduct. Several characteristics were desirable, and not a few were considered injurious. Not surprisingly, friendliness and a cooperative nature were universally appreciated, as was the ability to take practical joking and teasing in stride. The technicians' work-

---

[3]The National Institute for Automotive Service Excellence, a national nonprofit organization, tests and certifies the competency of automotive technicians. To become certified, technicians must pass written exams designed to test their technical knowledge.

day was filled with boisterous exchanges with peers, and neophytes were frequently targeted as the butt of a joke. Teasing relented gradually as neophytes were drawn closer into the community of practice. Hence, the joking and teasing were not unlike a sort of mild hazing intended to test neophytes' demeanor and patience as they inched closer to membership status. Neophytes who became defensive or withdrawn upon receiving such attention were viewed as "bad sports" who were less-than-promising candidates. As one technician noted, an unpleasant demeanor was a flaw that was not easily overlooked in even talented neophytes:

> Being friendly, cooperative is important . . . especially for an entry-level mechanic, because they're gonna be askin' for favors every day. They have to be easy to get along with, too. Some of the new guys we get are a little frustrating for me to get along with. Like, here's a person with good skills, they're good with their hands. They have the physical ability and the mental aptitude for it but . . . I don't want to work with them. There's too much friction. It's too hard to relax with this person. It's just not worth my time. (*technician, dealership*)

Patience is another behavioral characteristic that is necessary to win the approval of employers and peers. In the occupation of auto repair technician, patience was denoted by quiet diligence and emotional restraint. Virtually all practitioners were periodically confounded by impasses in their work. These could be an elusive electrical fault that defied repeated attempts at identification, a stripped head bolt lodged in the bowels of an engine, or a motor mount so corroded that no amount of torque or solvent could break it free. Occasionally technicians were held responsible for errors that occurred through no fault of their own. For example, several informants recalled instances of completing a laborious and difficult rebuild only to find that an equipment supplier or parts-room attendant had given them the wrong components at the outset. All informants reported feelings of frustration and outright anger when confronted by such mishaps.

Many technicians were tempted to give vent to their frustrations in these situations, and a few actually did—reports of shouting, swearing, spitting, kicking vehicles, throwing tools, and generally indulging in fits of temper were not uncommon. Although peers could empathize with the offending party, such behavior was never condoned. Employers considered it grounds for immediate dismissal, and peers shunned colleagues given to emotional outbursts. It was particularly risky for neophytes to behave in this manner, for their lack of experience could more easily give rise to problems and frustration and because they were watched more closely and indulged less than experienced employees. Far better was an approach that demonstrated patience:

> The fact is, sometimes you've gotta do things over. It may be an awful job, it may not be your fault, and you may have just finished swearing to yourself that you'd never do that job again. But you know what? You gotta do it. So don't bitch about it, don't have a fit. Don't throw your tools or kick the car. Count to

10 and just do it. . . The other guys will respect you for it. (*technician, indepen-dent shop*)

Communication

Communication with laypeople, and clients in particular, is unlike communi-cation with fellow technicians, other employees, and managers. In general, ex-changes with organizational outsiders were considerably more circumspect un-less the technician had a special relationship with the speaker. Tones were moderate; speech was clear and noticeably "clean"—free from profanity or any remarks that might give offense. Employers and technicians spoke approvingly of those who demonstrated "respect" for clients by listening carefully, being courteous, and attending to their concerns in a sincere and responsive manner. Moreover, interactions with clients were not occasions for erudition. Discourse had to be sufficiently specific and technical to explain the problem or repair and give the impression that the speaker was competent, but not so obscure that clients, who generally possessed little knowledge of automotive technology and repair, became befuddled.

A puzzled or nervous client is a liability in automotive repair. To success-fully engage in problem diagnosis and repair, workers must question motorists about their vehicle's symptomatic behavior and history in a manner like that of a physician with a patient. The speed and accuracy of diagnosis often hinged on a few scraps of information gleaned from a client's description of the problem. But confused, intimidated clients were less able or, in some cases, less willing to supply needed information. Informants confided that many customers were hesi-tant to reveal how little knowledge they actually possessed about automotive technology and, consequently, refused to say much of anything (see Nelsen, 1995). Thus, to guard against puzzling clients, technicians had to rid their speech of most technical jargon and, perhaps more importantly, rid themselves of the assumption that laypeople would probably understand what they were talking about. Effective communication called for the use of simple descriptions, fre-quent repetition, clarifying questions, and elucidating metaphors—communica-tion techniques that are unnecessary with peers.

In contrast, communication with community members (including some shop owners and managers) was far more technical and direct. Peers, managers, and such visitors as equipment suppliers shared membership in a speech community. Thus, technicians could reasonably assume that they understood technical prin-ciples and terminology as well as cultural norms condoning the use of joking, shouting, whistling, and profanity within the bounds of the community. The need to monitor one's speech and check behavior was reduced considerably. However, technicians could not assume that peers and employers would under-stand their actions and methods, particularly when doing something that seemed odd, unusual, or potentially unsafe. This is of particular concern to neophytes, who are subject to extreme scrutiny during the first months on the job. New hires could do much to avoid attributions of incompetence by communicating their intent before proceeding:

> You can't assume that other people understand why I'm doing something or what I'm doing. This is especially true if I know that I'm going to be doing something that's really obvious but strange looking. Sometimes I'll prepare people for what I'm about to do. I'll say, "This is what I'm going to do, and this is why I'm going to do it. I know it's going to look strange." And if it's something I'm not real sure about, I'll ask for a second opinion. . . . "Do you have a suggestion on a way that I can do this better?" Now, if new guys would learn to do that before they look foolish or before they get in trouble, it'd be much better. (*technician, repair franchise*)

Manipulation of Symbols

An important part of projecting a desirable occupational image is understanding how to identify and manipulate those ideas and objects that symbolize competence, professionalism, and membership in the community of practice. Various objects can symbolize competence but perhaps none more so than the automotive technicians' tools. In the field of auto repair, technicians are expected to supply their own hand and power tools and handheld computerized diagnostic devices. Employers provide only larger diagnostic devices such as oscilloscopes, permanent fixtures like hydraulic lifts, and special tools needed to repair a specific make of car. So critical are tools to a technician's livelihood that it was widely held that one could accurately judge a practitioner's technical skills and attitude from the condition of these objects. Tools in poor condition indicated a lack of ability and caring, whereas well-maintained tools suggested prowess and professionalism. Entry-level technicians were not expected to possess the vast collection of tools common among experienced workers nor to feature expensive brands of equipment in their kits. But they were expected to own the tools needed to perform basic repairs and to have tools that were of reasonable quality, neatly organized, and well maintained.

In fact, service managers and shop owners took the condition of a prospective employee's tools as an indicator of the candidate's promise—a box neatly stocked with well-tended tools was guaranteed to impress while tools in disarray or disrepair met with disapproval. Service managers and shop owners regularly asked to inspect applicants' tools during interviews. As one explained, "If the box looks like garbage, I figure the guy does garbage work. And I don't want him here." Clients also appeared to be impressed with tools, for technicians claimed that employers would strategically assign work bays most visible to the public to technicians who had neat, impressive collections. Upon a neophyte's arrival at a shop, the newcomer's tools once again became an object of attention. By casually borrowing an item from the newcomer's kit, experienced workers could appraise the selection and condition of the items within and form an immediate impression of their owner. Judgments were based even on the nature and condition of the case in which tools were kept. Metal boxes and rollaway chests that were clean and dent-free were admired; plastic boxes covered with grime and decals were disparaged. One technician recalled the negative impression he had unwittingly created by toting an unimpressive tool box:

> I walked into my first job carrying my tools in an old fishing tackle box. . . . I saw the older mechanics eyeing me, but nobody said anything until I was getting ready to leave a couple years later. One of the old-timers said, "Jim, when we saw you walk in with that tackle box, we bet amongst ourselves that you wouldn't last the month. We thought you must be stupid if you carried that thing around. But you surprised us!". . . . There's a good lesson in that. (*technician, dealership*)

Accessing, Disseminating, and Evaluating Informal Knowledge

An entry-level automotive technicians' informal education can be speeded up with the help of a thorough understanding of the cultural rules for accessing, disseminating, and evaluating informal knowledge. One type of understanding involves knowing where to seek information. Quite simply, not all peers are equally knowledgeable. Informal knowledge is distributed in the community of practice along two dimensions. First, it is distributed among members by tenure. Those who have the longest tenure at the firm or in the business will have the richest stores of firm-specific and industry-specific knowledge, respectively. Informal knowledge is also distributed throughout the community by technical specialty. Individuals working as transmission repairers are the logical source of information on shifting patterns; drivability technicians, on cold-start problems; brake installers, on rotor tolerances; and so on.

When a piece of information is needed, neophytes need to sift through the collective competencies of community members and identify the most appropriate source for knowledge. This is necessary not only to obtain the most accurate and reliable information but also to avoid appearing naive or uninformed by asking improper questions. For example, asking a lube technician whose experience is limited to changing oil and greasing fittings about a complex drivability problem would be viewed as absurd. However, if a neophyte discovers that, say, a transmission technician harbors an interest in drivability problems but seldom has an opportunity to display his knowledge, that person could become a valuable and enthusiastic informant. Individuals who have recently returned from training or who participate in continuing education courses are also good sources of information because they may be eager to demonstrate what they have learned. One technician took advantage of this opportunity by serving as an informal "study partner" for a peer who was studying for the Automotive Service Excellence (ASE) certification examinations.[4] Although not preparing for the tests himself, the neophyte quizzed his partner using practice booklets and manuals during breaks. This tactic proved doubly useful—the drills exposed the neophyte to a valuable source of formal knowledge and drew him closer to an indebted, more experienced peer. Discussions of the practice questions also provided the neophyte with opportunities for eliciting informal knowledge drawn from his peer's work experience.

Once knowledgeable individuals are identified, neophytes are wise to cultivate relationships with them. Although newcomers should attempt to win acceptance among all community members, it is advantageous to secure the goodwill of those noted to be especially helpful or expert. This can be done simply by subtly acknowledging their expert status in the community of practice. Practitioners identified as being unusually skillful are usually treated differently than their less gifted compatriots. This may be reflected in forms of address. For instance, in one shop the resident drivetrain expert was introduced in the following manner: "This is Tony. He's our transmission god." Another expert was referred to as "a walking encyclopedia" of automotive knowledge. Although seemingly humorous, these words were spoken with sincerity and reverence. Respect was also manifest in interactions—when experts spoke, others paused to listen, and the experts' opinions were not challenged casually. Technicians also noted that a potentially helpful informant may not be a peer. By lending an ear to a frustrated shop foreman, neophytes could quickly become a valued confidant:

> If the boss keeps ignoring what the foreman's saying, and the foreman knows he's right, he's done the job over and over again, but the boss is thinking bottom line or thinking about sales or something else—the foreman will unload to somebody. And if it's that new hire, that's good—it builds a bond. I've seen that work out quite well. The boss never listens to the guy who's managing the shop. . . . Play into it. Work with the guy who's supervising you directly. And as a result, your life gets easier. (*technician, dealership*)

Relationships with knowledgeable peers are likely to be short lived unless neophytes understand and obey the rules of disseminating informal information. These concern how one should exchange information: rules of listening, taking turns, and not saying more than you know. Given their inexperience and provisional status, neophytes were expected to listen attentively and not interrupt excessively or speak out of turn when conversing with more senior workers. Joking and a bit of good-natured bragging were acceptable, even encouraged, but delivering advice that one was unqualified to give was frowned upon. Rules of information exchange also governed when one should seek information. Neo-

---

[4]"ASE" refers to the National Institute for Automotive Service Excellence, a national nonprofit organization that tests and certifies the competency of automotive technicians. To become certified, technicians must pass written exams designed to test their technical knowledge.

phytes were expected to refrain from making inquiries when the informant was rushed or engrossed in a complex problem, if possible, or to ask only short straightforward questions during such times. Break times and lulls in the work-day provided better windows for seeking detailed answers to complex questions, and the answers received during these times would usually be far more descriptive and extensive.

A final type of understanding concerns the ability to evaluate information. The validity and accuracy of information obtained from both formal and informal sources could prove unreliable with surprising frequency. Thus, accepting any information at face value was to court disaster. Neophytes must therefore retain a healthy but quiet sense of skepticism and develop the ability to carefully weigh information gathered. If an answer or passage recorded in a manual didn't seem right, technicians were expected to follow their hunch to determine if the suspect data were indeed faulty. As one technician noted, this process required both resourcefulness and determination:

> There's no one source of information that's going to be 100 percent correct. [Entry-level technicians] have to develop the ability to draw from different resources. I do it myself. I'll go ask somebody, and if I don't get a complete answer, or I'm not happy with the answer, or I don't understand it, I'll ask someone else or go to the book [manual]. And maybe I won't like what I see in the book either, so . . . I might go to a CD-ROM compilation. Or I might just need to see a good picture. . . . If the illustrations aren't in the book, maybe I can go find a similar-model vehicle and pop the hood [to] take a look at that one. That might mean a trip down to the dealer if it's not a late model. Or maybe a call to the dealer. These are all techniques I've had to use. (*technician, independent shop*)

Technicians related numerous tales in which they saved their reputation for safety, technical skill, and good sense by evaluating a passage of text or a piece of advice that struck them as odd before acting on it. However, they also warned that neophytes' investigations should be conducted in a discreet, low-key manner to avoid giving the appearance of second-guessing more experienced colleagues. As one explained, "This is one time when it's important to be quiet and go about your business."

Knowledge of Rules Governing Exchange of Assistance

Virtually all entry-level technicians require considerable help. This can consist of simple gestures, such as showing the newcomer where supplies and equipment are located, to elaborate favors, such as offering detailed demonstrations of repair procedures. Experienced peers are fully aware of the newcomers' need and are generally willing to assist. However, exchanges of assistance are governed by cultural rules. Newcomers must observe these rules to avoid wearing thin their peers' good will.

For example, requests for assistance should be distributed throughout the shop to avoid overtaxing anyone in particular. When assistance is rendered, recipients should be attentive and make an effort to learn from the experience. It is not expected that a neophyte will retain complex information after a single hearing or viewing. But it is assumed that after two or three exposures the information will become embedded in memory. Technicians complained that nothing was so annoying or ill tolerated than "a new guy who asks the same damn question over and over." In fact, such behavior was interpreted as a sign of general incompetence or an uncaring attitude.

It is important for recipients to show gratitude when assistance is rendered and to adhere to the norms of reciprocity that govern such exchanges. These norms specify an even exchange of assistance or other favors. Of course, the entry-level technicians' inexperience places them in a relatively poor position to reciprocate with exchanges of technical assistance, so they must discover other ways to make up their social deficit if they are to continue receiving aid. Entry-level technicians devised ingenious ways of settling their debt with peers. For example, one made a habit of passing a plate of home-baked cookies among peers several times a week. A second voluntarily swept clean the work areas of experienced technicians at the end of each day. A third reported treating his co-workers to an occasional fast-food lunch. And one technician fulfilled his social obligations by occasionally purchasing new tools for helpful colleagues:

> It's a good idea to "buy your way in," like I did. If you borrow their tools, you might want to buy them a tool. Like, hand them a flashlight and say, "Here—I noticed your flashlight is busted, so I bought you a new one. Thanks very much for letting me borrow your tools and thanks for all your advice." Let 'em know that their help pays dividends. (*technician, independent shop*)

Of course, one must take care when fashioning such strategies; overt sweeping expressions of gratitude may be viewed as manipulative attempts to curry favor while perfunctory gestures could seem insulting. Although the actual methods used varied, acceptable means of repaying a social debt were always subtle, modest, and, perhaps most importantly, sincere.

Knowledge of Ideal and Practical Demands

In many cases there are "official" and "unofficial" ways of accomplishing tasks. The former are the methods decreed optimal by authoritative sources: manufacturers, suppliers, employers. Official procedures are featured in standard operating procedures, technical service bulletins, manuals, and other textual sources. Unofficial methods are the procedures that technicians themselves fashion through experience, experimentation, and judicious application of informal knowledge. These are embedded in heuristics, shortcuts, and makeshift measures. For instance, technicians routinely employ shortcuts by substituting procedures of their own design for those in manuals, and they omit steps specified in a diagnostic or repair procedure deemed unnecessary for achieving desired results. Although unofficial methods can be more efficient or effective than official methods, they may not carry authoritative approval. Therefore, becoming a competent practitioner implies learning not only the methods themselves but also which method is deemed appropriate for a given situation.

Myriad factors guide the selection and application of repair methodologies. For example, workers must be sensitive to employer preferences—some employers frown on informal methods while others encourage their use. In some cases, managers made their desires explicit:

> When I first started, I was fresh outta [community college] and thought I knew my stuff. But when I was doing my first brake job, I went to the boss and said, "Where's the seal driver?" The boss said, "The what?" "You know, the seal driver . . . to drive these wheel seals in." He goes, "Son, come over here." He got a 2 x 4 and a hammer and says, "Watch this." And he showed me how most mechanics put it in without the special tool. I felt like a fool! I've always remembered this, and that's why I try to tell young guys there's a by-the-book way and there's the way they do it in real shops. Know the difference. (*technician, independent shop*)

If managerial preferences were less obvious, neophytes could pick up shop norms by watching peers to see what fellow workers did and when they did it. A well-placed question to peers could also secure the needed information. In fact, experienced technicians considered such questions to be indicative of "shop savvy"—an understanding of and appreciation for the way work is really done in shops to save money, effort, and time. Demonstrating this knowledge helped neophytes shed the image of "being green"—naive and inexperienced—and speeded their acceptance into the community of practice. In contrast, consistently choosing and applying methods that technicians considered inappropriate—even if these are formal methods deemed optimal by manufacturers and employers—put neophytes at risk of being viewed as less than promising.

This did not mean that neophytes could apply informal methods freely, however, for cultural rules specify who can use informal methods as well as when. Experienced technicians agreed that neophytes should refrain from taking shortcuts unless they had accumulated enough knowledge and experience to make informed detours. Similarly, neophytes were expected to avoid attempts at experimentation and innovation in work practices until they had mastered formal procedures and demonstrated their competence on repeated occasions.

THE FINISHING SCHOOL—AN OLD IDEA REVISITED

To date, discussions of workplace readiness and the perceived shortfall of skills among high school graduates have revolved around a delimited range of knowledge and skills. Most prevalent are complaints about the lack of basic literacy and numeracy, followed by reports of a widespread lack of technical skills—knowledge of technology (computers in particular), critical thinking skills, and the like. However, the foregoing discussion suggests that social capital also is an indispensable part of the workers' portfolio of skills and knowledge. These skills help entry-level automotive technicians communicate effectively, adapt their behavior to meet the practical and social exigencies of the workplace, and simultaneously avoid attributions of incompetence that impede employability and build relationships that facilitate learning and teamwork. Given the importance of such knowledge, it may be advantageous to provide structured opportunities for acquiring social capital in vocational schools. But what must be done to provide such opportunities?

Once again, the example of the finishing school is instructive. Recall that these schools were effective vehicles for imparting social capital because they circumvented three curricular and pedagogical shortfalls that often plague modern schools. First, the schools provided ample opportunities for students to experience social dynamics characteristic of adult roles in realistic settings. Second, these experiences were supplemented with formal instruction in social skills and knowledge and structured opportunities for practice. Finally, the social capital imparted in finishing schools was entirely consistent with that required in real-world settings. To effectively inculcate the social skills and knowledge required by today's practitioners, vocational schools must also skirt these shortcomings. This implies that schools must do the following: provide opportunities to experience social dynamics in realistic work settings, supplement experiential learning with formal instruction and structured opportunities for practice, and achieve congruence between social capital valued in schools and in the workplace.

Provide Opportunities to Experience Social Dynamics in Realistic Work Settings

To become socially adept, students must experience firsthand the social dynamics of the workplace. Many vocational schools do a fair job of replicating the physical environment found in work settings: classrooms may look like shop floors, laboratories, and examination rooms; tools and instruments plied in real work settings are used; and students engage in the sort of tasks they will soon perform. But these settings are typically devoid of the kind of people the entry-level technician can expect to encounter on the job. Clients, managers, suppliers, and experienced practitioners are conspicuously absent. As a result, teachers are the only resource for building social capital available to most students. If instructors have some practical experience in the field, they can be a valuable source of information. However, in some school settings, students will interact with a single vocational instructor throughout their training or have few chances to mingle with others. Consequently, students may be exposed to the experiences and social knowledge of only a single former practitioner. It is unlikely that any teacher's experiences encompass the full range of social capital a student could possibly be called on to exhibit.

Replicating the social dynamics of the workplace in school therefore requires creating opportunities for sustained social interaction with people commonly found in the workplace. One means of accomplishing this goal is through increased use of internships, externships, apprenticeships, and other collaborative learning efforts between schools and employers in local labor markets. In addition, schools could seek ways to introduce social actors into the classroom. Encouraging a group of local employers to release a practitioner from his or her duties for a few hours every week would be a start. These advisers could circulate during practice activities, offering guidance, commentary on students' behavior, and, perhaps most importantly, an example of how full-fledged members of the occupational community of practice should behave. Managers and employers could also make regular appearances in the classroom, not to lecture but to interact informally with groups of students as they work. Retired practitioners also represent a valuable source of social guidance, and such individuals may readily volunteer a few hours each week in the classroom.

Supplement Experiential Learning with Formal Instruction and Structured Opportunities for Practice

Internships and other occasions for sampling social dynamics provide excellent opportunities for practicing social skills in actual work settings. However, internships alone can prove inadequate for the same reason that medical residencies and craft apprenticeships often fall short of the mark—namely, few deliberate attempts are made to inculcate this knowledge during the training experience. Hence, students with natural talents in this area may excel and receive more or better opportunities for learning while their less fortunate peers struggle for recognition and acceptance. Vocational schools could do much to level the social playing field by adding formal instruction in occupationally specific social skills to academic curricula and by creating situations in which students could practice.

In the case of automotive repair, such instruction could be slipped into existing lesson plans with relative ease. For example, a discussion of the cultural significance of tools and tool maintenance could be added to demonstrations on safe and effective use of tools and implements in the shop. It is likely that, once appraised of the symbolic importance of tool care, students may see the chores of tool maintenance and shop cleanup in a somewhat different light. Lectures on the rudiments of asking questions, seeking assistance, projecting a professional image, and repaying social debts could also be featured. Students could be graded on their social proficiency as well as classroom performance to instill a respect for these skills.

Similarly, a short module could be added in which students have the opportunity to practice interaction and diagnostic questioning with volunteers recruited to play the role of customers in repair shops. After a few brief demonstrations by the instructor, students would take a turn at interacting with the "customer," who could challenge students by behaving in a nervous, puzzled, officious, or obnoxious manner. These sessions would be observed by students, teachers, and, ideally, practitioners and employers, who would critique each student's performance and offer alternative approaches. Students could also engage in role play to practice social skills in problem solving and conflict resolution. These lessons would logically precede internships or other forays into actual work settings.

Achieve Congruence Between the Social Capital Valued in Schools and the Workplace

Formal instruction, practice sessions, and other well-intentioned efforts to impart social capital in schools will be pointless if the social skills these impart are not those needed in the workplace. Care must be taken to ensure that acculturation in the classroom is congruent with that of the occupation for which students are preparing, for a basic lack of familiarity with the cultural rules and norms extant in the workplace can blunt pedagogical tools that are otherwise effective for imparting this knowledge.

Evidence for this conclusion can be drawn from recent efforts to include social instruction in postsecondary vocational programs. In response to complaints from industry that technically skilled graduates frequently lack interpersonal and written communication skills and an awareness of ethics and values, the American Association of Community and Junior Colleges has spearheaded efforts to include social instruction in vocational training (see Rzonca et al., 1995:153-154). Under the association's direction and with financial support from the National Endowment for the Humanities, a few pioneering community colleges have supplemented technical training with humanities courses. Although it is too soon to fully assess the courses' impact, employers have already objected to their content and relevance (Collins, 1991). The problem appears to stem, at least in part, from a discrepancy between the social capital that academics think employers want (and that academics are prepared to teach) and the social capital that new employees actually need. Humanities courses discuss generally useful ideas, attitudes, and behaviors but not the occupationally specific skills and knowledge that students will be called on to exhibit upon entry into the workplace.

SUMMARY

My studies of the automotive repair field suggest that employers can unwittingly perpetuate such misunderstandings. During interviews, subjects were routinely asked to comment on the skills and knowledge required of entry-level automotive technicians. The comments of shop owners and service managers echoed themes surprisingly similar to those of employers in general—all were unanimous in the opinion that "values" and "having a good attitude" were absolutely critical for being hired and for continued success on the job. However, only upon closer questioning and sustained observation in the workplace did it become apparent that service managers were not referring simply to generally useful values, ethics, and behaviors but also to the ability to appreciate and observe occupational norms and cultural rules. This experience suggests that it is important not to accept such terms at face value and to be clear when stating employment needs. To develop effective vehicles for social training and acculturation in the classroom, educators must acquire a detailed understanding of the social capital needed by entry-level workers. This requires detailed cultural studies of occupations and work practice produced with input from employers, managers, and, perhaps most importantly, practitioners themselves.

REFERENCES

Aerospace Education Foundation
   1989   *America's Next Crisis: The Shortfall of Technical Manpower.* Arlington, VA: Aerospace Education Foundation.
Barley, Stephen R.
   1985   The Technician as an Occupational Archetype: Observations on the Changing Nature of Work for Theories of Organizing. Working paper, National Center for the Educational Quality of the Workforce, University of Pennsylvania, Philadelphia.
Barley, Stephen R., and Beth Bechky
   1994   In the backrooms of science: The work of technicians in science labs. *Work and Occupations* 21:85-126.
Barley, Stephen R., and Bonalyn J. Nelsen
   1995   *The Nature and Implications of Infrastructural Change for the Social Organization of Work.* Technical report. Washington, DC: Office of Technology Assessment.
Barton, Paul E.
   1990   *Skills Employers Need: Time to Measure Them?* Princeton, NJ: Educational Testing Service.
Becker, Howard
   1972   School is a lousy place to learn anything. *American Behavioral Scientist* 16(1):85-105.
Brown, John Seely, and Paul Duguid
   1991   Organizational learning and communities of practice: Toward a unified view of learning, working and innovation. *Organization Science* 2(1):40-57.
Cappelli, Peter
   1995   Is the "skills gap" really about attitudes? *California Management Review* 37(4):108-124.
Carnevale, Anthony P., Leila J. Gainer, and Ann S. Melzer
   1988   *Workplace Basics: The Skills Employers Want.* Washington, DC: U.S. Department of Labor and the American Society for Training and Development.
Collins, J.
   1991   A Description of an Attempt to Integrate the Humanities into Occupational Curricula at Kirkwood Community College. Unpublished master's project, College of Education, University of Iowa.

Committee for Economic Development
  1984   *Investing in Our Children.* Washington, DC: Committee for Economic Development.
  1991   *An Assessment of American Education: Views of Employers, Higher Educators, the Public, Recent Students, and Their Parents.* New York: Louis Harris Associates.
Gerholm, Tomas
  1990   On tacit knowing in academia. *European Journal of Education* 25(3):263-271.
Gorman, Christine
  1988   The literacy gap. *Time* December 19:56-57.
Jackson, Philip W.
  1968   *Life in Classrooms.* New York: Holt, Rinehart and Winston.
Kusterer, Ken C.
  1978   *Know-How on the Job: The Important Working Knowledge of "Unskilled" Workers.* Boulder, CO: Westview Press.
Mateyka, James A., Jason D. Lee, and Arthur Chiang
  1988   The Auto Service Industry: Winners and Losers in the 1990s. Technical paper no. 880394, Society of Automotive Engineers, Warrendale, PA.
McBride, Sarah Davis
  1992   Ornaments of education: The material world of National Park Seminary. *Washington History* 4(1):47-68.
National Commission for Excellence in Education
  1983   *A Nation at Risk: The Imperative for Educational Reform.* Washington, DC: U.S. Government Printing Office.
Nelsen, Bonalyn J.
  1995   Managing the Anomalous Cultural Position of Skilled Service Workers: Observations from the Field of Auto Repair. Working paper, National Center for the Educational Quality of the Workforce, University of Pennsylvania, Philadelphia.
Nelsen, Bonalyn J., and Stephen R. Barley
  1994   Toward an Emic Understanding of Professionalism Among Technical Workers. Working paper no. WP29, National Center for the Educational Quality of the Workforce, University of Pennsylvania, Philadelphia.
Rzonca, Chet, Douglas Gustafson, and Sandra Boutelle
  1995   Vocational education: Meeting manpower needs and providing student opportunities. Pp. 139-160 in *The New Modern Times*, David B. Bills, ed. Albany: State University of New York Press.
Schon, Donald A.
  1983   *The Reflective Practitioner.* New York: Basic Books.
Sternberg, Robert
  1993   Intelligence is more than IQ: The practical side of intelligence. *Journal of Cooperative Education* 28(2):6-17.
Wagner, Richard K.
  1987   Tacit knowledge in everyday intelligent behavior. *Journal of Personality and Social Psychology* 52(6):1236-1247.
Wagner, Richard K., and Robert J. Sternberg
  1985   Practical intelligence in real world pursuits: The role of tacit knowledge. *Journal of Personality and Social Psychology* 48:436-458.

5

Manufacturing the New Worker: Literate Activities and Working Identities in a High-Performance Versus a Traditionally Organized Workplace

Glynda Hull

INTRODUCTION: THE SKILLS DEBATE ON THE FACTORY FLOOR

While reports in the 1980s (e.g., National Commission on Excellence in Education, 1983) called attention to the ways in which schoolchildren were performing poorly at reading, writing, and math, worry has focused more recently on adults already in the work force or young people about to enter it. This time, the perceived deficits in workers' "basic" and "higher-order" skills have been linked to lowered productivity in the workplace and a lack of competitiveness in the international market (U.S. Department of Education and U.S. Department of Labor, 1988; Carnevale et al., 1988; Lund and McGuire, 1990; for critical reviews see Hull, 1993; Gee et al., 1996; Darrah, 1996). The claim is that in order to be competitive U.S. industries must adopt new technologies and new forms of work organization often labeled "high performance," in contrast to more traditional Taylorist models (Commission on the Skills of the American Workforce, 1990; Secretary's Commission on Achieving Necessary Skills (SCANS), 1992; Sarmiento and Kay, 1990; Appelbaum and Batt, 1993). The demand is that schools support these changes by teaching the knowledge and skills thought to be needed in restructured, technologically sophisticated workplaces (SCANS, 1992; see Marshall and Tucker, 1992). There is a developing consensus, then, that what is needed is a new kind of worker.

Definitions of what constitutes high-performance workplaces vary, but these workplaces are usually assumed to require greater collaboration and communication among workers, to provide increased opportunities for the exercise of different and more complex skills and literacies, and in general to give frontline workers more responsibility. In addition, it is claimed that companies aiming to become high performance will need to make larger investments in training and offer higher salaries for the payoff of increased skills and productivity (see Commission on the Skills of the American Workforce, 1990; Carnevale et al., 1988; SCANS, 1992; Appelbaum and Batt, 1993; Brown et al., 1993). In this atmosphere of change there is a tendency to speak about U.S. workers pejoratively—to worry that our increasingly "nonmale, nonwhite, and nonyoung" (Ehrlich and Garland, 1988) work force is poorly trained and poorly skilled and therefore ill equipped to cope with new workplace demands (see also U.S. Department of Education and U.S. Department of Labor, 1988; Carnevale et al., 1988).

Despite such claims about the skills, including the literacies, required in reorganized, technologically sophisticated workplaces, as well as about the skills that workers are assumed to lack, little is known about the actual demands of these workplaces or the kinds of training that new jobs might require. (For a review of existing research, see Hull et al., 1996; for recent examples of research on literacy, skills, and work, see Hull, 1997.) In fact, most of the complaints about worker "illiteracy" arise not from detailed observations of work but from surveys and anecdotal reports that rely largely on the perspectives of managers (Baba, 1991; Darrah, 1996; Appelbaum and Batt, 1993). It is not clear, then, just what literate capabilities are required in the new workplaces or even what literate capabilities workers possess or lack— although such information would seem to be crucial for reconceptualizing secondary and postsecondary schooling, vocational training, and workplace education efforts.

This chapter is drawn from a larger research project designed to fill in some of these gaps. The aims of the project were several: to develop a methodology for investigating literate activities in workplace settings; to document the actual literate activities in a high-performance workplace versus a traditionally organized one; to document the work activities associated with self-directed work teams and high-performance work; to make recommendations about literacy education and training for the present;and to find innovative ways to introduce educators, researchers, and laypeople to the changing face of work.

This chapter focuses on a subset of the larger project having to do with literate activities and working identities. Current public debates and concerns about skills and skill requirements are, I would argue, efforts to develop a national consensus about new working identities—the ways of thinking, acting, talking, and valuing that are believed to be appropriate for the new worker. As we will see, a literate identity is an important aspect of a worker's sense of himself or herself in a high-performance workplace. But, as we shall also see, it is perilously easy for companies to so structure and constrain work activities that—even at a high-performance plant—the identities that workers develop around literacy are conflictual and limiting.

BACKGROUND: THE VALLEY OF HEART'S DELIGHT

The landscape is flat, hot, suburban, and bland—a seemingly endless juxta-position of shopping centers, parking lots, tract housing, freeways, and electronics firms. If you look to the east, the Diablo Mountain Range is always in view; to the west and out of sight are the southern reaches of the San Francisco Bay. Just 50 years ago this whole area was verdant with olive groves, vineyards, and orchards of apricots and walnuts. The quintessential land of milk and honey, it was dubbed by residents the Valley of Heart's Delight. Today this 25-mile strip of the San Francisco peninsula is home to some 2,000 high-tech firms and some 200,000 workers. It is Silicon Valley, and although one can find examples of industries other than electronics here, the area now belongs to the design, manufacture, and assembly of computer boards, chips, and components.

Silicon Valley is held up as a major economic success story in the United States and, as such, has gotten its fair share of attention from presidents, queens, and more ordinary visitors such as researchers. A recent example is Saxenian's (1994) study of the unique local industrial environment that allowed young entre-preneurs to parlay their considerable technical know-how into multi-million-dollar empires. And there have been a host of popular accounts of individual visionaries, inventors, and their companies, such as Rose's *West of Eden* (1989), a look at part of the history of Apple Computer. What is less common in the literature on the region are studies of frontline workers, the men and women who manufacture silicon chips and assemble circuit boards and do the actual work of production (for an exception to this tendency, see Hossfeld, 1988; see also Rawls and Bean, 1993, for a brief history). They constitute 80 percent of the Silicon Valley work force. Implicit here, of course, is the extreme segmentation of the valley's work force into highly skilled technical and professional workers at the top, and the much more numerous production workers, often recent immigrants from Asia and Latin America who do not earn a lot more than the minimum wage and for whom opportunities to advance are few. Nonetheless, such workers are increasingly expected to cultivate new skills, acquire new knowledge, and par-ticipate in new work practices, such as self-directed work teams—in short, to develop new working identities. They are the focus of the current study.

I examined one subset of the computer industry, circuit board assembly, an instance of contract manufacturing. We often hear that the most prevalent job in recent years is the temporary one, a trend that provides workers little job security and few benefits (such as health insurance) but that enables corporations to adjust their labor overhead to the ebb and flow of the market (for a critical look at this trend, see Parker, 1994). A parallel phenomenon to temporary hiring is contract manufacturing, also called "outsourcing," and in fact, contract manufacturers depend heavily on temporary workers. Contract manufacturers perform services for other companies, often central services that were once performed by the companies themselves. For example, while big computer companies like Apple and IBM used to assemble all their own circuit boards in house for their own products, it is now customary to farm out this aspect of their production.

Being a contract manufacturer has particular implications for doing business and has ramifications as well for the skills its work force is called on to develop and use, especially literacy. A company chooses one contract manufacturer over another because of lower costs, higher quality, and productivity, so there is much ado in these companies about minimizing defects and speeding up production. Because technology changes so quickly these days, a contract manufacturer's customers can be expected to be particularly demanding, calling for changes in circuit boards that are already in production and regularly returning old boards to be reworked and updated on short notice. Recordkeeping on such occasions is paramount: customers want to know what changes were made on which boards on what dates and by whom; paper trails are thick. Customers also want to be assured of a certain level of competence before they bring their business, and thus, circuit board assemblers, like a growing number of other U.S. and European firms, vie to be certified by international standards. These agencies enforce stringent procedures concerning documentation, so that factories are practically afloat in a sea of paper. It is customary for every single procedure that takes place within such a certified factory to be written down and documented, and workers' activities and their work practices are expected to match the printed account and are regularly audited to ensure that they do so.

My research team and I studied two Silicon Valley circuit board assembly factories, one a high-performance workplace and the other a traditionally organized one.[1] The traditional factory we called EMCO, for electronics manufacturing company. The other we named Teamco, a pseudonym that highlights the company's recent investment in self-directed work teams. What was remarkably fortunate about this choice of companies is that, aside from their policies and practices regarding work organization, EMCO and Teamco were very similar. In fact, I knew some frontline workers who were working simultaneously at both places, just on different shifts, though this was a violation of both factories' policies. Other employees—line workers, engineers, managers—had previously switched from one company to the other, and employees continued to do so as the study progressed. EMCO and Teamco are both quite successful, posting profits in the billions. They are both international, having plants not only in the Silicon Valley but in various countries worldwide. Indeed, they are both large, employing thousands of employees nationally and internationally. Their California factories are both multicultural and multilingual, drawing on work forces composed

---

[1] It is important to note that this dichotomy is in some ways a false one, for a company can at one and the same time embrace features of high-performance work organizations and traditionally organized ones. To further complicate matters, companies sometimes "talk the talk" but do not "walk the walk." That is, they claim to follow the high-performance model but in actuality rely on quite traditional practices.

mainly of recent immigrants. This striking similarity means that the study was not an apples-and-oranges comparison, the juxtaposition of two essentially different work settings. Rather, the similarities made it possible to hone in with confidence on the differences in literacy requirements and practices that were associated with the factories' different perspectives on work organization and the roles and identities of frontline employees.

A NOTE ON METHODS

Rather than relying on "grand tours" of the workplace, which can result in a limited and distorted view of workers' and managers' roles and activities (Darrah, 1990; Spradley and McCurdy, 1972), this project drew on ethnographic methods that allowed the investigation, in close detail, of the perspectives and understandings of the various stakeholders in the two workplaces. Fieldwork took place during a 3-year period, 1993 to 1995. Most data came from observations and interviews, the majority of which were audiotaped or videotaped. We also participated in the work of the factories on occasion, assembling the simpler products or helping out with literacy-related duties. One long afternoon, for example, I spent almost entirely on my knees along with the lead of one of the "hand-load" lines, meticulously combing the files of each set of manufacturing process instructions for each assembly in the plant. Our task was to determine the exact number of components that workers were expected to load for each assembly, figures that would then be plugged into a new formula for determining "standard times," or how fast people needed to work. This task, like many other new responsibilities, grew from the company's interest in making teams accountable for improving productivity. (For a detailed explanation of methods and the sociocultural approach that informed the research, see Hull et al., 1996.)

Our public and official role in the factories was to be "researchers," a group from a local university studying the literacy requirements of work. In some ways, however, our roles went beyond the usual notions of "participant observation," crisscrossing the boundaries traditionally set between researcher and researched. Members of the research team frequently provided personal assistance to individuals. Since many workers were recent immigrants whose English was shaky, we offered ourselves, and were regularly relied on, as language intermediaries. Once a worker who moonlighted in a Chinese restaurant brought in a menu so that we could record the English pronunciation of "pot stickers" and "vegetable fried rice." I intervened on many occasions for a young supervisor, an ethnic Chinese who grew up in Vietnam but had developed an American penchant for credit cards and mail-order houses. Her query of "what is sweepstake?" began a months-long saga of negotiations with a disreputable mail-order house to return $899 worth of pens. We read and commented on essays from night school, interpreted traffic tickets and insurance policies, ventured opinions regarding medical options, and exchanged business cards with anxious parents happy to know a professor from the university where their sons and daughters were enrolled or had aspirations of attending.

Our roles as language and cultural brokers helped people to trust us, people from whom we were separated by vast cultural and social gulfs. We became their friends as they became our informants, and these relationships helped us immeasurably as we attempted to understand work activities and social positions on the shop floor. In the same way, then, that a factory can be understood as the product of multiple influences—its industry, its local history, the current economic climate, the vision of its managers—so can the attitudes, abilities, and actions of workers be usefully interpreted in light of their work and educational backgrounds, their individual styles and creativities, their cultures and genders.

Fieldwork at EMCO (approximately 100 visits from May 1993 through September 1994) resulted in over 200 hours of audiotape of interviews and work-related activities in all departments; 6 hours of videotape of training, manufacturing, and a team meeting; a database of all employees' education and work experience; and a wide-ranging collection of documents—process instructions, engineering changes, assembly drawings, performance reviews and disciplinary notices, quality alerts and requests for corrective action, supervisors' passdowns, workers' notes and drawings, meeting agendas, interoffice memos, and much more.

Fieldwork at Teamco (approximately 200 visits from September 1994 through November 1995) yielded more than 300 hours of audiotape of work in all departments and of training, interviews, and a variety of meetings (including those of self-directed work teams and related committees) and approximately 100 hours of videotape of self-directed work-team training, meetings, and related committees and of self-directed work-team competitions and presentations to management. Also, as in our fieldwork at EMCO, we collected a wide range of documents, from the training curriculum, from team meetings, and from the factory floor—including process instructions, time standards, workers' notes and drawings, quality and productivity data, meeting minutes and agendas, and management assessments of team goals.

From these abundant data, I have selected two stories to tell, two narratives that demonstrate in dramatic form the literate activities that were available to, expected of, or withheld from frontline workers at EMCO and Teamco. I present these narratives in some detail, introducing the workers who figure prominently in them, providing excerpts from their conversations, and describing and summarizing their work or training activities. After these narratives I will turn to a more formal analysis of the literacy practices that were a part of the work of circuit board assembly, as well as the practices that distinguished work at the traditionally organized factory from work at the high-performance plant.

A SNAPSHOT FROM THE FLOOR

It is important, if we are to understand how literacy does and does not function on the shop floors of EMCO and Teamco, to know something about the work of circuit board assembly, for this work structures the reading and writing that gets done in these factories and gives literacy its purpose. Before turning to case studies from each of the factories, I offer a glimpse, a broad sweep, of the work that people do on such a manufacturing floor. We will catch this glimpse by following a "bare board" and a kit of components (integrated circuits, diodes, resistors, capacitors, brackets, nuts and screws, and so on) across the manufacturing floor on their way to becoming completed printed circuit boards. This is a generic description, one that generally fits the circuit board assembly process at both EMCO and Teamco.

Work begins in the storage and shipping department, where bulk components arrive and a "kitting" crew consults various documents—manufacturing schedules, manufacturing process instructions, bills of materials, approved vendor lists—to determine how many of which components are to be placed on which boards. The crew then makes up kits of those components, kits that will be picked up as needed by materials handlers from the various departments. Out on the floor the bare boards begin in an area referred to as "pick and place" or as "surface-mount technology" (SMT), which consists of lines of robots. A worker programs the machines to either spread solder paste or squirt daubs of epoxy on the board and then place the right components in the right spots. The boards, with components in place, continue along an automated line through an "oven" or reflow machine, which heats up and solidifies the solder. Although it is possible for a single person to load the machine, monitor the process, and catch the boards at the end of the line, it is more common for two people to share these responsibilities, with the person who catches the boards acting as an inspector to see that all parts were placed on the board properly. Roving inspectors also conduct spot-checks here and throughout the plant.

A worker (a "materials handler" on some shifts, a pick-and-place "lead" on others) places the boards on trays or in sectioned bins called "totes," sets the trays or totes on carts, and wheels the carts to a washing machine. (At EMCO, a movement log is filled out in triplicate and filed to document this and all transfers of materials in the plant; at Teamco a one-page "traveler" is filled out to accompany the cart, but the boards are also scanned at certain points to track them along the manufacturing process.) Another crew of one or two runs the boards through the wash, puts them back into bins, then puts them on carts, and wheels them to either "auto-insertion" or "stuffing" (also known as "hand-load"). Though board designs rely increasingly on SMT, all boards still contain at least some "pin-through-hole" components, components that have small wire "legs" or "leads" that stick through small holes in the board and are wave soldered or hand soldered on the back side of the board. Some of these through-hole components are placed by machine in the auto-insertion area after going to SMT, others by hand in the stuffing (hand-load) and mechanical assembly areas. Stuffing is a line of perhaps a half dozen workers who hand place more components on the board, components that because of their size, shape, or other characteristics, could not be placed during the earlier stages of the process. The components added in auto-insertion, hand-load, or mechanical assembly require soldering and so are moved, according to the customer's specifications, either to the wave-solder area or to the area known variously as "second ops" (second operations) or "touch-up." Staffed by one to three operators, the wave-solder machine makes it possible to solder the leads of through-hole components en masse—an important time saver when a single connector might have a hundred leads or when a board might have a few hundred small through-hole components, each component with at least two leads.

Second ops is the most labor-intensive part of the plant. It is here that workers (usually women) perform the hand soldering known as touch-up (adding final components) and rework (removing and/or replacing components). Second ops also includes some hardware assembly, where workers screw brackets to boards, add bar code labels, and snap in components that do not require soldering or that cannot be subjected to the wave-solder process. The assembled boards are then "shipped" to another department for in-circuit and functional testing and quality inspection. Depending on the results, the boards are next either sent back for rework or packed and shipped out.

Surrounding and interacting with the manufacturing process described here is the work of designers, engineers, and managers of various kinds—the people who prepare for and oversee the manufacturing process and who interact with customers, vendors, and employees at other plants owned by the corporation.

"OPERATOR BRAIN DEAD": A READING PROBLEM AT TEAMCO

The first narrative that I will tell to demonstrate the literacy activities and literate identities of workers in circuit board assembly has to do with a literacy problem, a documented instance of EMCO workers who apparently failed to read or follow instructions and thereby almost made a production mistake that would have had serious repercussions for an important customer. This story began one evening during EMCO's second shift while I was "shadowing" a process engineer, Wade. (See Figure 5-1 for the chronology of this event.) This engineer, who usually worked during the day, was on special assignment to the second shift that evening. I followed Wade about as he made his rounds in the plant, stopping to check with the leads in each department to see if all was well, and I sat with him as he completed his main project for the shift, the construction and assignment of a rework task.

The rest of this paper contains a number of transcriptions of conversation. I use the following transcription conventions:

[ ]	researcher's explanation
( )	researcher's best guess
(xx)	unintelligible word or phrase
=	overlap (simultaneous speech)
==	latching (one speaker following immediately after another)
-	cutting off word or phrase
caps	stress
::	fluctuating intonation
..	pauses of less than 0.5 seconds
[2]	pauses timed precisely (2 seconds)
...	omitted talk

One of EMCO's major customers had returned a batch of boards that EMCO had already assembled; the boards were to be upgraded and altered according to the customer's current specifications, and the relevant paperwork was to be updated, approved, and appropriately distributed and filed. This kind of rework task is common in circuit board assembly, for computer companies are continually

9/22 The TASK

Process engineer, Wade, sorts a box full of 35 or so printed circuit boards that have been returned from a customer for modifications or "rework" to bring them up to current specifications.

9/24 The PROCESS

Rework begins; line workers solder, etc., create new labels, affix labels, and eventually send the completed boards to testing.

9/28 The PROBLEM

Engineer Wade discovers the boards have been labeled improperly; investigates, talking to the supervisor, the line workers, his boss, other managers; issues a "Corrective Action Report" or "CAR" to the appropriate supervisor; puts other boards on hold.

9/29 The SOLUTION

Supervisor meets with workers who did the rework to "retrain" them; Wade releases the remaining boards to the floor; new labels are made and Wade himself puts them on the boards; boards are released to the testing department.

FIGURE 5-1   Chronology of the "label problem."

improving the design of boards that are already being produced. The challenge for a contract manufacturer like EMCO, then, is to simultaneously maintain production and to update the old boards that have already been assembled—and to do so quickly and accurately.

The boards the engineer showed me that evening, which arrived in a batch of 35 in one big box, each board worth about $600, were not all alike; that is, they represented five or six different versions of the same board, each version manufactured at a different point in the design process. Wade therefore had to examine every board singly and sort each into appropriate categories. He made handwritten notes to himself, listing individual boards by their serial numbers, notes he would later convert into instructions for the workers. As he explained, "The operators [employees who would perform the rework on the boards] will not have to look at it [each board] and try to decide what, which board. Just look at the number and know what (it takes. Checklist." Having completed his sorting and note taking, he remarked that the rework would probably be done by a couple of operators and stretched out over several shifts. He said he would check the first few boards for "workmanship" but would leave the main inspection for the test and quality departments.

During the next week members of the research team observed the rework that was done on a subset of the 35 boards, three especially complex "mother boards" that were designated "hot" or high priority; the oldest in the batch, these were the boards the customer wanted returned pronto. We observed the addition of a green wire, as directed in the instructions, by one worker, and another worker explained what she had done on the board, characterizing the rework as "straight-forward." (For the specific rework directions, see Figure 5-2.) This employee added that all that remained, before the boards were sent to the test department, was the addition of a datecode label (also as mentioned in the directions), and another worker set off to make the new labels.

We saw nothing that struck us as unusual during this process, but when Wade, the engineer, checked on the progress of the boards a few days later as he had said he would, the fur flew. "See the little jumper wires I referred to on the instructions," he started to say approvingly as he showed me one of the completed boards. Then he paused and noted quietly, "We got a problem here though. The instruction says to make a datecode label of A-3337. . . . Need to reject these."

Jamal, the lead in the test area, perhaps taken aback by Wade's consternation, pointed to the rework instructions and said to Wade, "I think this is your instructions." "I know," Wade replied, "and they didn't follow them."

It was not that the workers had done the actual repair of the boards incorrectly. In fact, as Wade would later point out, their handwork was so superb that the three boards were virtually identical, just as they should be. Rather, the problem was with the datecode label, a tiny identification affixed to every printed circuit board. (See Figure 5-3 for a replica of the actual label and Figure 5-4 for

---

2ND OPERATION

For serial number 032 only, remove diode at location Z3.

FOR ALL ASSEMBLIES, PERFORM THE FOLLOWING REWORK

Remove IC at location U16 (74BCT2440).
Hand solder part number 1820-6307 (74HCT244) at location U16.
Lift pin 19 of U17.
Lift pin 11 of U34.
Connect the following pins using #30 AWG green jumper wire.
Insulate lifted pins with sleeving.
U24 pin 1 to U34 pin 11
U34 pin 10 to U17 pin 19
Tack PAC wires every 1/2 inch.

HAND CLEAN REWORKED AREA

Remove M8 revision of the BIOS IC at location U22.
Install M9 revision of the BIOS IC at location U22.
Make new datecode label (A-3337).
Apply new datecode label over old datecode on serial number label.
Do not cover old serial number or assembly number of the label.
Send assemblies to test.

TEST

Perform ICT if possible and functional. Record debug time spent and
any rework performed on data sheets.

FIGURE 5-2 Excerpt from instructions for board rework and datecode label replacement.

an enlargement and explanation.) The parts of the label include the datecode (which indicates the version of the board—in this case "B"—and the week and year it was manufactured—in this case the 37th week of year 33, meaning 1993) and the serial number, the unique identification number for that particular board. Wade's instructions had directed the workers first to "make new datecode label (A-3337)" and then to "apply new datecode label over old datecode on serial number label." He further directed, "Do not cover old serial number or assembly number of the label" (see Figure 5-2). The workers' mistake was threefold: they had removed and discarded the original label; they had generated a whole new datecode label with a new serial number; and they had changed the version number on the new label from A to B.

PCA P/N 5063-0488
B-3337 S/N000720

FIGURE 5-3   Datecode label: actual size.

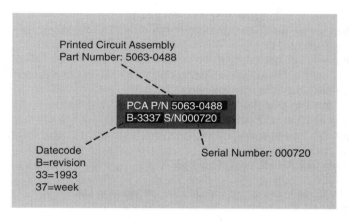

FIGURE 5-4   Datecode label: explanation of parts.

Upon discovering the mistake, the engineer hurried down to the shop floor to find out what had happened. He called to the lead in the second-operations area:

Wade:	Marisa! (pause) RSD madre?[2]
Marisa:	Yes.
Wade:	RMAs? [rework instructions]
Marisa:	Right.
Wade:	Did you make the stickers?
Marisa:	The sti-, yes.
Wade:	Day shift? Porqué no A? How come there's no (xx) serial number? (What did you do with the old) serial number? (Did you just) put new serial number for everything? Why did you=
Marisa:	=I do not touch those. Who was the person?

At this point, visibly alarmed, Marisa went to consult the operators who worked on the three boards, and they spoke together in Spanish for a moment, but nothing seemed to be resolved. Wade then instructed Marisa: "You're getting 30 more

---

[2]Wade is monolingual, but he prided himself on learning and using a few words from each of the several languages spoken in the factory.

RMA boards out here. We have to know what serial number it is. . . . Looks like somebody took the old serial numbers off them. Now we can't tell what serial numbers they are. Now we got problems. They're gonna be on hold until I have time to check 'em out. Make sure this doesn't happen on the rest of them, okay? I need to go talk to Celia [Marisa's supervisor]. . . . Gracias." With this, Wade strode off to break the bad news elsewhere.

At this point I was still somewhat mystified by the degree of consternation that accompanied the label problem, for surely, I thought, the labels could simply be reproduced and the error corrected. But this was not the case. As Wade explained several times over the course of the next half hour: [To the researcher] "Now we've lost traceability on these boards. . . . Basically I do not know how I can identify them now. . . . This is kind of serious because it's an irretrievable thing that you can't really fix. . . ." [to the quality engineer] "This is, this is kind of serious because the traceability is important and now we've lost it."

The concept of "traceability" is central to EMCO's successful dealings with its customers. As a contract manufacturer, the company must keep exact records on all of its products, including recurring updates and modifications, and the recordkeeping applies to individual boards as well as to types of products. In this case the three mother boards had been taken out of particular systems, and the customer expected to replace each board accordingly. (The program administrator in charge of this particular customer toyed only fleetingly with the idea of a cover-up: "So now what do we do? We could fake it . . . but that would come back to haunt us.") It is significant that "traceability" is inexorably linked to literacy. And it is important to note as well that some employees at EMCO understand and participate in this practice and that others don't, despite the fact that it has implications for the work of almost all.

By the end of the day Wade had written a "corrective action report" to Marisa's supervisor; that is, he had put the problem in writing and the offenders on notice. He had also spoken to the supervisor, who promised to take the issue up with her shift at their meeting in the morning. He had stopped production on the remaining batch of 30 or so boards, for fear the same mistake would be repeated. And he had carried out his own detective work, managing to figure out which board was which among the three in question. The next day he supervised the creation of new datecode labels, checked them, and pasted them on the boards himself, and then he released the remaining boards to the floor.

What interested me most about this small drama was how the mistake had occurred, especially since the error was apparently connected to workers' failure to read, understand, or follow written instructions. When I asked Wade how he thought it had happened, the following conversation occurred:

Wade: Probably related to another acronym we have here, "OBD."
Researcher: I hesitate to ask.

Wade: It stands for "operator brain dead."
Researcher: Uhh-oh.
Wade.   Occasionally we run into that, not too often.

When he described the problem to Frank, a fellow engineer, Frank observed that the operators must not be reading the instructions. Wade replied: "Well, they may be reading them, but they're definitely not following them." Later in the conversation Wade complained: "We've got to make them [the workers] understand that maybe they should read these things and follow them. I don't do them [write the instructions] just to justify my existence."

Apparently, Wade was not sure whether workers had failed to read the instructions or had read them and failed to follow them; but it was six of one and half a dozen of another to him, and in any case an example of the malady he referred to several times as "OBD." This view was, however, inconsistent with Wade's overall characterization of the workers as competent, even too competent: when trying to distinguish the three boards one from another, he noted that the rework was so finely done that he could not tell the boards apart through physical evidence. And at various times he offered other examples of the workers' expertise.

Another possible explanation, one that perhaps would occur most quickly to literacy specialists, is that the text that workers were expected to read was unclear, ambiguous, or vague. In fact, the program administrator offered this explanation when he first heard about the label problem, albeit jokingly:

Rod: So this must reflect on the instructions provided by the, uh, the engineer, I guess the cognizant engineer.
Wade: I keep telling you I'm not cognizant. [more quickly] You've got the instruction that says in there==
Rod: ==Yeah, yeah, do not cover up the old number. So now what do we do?

Since Wade was responsible for writing the rework instructions, Rod could not resist the chance to tease him about his prose. Surely, the instructions (see Figure 5-2) could have been worded more clearly. It is also important to note that the frontline workers weren't allowed to construct or alter manufacturing process instructions, these most important of factory documents, so they were continually at the mercy of Wade's prose and that of other engineers. Incomplete, inaccurate, or obsolete instructions were something we heard many complaints about, although the workers grew accustomed to deciphering or to working around these on a daily basis.

Another interpretation that relates to language has to do with the fact that this was a largely immigrant, in fact largely Korean, work force. The perception was that most of the Korean workers and many of the other immigrants could not speak English, could not understand English, could not read and write English, and, furthermore, were not all that interested in learning how. "What could help us here," said one manager, "is an intense ESL [English-as-a-second-language] program. The Koreans would resist that—my impression—none of 'em ever said that. I just have this feeling they would not be receptive. The women were going to ESL class and for some reason they just discontinued that." In fact, some of the Korean women were so interested in learning English that they were attending a literacy program especially for Asian immigrant women after work in a different city some miles away.

Here is what Sook Yoo, one of those women, had to say (through an interpreter) about not speaking English well: "I think there is a reason why we do not speak English that well. When we started working at EMCO, our starting pay was so little. But since we did not speak much English, we just took the starting pay. We started working and stayed for a while, but since the pay was so little, there was no time for us to study, realistically, because the pay was so minimal. . . . And we were so busy trying to survive. Since we came up that way, even now, we do not have a lot of money, and we are leading a hard life."

Sook Yoo and the other women in the literacy class went on to explain that in their community people resist governmental assistance, proudly preferring to earn the little they get. This, plus the value placed on higher education for their children, often necessitates taking two jobs. The result is too little money, too little time to learn English. Not being able to speak English, they pointed out, means not being able to defend yourself in the workplace when you're accused of a mistake, and, most importantly, it means a greatly reduced chance of promotion, even when you do your current job very well. There are no Korean supervisors, they observed, in this high-tech workplace where international certification standards require that manufacturing process instructions be written, read, and communicated in English. They wished that the company had continued to provide English classes on site, but the classes had suddenly been discontinued. Sook Yoo concluded: "So we lost the chance to learn English, and now we are too old."

The manager was right, then, that there certainly were some workers, mostly Korean, who did not speak much English, but he was way off base in assuming that they did not want to learn. I should also point out that it is not necessarily the case that workers who do not speak much English do not understand much. Over and over my research team found that workers in factories like EMCO understand much more than is apparent. As one employee put it, many workers "cannot speak nice but understand." Further, in our fieldwork at EMCO and Teamco, we regularly observed workers translating for each other; indeed, leads for the various areas and lines at EMCO were chosen in part because they are bilingual and can serve as literacy and language brokers. At both factories immigrants with limited English skills appeared to meet their companies' quality and productivity goals despite the fact that not all of them speak, read, or write English well. I am not arguing that things would not be easier overall if everyone in a plant spoke and was literate in the same language; however, work does get done quite competently even when this is not the case. We should not, then, automatically assume that limited English was the reason the three boards were mislabeled.

Let us turn now to explanations provided by employees who worked on the shop floor. The first shift's supervisor, Celia, on whose watch the label problem occurred, believed her workers read the instructions too quickly to notice what was salient and that they did so because they were mistakenly in a rush to finish the boards so that they could be moved to another department: "They know that they have to read. Each RMA [rework instruction] is usually always different. In this case they read it but read it so fast that they did not comprehend everything that . . . needed to [be done], so they missed it. . . . They feel like it's a shift type of thing. They need to produce enough assemblies. Whatever they touch and work on, they need to move it on to test. It's a quota-type thing. It isn't."

Thus, this supervisor attributed the label error to another error, the workers' belief that if any boards were waiting for them on their shift, they should be moved on to the next step in the manufacturing process, to the next department, as quickly as possible. Although this supervisor made a point of insisting that quality was most important and that the workers were wrong in thinking there was some kind of quota they needed to reach on a given day, my research team observed plenty of instances in which workers felt pulled in two directions—high quality versus high productivity. "Push, push, push," one worker said of another supervisor's modus operandi. At Teamco the complaint was similar: How can I keep my quality high if I must work faster and faster? Thus, this tension is a fact of life that workers have to cope with, even when it remains unacknowledged, and, conceivably, it could have had something to do with the label problem. But let us ask the workers themselves.

Marisa, the lead in the hardware department, was the person who made the incorrect labels and passed them to another worker, Tran, to be affixed to the boards. She first commented, "It's too bad that you [the researcher] have to find out about these boards. We are not supposed to make mistakes like that." She had several explanations for the problem, the first resembling the supervisor's analysis in that it also focused on time—work that day had been hectic: "It was so busy that day . . . and besides they tell me, 'Oh, we have these three boards' and they said 'we need to ship these three boards.'" Clearly, Marisa thought the boards were "hot," that they had to be shipped pronto, so she may have given the written instructions short shrift. She also pointed out that Tran, the worker who actually pasted the labels on the boards, was new and that she had not had time to train him sufficiently. Next time, she promised, she would have an experienced person work on the special boards.

Marisa's other explanation had to do with how work was organized on the floor, especially the literacy requirements of work. It seems that one worker in Marisa's department, Mrs. Kim, always read the entire set of instructions for each board and let people know if anything special was required. On the day the three mother boards were reworked, Mrs. Kim was absent, and the person who took over her job did not act as the literacy broker for the rest of the workers. "She just read her part," Marisa complained. "Mrs. Kim always reads the whole thing and then she tells you." Not alerted to the special directions, Marisa made new labels according to the customary process.

Interestingly, if Marisa had read the instructions herself, she would certainly have known what to do in a procedural sense—leave the old datecode label on the board; prepare a new, smaller label with a new month and year; and paste it on top of the old one. Marisa would also have understood that the process was done this way because the customer wanted it done this way. However, as will be clear from the following transcript, she would not have understood the role and importance of such documentation in the all-important practice of maintaining traceability:

Researcher: Do you have to understand what the numbers [on the label] mean?

Marisa: Yes, this is the datecode. We're supposed to leave old label. Customer wants to change new datecode. I make small label with datecode and cut it and put it on top of the other one.

Researcher: Why is that so important to the customer?

Marisa: We're not supposed to remove the old label. That one, we're supposed to leave it on there.

Researcher: Do you understand why they care that much about whether the old label's there?

Marisa: Uhhhmm, not really, but we just have to follow what the customer wants if he, they, say "I want you guys to remove that label, we just want to leave it alone, just change datecode."

Researcher: Do you understand why it's such a big deal?

Marisa: I not really understand that.

It is quite significant, I would argue, that workers like Marisa were expected to read and follow directions but not to understand their significance. This suggests another reason for the error, not having access to global knowledge about the manufacturing process that makes tasks understandable and meaningful. If Marisa had understood the relationship between labels and traceability, and if she had understood the role of traceability in contract manufacturing, she might have paid more attention to instructions to make particular datecode labels.

The last worker interviewed about the board problem was Tran, the person who had pasted Marisa's incorrect labels on the board. His explanation for his part in the mishap was simple—reading directions was not part of his job:

Tran: Only the lead take care.

Researcher: Only the lead takes care?

Tran: When I'm not lead, I'm not looking.

Researcher: Not looking at the MPI? [manufacturing process instructions]
Tran: Yeah. Only the lead take care.
Researcher: Did anybody ever show you how to read the MPI?
Tran: No, they did not show.

Even as a new employee, Tran recognized what I had learned from the managers early on in the study: EMCO's policy was that only workers designated as "leads" for each line or area are responsible for reading written instructions; they are then supposed to spread the word orally. As we saw with Marisa, sometimes employees work out an informal system whereby someone besides the lead is the literacy broker. But the official policy—which originated in large part as an attempt to compensate for what were perceived to be English-as-a-second-language problems, especially among the Korean workers "who weren't keen on learning English"—was that only the leads were required to read. Thus, Tran, did not feel compelled to read Wade's rework instructions and could not be blamed for his choice, given EMCO's policy on literacy responsibilities.

The story of mistaken labels and my subsequent analysis of the possible reasons for the mistake suggest that it may indeed matter, and matter a great deal, that work is organized so that frontline workers are not supposed to read. It would seem that not only should frontline workers be expected to read, but they will also need to possess a greater knowledge of the plant's operation and the industry's practices if they are to accurately interpret what they will need to read. Thus, one could argue that being fully literate in such a manufacturing environment goes beyond being able to decode instructions on how to apply a datecode label and includes as well global knowledge about the industry—such as understanding the important concept of traceability.

It is clear that frontline workers at EMCO do not ordinarily think of literate activities as central to their work or, to put it another way, they do not construct working identities—ways of thinking, acting, talking, and valuing—that have much to do with literacy and print. And it is clear that supervisors and engineers do not expect or encourage frontline employees to develop literate identities as workers. All this is quite an irony, given the trend toward excessive documentation in such workplaces and the central role that such documentation appears to play in the manufacturing process.

"YOU HAVE TO WRITE IT DOWN": THE LITERATE PRACTICES OF TEAMS[3]

The narrative from EMCO suggests the importance of literacy in circuit board assembly, even at a factory deemed to be traditionally organized. Furthermore, at EMCO work was actually arranged so as to require as few literate responsibilities as possible of the frontline workers. I have illustrated how such

---

[3]This section is based partly on Gee et al. (1996).

an arrangement can spell trouble. Let us now turn to a second company and a different story. At Teamco every frontline worker is required to be a member of a self-directed work team. Teamco represents, in fact, a dramatic turnaround from the first factory in terms of training policies, work organization, and the responsibilities and roles of frontline workers. One might say that Teamco has attempted to create a new work culture and, in so doing, has wanted to foster new working identities among its employees. In such an environment one would certainly expect the development of new and different literacy demands, new literate practices that keep pace with the development of new work practices. We will thus want to ask, as we proceed with this story, how the literacy and work practices at Teamco compare with those at EMCO. What sorts of forums or spaces are made available at Teamco for workers to take part in decision making and to display their newly developed or newly acknowledged literate and problem-solving capabilities?

Teams in this factory corresponded to work areas. That is, all the people who worked in shipping were on one team, all those in a hand-load line were on another, those in touch-up on another, and so on. Officially, each team was supposed to meet for a half hour each week, every week, although this varied greatly in practice. For instance, one team from the test department met unfailingly each Monday at 7:00 a.m. for an hour. I was aware, however, of other teams that met sporadically or only for the benefit of my research team and others that had yet to meet during our stay at the factory. Some supervisors or coaches, I soon learned, were less than enthusiastic about the team concept, and "hot jobs" or a heavy production schedule were apt to take precedence over team meetings. When team meetings did happen, they were held in a variety of places, partly dependent on the size of the team. Large teams of 20 people or so commandeered the training room, while smaller ones crowded into a cubicled conference room that abutted the factory floor or held their meeting at a table in the noisy cafeteria adjacent to the cubicles but off the factory floor.

Officially, team meetings were supposed to be conducted according to certain criteria. There was supposed to be a team leader and a minutes taker, and there always were in the meetings that my research team and I observed. These jobs were to rotate among members, which sometimes happened and sometimes did not. The team leader was not supposed to be the same person as the lead worker on the line or in an area, although this was sometimes the case, as we will see below. (Ironically, there were not supposed to be lead workers at all; these positions had been abolished with the advent of teams, when authority and responsibility on the floor were to be shared among all workers. However, in practice, leads were still leads and were recognized as such.) Each team had a binder in which minutes were recorded on printed forms. There was supposed to be an agenda for each meeting, and there were recommended forms of participation, such as brainstorming and saying "pass" if you had nothing to report.

Perhaps most importantly, team members were expected to engage in a seven-step problem-solving process, which had been covered in the self-directed work team curriculum. By means of this process, workers were supposed to analyze the causes of problems in their areas (through the use of fishbone diagrams, Pareto charts and such), implement and evaluate a solution, and measure the results—activities that certainly required considerable expertise with literacy, mathematics, and language, not to mention knowledge of manufacturing. Later, during building-wide and plant-wide competitions, selected individual teams were expected to present the results of their problem-solving activities to management; they were judged then on their presentation style as well their results.

One other team activity is worth previewing before we eavesdrop on an actual team meeting. Shortly after I began my observations of teams, management announced plans to link self-directed work teams directly to productivity and quality results, and these results to compensation. This was done by requiring all teams to set specific quality and productivity goals for each fiscal quarter—that is, all teams completed a form containing graphs of their previous quality and productivity percentages and a rationale for their future goals—and by rewarding those who met their goals with a bonus. Team leaders were expected to compute quality and productivity on a daily basis, to record these scores daily in a computer program with a security system (to prevent cheating), and to report back to the team, so that problems affecting the teams' scores might be solved. Then, at the end of the quarter, the money available for bonuses would be divided equally among teams who had met their goals; those who had not met their goals would receive nothing.

There was naturally some interest and worry on the part of workers about this new system. In the past, bonuses of varying amounts had simply appeared in the pay envelope of some individuals. Under the old system the rationale for determining bonuses was never made explicit, though everyone had a theory— it's how much overtime you're willing to put in or it's how well you get along with your supervisor. With the advent of teams, individual performance would cease to be rewarded in favor of the team unit; no matter how hard an individual might work, his or her fortunes would rise or fall with those of the team. It follows, then, that one important potential activity for team meetings would be setting goals and monitoring weekly performance on quality and productivity, with an eye toward determining whether or not team performance was likely to result in a team bonus.

The story I tell here is the gist of a half-hour meeting of the "Acon" team. This team was from the hand-load area, an area of the plant that does not require much training, although all employees in this area must take basic electronics at Teamco Tech once they become permanent hires. Workers in this area place components on boards by hand. This work begins when a line is assigned a batch of boards from a customer (such as Intel, Hewlett-Packard, or Apple). The lead decides how to apportion the work among the six people in her line—that is, how many and what kind of components the first person in the line will load, and so forth. The boards are pushed from one end of the line to the other, with each worker incrementally adding a different set of components. In front of each worker is a color-coded diagram, indicating schematically which parts should go where.

The last person on the line is the "QC," or quality control; she inspects the work done by the others and, when necessary, refers to a set of manufacturing process instructions, the major document on the floor, as does the lead. Written by engineers, these instructions describe what workers are supposed to do in each factory department or area in order to assemble a given circuit board. After inspection the QC loads the boards onto a cart, and they are wheeled off to the next department. While the others are assembling and inspecting the parts, the lead worker continues to organize the work, troubleshoot, or help out on the line. The pace is intense; there are time standards for each board and contradictory pressures on the workers, given team goals, both to work faster and to work cleaner, increasing productivity and decreasing defects.

This hand-load team called itself "Acon" after a major customer. It consisted of seven women, all of them immigrants. Two of the women, Xuan and Eva, play a big role in the team meeting that I will soon discuss. Xuan is of Chinese heritage. She grew up in Vietnam and speaks Vietnamese as well as Cantonese fluently but lacks confidence in English, which she began to acquire when she arrived in the United States 4 years ago. Young, in her 20s, is small and soft spoken, and although she is the lead of her hand-load line and in charge of her team's meetings as well, she often has trouble influencing the workers to participate in team activities. The supervisor of the hand-load lines reports that Xuan has no desire to promote, but I noticed that Xuan routinely and ungrudgingly took on more and more responsibilities regarding teams and their reporting requirements and that she became quite adept at the growing paperwork surrounding goal setting. She also used every opportunity to learn English, although shyly. Her team had the best quality and productivity scores of the hand-load area, with almost perfect quality scores, or zero defects, and productivity that sometimes exceeded 100 percent. Xuan was engaged to be married; she and her fiancé were planning a traditional Chinese wedding celebration at a local restaurant in the coming year.

Eva, the most recent hire in Xuan's hand-load line, is originally from the Philippines. Her English is very good, and because of this she was the informal spokesperson for the team, despite the fact that Xuan was its leader and Eva, the most recent hire. Eva was also responsible on most occasions for taking minutes during the meetings. Married with two children, she often commented that she has two jobs, one at Teamco and one when she went home to be a wife and mother. Eva was hired initially as a temporary, as are all workers at Teamco, and during the time that I knew her, she was very proactive in attempting to be made permanent. When all the other members of her line refused to take on the tedious, eye-straining job of quality inspector, she eventually volunteered for it, for the supervisor had hinted broadly that it would help her chances of becoming a permanent hire. Although she claimed to be afraid to talk to the supervisor and often asked me to intervene on her behalf, Eva was quite outspoken at team meetings and on the line, so much so, in fact, that she regularly offended some of her co-workers. Eva was made permanent about 5 months after she was first hired, earlier than is the norm.

The meeting we will examine here took place after the Acon team had been meeting regularly for 4 months. Most, but not all, of the team members had completed training on how to participate in self-directed work teams; one notable exception was Eva, who as a recent hire was still classified as a temporary employee and was ineligible for the training. The meeting was held in the cafeteria at 2:00 p.m., 1 hour before the day shift ended, while workers from various departments were milling about the room. I had attended almost every meeting of the Acon team thus far, had gotten to know everyone, and was viewed by most as a friendly resource, someone who could give advice about literacy-related team activities and someone to whom it was safe to complain.

This meeting of the Acon team began, as they all did, with our exodus from the shop floor to the cafeteria. Team leader Xuan went around from station to station, quietly but insistently announcing in a high-pitched voice, "Team meeting, team meeting!" I walked with Eva, as was our custom, for she enjoyed providing quick summaries of what had been happening the previous week. Eva confided that she had given Lan, her supervisor, an "ultimatum" about being made permanent. When I asked what she had told her exactly, Eva confessed that she had written her a note, being afraid to speak to her face to face, and that she had explained she would have to leave Teamco were she not made permanent soon. The group gathered around a cafeteria table in the usual manner, with Xuan and Eva at one end next to me, the others grouped near us, and Mrs. Chen, the pariah of the group, some distance away. The first part of the meeting was a recital of the week's problems, common fare for any hand-load line. There was the big board that required each person on the line to load 59 components apiece, and the additional problem of having had 20 of these boards returned to the line because certain parts had been reversed. There was the problem on another board of "mixed parts," the mistaken use of one part that is the same size and color as another but that has a different value, and a problem with "bent legs," the disturbance of the tiny wires protruding from components that fit down into the board. Here is an excerpt:

Eva:	[to researcher] Oh, we're having a hard time doing the Lexicon, the big board. The one Lan told you had more than 300 components.
Xuan:	375.
Eva:	One person [has] to load 59 components at every station.
Researcher:	One person?

Eva:	We spent 2 hours finding our own location.
	[Much laughter]
Xuan:	Yeah ( ) the location, 1 minute, the other side [miming with her hands finding the locations on the board]
Eva:	We did about 20 boards from 8 to 3, and then the next, the following day, they returned to us, reverse [meaning the line had made a mistake, putting the parts on in the wrong direction]. [Laughter]

All this talk proceeded casually, with much laughter and joking and with no one taking control of the meeting or enforcing an order of business, though Eva with her good English and strong personality tended to dominate. Interspersed among the discussions of typical hand-load problems were other topics of interest—a startled realization that someone had forgotten to bring the book for taking minutes, a critical observation about the short dress of a cleaning person who walked past the table, a report of a rumor that more production lines were soon to be added, a complaint about a noxious smell in the wave area.

After Eva mentioned John, a Filipino worker who said he did not want to work in the wave area because of the smell, there was a pause of several seconds until Xuan brought up the issue of productivity. One day the previous week, it seems, their line had had a productivity score of only 55 percent, which was below their stated goal for the quarter. Xuan explained that "the lady," by whom she meant the female engineer, thought the calculation might be wrong, that it should be higher, and Eva urged Xuan to make the correction. However, Xuan stated that it was too late, implying that once recorded, the score could not be changed. Here is their exchange (which includes overlapping and interrupted conversational turns):

Eva:	Did you check the lady about the 55 percent =
Researcher:	= Mhm =.
Eva:	=of what we did ah just any -
Mai:	Just any -?
Eva:	And he told you to check it to the lady. So did you check it?
Xuan:	Yeah, I check already.
Eva:	What did she said?
Xuan:	She said it might wrong you know because hand-load they write in the mechanical ( ) that's why=
Eva:	=That's what, so how many percent now?
Xuan:	(50) percent. [slight pause] You cannot change it.
Eva:	Aaaaaahhh.

After this exchange Xuan continued to focus the group's attention on poor productivity, pointing out that one day this current week the line's score was only

57 percent. Eva's agitated question of "why, why, why?" brought a quick and spirited explanation constructed jointly—in fact, almost simultaneously—by several people on the team. (See the complete transcript of this discussion in Appendix 5-A.) It seems that the Acon line had been asked to load components on a new board, the Acuson, during a period of enforced idleness. (A machine was down, making their customary boards unavailable.) The Acuson was a board ordinarily loaded by another line, and the Acon team was not familiar with it. The board was especially complex, requiring 21 tiny transistors and much tedious masking. There were only five people on the Acon line to do this work, whereas the line that usually loads this board has seven workers. Nonetheless, the Acon line managed to complete 120 Acuson boards, working 2 hours of overtime. Yet their productivity was below their goal. This conversation indicates how savvy these workers were as a group, even those like Mai, whose spoken English was quite limited and who did not ordinarily participate much in meetings: they knew precisely why their productivity was low for that day and could marshal all sorts of details and evidence in support of their explanation, albeit in what might be viewed as a random and rowdy manner.

The next topic at the meeting was how to document this problem. Eva stated loudly to Xuan, "You have to put a note on the paper. . . . You have to give them a reason," meaning that Xuan should take care to write down on their score sheet an explanation for the low productivity score for that particular day. Xuan defended herself, saying she usually writes these things down but on that day she simply forgot. Eva retorted with spirit that Xuan may have forgotten to write, but she will remember the bonus—and maybe the team won't get one:

Eva:	Then you have to make a note at the back and tell tell them the reason why is our productivity is so low that day. So they will give us credit for that==
Xuan:	==I know, yeah, this time I forgot.
Eva:	Ay-yai-yai! Oh::
	[much laughter all around]
Eva:	Did you see every time, did you see every time we have a meeting or something else I put a note on my paper?
Xuan:	Yeah==
Eva:	==Yeah, you have to do that all the time.
	(17 related turns omitted)
Xuan:	I write a note already.
Researcher:	Good.
Xuan:	But that Acuson I forget [laugh].
Researcher:	[laugh] You forgot the Acuson.
	[Much laughter]
Researcher:	Okay.
Eva:	You'll remember the bonus ( ).

Eva: [Much laughter]
            [teasingly] Maybe we do not receive any.
            [Much laughter]

The meeting began to wind down. Eva asked jokingly whether anyone had been fighting—"everybody fighting?"—a reference to the rather steady history of conflicts between Mrs. Chen and the rest. Mrs. Chen responded that "everybody tired," which prompted a whispered conversation about her rumored wealth and some raucous comments on what she could do about her high blood pressure. Eva then turned the conversation one last time back to their productivity for the week, asking Xuan, "How many percent we have this week?" Although she did not have the numbers at hand, Xuan, with help from the team, was able to reconstruct from memory their scores for the first 3 days of the week: 77 percent on Monday, the infamous 57 percent on Tuesday, and 75 percent on Wednesday. The data had not been analyzed for Thursday, but the group felt confident that their score was fine for that day. I averaged these data and reported that their score was 69 percent thus far for the week, well above their quarterly goal of 60 percent. Xuan then consulted a little black notebook she always carried in her pocket and announced that for the entire quarter thus far their productivity average was 82 percent but that their quality was poor and still a problem. No one commented. The half hour set aside for the meeting had passed, and the Acon team wandered back to the floor, chatting in groups of two and three as they walked.

This meeting of the Acon team certainly does not fit the usual notions of a formal meeting, at least the notions of those accustomed to some variation on Robert's *Rules of Order*. Nor does it abide by the guidelines set up by Teamco through its self-directed work team curriculum. There was no agenda; there was no apparent order of events. There was no problem-solving à la fishbone diagrams and Pareto charts or any other reminder of the self-directed work team classes. There was really no one in charge. People wandered in and out of the conversation, paying attention to what interested them, ignoring the rest. Talk was simultaneous, overlapping, and latched, as one person repeated the words of the current speaker or finished someone else's sentence or interrupted or talked on top of another. There was much laughter and joking. One member of my research team who had lived in Southeast Asia and speaks fluent Vietnamese told me that the meetings transported him to Vietnam, that the participants were very "close" to that culture, not yet being completely Americanized, and that they seemed to draw on common Vietnamese participant structures. It seemed to me, as well, that there was something reminiscent here of kitchen table conversations among women everywhere, something most of us have witnessed or experienced.

Although the meeting may have appeared chaotic, it is important to note that some important work of the team was getting done. One can point, for example, to the litany of hand-load problems at the beginning of the meeting, dutifully noted in the minutes—reversed parts on board number 158294, bent legs on number 4929194—a significant step in identifying and documenting the line's quality problems. Then there was the jointly constructed explanation for their team's low productivity on one particular day—they were working on a complex board foreign to them, and their line was short the requisite workers. This explanation allowed them to account for a problem if not fix it. And then there was the team's discussion of how to document extenuating circumstances so as not to be penalized on their productivity record and ultimately their team-based bonus—team-worthy activities all. The fact that so much work was accomplished in this informal, folksy gathering, and that there was participation by workers who did not speak in other forums that I observed, makes one wary of preconceived notions of what counts as a good meeting. Indeed, I witnessed less lively, more dreary gatherings of other teams that did abide by the letter of the law for how to conduct a meeting but appeared to accomplish less.

Another indication that the Acon workers were acquiring the sensibilities to operate as a team is their attention to documentation. The enormous reporting apparatus associated with productivity and quality scores for teams—alluded to in the above transcript, especially in Eva's comments—underlines the increasing role of literacy in this factory and the ways in which writing, reading, and computation took their place in day-to-day work events. Every week, it seemed, engineers or supervisors would invent a new form or revise an old one, most of them designed to enforce careful recording and analysis of data collected on productivity and quality rates. The data were then transferred to computer programs, which generated the myriad graphs and charts that lined the walls of the cubicles on the perimeter of the factory floor.

For the most part, leads buckled down and mastered the massive new reporting requirements, attending the meetings in which new forms and methods of calculation were introduced, computing their scores and filling out their forms each day after work, keeping a bottle of "Wite-Out" nearby, and acquiring the technological sophistication needed to wade through and modify vast computerized databases. They also groaned—"No, not another form! So much paper!"—and noted that the paperwork was an additional burden in an already burdened workday. Workers were quick to notice the ways they could turn paperwork to their advantage. Eva's zeal to write down explanations for the team's low productivity is a good example. Xuan's little black book of important numbers and facts is another. And when faced with strict reporting requirements that rigidly divided the day and the work into unworkable segments, workers learned to fudge, altering what they reported so that it would fit the forms.

One could say, then, that a part of the new working identities of people on the front lines at Teamco had much to do with literacy and numeracy. All of a sudden, not only were hand-loaders expected to be quick and accurate at their work, they were also, with the advent of teams and new systems of reporting and monitoring, supposed to conceptualize their work differently. They were now to include as part of it an understanding of goals, goal setting, calculations, and reports and all the literate acts these activities entail. Put another way, workers were asked to conceive of themselves not just as employees who performed the physical act of placing components on a board but also as thinkers, as people who monitored their own hand-loading rates, reflected on and analyzed their problems, and reported on this through print and through presentations.

However, there is more to the literacy practices and the working identities at Teamco, a darker side of the story. I have cited some instances of workers' taking charge of literacy, so to speak, not only acquiring the various practices valued at the company but also turning writing to their own purposes—creating a paper trail, documenting a reasonable explanation for their low productivity on a given day. I must point out, however, that for the most part the kind of literacy valued in the factory emphasized self-monitoring, not self-direction, and that workers had no choice but to abide by rigid documentary rules—recall Xuan being resigned to the fact that, once entered into the computer, her team's productivity score could not be changed even if it was wrong. Leads spent inordinate amounts of time counting, figuring, and tabulating, all in service of accountability. While self-directed work teams were supposed to be empowered to solve their own problems, managers and engineers appeared so compelled to measure and document quality and productivity, to find ways to quantify the teams' work, to keep tabs and to keep track—all through literacy-related activities—that workers were left very little room to maneuver.

One more literacy-related example will make this point. I have already mentioned that manufacturing process instructions were the central documents on the shop floor. These instructions were written by engineers, and there was a set of them for each individual circuit board. They outlined the manufacturing process from beginning to end, for each department or area, and listed the type, amount, and serial number of each component to be affixed to the board. These central documents were consulted when engineers determined standard times, or how long it should take to complete a given piece of work on a board. These standard times, of course, influenced productivity scores. It was well known on the factory floor that manufacturing process instructions were often wrong or outdated. Busy engineers did not always have the time to make corrections, or they overlooked tiny details that made the difference between a board that worked and one that failed or between achieving one's productivity goal for the day and missing it. Despite the fact that the engineers knew about the problems with the manufacturing process instructions, workers were absolutely prohibited from changing them, from making an alteration even of the smallest kind.

On one afternoon I was watching Xuan as she studied one manufacturing process instruction. She eventually found the problem she was looking for—the author had mistakenly written a "1" where an "11" should be in the column listing the number of components. This simple mistake had major implications for Xuan's line in terms of productivity calculations. It obviously takes 11 times longer to load 11 components than it takes to load 1; the group's "standard time," or the amount of time allotted for assembling that board, was thus way off kilter, and so would be their productivity—if they went ahead and assembled the board as it should properly be done. I reached over with a pencil and attempted to write in the other numeral, whereupon the usually mannerly Xuan gave a startled shriek and ordered me away, explaining that we must not, and the workers must not, nor even could Lan the supervisor, modify a manufacturing process instruction. She and her group went ahead and did the boards correctly and suffered the consequences. But other workers took different approaches: A couple of test operators found one engineer especially difficult to work with whenever they approached him about errors or omissions in his test process instructions, so they quit telling him and instead took to troubleshooting the test process instructions themselves and working from the revisions they had penciled in in their own notebooks. In other cases, workers refused to make changes they knew were needed when the manufacturing process instruction was incorrect, even if the engineer gave verbal permission to do so. "Do not go by verbal, go by written," Mr. Marco warned his group again and again, having been burned once too often.

In some ways, I would argue, the literacy practices of the factory—who was enabled to read and write which documents for what purposes on which occasions—were a window on the work practices of the factory as a whole and the hierarchical structures that governed them. Despite the fact that Teamco required its work force to organize around teams, required those teams to meet, and required them to solve problems and to continually find ways to improve and document their quality and productivity—despite the fact that it claimed to want a thinking work force, a self-directed, and empowered one—I saw continual evidence that workers received a conflicting message, that they were in fact quite constrained in terms of the actions they could take, the decisions they could make, the influence they could have, and the literacies they could practice. While the working identities of people on the front lines of this factory increasingly included a sense of their work as "intellective" (Zuboff, 1988) and as connected to, directed by, and shaped in relation to written texts, their sense of themselves as workers continued to fit the old mold. They were employees very much in the grip of a hierarchy that insisted on self-monitoring but allowed very little self-direction.

FORMAL ANALYSES OF LITERATE ACTIVITIES

Thus far in this chapter I have offered narratives, tales of two factories, if you will. Through them I hoped to provide a detailed and nuanced sense of what work is like in circuit board assembly and the role of literacy in that work as well as a feel for who the workers are. So much talk about "skills" is done acontextually these days, with scant reference to actual situations, particular workplaces, and real people. This way of talking about skills has a tendency to misrepresent the nature of working knowledge and leave us with pat, inaccurate skill lists and related curricula. Thus, I hope that my narratives, which try to locate what people are required to know and do as workers within the social, cultural, and political worlds of the factory, will serve as a corrective to the tendency to always speak generically of skills.

In the following section I try to go beyond the broad characterizations that are possible through narrative accounts and present an analysis of the literate requirements of work in finer detail. Because my research team relied extensively on audiotaping and videotaping its data collection, it was possible in most cases to transcribe quite precisely the talk that occurred in meetings, in training sessions, and on the shop floor. (See, for example, the transcript provided in Appendix 5-A.) These transcriptions, supplemented by field notes and documents, were coded inductively according to the functions that reading and writing served. That is, my research team and I noted any use of or reference to reading or writing, and drawing on our knowledge of the situation, the participants, and the activity, we determined the function that use served in that particular instance. As we analyzed more and more transcripts, we added to and emended this emerging taxonomy of literate functions. At the end of our analysis, we had identified approximately 80 functions that literacy served at EMCO and Teamco; these are listed in Appendix 5-B.

Making sense of this analysis required one more step. Taking our list of 80-odd literate functions, and again working inductively, we grouped like categories together. For instance, the literate functions copying and labeling were put in the same list, and the functions creating hypotheticals and problem solving were grouped together in a different one. When we were finished, we had created seven broad meta-categories of literate functions: performing basic literate functions; using literacy to explain; taking part in discourse around and about texts; participating in the flow of information; problem solving; exercising critical judgment; and using literacy to exercise, acknowledge, or resist authority. The meta-categories and their members appear in Appendix 5-C.

Then it was a matter of returning to the analyses of work events on the shop floor, training classes, and team meetings and re-presenting these according to the meta-categories. The resulting worksheets allow one to see, almost at a glance, which participants in which situations used literacy in which ways and with what frequencies.[4]

Before going on to discuss what this kind of literacy analysis makes visible, I should provide some caveats on using the taxonomy. The meta-categories represent robust tendencies rather than hard and fast rules. That is, depending on the context, any literate function, although usually an example of one particular

---

[4]In addition to analyzing the functions that literacy served in team meetings, work events, and training sessions, my research team and I developed two additional coding schemes, one centering on team meeting activities and a second on classroom activities.

meta-category, might fit better into another. Thus, the meta-categories suggest primary allegiances, but less frequently any function can be used in a variety of ways. Further, almost any function might fit into the last meta-category—that is, using literacy to exercise, acknowledge, or resist authority—again depending on context. One warning, then, is that the meta-categories should not be used as just another set of skill lists but rather as a heuristic for analyzing and understanding literate activity.

A second caution has to do with the ordering of the meta-categories into a continuum, beginning with performing basic literate functions and ending with using literacy to exercise, acknowledge, or resist authority. The performing basic literate functions meta-category includes uses of literacy such as *copying, keyboarding, proofreading,* and *labeling.* The final meta-category includes literate functions such as *gaining consensus, gauging reactions,* and *requesting action.* One of my greatest worries in offering the meta-categories in this particular order is that they will be read as representing a kind of developmental progression. That is, some educators, researchers, or laypeople might infer that first workers (or students) need to master the basic literate functions; then they progress to the second category of using literacy to explain; eventually they will be sophisticated enough to engage in those functions in the last meta-category, using literacy to exercise, acknowledge, or resist authority. Nothing could be further from what my research team and I found in our fieldwork or how I intend the taxonomies to be used. It is true that the meta-categories are ordered according to a progression, but this progression has to do with rights and opportunities for exercising literate abilities.

As I will illustrate in the following section, we saw both workers and managers engaging in literate activities from all seven meta-categories. However, the categories on the left-hand side of the chart—performing basic literate functions and using literacy to explain—are the categories most often associated with and available to frontline workers. The categories on the right-hand side of the chart—exercising critical judgment and using literacy to exercise, acknowledge, or resist authority—are the categories most often associated with and available to those in positions of authority, such as supervisors, managers, and engineers. In other words, the meta-category chart and the continuum it represents lay bare how patterns of literacy use are linked to structures of authority.

Literacy Finding 1: Much Ado About Literacy

In recent years there has been much ado about increasing skill requirements in the workplace, literacy included and literacy in particular. I think that this assessment, at least in its broad outlines and general direction, is accurate. There can be no doubt about it—both EMCO and Teamco were awash with literacy. Or to mix metaphors, literacy provided the frame, the scaffolding, the superstructure within which work got done at these circuit board assembly plants. My evidence for this claim is the 80-odd functions that we saw reading and writing serve on the factory floors, in meetings, and during training sessions. This number suggests something of the remarkable diversity of the literate activities in these work-places. But I can give a richer sense of this range by turning to a few examples that highlight some of the functions and also the seven meta-categories into which the functions are grouped.

Let's first review the Acon meeting from Teamco. You may remember my characterizing the meeting as kitchen table talk among a group of women. Acon team members showed little awareness of (or perhaps it was interest in) the expected conventions for running a meeting. But even at this quite informal gathering of workers from the lowest prestige and, some would say, lowest-skilled area of the plant, I identified some 44 instances of literacy representing functions from four of the seven meta-categories—performing basic literate functions; taking part in discourse around and about text; exercising critical judgment; and using literacy to exercise, acknowledge, or resist authority. The most frequently used category was taking part in discourse around and about text, as the lead, Xuan, and the unofficial team spokesperson, Eva, repeatedly *referenced* documents they had on hand or *cited* documents, such as quality reports, that played an important role in their work. Particularly noteworthy was their discussion of the necessity of documenting problems on the line so as to protect and defend their productivity scores. "You have to make a note at the back and tell, tell them the reason why . . . our productivity is so low that day," Eva insisted to Xuan. "Did you see every time, did you see every time we have a meeting or something else I put a note on my paper?" she continued to scold. In their exchange Eva *invokes* a rule about recordkeeping and at the same time *admonishes* Xuan to do a better job of this literate responsibility. She also raises the specter of the team's possible failure to meet productivity and quality goals and the related failure to get a bonus—all because the team leader had not made the required written accounting of the circumstances surrounding the team's low scores. These are examples par excellence of a sophisticated understanding and use of literacy to exercise, acknowledge, or resist authority.

At EMCO, as well, there were instances of literate activity from each of the major categories. In one such instance a lead worker, Eduardo, struggled to correct an obsolete document. In this work event I identified instances of each of the literacy meta-categories—from performing basic literate functions to using literacy to exercise, acknowledge, or resist authority. Especially notable were the high number of instances in the meta-category taking part in discourse around and about text and in exercising critical judgment. Many of the instances of the latter involve Maggie, the supervisor, and Eduardo *interpreting* the engineer's documents, *evaluating* proposed solutions, and *critiquing* the engineer's obsolete documents. In the following excerpt, Maggie and Eduardo had been working at the problem for some 200 lines of transcript. They have examined all the documentation and have brainstormed a number of possible solutions. Here Maggie is *perusing* the manufacturing process instructions, rereading parts aloud, while Eduardo is *contextualizing* the activity, providing background on the various shifts' work on the board. Next they look at the assembly drawing again, *critiquing* it and then *referencing* the manufacturing process instructions to discover the last time the documents were updated.

Maggie:	Uh huh. [reading from manufacturing process instructions] "Install Q 6, 7, 12, and 13 with mounting hardware after solder flow." After solder flow . . . [.06] hmmm. "See detail A. Add CR 1 after solder flow."
Eduardo:	I guess the last time we di- day shift did this one-
Maggie:	Oh, okay.
Eduardo:	Day shift did this one.
Maggie:	After solder flow. Mm hmm.
Eduardo:	They put on this one and then they just put the hardware on these two. See, but that's the deficiency, they've been putting on the different part, and see this one, now no detail of this one should be cut in the middle; this one should be bent like this. That's what I'm saying. "Just follow the drawing," but this much different.
Maggie:	Yeah, the draw- the drawing is definitely wrong. And how old is this manufacturing process instructions? [Reading a date on the manufacturing process instructions] "4/26/94 update BOM [bills of materials]." This is 8/13 when they initially released this to manufacturing.
Eduardo:	The drawing says 1979.
Maggie:	[laughs] Bingo! See, this. . . .

In summary, then, there was evidence at both EMCO and Teamco—at traditionally organized and high-performance factories—to suggest that literate activities are woven throughout the work of today's circuit board assembly. Now let us turn to the patterns of literacy use that distinguish one factory from the other.

Literacy Finding 2: The High-Performance Hoopla

The popular discourse on high-performance versus traditionally organized factories has generally assumed that high-performance work requires more and different skills. In terms of literacy and in broad strokes, I have found this to be the case. Despite the fact that we saw instances of literacy from all of the metacategories at EMCO, the traditionally organized factory, there were striking differences as well. In essence, literacy use at EMCO among frontline workers was restricted according to position; leads got to exercise literate abilities to a certain extent, but work was organized in such a way that the masses of frontline workers did not get to do so. Further, at EMCO literate functions on the right side of our continuum—using literacy to exercise, acknowledge, or resist authority; exercising critical judgment; and solving problems—were much more likely to be performed by supervisors, managers, or people in traditional positions of authority. At Teamco, on the other hand, a wider range of workers were called on to exercise a wider range of literate abilities across the continuum. In particular, I saw more instances of frontline workers performing literate functions associated with the right side of the continuum, the power side. This occurred mainly through the opportunities and intellectual space provided in team meetings.

To consider these points in more detail, let us return to the narrative about EMCO labels presented earlier. In this event were instances of each of the literacy meta-categories—from performing basic literate functions to using literacy to exercise, acknowledge, or resist authority. However, it is noteworthy that the only person to participate in this broad range of literate activities was the engineer. Wade performed a variety of basic literate functions, such as *recording*, *tallying*, and *matching*. Readers will recall, for example, how he sorted the box of returned boards and wrote down identifying information about them. But Wade participated in many other literate activities, too— *explaining* the literate problem of labels to a variety of personnel, *citing* literate rules about how to write corrective action reports, *instructing* workers and their supervisor about how to create correct labels, *brainstorming* to solve the problem of the mistaken labels, *reprimanding* workers in writing. Astonishingly, the only literate activities that one worker, the lead Marisa, participated in during the labels event were in performing basic literate functions—*keyboarding* and *copying*—and participating in the flow of information—*clarifying* her role in the labeling process.

There were occasions when workers at EMCO got to do more, especially certain leads (as we saw above with Eduardo), but in general literacy practices were quite restricted at this factory. In virtually all our analyses, line workers were absent across the categories. At Teamco, on the other hand, we saw instances of a wide range of literacy activities during the meeting of the Acon team—and this was a relatively literacy-poor example compared with others we observed. Let me refer briefly to another meeting, this one by the wave-solder team. The beginning of this particular meeting was dominated by a few workers—the lead of the meeting and a technician who served as a self-appointed informal facilitator. Eventually, however, an invitation into the discussion—that is, into both the team's immediate discussion and the larger ongoing discussion within the workplace—was explicitly extended to all of the team members when Carlos first brought to their attention the issues raised in a weekly quality meeting. The team members took up his invitation, especially when Carlos *proposed* and facilitated the construction of a fishbone diagram of one problem. Carlos exercised the authority he had as technician and team patriarch by first *proposing* the brainstorming and diagramming and then facilitating it even after the team leader ignored the idea. His help we coded as *coaching*, or facilitating a literate activity or the understanding of a representation, a function of the meta-category participating in the flow of information.

When Carlos raised the quality issue, the concern about solder balls, Yiheng joined the conversation for the first time, *perusing* and *citing* the quality report, *signifying* his familiarity with the assembly referred to in the report, and *conjecturing* about the possible causes of the problem. Leon and Dai likewise took part in discourse around and about the text (in this case the quality report) and joined in the problem-solving effort, adding to the flurry of *conjecture* about causes. Hoang also entered the conversation, *requesting* and *perusing* the report. It was during this section of the meeting that Leon, always active in team discussions, began participating in new ways by *providing linguistic assistance* for Yiheng. Though this assistance was more obvious in later sections of the meeting, it began here with his *miming* particular processes as a way of helping Yiheng stay afloat in the conversation.

The range of participation in the meeting increased during the formal brainstorming session (the fishbone diagram) and the subsequent listing of solutions to the brainstormed (or fishboned) causes of the solder-ball problem. For the most part, over the course of the meeting the team members' participation fell into the meta-category taking part in discourse around and about text. As with the other meetings and events we analyzed, this was the most frequently used category—a full two-thirds of the more than 150 instances of literate activity in this meeting represented functions in this category, with team members repeatedly *perusing* and *referencing* the documents on hand and *citing* assemblies, their profiles, and machine settings and adjustments. But in this section of the meeting, with the introduction of the formalized process, the *perusals*, the *references*, the *citations* took on a different weight, a different function. As part of the brainstorming, the team members helped to shape the lists and diagrams as they referenced them and then let these new representations shape their understanding of a work process. And so perhaps more significant than the several instances of taking part in discourse around and about text were these fewer instances of problem solving: specifically, six of the nine team members present participated to some degree in *brainstorming*, collaboratively constructing a representation for heuristic purposes. The brainstorming session was a swirl of literate activity, with workers constructing representations, clarifying proper categories for ideas offered, referencing items on the list, and citing a variety of representations and literate activities, all this within the framework of a particular work process in which they variously participate.

Thus, the workers in this meeting were offered an opportunity to participate as a group in troubleshooting the work processes they were a part of, while the frontline workers in the EMCO events were kept out of discussions of work processes and at a distance from texts. It is interesting to note that although the lead, the technician, and the senior operator dominated the meeting, when the rest of the workers did participate, not only were they taking part in discourse around and about text, simply *receiving instructions* or *requesting clarification*, but with the help of a skillful facilitator such as Carlos, they were also participating to some degree in problem solving and in further understanding the larger work processes of which their particular tasks were a part.

On the basis of such literacy analyses it is clear that, while literacy was everywhere at both factories, at Teamco more literate activities were expected of a wider range of workers. At EMCO the leads were the only frontline workers with any responsibilities for literate activity, while at Teamco virtually all workers were expected to develop literate sensibilities, and a rather impressive range of workers read, wrote, and talked about texts for a rather impressive range of purposes.

Literacy Finding 3: Caveats and Qualifications Regarding Literacy Rights and Responsibilities

The public discourse about high-performance work environments rarely ventures beyond blanket pronouncements on the benefits to be gained from self-directed work teams and the "learning organization" or uncritical praise for particular factories that have chosen this route. In my research, though, I have been able to look deeply at the implementation of teams at a highly regarded company and in so doing to probe beyond the company's public persona and to document problems and challenges as well as successes. In essence, what I found is that Teamco, despite its high-performance ideals, actually placed considerable constraints on the exercise of literate abilities—because it placed serious constraints on workers' rights and responsibilities in general. While claiming to empower its frontline workers, Teamco generally continued to maintain traditional roles and relationships between workers and management, and this established hierarchy shaped and constrained literacy practices.

Earlier, in the context of information about the Acon team meeting, I discussed the ways in which the literate practices of teams were constrained. Another place where traditional roles were most apparent at Teamco was the training room, where workers went to learn how to participate in self-directed work teams. While the teacher of these classes generally engaged in activities in which literate functions spanned all of the meta-categories, students in the class were severely constrained in their literate activities. They *recited;* they *received instruction;* they *recounted;* they *completed forms;* they did a bit of minimal *explaining* around literate tasks. But in a class designed to induct them into self-directed work teams, they engaged in virtually no activities that required literate problem solving or that required them to exercise critical judgment. We would have thought the training classes, where workers momentarily escaped from time pressures and from what one manager called the "brutality" of the factory floor, would have been the prime place for modeling, practicing, and trying on the new activities expected of team members, including activities leading to an identification with factory literacy, activities with numbers, forms, reporting, and the written word. But this was not the case.

In the team presentations I analyzed, where frontline workers stood before management and offered up information on the data they had collected and analyzed, I likewise expected to see a great deal of literate activity that could be categorized as problem solving or exercising critical judgment. But here, too, workers seemed fairly limited. Predominantly in these sessions, presenters used literacy to explain and to take part in discourse around and about text. Perhaps because these sessions were viewed early on as performances rather than as genuine dialogues between workers and management, there was small expectation that workers would exercise those literate abilities associated with the right-hand side of our meta-category continuum and little incentive for them to do so.

CONCLUDING THOUGHTS

Previous studies of literacy at work—even qualitatively oriented ones—have been content with characterizing literate activities with broad brush strokes. One of the best-known early examinations of literacy at work—Diehl and Mikulecky (1980)—categorized literate activity as either reading to know or reading to do. These authors suggested that "reading to do" characterizes literate activity in the workplace, while "reading to know" is what children do mostly in school. Thereby, they usefully questioned the commonplace assumption that reading is reading is reading. In contrast to this early work is the taxonomy described in this chapter, which paints a more detailed and complete picture of the nature of literate activity at work than most studies to date. To be content now to say that reading at work in the main consists of "reading to do" is to overlook the many different functions that reading serves when people are reading in order to accomplish a task, as well as to underestimate the importance and prevalence of literacy in the workplace. Moreover, the categories "reading to do" versus "reading to know" give no sense of the political nature of literate activities in the workplace. The kinds of literate activities that a person engages in at a workplace may have more to do with workers' rights and responsibilities and the limits and constraints set by the company hierarchy than with the nature of the work per se. Thus, I believe that this study indicates how very important it is to be precise and detailed when describing the functions that reading and writing serve in the workplace and to be clear about how those functions relate to workplace hierarchies and power structures.

The study further illustrates, I believe, the value of ethnographic and qualitative research for understanding the skill requirements of work and, conversely, suggests the ways in which studies that are based primarily on survey data or "grand tours" of the workplace may be misleading. When we first began our research at EMCO, the plant manager assured us that literacy was not very important at the factory and pointed out that most people there could not even read English. As I have demonstrated, he was wrong on both accounts. Even at Teamco, with its intense interest in the team concept, the role and importance of literacy went unrecognized. Yet we have seen that both factories were awash with paper and that at Teamco an important part of being an effective team member was developing what I have called a "literate identity."

The project also complicates the notion of high-performance work environments. Appelbaum and Batt (1993) observed with a critical eye that the U.S. response to workplace innovation has been to try it piecemeal, adopting a few isolated practices associated with quality enhancement programs rather than the whole ball of wax. This characterization, while accurate for many companies, I am sure, does not quite get at the problems I saw surfacing at the high-performance factory. It is hard to imagine a much more whole-hog approach to reorganization around teams than Teamco's. What seems to be the case for that factory, and I suspect for others, is that it is quite possible for high-performance innovations such as self-directed work teams to coexist comfortably with Taylorist hierarchical work processes and Taylorist notions of how to introduce change. Teamwork at this high-performance company was directly connected with, and its success completely measured by, the improvement of quality and productivity rates. But this did not mean that workers performed their jobs differently or that the traditional plant hierarchy was rearranged or challenged. Those interested in workplace reform and high-performance innovation have a long row to hoe, both in implementing change and in understanding and circumventing resistance to it.

In this paper I have illustrated the ways in which literacy is part of the texture of circuit board assembly. I would venture that similar portraits will emerge from research in other industries, since modern literacy requirements in manufacturing seem to be driven by an almost universal interest in and need for certification and recordkeeping. A new requirement for today's world of work, then, is developing a literate identity as a worker—becoming adept at and comfortable around the paperwork that is part and parcel of everyone's work now on the manufacturing floor, learning to conceptualize one's work in terms of its written representations, and being able to master and manipulate the social rules that govern literate activities in the factory.

It is still customary to talk about literacy in terms of basic skills and to urge schools, vocational programs, and adult literacy classes to teach these fundamentals. But my research argues for a vastly different way of viewing workplace literacy. I have shown the remarkable variety and number of functions that reading and writing serve in circuit board assembly. What will also surprise people about this list is how small a portion of the functions fall into the category of "basic," by which I mean relatively simple, self-contained tasks: copying, labeling, keyboarding, tallying. The continuum of literacy functions quickly expands first to include categories in which the purposes that literacy serves are more complex—using literacy to explain, taking part in discourse around text, participating in the flow of information, problem solving—and then to include categories in which literacy is more obviously connected with issues of power—using literacy in the exercise of critical judgment, using literacy to acknowledge, exercise, or resist authority.

Workers don't need just the "basics," whether those basics are cast in a traditional mold of reading, writing, and arithmetic or recast as higher-order thinking skills or other decontextualized competencies posted on various skill lists. I have observed workers using literacy for purposes that run the gamut of the categories. Indeed, my argument is that a literate identity means being able to do precisely that—that is, to dip appropriately as needed into a wide and deep repertoire of situated ways of using written language and other forms of representation in order to carry out a work-related activity.

Happily, virtually all of the workers my research team and I observed were able to rise to the occasion. There was no literacy crisis at EMCO or Teamco. Despite having to traverse boundaries of culture, language, class, gender, ideology, and work hierarchy, these workers for the most part have taken on the challenge of developing a repertoire of literate practices, and they are meeting it successfully.[5] One need only recall the picture of the frontline worker, the recent immigrant, standing before a roomful of managers, reciting from her graphs and charts, to recognize and appreciate the task and the achievement. In fact, the most formidable challenge for workers is not, I would argue, developing a literate identity but being perceived as capable of doing so, being viewed as fit for the occasion.

It is almost a truism of current literacy theory that reading and writing are connected to power, but rarely have researchers traced those connections empirically. This project has demonstrated that particular functions for literacy—high-prestige functions such as those associated with exercising judgment and problem solving—are most often associated with and available to those in positions of authority, such as supervisors, managers, and engineers. On the other hand, certain other functions that literacy serves—lower-prestige purposes such as accomplishing simple, discrete tasks or using literacy to explain—are most often the categories associated with and available to frontline workers. Taking part in literate activities is not always so much a question of ability, then, as it is a question of rights and opportunities. In other words, patterns of literacy use are generally linked to structures of authority. What this means, practically speaking, is that skills change when authority changes. Thus, one reasonable measure of whether a factory is truly high performance—whether workers are actually imbued with the power to solve problems and to direct themselves—lies in the types of literacy workers are able to practice.

---

[5]Exactly how they did so, how workers organized themselves individually and collectively to get their work done, including literacy-related tasks, will be the topic of a future paper.

ACKNOWLEDGMENTS

The larger project upon which this chapter is based was funded by the National Center for Research in Vocational Education and the National Center for the Study of Writing and Literacy. I especially thank the directors of those centers, W. Norton Grubb and Sarah Warshauer Freedman, respectively, for their sustained and helpful interest and guidance. For a more detailed account of the larger project on which this chapter is based, see Hull et al. (1996). The research team for the larger research project included Kathy Schultz and Berkeley graduate students Meg Gebhardt, Mark Jury, Mira Katz, Craig Wilson, and Oren Ziv.

APPENDIX 5-A: ACON TEAM EXPLAINS ITS LOW PRODUCTIVITY*

Researcher: It's still fifty=six=
Xuan: =But= this week- this week had 1 day is fifty-seven, right?
Woman: =Yeah=
Researcher: =Ah, why?= Ah, why?==
Eva: ==Why?
Xuan: Becau- . . . us don't have job, right?
Mai: Yeah [rapid speech] (Le-=e-e-he)=
Xuan: =Acuson= board
Eva: ==Oh:: yeah==
Mai: ==Acuson board==
Xuan: ==[xx]== very slow
Eva: Yeah::
Mai: One hundred twenty
Eva: We did a=
Mai: =wh-=
Eva: =Acuson board I think==
Mai: ==1 hour -1 hour=
Eva: =Wednesday=
Mai: [rapid speech] Twenty boards -an hour=
Researcher: =Ah, when you- said you did twenty boards -that day=
Woman: =[laughter]=
Researcher: ==Is that the day you're talking about? The day you -did twenty=
Mai: =[xx]- First number wa- was -[xx]=
Eva: =No, that's- different this week
Researcher: Oh, this week. Oh, oh, oh, -that was last week=

---

*See the section "Operator Brain Dead: A Reading Problem at Teamco" for an explanation of transcription conventions used here.

Xuan: =I think we did sixty- twenty boards==

Eva: ==We didn't have boards== because the melting machine was down=

Mai: =[xx]=

Eva: =and they let us do the Acuson board, and we spent- I don't know how many hours we did their board

Researcher: Isn't- you don't -usually do Acuson-=

Xuan: =(They give us)- 2 hour- you're not- overtime 2 hour they have eighty boards, but us how many, how-==

Mai: ==One hundred twenty

Xuan: One hundred twenty, but how-==how long=

Mai: =how hour=

Xuan: =How long?=

Mai: I don't know how long

Eva: I remember it==

Hoa: ==may- =maybe it's-==

Xuan: ==5 hour

Eva: =5 hour, yeah=

Mai: =maybe it's 5= =maybe 5=

Eva: =maybe 4 to 5 hour=

Mai: =maybe so:

All: [laughter; comments in Vietnamese]

Researcher: Why though? I mean-

Eva: Because it's- there so many defect boards=

Woman: =[Vietnamese]

Researcher: You're not used to doing that?==

Eva: ==No, because that's- this is Acuson board==

Researcher: ==Oh:, so you don't =do that Acuson board=

Eva: =it's not our board=

Researcher: It's not =what you=

Eva: =We're just trying= to help it because we don't have any board to do

Researcher: So it took you a long time; that made your productivity low

Eva: Yeah

Researcher: Would- Hmm==

Hoa: ==[high pitched] Yeah

Researcher: So==

Woman: ==[Vietnamese] [.03]

Xuan: Just how- how many person?

Eva: =ten=

Mai: =one=

Woman: [Vietnamese]

Mai: One, two, =three, four,=

Xuan: =Acuson boa-=
Mai: ==five. five==
Xuan: ==five people==
Mai: ==five people
Xuan: Nah: =[Vietnamese]=
Mai: =five people [Vietnamese]=
Researcher: Oh, Acuson usually has seven==
Mai   ==Yeah [xx]
Researcher: And you- just five of you guys
Mai: Yeah =[Vietnamese]=
Xuan   =[Vietnamese]=
Mai: Twenty, twenty, twenty, twenty-one==
Eva: ==transistor- twenty pieces of transistor=
Woman: =Oh::=
Eva: =you have to put masking on it, and=
Researcher: =Oh=
Eva: =[xx]=
Xuan: =each one= but it's hard, you know. You need to pick the
               (straight). If you (fall down) like that you cannot make it==
Eva: ==That's why we're very very slow==

APPENDIX 5-B: TAXONOMY OF FUNCTIONS OF LITERACY AT EMCO AND TEAMCO

Literacy Codes	Description
Actioning	Accepting or assigning responsibility by committing in writing.
Admonishing	Admonishing an individual or group about possible or actual violations of documented procedures.
Analogizing	Comparing representations, processes, or activities in order to illustrate a point or to facilitate understanding.
Assessing	Assessing an individual's or group's understanding of a representation or literate activity.
Assigning	Assigning responsibility for authoring a representation.
Bestowing blessings	Declaring a literate activity good and worthy of time spent.
Brainstorming	Individually or collaboratively constructing a representation for heuristic purposes.
Calculating	Doing calculations (whether adding and subtracting or figuring standard deviations) not in service of one's self but as an integral part of literacy-related problem solving (e.g., for setting, adjusting, or justifying production schedules or team goals).
Categorizing	Sorting something in order to classify.
Certifying	Using a representation to attest to an individual's particular competence(s).
Citing	a) Referring to a representation that is not at hand; b) referring to a literate activity not at hand.
Coaching	Facilitating a literate activity or the understanding of a representation.
Completing forms	Completing routine forms.
Conjecturing	Inferring, theorizing, predicting, or guessing based on limited data.
Constructing rules	Constructing a rule regarding the use or interpretation of a representation or literate activity.
Contextualizing	Providing an historical or situational context for a representation or literate activity.
Copying	Copying a representation from one medium to another without qualitatively changing the representation.
Correcting	Ridding a representation of errors.
Creating hypotheticals	Creating a hypothetical comparison of representations or literate processes or activities.
Critiquing	Showing or expressing disapproval of or finding fault with a representation or literate activity.
Deferring	Yielding to the opinions or direction of another regarding a representation or literate activity.
Demonstrating	Demonstrating a literate activity for purposes of explanation, clarification, or instruction.
Disputing	Questioning, doubting, debating, and/or resisting the opinion or direction of another regarding a representation or literate activity.
Dramatizing	Explaining a representation or literate process by using a fictionalized example.
Elaborating	Explaining a representation by drawing upon details not present in the representation.
Evaluating	Evaluating the quality of a representation or literate activity.

Literacy Codes	Description
Exhibiting	Demonstrating a point by passing around a sample representation, as in show-and-tell.
Explaining	Using or referring to a representation or literate activity in explaining something to another person.
Fudging	Creating a deliberate misrepresentation.
Gaining consensus	Gaining and recording group agreement.
Gauging reaction	Considering alternate interpretations of, reactions to, and potential fall-out from problem solutions.
Giving direction	a) Writing directions for what to do; b) telling another what to do with respect to a literate activity.
Giving instruction	a) Writing instructions for how to do something; b) Telling another how to go about a literate activity.
Giving a show-and-tell	Demonstrating by passing around a sample representation, as in show-and-tell.
Granting permission	Granting permission to alter or transfer a controlled representation or to revise or engage in an alternative to a controlled literate activity.
Highlighting	Emphasizing an aspect or aspects of a representation or literate activity.
Identifying	Matching the physical with the representation.
Illustrating	Using a representation to illustrate a point.
Inferring	Inferring or predicting consequences based on an understanding of causes and effects.
Interpreting	Understanding a representation in terms of its purpose or function a) within a work process or b) within the organization's hierarchical structure.
Invoking	Invoking an organizational rule, script, procedure, or personal understanding of how to carry out a literate activity.
Irony	Drawing on understanding of another literate function to make a joke.
Justifying	Drawing on forms of representation to justify a course of action.
Keyboarding	Entering any type of information using a keyboard.
Labeling	Creating a representation in order to identify.
Locating	Looking for a particular representation, which should exist, to satisfy a particular function.
Looking something up	Finding information in a document.
Matching	Checking that a physical item and a representation match.
Miming	Gesturing to represent another representation or a literate activity.
Note taking	Taking notes during work processes, class, or training for personal reference later. (Notes may serve any of a variety of functions, including highlighting, translating, reminding, simplifying, and correcting.)
Perusing	Reading or studying a representation.
Planning	Working from a representation to plan a course of action.
Practicing	Participating in literate activity solely for purpose of becoming proficient at process; "product" not intended for use.
Presenting	Using a representation to structure an oral presentation.
Problem solving	Drawing on literate and/or numerate resources in conjunction with background knowledge to construct a problem solution.
Proofreading	Scanning a representation for errors.

Literacy Codes	Description
Proposing	Creating a representation to propose an idea or course of action or proposing the creation of a representation as a course of action.
Protecting	Using a document to protect oneself from blame—assigning responsibility to another, documenting course of action, etc.
Providing linguistic assistance	Aiding someone in decoding and/or pronouncing written material.
Quoting	Drawing on or invoking company discourse to legitimate an idea, suggestion or position.
Receiving instruction	Receiving instruction on how to do something.
Reciting	Reciting from a written text (e.g., blackboard, workbook, flipchart, overhead).
Recording	Making note of an action.
Recounting	Reviewing, with some narrative detail, a literate activity.
Referencing	Referring to representations, literate activities or processes at hand.
Reflecting	Reflecting on some aspect (e.g., process, intention, efficacy) of a literate activity some time after the activity has been completed.
Representing	Creating a representation of something else.
Reprimanding	Writing a document that can have a disciplinary consequence.
Requesting action	Writing something to request action from another.
Requesting and/or providing clarification	Requesting and/or providing clarifying information about a representation or literate activity.
Requesting documentation	Requesting a representation for use or perusal.
Requesting permission or approval	Requesting permission to alter or transfer a controlled representation or to revise or engage in an alternative to a controlled literate activity; requesting approval of such an alteration.
Revising	Modifying or updating a process or document.
Role playing	Taking on the role of another person in order to enact a scripted hypothetical work scenario.
Seeking direction	Seeking direction from some authority in carrying out a literate activity.
Seeking instruction	a) Seeking written instructions; b) seeking instruction from another in how to carry out a literate activity.
Signifying	Matching up two signs for the same object.
Summarizing	Recapping the content of a representation or using a representation to recap a process or activity.
Tallying	Doing calculations to serve limited literacy-related ends (e.g., to complete forms) in isolation from the larger problem-solving contexts for which the data will be used.
Translating	Translating from one representation to another.
Validating	Sanctioning an idea or action proposed in or through a representation.
Verifying	Checking one's understanding of a representation, literate process or activity.

APPENDIX 5-C: META-CATEGORIES OF LITERATE FUNCTIONS AT EMCO AND TEAMCO

Performing Basic Literate Functions	Using Literacy to Explain	Taking Part in Discourse Around and About Text	Participating in Flow of Information	Problem Solving	Exercising Critical Judgment	Using Literacy to Exercise, Acknowledge, or Resist Authority
Completing forms	Analogizing	Citing (a) (b)	Coaching	Brainstorming	Assessing	Actioning
Copying	Contextualizing	Constructing rules	Constructing rules	Calculating	Bestowing blessings	Admonishing
Correcting	Demonstrating	Highlighting	Giving instruction (a) (b)	Categorizing	Certifying	Assigning
Identifying	Dramatizing	Miming	Invoking	Conjecturing	Critiquing	Constructing rules
Keyboarding	Elaborating	Perusing	Practicing	Creating hypotheticals	Disputing	Deferring
Labeling	Exhibiting	Presenting	Providing linguistic assistance	Gauging reactions	Evaluating	Fudging
Locating	Explaining	Quoting	Receiving instruction	Justifying	Highlighting	Gaining consensus
Looking up	Illustrating	Recounting	Requesting/providing clarification	Planning	Inferring	Gauging reactions
Matching	Role playing	Referencing	Seeking direction	Problem solving	Interpreting	Giving direction (a) (b)
Note taking	Show-and-telling	Reflecting	Seeking instruction (a) (b)	Representing	Irony	Granting permission
Practicing		Signifying		Revising	Validating	Interpreting (b)
Proofreading		Summarizing			Verifying	Invoking
Providing documentation						Irony
Reciting						Proposing
Recording						Protecting
Requesting documentation						Reprimanding
Tallying						Requesting action
Translating						Requesting permission or approval

NOTE: See Appendix 5-A for description of the functions listed here.

REFERENCES

Appelbaum, E., and R. Batt
1993   *Transforming the Production System in U.S. Firms.* A report to the Sloan Foundation. Washington, DC: Economic Policy Institute.

Baba, M.L.
1991   The skill requirements of work activity: An ethnographic perspective. *Anthropology of Work Review* 12(3):2-11.

Brown, C., M. Reich, and D. Stern
1993   Becoming a high-performance work organization: The role of security, employee involvement and training. *International Journal of Human Resource Management* 4(2):247-275.

Carnevale, A.P., L.J. Gainer, and A.S. Meltzer
1988   *Workplace Basics: The Skills Employers Want.* Washington, DC: U.S. Department of Labor and American Society for Training and Development.

Commission on the Skills of the American Workforce
1990   *America's Choice: High Skills or Low Wages!* Report of the Commission on the Skills of the American Workforce. Rochester, NY: National Center on Education and the Economy.

Darrah, C.N.
1990   An Ethnographic Approach to Workplace Skills. Unpublished manuscript, Department of Anthropology and Cybernetic Systems, San Juan State University, San Juan, CA.
1996   *Learning and Work: An Exploration in Industrial Ethnography.* New York: Garland.

Diehl, W., and L. Mikulecky
1980   The nature of reading at work. *Journal of Reading* 24:221-227.

Ehrlich, E., and S.B. Garland
1988   For American business, a new world of workers. *Business Week* Sept. 19:107-111.

Gee, J., G. Hull, and C. Lankshear
1996   *The New Work Order: Behind the Language of the New Capitalism.* Boulder, CO: Westview Press.

Hossfeld, K.
1988   Divisions of Labor, Divisions of Lives: Immigrant Women Workers in the Silicon Valley. Unpublished doctoral dissertation, University of California, Santa Cruz.

Hull, G.
1993   Hearing other voices: A critical assessment of popular views on literacy and work. *Harvard Educational Review* 63(1):20-49.

Hull, G., ed.
1997   *Changing Work, Changing Workers? Critical Perspectives on Language, Literacy, and Skills.* Albany, NY: SUNY Press.

Hull, G., M. Jury, O. Ziv, and M. Katz
1996   *Changing Work, Changing Literacy? A Study of Skill Requirements and Development in a Traditional and Restructured Workplace.* Final report. Berkeley, CA: National Center for Research in Vocational Education.

Lund, L., and E.P. McGuire
1990   *Literacy in the Work Force.* New York: The Conference Board.

Marshall, R., and M. Tucker
1992   *Thinking for a Living: Education and the Wealth of Nations.* New York: Basic Books.

National Commission on Excellence in Education
1983   *A Nation at Risk: The Imperative for Educational Reform.* Washington, DC: U.S. Government Printing Office.

Parker, R.E.
  1994   *Flesh Peddlers and Warm Bodies: The Temporary Help Industry and Its Workers.* New Brunswick, NJ: Rutgers University Press.
Rawls, J.J., and W. Bean
  1993   *California: An Interpretive History,* 6th ed. New York: McGraw-Hill.
Rose, F.
  1989   *West of Eden: The End of Innocence at Apple Computer.* New York: Viking.
Sarmiento, A.R., and A. Kay
  1990   *Worker-Centered Learning: A Union Guide to Workplace Literacy.* Washington, DC: AFL-CIO Human Resources Development Institute.
Saxenian, A.
  1994   *Regional Advantage: Culture and Competition in Silicon Valley and Route 128.* Cambridge, MA: Harvard University Press.
Secretary's Commission on Achieving Necessary Skills
  1992   *Learning a Living: A Blueprint for High Performance.* Washington, DC: U.S. Department of Labor.
Spradley, J.P., and D.W. McCurdy
  1972   *The Cultural Experience: Ethnography in Complex Society.* Palo Alto, CA: Science Research Associates.
U.S. Department of Education and U.S. Department of Labor
  1988   *The Bottom Line: Basic Skills in the Workplace.* Washington, DC: U.S. Department of Education and U.S. Department of Labor.
Zuboff, S.
  1988   *In the Age of the Smart Machine: The Future of Work and Power.* New York: Basic Books.

6

Twenty-First Century Measures for Twenty-First Century Work

Kenneth Pearlman

INTRODUCTION

This paper explores the possible roles of assessment in promoting and facilitating the development of skills required in the emerging world of work. The paper draws heavily on earlier work (Pearlman, 1993, 1994a,b) and develops the following basic arguments:

1. "Skill" is not a singular or unitary concept. There are a number of skill types with differing implications for how we conceptualize skill gaps and skill transferability.

2. The meaning and value of work in the twenty-first century, especially in emerging high-performance organizations, will be increasingly dependent on emerging theories of job performance and on the meaning of the term "contextual performance." Contextual performance (as distinct from job-specific, technical or task performance) involves activities that, whether or not they are formally prescribed (part of a job description), are not specific to a particular job or area of work specialization but rather support the organizational, social, and psychological environment in which job-specific or technical or task performance occurs (see also Resnick, Chapter 11, this volume). This definition encompasses such activities as facilitation of peer, team, or unit performance; commitment to, promotion of, and generation of enthusiasm for organization or unit goals, practices, and policies; organizational "citizenship" or image—enhancing behavior; and various forms of prosocial, service—oriented, or organizational commitment behavior, which simultaneously implies the avoidance of behavior that would harm the organization or work unit. In other words, contextual performance is the "surround" of what we have traditionally thought of as "real" job performance.

As the emerging workplace increasingly blurs distinctions among jobs, and even threatens the very concept of a "job" (Bridges, 1994; Pearlman, 1995), contextual performance becomes increasingly important to organizational survival—it is the organizational analog of the medium becoming the message.

3. Cross-functional skills such as teamwork, communication, leadership, coaching/mentoring, conflict management, negotiating, customer service, decision making, managing resources, and information gathering and analysis are among the most important for effective contextual performance and employment stability and security for workers. Unfortunately, such skills are also the most problematic to define, assess, and develop, largely due to the absence of rigorous, comprehensive, work-analytic or construct-oriented research on such skills. There is as yet no systematic mapping of such skills to either the content or the context of the emerging workplace.

4. The utility of programs and initiatives designed to shape and motivate the education, training, or development of the skills and knowledge needed in the emerging workplace depends on research and information that is incomplete in several key respects, such as the relative importance and the relative trainability of different types of skills.

5. The above points present numerous challenges for assessment, the most urgent of which is the need for technically sound and widely deployable measures of cross-functional skills. On a system level, there is a need for better integration of the three conventional roles of assessment: diagnosis (enabling inferences regarding what has and has not been learned); prediction function (enabling inferences regarding future performance or behavior); and evaluation (enabling inferences regarding level, status, or progress of either individuals or institutions, which can influence the degree and direction of individual and institutional investment in skill, knowledge, and ability development).

The remainder of this paper builds toward a vision of twenty-first century assessment that links four key themes: the changing demographic and organizational context of work, changing concepts of skill and competence, the need to map changing skills definitions to changing definitions of work, and the resultant (and formidable) challenges to assessment posed by these changes. To set the stage for this analysis, I begin with a brief review of the legislative, policy, and research contexts.

BACKGROUND

ITEM: A report issued recently by the National Association of Secondary School Principals (1996) proposed that an employer dissatisfied with a recent high school graduate's job performance should be able to send the employee back to high school for additional training. This was one of several recommendations for sweeping structural changes in our education system included in their study, *Breaking Ranks: Changing an American Institution.* The report states that:

buyers can get [faulty products] fixed or replaced if they do not work properly. We understand the difference between inanimate objects and human beings, but that does not excuse high schools from the obligation to guarantee the quality of the young people they educate.

The report said that personnel managers often complain about the deficiencies of 18 and 19 year olds who cannot do simple arithmetic and lack basic writing skills. Forcing the schools to guarantee their "product"—symbolized by the diploma—would encourage them to raise their standards for graduation. A dissatisfied employer could file a complaint with the high school. If the young person's education was deficient by entry-level standards, the high school would have to provide additional training or arrange for the graduate to attend classes at a local community college or in a special remedial program.

ITEM: In a speech at an October 1993 Business for Social Responsibility Conference, the renowned Massachusetts Institute of Technology economist Lester Thurow expressed his ambivalence about Motorola University, widely regarded as one of the best-private sector training enterprises in the country: "On one level," he said, "I think it is the most fantastic thing any big company has ever done in America. On another level, it tells the local school system, 'You don't have to perform because even if you turn out a lousy product, we'll re-educate them later,' so you deliver a very bad signal to the system." Thurow cited the work of John Bishop at Cornell University, who has argued against the use of the Scholastic Aptitude Test (SAT) for making college admissions decisions in favor of wide-range achievement tests and Advanced Placement tests (Bishop, 1988). Bishop holds that use of the SAT by colleges and universities gives American high schools an excuse for failure by, in effect, sending the message that no matter how poor a job has been done by the K-12 education system, a student with a high IQ will be accepted anyway. Thurow argues, as does Bishop, that universities should insist that high IQ is not a substitute for performance and should let high schools know that they will be judged on performance, not whether they have high-IQ students. Thurow went on to make the point that it is only through well-conceived and well-designed *systems*, and systematic *national* efforts to change our philosophy and approach to education and training in this country that we will be able to begin to offer the type of "product guarantee" now increasingly being sought by employers and educators alike.

ITEM: A recent report of a survey of New Jersey employers conducted for the New Jersey Business-Higher Education Forum (Van Horn, 1995:22-23) concluded that:

> there is wide agreement that more must be done to strengthen the bond between higher education and employers. Many employers say they are having difficulty hiring college graduates who have the skills they need. Employers are placing greater emphasis on teamwork, communications skills, problem-solving, and creative thinking. Business people often say that faculty members do not know enough about the world of work and are thus ill-prepared to teach necessary work

skills. . . . Many postsecondary institutions are responding to employers' concerns, but significant resistance persists. Leaders from higher education complain that employers do not adequately communicate what they need from college graduates. . . .

Some academics resent what they regard as crass attempts to transform colleges and universities into "vocational schools" and to subvert the nobler purpose of education for its own sake. Suspicion and resentment are fueled because the pressure for greater higher education/workplace connections is coming primarily from business leaders and politicians rather than from the faculty and academic administrators. . . . Significant progress has been made on the crucial step of stipulating the knowledge, skills, and abilities vital to employers. A consensus is emerging on the basic elements. Efforts by industrial sectors to specify clusters of necessary skills are promising and could contribute lessons for other areas of the economy. Less progress has been made on assessing the performance of college students in acquiring the skills and abilities desired by employers. Designing such measures is difficult and also problematic because many of the desired skills and abilities are not taught in colleges and university classrooms and laboratories. . . . Questions still must be resolved about what should be taught in schools, what should be taught on the job, and what cannot be taught at all.

These represent but a few of the most recent examples of a series of alarms that, beginning with the widely cited 1983 report *A Nation at Risk: The Imperative for Educational Reform* (National Commission on Excellence in Education, 1983), have been sounded over the past 15 years by various federal and state governments, special commissions, and task forces (Johnston and Packer, 1987; National Center on Education and the Economy, 1990; National Governors' Association, 1992; Secretary's Commission on Achieving Necessary Skills [SCANS], 1991). These reports reflect a widely perceived national crisis—the growing gap between the demands of a new American workplace driven by the emerging global economy and the supply of workers who possess the skills and knowledge to function effectively in such a workplace. It is a crisis that has called into question the efficacy of our education system—both K-12 and postsecondary education—as well as the way we assess the capabilities of individuals and the effectiveness of educational and training institutions.

At the national level, this crisis has been the impetus for a number of federal initiatives over the past several years, each directed in one way or another toward remediation of America's perceived "skills gap" and the attainment of "a high-performance economy—one characterized by high skills, high wages, and full employment—in which every human being's resources are put to their best use" (SCANS, 1992).

Secretary's Commission on Achieving Necessary Skills

The Secretary's Commission on Achieving Necessary Skills (SCANS) was chartered as one aspect of the "America 2000" strategy to achieve a set of national goals in education agreed to by the president and the nation's governors (SCANS, 1991, 1992). SCANS was asked to examine the demands of the workplace and the capacities of young people to meet those demands. Specifically, it was asked to define the skills needed for employment; to propose acceptable levels of proficiency in those skills, to suggest effective ways to assess proficiency; and to develop a dissemination strategy for the nation's schools, businesses, and homes. SCANS found that more than half of the nation's students leave school without the knowledge or foundation required to obtain and hold a good job. This is directly attributed to the workplace changes that have resulted from globalization and new technology growth, creating conditions that have fundamentally changed the terms for entry into the workplace.

The centerpiece of the SCANS work is the delineation of a set of five "competencies" (productive use of resources, interpersonal skills, information, systems, and technology) and three categories of "foundation skills" (basic skills, thinking skills, and personal qualities) believed to lie at the heart of job performance and to reflect essential preparatory requirements for all students, both those going directly to work and those planning further education. The vision was for this work to constitute the blueprint that would drive needed changes in education (curriculum development, school organization, teacher training, and instructional materials and technology); the workplace (work-based learning, public-/private-sector training coalitions), and associated assessment systems (a national assessment system that helps students understand what they need to learn and that certifies achieved levels of the SCANS skills and competencies). An ongoing National Job Analysis Study is being conducted by American College Testing to pursue further validation and elaboration of the SCANS framework (American College Testing, 1994).

Advisory Panel for the *Dictionary of Occupational Titles*

The Advisory Panel for the *Dictionary of Occupational Titles* (APDOT) was chartered in 1990 to recommend to the secretary of labor strategies for collecting, analyzing, and disseminating occupational information to revise or replace the aging *Dictionary*. This initiative, like SCANS, grew out of the recognition that investment in people's skills and restructuring of workplaces into high-performance organizations were critical to our country's ability to remain competitive in today's global economy. Moreover, it was recognized that the development of a national occupational information system—one that provided a common language for describing both people (i.e., skills, abilities, and knowledge) and work (both content and context)—was in turn an essential requirement for meeting such needs. A major output of APDOT was a "content model" (see Appendix) that provides, in some detail, a framework or taxonomy, for the collection, assessment, and dissemination of occupational information that is both worker oriented (skills, knowledge, abilities) and work oriented (work tasks and outputs, as well as the surrounding work, organizational, and labor market context) (APDOT, 1993). APDOT's vision was that this content model, when fully operationalized and deployed in the form of an automated database available in multiple media and formats, would form the basis for a national occupational information infrastructure, based on a common language of person- and work-related information, that would support a myriad of applications and work-force investment strategies involving skill and knowledge development, education, assessment, and vocational and career counseling. A prototype of this system, covering about 20 percent of the occupations in the U.S. economy, is nearly complete (American Institutes for Research, 1995).

Goals 2000 and Skills Standards

In 1994 the Clinton administration launched a collaborative effort between the U.S. Departments of Labor and Education to promote the development of a nationwide system of voluntary, industry-based skill standards. The Goals 2000: Educate America Act established a National Skills Standards Board to encourage, promote, and assist partnerships representing business, labor, educators, and others in the development of industry-related skill standards. This initiative was an outgrowth of the recognition that there is currently little systematic connection between the skills needed in the workplace and those imparted through education and training. The problem is exacerbated by the limited range of nationally recognized credentials. These problems result in increased hiring and training costs, restricted employment opportunities, lack of quality assurance, and a direct threat to the country's ability to compete effectively in the emerging and rapidly changing global economy.

The stated purpose of a national system of industry-based skill standards is to identify the knowledge, skill, and ability levels needed for successful workplace performance. Such a system would also ensure a common, standardized way to classify and describe the skills needed for particular occupations and would utilize a variety of evaluation techniques to assess the skills possessed by individual workers. In so doing, it would aid communication among employers, educators, trainers, and workers regarding specific skill levels and needs and would ensure that workers have the portable skills required in today's dynamic economy. The development of broadly defined skill standards is viewed, in the words of then-Labor Secretary Robert Reich (1991), as "the cornerstone of [a] work force development system," which, when linked to educational standards, "will help create a seamless system of lifelong learning opportunities with certificates of mastery and competency that are accepted and recognized by employers" and which will "enhance America's ability to match skills and jobs."

There are many anticipated advantages of a system of voluntary, industry-driven skill standards and certification. For industries it would be a vehicle to inform training providers and prospective employees of the skills required for employment. For employers it would reduce the costs and legal risks associated with the assessment of job candidates and would make employment decisions more objective. For unions it would increase members' job security through access to competency-based training and certification. For workers, it would protect against dislocation, enable them to pursue career advancement, and enhance their ability to reenter the work force by having a work portfolio that is based on training to industry standards. It would help trainers and educators determine appropriate training services to offer. It would help government to protect the integrity of public expenditures by requiring that employment-related training meet industry standards where they exist.

The fundamental challenge of Goals 2000 is how to most effectively ensure that today's and tomorrow's students and workers can acquire and maintain the skills necessary to be productive in a rapidly changing workplace and thereby contribute to the country's continued competitiveness in the emerging global economy. To accomplish this, Goals 2000 has adopted the strategy of building a national system of skill standards and skill certification intended to focus, motivate, and reward the skills that are to be learned on the job, in training, and in school. It has further adopted the strategies of addressing this issue using (1) job families or occupational clusters, as opposed to individual jobs or occupations, as the primary units of analysis within which skill standards and certification criteria would be developed and (2) skills that are sufficiently broad so as to be transferable across relatively wide ranges of work.

School-to-Work Opportunities Act

The 1994 School-to-Work Opportunities Act provides seed money to states and local partnerships of business, labor, government, education, and community organizations to develop school-to-work systems. Rather than creating a government program, the intent of this law is to establish an infrastructure for a national system based on existing models of school-to-work transition, such as career academies, youth apprenticeships, technical preparation, and cooperative education. The law allows states and their partners to work together in efforts at education reform, worker preparation, and economic development to create a system that will prepare young people for the high-wage, high-skill jobs of the emerging twenty-first century workplace. The legislation prescribes no single model of how to accomplish this; rather, it encourages states and their partnerships to design school-to-work systems that make the most sense for them. However, all such systems would share the common goal of providing every American student with (1) relevant education (allowing students to explore different careers and see what skills are required in different work environments), (2) skills (obtained from structured training and work-based learning experiences), and (3) valued credentials (establishing industry-standard benchmarks and developing education and training standards that ensure that proper education is received for each career).

In addition, the legislation sets forth three elements viewed as fundamental to efforts to create a national school-to-work system: school-based learning, work-based learning, and connecting activities. School-based learning involves curriculum restructuring so that students can see the relationship between academics and work. It includes such elements as project work in teams, teacher-employer interaction, and workplace-relevant interdisciplinary teaching. Work-based learning involves (1) employer-provided learning experiences to develop broad transferable skills and (2) the study of complex subject matter and important workplace skills (e.g., teamwork, problem solving, meeting commitments) in a real-life "hands-on" environment that provides feedback and mentorships. Connecting activities include program coordination and administration, school and business staff exchanges, and career counseling.

The above initiatives address the challenge of how best to ensure the continued competitiveness of the American economy in the global marketplace through investment in a highly competent, knowledgeable, skilled, and flexible work force. Central to all of these initiatives are issues of skills, skill transferability, skill standards, changes needed in our systems of education and training, the nature of work and work performance, and the role of assessment. Significantly, each of these initiatives, implicitly or explicitly, recognizes the need for *systems* that integrate and leverage these elements in an optimal way. This implies the need for theories, conceptual models, or frameworks by which the nature of these elements and their interrelationships can be understood.

SKILLS

Skill is not a unitary concept. In fact, there is currently no single, generally accepted definition of "skill" in the professional or scientific literature. The term has been used to refer to a wide range of personal characteristics, traits, work preferences, broad aptitudes, basic abilities, generic competencies, specialized skills, and specialized knowledge, creating a contemporary tower of Babel in that the same terms are often used to denote different classes of skills and different terms are often used to denote the same classes of skills. This lack of an accepted vocabulary or a "common skills language" has been a major obstacle to developing appropriate strategies for addressing many critical skills issues, such as transferability, gaps, and the setting of standards.

As one example of this problem, consider the lack of clarity that permeates many current discussions of the growing "skills gap" in this country, a term used to refer to the difference between the demand for and the supply of "work-ready" people. At times the skills gap involves or implies problems in fundamental aptitudes or abilities (e.g., seen as current work-force literacy and numeracy deficiencies). At times it involves problems in relatively generic or cross-functional skills (e.g., seen as the need for greater degrees of interpersonal, teamwork, and decision-making skills among production workers who have been reorganized into semiautonomous teams). And at times the gap refers to problems in very specialized skills or knowledge (e.g., seen as the need for workers to become knowledgeable about and proficient in the use of new technology). More recently, it has become apparent that the gap of greatest concern to many employers is not about skills at all but about attitudes and personal qualities, such as integrity, reliability, and dependability (Cappelli, 1995; National Center for the Educational Quality of the Workforce, 1994; Zemsky, Chapter 3, this volume). The lack of clarity and specificity about the origins and meaning of the concept of a skills gap makes it difficult to propose appropriate corrective policies.

Multiple Categories of Skills

This problem was recognized in the content model developed by APDOT and shown in the Appendix. The model defines the specifications for a comprehensive occupational information infrastructure intended to have utility for multiple work-force investment initiatives. Rather than attempting to define skills in a unitary fashion, the content model proposes a set of five categories of skills-related information as a provisional framework for defining and understanding the full range of attributes commonly referred to as skills. These five categories are (1) aptitudes and abilities, (2) workplace basic skills, (3) cross-functional skills, (4) occupation-specific skills, and (5) occupation-specific knowledge. An additional category, personal qualities (defined as "an individual's characteristic, habitual, or typical manner of thinking, feeling, behaving, or responding with respect to oneself, others, situations, or events) was not considered by APDOT as part of the set of skills-related information descriptor categories because it refers to personality traits, values, and attitudes rather than skills per se. It is, however, potentially relevant to the present discussion.

These skills-related information categories can be conceived of as a continuum that varies in the level of description and application. At one end of the continuum are the very general and relatively few aptitudes, abilities, and basic workplace skills, consisting of perhaps 15 to 30 elements, that are expected to be applicable to very wide ranges of jobs. At the other end of the continuum are the fairly specific and relatively many occupation-specific skills and occupation-specific knowledge, consisting of thousands of elements, that are expected to be applicable to relatively narrower ranges of jobs. The cross-functional skills represent a moderate level of generality and a moderate number of elements (perhaps 30 to 50), and encompass skills that are expected to be applicable to relatively wide ranges of jobs but that fall far short of the presumably near-universal applicability of such basic workplace skills as reading and writing. The human attributes denoted by such terms in fact differ in a number of important ways, as discussed below.

How Broadly or Narrowly Attributes Are Defined and Described

Skills-related attributes vary in the degree of generality or specificity with which they are defined. For example, verbal ability represents a broader level of description than reading comprehension skill, which in turn represents a broader level of description than the ability to read and understand corporate real estate contracts. Similarly, skill at carpentry represents a broader level of definition than skill at inside finishing, which in turn represents a broader level of definition than skill at hanging interior doors.

Applicability and Relevance (or Transferability) Across Different Jobs

Different classes of attributes also differ in terms of their applicability and hence transferability (or portability) across jobs and job families. For example, a skill such as organizing and prioritizing work tasks is obviously applicable to a much wider range of jobs than such a skill as repairing watches. Basic skills such as reading and arithmetic computation are nearly universally applicable, whereas highly specialized knowledge, such as knowledge of the physical properties of solenoid magnets, is relevant to very few jobs.

Modifiability or Trainability of the Attribute

A skill or attribute's trainability refers to how well it lends itself to being learned quickly or to higher degrees, successfully transferred from the learning setting to the application setting, and retained over time. There is evidence that personal qualities (personality traits, values, and attitudes) and general aptitudes and abilities are trainable or modifiable to very limited degrees and only with substantial investments of time and effort (Ackerman and Humphreys, 1990:260; Gottfredson, 1986b:386-389; Humphreys, 1989). Basic workplace skills, cross-functional skills, and occupation-specific skills and knowledge, on the other hand, are, by definition, acquired and hence trainable but within limits defined by an individual's degree of general aptitudes and abilities and possession of the particular personal qualities that underlie or are related to the attribute to be trained (Hunter, 1986). In addition, the trainability of such skills varies as a function of their complexity, with simpler, less abstract knowledge and more routinized skills more readily trainable than more complex, more abstract knowledge and more dynamic or adaptive skills, such as those that require frequent or constant adaptation to changing situations or conditions (Ackerman, 1987; Kanfer and Ackerman, 1989).

Applicability or Relevance of an Attribute to Different Settings or Purposes

Not all types of attributes are equally applicable or relevant to different purposes. For example, in the employment domain it is appropriate to use measures of aptitudes and abilities and/or basic workplace skills to select among inexperienced applicants (such as recent high school graduates) for jobs in which they will receive subsequent company training (e.g., entry-level computer programming). This is because the goal in such a situation is to identify individuals with the highest *capacity* or *potential* for mastering the training. It would make no sense to test programming skill or knowledge in such a situation. On the other hand, a test of programming skill or knowledge (i.e., a measure of developed skills or knowledge) would be appropriate for selecting among applicants with prior computer programming experience for higher-level programming positions. As another example, Bishop (1988) has argued that measures of developed skill and knowledge are more effective incentives for learning than are aptitude measures. In addition, various categories of skills-related information also differ in the degree to which they lend themselves to the setting of skill standards and the establishment of skill certification criteria. There is evidence to support the view that both meaningful definition of a particular attribute and meaningful determination of an appropriate required level of that attribute (e.g., to certify attainment of some established performance or knowledge level) are more feasible for fairly specialized skills or knowledge than for more general attributes, such as aptitudes and abilities, personal qualities, and cross-functional skills.

The Manner in Which Attributes Can Be Measured

There is a wide variety of methods and techniques by which human attributes can be measured or assessed. These include paper-and-pencil tests, physical ability tests, performance tests, assessment centers and job simulations, work samples, interviews, structured training and experience evaluations, trainability tests, personality tests, direct job performance observation and assessment, direct training performance assessment, education or training course grades, level of education, amount of experience or seniority, and work product assessment. Such techniques, however, are not equally applicable to different categories of worker attributes. For example, paper-and-pencil tests, which can provide reasonably good measures of certain kinds of specialized factual knowledge, do not lend themselves to measurement of various types of interpersonal skills (such as teamwork, leadership, and persuasiveness) or oral communication skills (such as speaking and listening skills).

The Reliability and Validity with Which Attributes Can Be Measured

Different categories of worker attributes also vary in the degree of precision or stability (reliability) and the degree of accuracy (validity) with which they can be measured. In general, aptitudes and abilities, basic workplace skills, and occupation-specific skills and knowledge can be measured with reasonably high degrees of reliability and validity when assessed using appropriate methods. In general, personal qualities (personality traits, values, and attitudes) can be assessed with somewhat lower (but generally acceptable) levels of reliability, although validity can vary widely depending on the specific method of assessment used and the specific purpose of the assessment, (e.g., validity tends to be higher when such measures are used for purely diagnostic or developmental purposes than for personnel selection purposes). The measurement of many cross-functional skills (such as organizing, planning, fact finding, and information analysis), particularly the "softer" skills (that is, interpersonally oriented skills such as teamwork, negotiation, leadership, and persuasiveness) is presently problematic for a number of reasons detailed later in this paper.

WORK

The historic changes that have been occurring in the workplace over the past decade or so are discussed in great detail in numerous sources (e.g., APDOT, 1993; Coates et al., 1990; Johnston and Packer, 1987; Meridian Corporation, 1991; Offerman and Gowing, 1993; Pearlman, 1995; Reich, 1991). These trends and changes can be summarized in terms of two major categories: changing demographics and changing organizations.

Changing Demographics

This refers to the changing characteristics of workers and can be characterized in terms of the following key trends or issues:

• *The Changing Age Distribution of the Work Force.* Significantly fewer young people will be entering the job market than in the recent past, leading to a shrinking pool of entry-level talent and greater competition among organizations for their services.

• *The Changing Gender, Ethnic, and Cultural Composition of the Work Force.* This reflects slower U.S. population and work-force growth coupled with rapid *world* work-force growth, resulting in increasing work-force diversity, with more women, minorities, and immigrants composing the available labor force and white males composing only 15 percent of the projected net increase in the work force over the next 10 years.

• *Anticipated Skill Shortages in Critical Areas and Industries.* This refers to the much-written-about skills gap, wherein the need for increasing types and levels of skills in a society of rapid technological advances and change will far outstrip the available types and levels of skills available in the applicant population (see also Holzer, Chapter 2, this volume). The problem will be exacerbated by the projection that typical American workers will face three to four career changes during their work lives.

• *Changing Lifestyles of Workers.* This includes a dramatic increase in single-parent households, increasing numbers of dual-income families, and a growing underclass of disadvantaged disaffected people.

• *Changing Job Attitudes of Workers.* These include an increased desire for autonomy, self-development, and balance between work and family life.

• *Increasing Size of the "Contingent" Work Force.* This refers to temporary and part-time workers, contractors, consultants, "life-of-project" workers, and leased employees with less loyalty to a given organization. This will result in different types of working relationships (e.g., remote supervision, flexible working arrangements, telecommuting) and will make it more difficult to maintain the shared vision and culture essential to a customer/service focus.

Changing Organizations

This refers to the changing characteristics of the broader economic context, the organizational context, and the immediate work and job context in which work is performed and can be characterized in terms of the following key trends or issues:

• *An Increasingly Global Economy.* In this economy the viability and profitability of organizations will become increasingly dependent on their ability to penetrate and compete in foreign markets. This will necessitate not only greater understanding of foreign clients, markets, and suppliers but also the ability to manage increasingly diverse elements within one's organization. In addition, global competition for labor resources (i.e., young, well-educated, mobile workers from other countries) will increase.

• *An Increasing Infusion of Technology.* This infusion of technology (e.g., computer use, advanced telecommunications) will occur at all levels and in all types of work, resulting in changed ways of working and alteration of traditional concepts of work and time.

• *The Continued Shift from a Manufacturing to a Service Economy.* This will result in a continued decline in production-oriented jobs and a continued increase in service-oriented jobs.

• *Increasing Value Placed on Intellectual Capital.* Intellectual capital, the aggregate knowledge and skill base of the work force, will increasingly become a key competitive advantage for increasingly knowledge-intensive businesses and work enterprises.

• *The Changing Size and Structure of Organizations.* This is evidenced by many company failures and frequent downsizings among the survivors. In addition, there will be much restructuring into flatter organizations with fewer layers of management and fewer people at upper levels; increasingly decentralized decision making; greater reliance on purchased components and services; and increasing numbers of mergers, acquisitions, buyouts and various strategic networks and alliances—which will result in highly dynamic and ever-shifting corporate cultures.

- *The Increasing Use of Work Teams.* This occurs as work tasks and activities become more knowledge based, service oriented, interdependent, and demanding of decision making at the point of production as a result of increased pressure for performance brought about by both new technology and global competition.

TWENTY-FIRST CENTURY WORK

Changing demographic and organizational contexts of work will necessitate shifts in human resources planning and strategy, especially in the following areas.

Retention of Skilled Employees

Organizations will need to increasingly focus on retaining skilled employees to cope with anticipated skill and labor shortages. This implies increased importance on attending to issues of worker satisfaction (i.e., worker interests and values) and hence an increased focus on vocational and career guidance to promote the entry and migration of people into areas of work they will find satisfying and rewarding.

Career Lattices

The development of "career lattices" (worker development within and across occupational and organizational levels, rather than upward development) will become more important as organizations streamline and restructure, resulting in fewer promotional opportunities and more career plateauing. This will necessitate a broader and deeper understanding of job and occupational interrelationships, so that there are clear "road maps" of skill and knowledge requirements within and across occupational areas.

Effective, Flexible Organizational Training and Retraining

The need for effective and flexible organizational training and retraining strategies and methods will increase in importance as organizations seek to adapt to rapidly increasing technology demands and rapidly changing work environments and organizational needs and as they seek to maximize returns on their investment in workers (particularly in view of likely escalating recruitment and selection costs). This further implies that organizations will need to place greater emphasis on the selection for or development of transferable skills, that is, skills that are likely to have applicability across different areas or families of work and jobs (e.g., the cross-functional skills and generalized work activities defined in the APDOT content model).

Selecting Employees Who Can Learn

The identification and selection of individuals with both the capacity and the motivation to learn, to be trained (to maintain currency of skills and knowledge within their area of work or specialization), and to be retrained or "reskilled" (to acquire skills and knowledge related to new areas of work) will increase in importance as organizations attempt to build and retain their intellectual capital.

Selecting for or Developing Cross-Functional Skills

To the degree that work tasks and activities across different jobs and functions become increasingly interdependent, organizations will need to place greater emphasis on selection for or development of various skills related to effective team performance and the ability to operate within increasingly networked and decentralized structures (e.g., interpersonal and communication skills, negotiating skills, conflict management skills, and information gathering and analysis skills)—most of which are subsumed, in the APDOT content model terminology, by the category of cross-functional skills.

Contextual Aspects of Performance

Organizations will increasingly need to attend to the contextual aspects of performance (i.e., behaviors that facilitate the performance of others and of the organization as a whole) as a way to enhance the quality of work life in an organization (related to the retention of skilled employees) and to maintain competitiveness and service quality in an increasingly less forgiving and results-oriented climate. This implies an increasing need for worker assessment, selection, and development for attributes—such as teamwork, leadership, and service orientation—related to these aspects of performance,

Toward a Conceptual Model of Work and Performance

Figure 6-1 displays in schematic form a general model of work performance (originally presented in Pearlman, 1994b) that integrates the key elements considered thus far here. The model provides a theoretical framework for understanding the components and the direct and indirect antecedents of work performance in the emerging twenty-first century workplace. It is based largely on, and represents an attempt to synthesize, the recent job performance theory development work of Campbell et al. (1990, 1993), Schmidt and Hunter and their associates (Hunter, 1983, 1986; Schmidt and Hunter, 1992; Schmidt et al., 1986), and Borman and Motowidlo (1993). The labeling and description of much of the model and its terms are designed to be consistent with APDOT content model terminology, and the variables and relationships depicted are intended to be generally consistent with the conceptual structure and empirical evidence de-

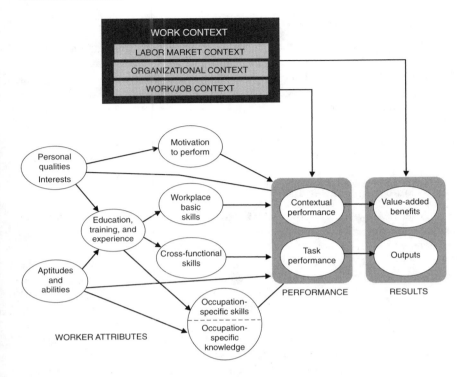

FIGURE 6-1   General work-performance model.

scribed by the authors cited above. The proposed model's chief extensions of previous work lie in its integration of the role of the work environment, its emphasis on contextual performance, and its greater elaboration of the role of different classes of worker attributes and skills-related information categories, a development facilitated by the APDOT content model.

This general work performance model proposes the following definitions and relationships.

Two Components of Performance

There are two distinguishable aspects or components of performance: task performance and contextual performance. Task performance is the performance of formally prescribed and recognized tasks and activities required by a specific job. Contextual performance (see also Borman and Motowidlo, 1993) is the performance of activities that are not specific to a particular job and that support the organizational, social, and psychological environment in which task performance occurs.

Results

Results (which refer to the effectiveness or evaluation of the *outcomes* of performance) are distinct from performance and are determined jointly by (1) a worker's task and contextual performance and (2) certain characteristics of the work environment (see Campbell et al., 1993). Final results can in part be subject to the influence of factors beyond a worker's own performance or control. For example, good sales performance may not result in a high proportion of closed sales in a depressed market or territory and may not result in high profits if selling prices have been temporarily lowered as a strategy to increase market share.

Two Components of Results

There are two distinguishable aspects or components of results: outputs and value-added benefits. Outputs are related to the more formally recognized, objectively measured, and more or less concrete deliverables for which a worker is held accountable; outputs tend to have immediate, short-term consequences (e.g., the work outcomes defined in the APDOT content model, such as products produced, services rendered, sales and profits). Value-added benefits are related to less formally recognized, more subjectively measured, less concrete outcomes, and these tend to have more indirect and longer-term consequences (e.g., customer and employee satisfaction, enthusiasm, and loyalty). It is further hypothesized that the effectiveness of task performance is a direct determinant of outputs and an indirect determinant of value-added benefits, while contextual performance is a direct determinant of value-added benefits and an indirect determinant of outputs.

The value of defining two components for both performance and results stems from mounting evidence that in each case the two components have somewhat different antecedents (e.g., contextual performance is influenced more by personal qualities and task performance more by general cognitive abilities), are hence selected for and developed or improved in different ways, and have different kinds and amounts of value to an organization. In particular, there is growing evidence for the increasing strategic importance of contextual performance and value-added benefits owing to the various emerging demographic and workplace trends described above. As one example, the growing skills gap (the difference between the demand for and the supply of skilled workers) has substantially increased the strategic value of maintaining high job satisfaction among employees as a way to retain highly skilled workers, something that has become an increasingly critical competitive advantage. This implies that human resources strategies and programs need to place increasing emphasis on the contextual aspects of job performance and the value-added benefits of results. Unitary definitions of performance and results would mask these differences, whereas recognizing, identifying, and highlighting these distinctions enables an organization to capitalize on them in various human resources strategies and programs, including the types of skill investment initiatives that are the backdrop of this paper.

Determinants of Task Performance

Task performance is determined jointly by an individual's environment-congruent occupation-specific skills, occupation-specific knowledge, basic workplace skills, aptitudes and abilities, and (through its effect on performance as a whole) motivation to perform. Contextual performance is determined most directly by an individual's environment-congruent cross-functional skills and (through its effect on performance as a whole) motivation to perform, and personal qualities and interests. "Environment-congruent" is used in this context as equivalent to "work- or job-related"; that is, it denotes whatever worker attributes are required by the work system or job design characteristics—including specific job, role, or task demands—of the immediate work or job context.

Determinants of Motivation

An individual's motivation to perform is determined jointly by certain characteristics of the work environment (e.g., recognition and reward systems, the presence of goals or performance standards) and certain environment-congruent personal qualities and interests (e.g., high-achievement orientation and entrepreneurial interests for sales jobs). In formulating job performance theory, Campbell et al., (1993) defined motivation in a manner consistent with its conventional representation in the literature, that is, as involving the direction, amplitude, and duration of volitional behavior. Specifically, they define motivation as the combined effect of three choices-to expend effort, the level of effort expended, and persistence in the chosen level of effort expenditure. The present model goes slightly further in positing the general categories of such antecedents (work context, personal qualities, and interests), at which level the model remains consistent with most major theories of motivation, which generally differ primarily in terms of the specific variables or elements of focus within these broad categories.

Skills and Knowledge

Cross-functional skills, workplace basic skills, and occupation-specific skills and knowledge are attributes that are acquired as a function of an individual's education, training, and experience, which are intended to represent the major categories of an individual's formal opportunities to learn and practice.

An Ability-Experience Path

Both the opportunities for and the benefits or effectiveness of education, training, and experience vary as a function of the individual's aptitudes and abilities and possession of particular skill-related, knowledge-related, and learning-/motivation-related personal characteristics and interests. This postulate is a slight departure from the model hypothesized by Schmidt et al. (1986), which did not incorporate a path from ability to experience. The inclusion here of an ability-experience path or relationship is based in part on the rationale suggested by Borman et al. (1993) that an individual's abilities are likely to be recognized by the organization and used in part as a basis for assigning work and responsibilities, thus providing opportunities for experience.

The relationship between personal qualities/interests and experience is based in part on a similar rationale, namely, that an individual's opportunities for experience are partly created by the recognition by influential others of his or her job-related personal qualities (i.e., in addition to ability), such as integrity, trustworthiness, and conscientiousness. This view is supported by a survey (Michigan Department of Education, 1989) that found these and related qualities to compose seven of the top eight attributes (out of 86) ranked by over 3,000 employers for importance to entry-level employment. This relationship is also based on the hypothesis, consistent with the investment theory of ability (Catell, 1987), that people's skill-, knowledge-related, and learning/motivation-related personal characteristics and interests determine in what types of development (i.e., toward what types of specific skills or jobs) they choose to invest these attributes. For example, a person with altruistic needs or values and an interest in working closely with others is more likely to seek education, training, or experience in social work than in sales.

These relationships and hypotheses provide the rationale for one of the central theses of this paper, namely, the importance of cross-functional skills to effective contextual performance. From one point of view, this may be seen as discrepant with Borman and Motowidlo's (1993) discussion of contextual performance, which focuses on its likely antecedents in the domain of personal qualities. However, from the perspective of the present model of work performance, this thesis can rather be as an elaboration of their position, wherein many cross-functional skills (primarily those within the noncognitive domain) are viewed as, in effect, representing a more proximal (i.e., to performance) manifestation of such personal qualities. From this point of view, such cross-functional skills are the more immediate precursors to effective contextual performance—the outcome of the shaping or "investment" of various personal characteristics over time into work-related form.

In other words, this suggests a relationship between personal qualities and (contextual) performance within the noncognitive domain that is analogous to that found by Hunter (1983, 1986) within the cognitive domain, where the strong and well-established empirical relationship between general cognitive ability and task performance was shown to be largely indirect—a function of individuals' investment of their cognitive ability into the acquisition of occupation-specific knowledge, which is the stronger and more immediate antecedent of effective task performance. Thus, for example, the importance of many of the personal characteristics either found or hypothesized to be related to contextual performance (e.g., conscientiousness, extroversion, openness to experience, altruism, integrity, need for achievement, etc.) may in fact also turn out to be largely indirect—a function of the more immediate antecedents of effective contextual performance found in the corresponding cross-functional skills (e.g., teamwork, communication, customer service, negotiation, leadership, conflict management) into which these traits have been invested and shaped through training, education, and experience.

Quality of Worker Performance

Although not depicted graphically in Figure 6-1, the model also posits that the *quality* or *level* of worker performance (as distinct from the *content* of such performance as task or contextual performance) is a function of (1) the degree of congruence or match between the specific characteristics and demands (e.g., skill/ knowledge, role, results requirements) of the work environment and an individual's occupation-specific skills and knowledge, cross-functional skills, basic workplace skills, and personal qualities and interests (in other words the match between work requirements and worker attributes) and (2) the individual's *degree* of competency, proficiency, or possession of those required (i.e., environment-congruent) worker attributes. Said another way, this means that a worker's performance level is a function of his or her degree of possession of or proficiency in the attributes required by the work.

MAPPING SKILLS TO WORK

What percentage of U.S. workers need to know how to prepare a budget? Or need to know principles of electricity? What percentage of U.S. workers need to be able to do arithmetic computation to perform their jobs effectively? Or need good eye-hand coordination? Or need to be able to make effective oral presentations to groups? The answer to all these questions is unknown. Figure 6-2 shows how such data, if they existed, might be arrayed; it provides a sense of how useful such information might be, for example, in prioritizing different types of skills and knowledge as targets of national education- and training-oriented initiatives. An ideal analysis would require clear, precise operational definitions for skills and types of knowledge; would collect data at broad (e.g., aptitudes and abilities) and narrow (tasks, duties, and generalized work activities) levels of analysis; and would have available a host of associated contextual information (industry and organization type, job and work design information, etc.).

The closest approximation to such a national system is, or used to be, the *Dictionary of Occupational Titles* and various associated materials (U.S. Depart-

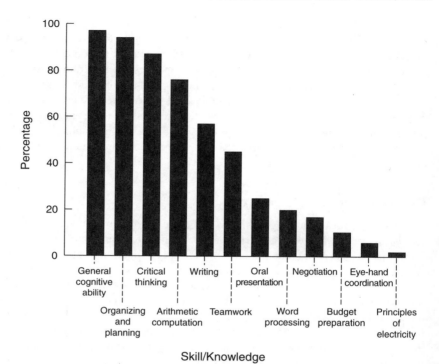

FIGURE 6-2   Skill requirements of U.S. jobs: Percentage of positions for which various skills and knowledge are required for effective job performance (hypothetical data).

ment of Labor, 1977, 1979a, 1979b, 1979c, 1981, 1991). Funding for them was radically reduced in the early 1980s, and since then these materials have not been updated to the degree necessary to ensure that the job information is current and fully reflects today's occupational spectrum. At present, we therefore have very little aggregate knowledge of the true underlying structure of job-related skills and knowledge across the occupational spectrum in the United States.

There is a great deal of empirical work of this type available for individual jobs and occupational areas, and there have been some noteworthy theoretical developments regarding the structure of work tasks (and, by implication, associated skills) within both industrial and cognitive psychology. However, neither discipline has an integrated body of empirically based outcomes in the form of a true skills (or knowledge) taxonomy applicable across the occupational spectrum (Pearlman, 1980). (Gottfredson's work in this area, 1981, 1983, 1986a, represented noteworthy steps in this general direction but was limited by the quality of the underlying *Dictionary of Occupational Titles* data available to her.) As a result, recent and current skill development initiatives, such as SCANS, Goals

2000, and School-to-Work, can be likened to attempts to lay down a complex road system—in the present context a network of paths that lead from unskilled to job ready for a range of work areas or occupations—before a survey of the land has been completed.

To be sure, the past few years have seen a significant number of studies, surveys, and reports that have attempted to address employers' concerns about the skills and qualifications of students entering the work force after high school or college (Bailey, 1990; Cappelli, 1992; Carnevale et al., 1988; Grubb et al., 1992; Michigan Department of Education, 1989; National Center on Education and the Economy, 1990; SCANS, 1991, 1992; Olsten Forum on Human Resource Issues and Trends, 1994; Van Horn, 1995). These studies have attempted to identify the worker skills, knowledge, and abilities most in demand in today's and tomorrow's workplaces. While the attributes identified in these studies have not been identical, most include in one form or another the following: reading/writing; applied mathematics; interpersonal skills (e.g., teamwork, leadership, customer service, negotiation); oral communication; information gathering and analysis; problem solving; critical/creative thinking; organizing, planning, and decision making; various technical or functional skills specific to an occupational area; and personal attributes (motivation, integrity, dependability, self-management).

It is interesting to note that, although this list spans several skills-related information categories of the APDOT content model (basic workplace skills for the first two items, cross-functional skills for the next six items, occupation-specific skills and knowledge for the next-to-last item, and personal qualities for the last item), the large majority of items represent cross-functional skills. It is also interesting to note that, despite widespread concern in recent years about the emerging twenty-first century workplace requiring "new" skills with which entry-level workers are not well equipped, little on the above list could qualify as new or different; rather, they are skills that have long been recognized as important for many, if not most, areas of work. What might be new is that many of the skills had formerly characterized higher-level occupations; now they are becoming increasingly relevant to a wider range of jobs, owing to the types of workplace changes described earlier (e.g., increasing team design of work, the trend toward flatter organizations, and the trend toward driving decision-making authority down to increasingly lower occupational levels). In other words, the issue is not new skills so much as changes in the relative prioritization or importance of existing skills across the occupational spectrum.

Despite the apparent usefulness of such study results, the information value of such studies and reports is significantly limited in terms of its utility for driving changes and reforms in education, training, and assessment. Most work of this type has not been grounded in a theoretically driven framework or based on methodologically rigorous procedures of work analysis. Rather, it has typically relied on surveys, focus groups, and inductive and qualitative data as the primary means for gathering this information and drawing conclusions about the importance of various types of skills. In some cases, attributes were not operationally defined or quantitatively linked to underlying information on work content. As a result, and as will be illustrated below, the skills derived from such work are in most cases insufficiently specified to be of optimal value for their intended purposes, such as the specification of education and training needs, assessment design, and standards setting.

In principle, the design of an optimal approach to such work is relatively straightforward. In broad terms (and assuming the use of professionally conducted and technically sound methods and procedures throughout), the major steps would consist of the following:

1. The systematic collection of work- or job-oriented information (such as tasks, duties, performance standards, and products and services, as defined in the APDOT content model) across a sample of occupations that was developed to be maximally representative of the current or emerging distribution of occupations throughout the economy. Ideally, such a sampling plan would be based on information that would permit additional stratification of the sample (in terms of the organizations sampled) based on important work-context variables, such as the degree of complexity of the work, the degree of task interdependence or team organization of work, and the use of technology. These data would be collected through a customized, structured job analysis questionnaire completed by a sufficiently large sample of appropriate local job experts (such as job incumbents or supervisors) representing multiple organizations for each occupation sampled.

2. Development of an optimal representation of the work content structure across the economy (i.e., an empirically derived job classification structure) through the use of quantitative cluster analysis procedures on the data collected in step 1.

3. On the basis of the results of step 2, derivation of worker-oriented information in terms of the various categories of skill related information and other worker attributes defined in the APDOT content model. This information would be derived for each occupation (or occupational area) developed in step 2. This would be accomplished by teams of trained analysts using anchored attribute-rating scales. This step assumes prior development of provisional taxonomies of the various skill-related information categories and development of improved and updated rating scales of worker attribute requirements.

4. Development of occupational/skill clusters at different levels of analysis (reflecting the various skill-related information categories of the APDOT content model) through the use of quantitative cluster analysis procedures on the analyst ratings completed in step 3.

Step 4 would produce a variety of clustering solutions, each providing a road map of transferable skills (i.e., skills important for multiple occupations or occupational areas) at a different level of analysis. The appropriate interpretation and use of such information for various purposes (e.g., identification of career lattices, prioritization of skills for standards setting or the development of education/training curriculum, and allocation of skills to different tiers of an integrated education/training strategy) will inevitably involve intensive analysis and discussion among appropriate experts and stakeholders in these various sectors of activity.

It can be observed that this suggested approach is essentially identical to the process that is now under way to implement the APDOT content model via development of a working prototype on a representative sample of about 20 percent of the occupational spectrum and the ultimate development of a new, automated *Dictionary of Occupational Titles*, to be known as O*NET (for Occupational Information Network) (American Institutes for Research, 1995). The results of the prototype development project, possibly in conjunction with American College Testing's current National Job Analysis Study (American College Testing, 1994), could serve as the basis for development of appropriate sets of required rating scales for the worker attributes needed for step 3.

Such an approach provides for the collection and analysis of a rich and broad array of occupational information that would be useful for multiple purposes. It would significantly advance our research and knowledge base regarding the underlying structure of job-related skills and knowledge, thus enabling the development of relatively sophisticated and multifaceted strategies and programs that could truly advance the objectives of the various federal initiatives described at the beginning of this paper in a scientifically and technically sound manner. Despite the cost and time such an approach entails, it is hard to overestimate the long-term value to the nation of a skill and occupational information source of this quality.

Table 6-1 presents a simplified hypothetical example of the results of such an approach to the mapping of skills to work. This table displays elements of four of the APDOT content model's skills-related information categories—aptitudes and abilities, cross-functional skills, occupation-specific knowledge, and the occupation-specific skills associated with one of the cross-functional skills (information gathering). The table shows which of these elements are significantly related to each of two jobs in two different industries. (The data are assumed to be derived through appropriate work and job analysis techniques.)

This table exemplifies how the degree of generality or specificity with which skills are defined affects the similarities and differences that can be observed among jobs. For example, if we were to look at the skill profile of each of the four jobs only in terms of the most general category of skills (aptitudes and abilities), we would conclude that all four jobs were essentially identical. However, if we were to include cross-functional skills in the profile of each job, we would begin to observe increasing differentiation among jobs; this differentiation would increase even further if we were to take into account occupation-specific skills and knowledge in making such comparisons. This illustrates how the degree of gen-

TABLE 6-1   Hypothetical Example of Occupational/Skill Clustering Scenario

Skill Category	Architecture/Engineering		Retail	
	Drafter	Administrative Clerk	Buyer	Administrative Clerk
Aptitudes/abilities				
Verbal	X	X	X	X
Quantitative	X	X	X	X
Spatial	X			
Cross-functional skills				
Organizing/planning	X	X	X	X
Information gathering[a]		X(A1, A2, A3, A4)	X(A1, B1, B2, B3)	X(A1, A2, C1, C2)
Negotiation			X	
Occupation-specific knowledge				
Pricing strategies			X	
Computer-aided design software	X			
Word processing software		X		X

NOTE: An **X** in a cell indicates that the skill is significantly related to the job.

[a]Codes for required occupation-specific information-gathering skills are shown in parentheses; code definitions are as follows: **A1** = ability to retrieve records of invoices paid; **A2** = ability to verify previous employment of job applicants by telephoning listed references; **A3** = ability to identify, locate, and acquire publications on recent technical developments in areas of interest to professional staff; **A4** = ability to research price information on CAD software; **B1** = ability to search on-line computer databases for market information on customer buying patterns; **B2** = ability to review merchandise catalogs, specifications, and price sheets to determine merchandise of highest value; **B3** = ability to interview alternative suppliers to determine availability, ordering and billing procedures, and delivery schedules for merchandise; **C1** = ability to obtain daily attendance figures from office supervisor; **C2** = ability to interview customers by telephone to obtain information on satisfaction with purchases.

erality or specificity of skill definition and analysis limits the potential degree of differentiation that can be made between jobs. It also shows how the breadth or narrowness with which skills are defined ultimately (i.e., after data collection) affects which skills are found to be relatively specific and which are more broadly applicable (i.e., transferable) and to what degrees. This in turn defines the content domain or breadth of applicability of such things as associated assessments, associated training, and associated skill standards and of the portability of certification.

Table 6-1 also helps us to understand the concept of transferable skills. Transferable skills can be defined as skills that have applicability (i.e., are important determinants of effective performance) across various ranges of occupations or occupational clusters. The identification of transferable skills is closely related to the development of career lattices, which are extremely important for issues of worker training and retraining. Career lattices are groupings of jobs within relatively homogeneous occupational levels (i.e., levels of complexity, difficulty, responsibility) that usually have some substantial subset of skills in common, so that individuals who possess most or all of the skills required for effective performance in one of the jobs in the lattice are likely to be able to effectively perform other jobs in the lattice with relatively modest amounts of additional training, education, or experience.

From this viewpoint it can be seen that occupational clusters created to maximize skill transferability will essentially result in the delineation of different types of career lattices. The degree to which particular skills are common to, and hence transferable across, a given range or set of occupations is established via the process of job analysis and subsequent clustering. It is through careful work and job analysis that the skills required of different jobs are identified, and through the clustering process (i.e., the specific method and grouping criteria used) that the degree of skill transferability is set. This implies that while the true underlying structure or "map" of skills across the occupational spectrum is something akin to a "state of nature" that is "discovered" through research and analysis, the manner in which the resulting information is used or harnessed is largely under the control of the analyst or researcher. Thus, occupational clusters can be created to reflect varying degrees (or tolerance levels) of within—cluster skill transferability.

Because cross-functional skills constitute the "middle ground" or intermediate level of the skill continuum from generality to specificity, they potentially represent the key to meaningful skill transferability across occupations and industries and hence are of high interest for the various federal initiatives described earlier and for school-to-work programs in particular.

However, even the relatively simple illustration of Table 6-1 reveals the underlying complexity involved in understanding and defining the transferability of cross-functional skills. This can be seen by considering information gathering, which is a good example of what is commonly viewed as a transferable skill of the type envisioned in the SCANS work and the Goals 2000 legislation. It is a likely target for the development, assessment, and certification of skill standards because of its broad practical utility in both educational and work settings and its typical neglect as an explicit part of K-12 education. It is also a skill that has been frequently identified as important to emerging high-performance workplaces in a number of recent employer surveys, as noted above.

When considered in light of the actual content and context of just the three jobs represented in Table 6-1, the seemingly simply defined and easily understood cross-functional skill of information gathering can be seen to represent widely varying types of both tast content and task complexity, and to subsume such varying processes as the following: simple retrieval of readily available information (as exemplified by occupation-specific skills A1 and C1); simple interviewing or questioning of individual sources based on structured guidelines for the content and sequencing of questions (skills A2 and C2); moderately complex interviewing or questioning of multiple sources on multiple related subjects requiring some improvisation of questions based on previous responses (skill B3); relatively simple price comparison research (skill A4); moderately complex price comparison and related research from written sources (skill B2); moderately complex questioning and scanning of multiple oral and written information sources (skill A3); and gathering of relatively complex quantitative data from multiple information sources requiring computer skills, database knowledge, and financial and market knowledge (skill B1).

This analysis illustrates the importance of underlying work content and surrounding work context for a full understanding of the meaning of any cross-functional skill; without this understanding it is not possible to target education, training, assessment, and related initiatives, such as the development of skill standards and skill certification programs. It also illustrates the limitations of simple surveys or focus group studies of employer-desired skills. Inevitably, the skills derived from such studies are insufficiently specified to be of optimal value for their intended purposes. This is because the skills receive unitary labels and definitions that do not reflect likely differences in work content (e.g., tasks, activities, outputs) or work context (e.g., complexity of functioning) across occupational areas of settings in which the skill is required. For example, the mere identification of, say, problem-solving, as and important employability skill, is of almost no value as a guide to the design of education curricula, training programs, or assessment tools regarding this skill—that is, without further elaboration of the work content and work context factors associated with a given application of the skill, without which it lacks essential definition.

While the need to account for differences in underlying work content in cross-functional skills may seem readily apparent, the effects of work context are perhaps less obvious and considerably less tractable. Despite its increasing importance to the meaning and understanding of twenty-first century work and work performance, work context is the least well developed and understood of any of the three major domains of work-related information (i.e., person-, work-, and context-oriented variables). While there have been some noteworthy attempts to systematize information on work context (e.g., Naughton and Outcalt, 1988; Wetrogan et al., 1983), none has really attempted to simultaneously and systematically tackle all levels and all facets of this domain. The previously mentioned work in progress on O*NET (American Institutes for Research, 1995), which is designed to operationalize the APDOT content model, could be the basis for significant advances in this area.

This is an area in need of much more research, with the goals of developing a comprehensive taxonomy of work context variables and ultimately, based on this, of general categories of work settings or situations (see Burke and Pearlman, 1988). Research of this type would tell us, for example, how many varieties of oral communication skill (or teamwork skill, or information-gathering skill, or decision-making skill) it is important to differentiate and define so as to reasonably represent the range of applications (content and context) of this skill across the U.S. occupational spectrum. It would reveal the degree to which such distinctions are driven more by, for example, industry segment (e.g., manufacturing vs. service), job complexity (e.g., in terms of information-processing demands), or task interdependence (e.g., working alone vs. working in teams) or some combination of these (or other work context variables). Without such a foundation we have little basis for developing national education, training, and assessment strategies directed toward the types of cross-functional skills that represent the keys to both organizational success in the twenty-first century workplace and employment security for the twenty-first century worker.

THE DILEMMA OF CROSS-FUNCTIONAL SKILL DEVELOPMENT

There are many unresolved training-related issues concerning cross-functional skills. The issues are complicated by the fact that such skills are linked both to aptitudes and abilities and personal qualities and interests (which set limits on their trainability, as discussed under "Trainability of Attributes" above) and to specialized skills and knowledge (which are often present or required in the application of a given cross-functional skill in a specific setting). For example, the degree to which an individual can be successfully trained in "negotiating skill" is in part limited by his or her underlying verbal ability. Moreover, although a meaningful generic definition of negotiating skill can be developed (e.g., "the ability to reach formal or informal agreements with, obtain commitments from, or arrange plans with other individuals or groups in a way that serves or promotes mutual goals or interests"), the effective application of negotiating skill within a particular job context will almost always entail mastery of a certain body of specialized knowledge that is different from job to job. This will in effect result in different operational definitions of negotiating skill for different jobs (or job families). Thus, for example, the meaning (as well as the complexity) of negotiation skill is substantially different for, say, an automobile salesperson and a labor contract negotiator.

The resulting dilemma from an education or training perspective is that, if such cross-functional skills are trained at the generic level, such training is not likely to be immediately transferable to a specific job or work setting (i.e., without the acquisition of the associated context- or occupation-specific knowledge). On the other hand, if such skills are trained in the context of a particular work setting (i.e., if the specific skills and knowledge associated with the use of a given cross-functional skill for a particular job are incorporated), such training is not likely to be immediately transferable to different jobs or settings, even those that require the "same" (generically defined) skill. Even newer and evolving training techniques (such as metacognitive skills training) that attempt to improve generic skills through contextual training of cognitive resource management and self-monitoring skills have failed to produce evidence that the skills learned through such methods transfer beyond the specific subject matter and information medium involved in the training (Gitomer, 1992).

Resolution of this dilemma may lie in an integrated education and training strategy wherein the generic components (or building blocks) of such skills are consciously built into primary- and secondary-school curriculum content and (perhaps more importantly) into modes of teaching and learning while the more specialized components are reserved for postsecondary education and employment-related training. This is clearly the direction of the contemporary educational reform movement in this country (SCANS, 1992), which argues for teaching in context, experience-based and application-oriented learning, integrated curricula, and so forth. This approach is also very similar in concept to, and hence highly compatible with, the three-tiered system of skill standards suggested by Tucker (1993), which essentially proposes an increasingly job-specific focus on skill development as one moves through primary and secondary education, to various forms of postsecondary education or training, and on to employer-specific or on-the-job training.

Moreover, such an approach could resolve a schism in the implicit model of education and training in this country. Under this model the development of aptitudes, abilities, and basic workplace skills has traditionally been the province of primary and secondary educational institutions, whereas the development of specialized skills and knowledge has primarily been the province of either specialized secondary-school institutions (such as vocational and technical schools), postsecondary educational institutions (colleges and universities), and employment settings themselves (i.e., through on- or off-the-job training). The intermediate category of cross-functional skills (such as organizing and planning, decision making, and especially such interpersonally oriented skills as teamwork, negotiation, speaking and listening, and coaching or mentoring others) has, unfortunately, largely been ignored as a specific target of systematic development efforts under this model.

The ultimate effectiveness of such an approach, however, depends on our ability to close or reduce two key knowledge gaps. The first, described earlier, concerns the absence of a structure or taxonomy of job-related skills and knowledge across the occupational spectrum that takes into account, or is built on, a taxonomic infrastructure of both work content and context. The second concerns our limited understanding of the malleability or trainability of the different categories of skills-related information discussed throughout this paper. Although the available research has allowed for deduction of some general principles in this regard (as noted under "Trainability of Attributes" in the earlier discussion of the training utility model) we lack the depth of understanding and overarching theory in this area that could support the development of much more focused and detailed skill development strategies than is presently possible. In the absence of a well-researched and "validated" taxonomy of work-related skills and knowledge that explicates both the hierarchical and lateral interrelationships among such elements while also shedding light on underlying characteristics related to trainability, our ability to design education, training, and assessment systems that optimize the content, sequence, and method of teaching and learning cross-functional skills will be limited, as will be the effectiveness of such systems. Only when armed with such systematic knowledge of this content and contextual skills infrastructure will we be able to meaningfully define the skills we wish to develop and appropriately "allocate" different categories and specific elements of these skills to different tiers of such a learning and assessment system so as to optimize individuals' skill and knowledge acquisition, retention, and transferability.

CHALLENGES FOR ASSESSMENT

The previously cited report of an employer survey conducted for the New Jersey Business-Higher Education Forum (Van Horn, 1995:15-17) states that:

> researchers are working to develop assessments of how well students learn [the] generic and specific skills and abilities sought by employers. . . . Thus far, no widely accepted tests have been developed. There are also disagreements about whether assessing and reporting on student skill acquisition is desirable. . . . The task of creating broadly accepted assessment tests is truly daunting. As one scholar observed, " . . . these questions go well beyond any experiences educators in the United States have had in the arena of assessment and public policy." [While] consensus exists on the importance of certain basic and advanced skills . . . *there is little knowledge or accepted measuring techniques for determining how well college graduates master those skills in communication and critical thinking* [emphasis added].

This quotation captures the fundamental challenges we currently face regarding the assessment of skills for the emerging twenty-first century workplace. As the quotation implies, these challenges can be viewed on two levels—one involving the development of tests or other assessment instruments needed to measure important skills, and the other concerning the manner in which the results of such instruments are used in broader systems or programs. The major challenge at the former level, as implied by much of the discussion here, is the development of technically sound and practically useful measures of cross-functional skills. The major challenge at the other level is the need for a more focused and systematic integration of three conventional roles of assessment: its diagnostic function (i.e., to enable inferences regarding what has and has not been learned); its predictive function (i.e., to enable inferences regarding future performance or behavior); and its evaluative and incentive function (i.e., to enable inferences regarding level, status, or progress of either individuals or institutions and thereby influence the degree and direction of both individual and institutional investment in skill, knowledge, and ability development). Obviously, these two levels of analysis are not independent. The nature and properties of assessment instruments set limits on their appropriateness and utility for different purposes, and the purposes of the assessment systems influence the design of instruments.

Measuring Cross-Functional Skills

Within the employment domain, cross-functional skills have most commonly been measured in assessment centers (Thornton and Byham, 1982). These centers use structured, standardized role plays in which participants engage in various group and individual activities that sample important domains of work behavior and worker functioning (e.g., communication, organizing/planning, decision making, negotiating, teamwork) while a team of trained assessors observes them. Cross-functional skills have also been measured through work or job simulations, structured behavioral interviews (Motowidlo et al., 1992), patterned behavioral description interviews (Janz, 1989), situational interviews (Latham et al., 1980), records of behavioral consistency or accomplishment (Schmidt et al., 1979; Hough, 1984), and low-fidelity simulations (Motowidlo et al., 1990), which are essentially multiple-choice situational judgment tests.

Within the education domain, cross-functional skills have been measured through what have been variously termed performance-based, alternative, or authentic assessments (Baker et al., 1993). The cross-functional skills typically assessed by such measures include decision making, organizing and planning, information gathering, oral communication, problem solving, and various types of interpersonal skills, such as leadership, teamwork, social sensitivity, behavioral flexibility, and negotiating skill. While the predictive validity of overall performance on such measures in the employment context has been fairly well established, less evidence is available regarding the predictive validity of their component dimensions (i.e., particular cross-functional skills). What does exist (see Table 5.12 in Thornton and Byham, 1982, for a summary of assessment center dimension validity) is generally favorable but is based on a relatively small number of studies. There are as yet few empirical reliability and validity data regarding the various forms of performance-based assessments in the educational context (Baker et al., 1993).

Despite useful levels of predictive validity, there is virtually no evidence bearing on the *construct* validity of the component dimensions of any of the approaches mentioned above other than assessment centers. That is, there is no evidence that the procedures are actually measuring the intended skills. (The Motowidlo et al., 1992, study is somewhat of an exception since it at least addresses the issue and presents some data relevant to convergent and discriminant validity of individual dimensions; however, the evidence they provide is not particularly compelling because of the similarity of the various processes used to differentially evaluate the dimensions.) For assessment centers, there is in fact a body of research bearing on the question of their dimensionality or construct validity in terms of both dimension-versus-exercise effects on overall performance (see Neidig and Neidig, 1984; Sackett and Dreher, 1982, 1984) and the underlying factor structure of dimensions (Russell, 1987). Such research has led to a conclusion of relatively weak construct validity for individual assessment dimensions and the likelihood that performance on the relatively large number of dimensions or cross-functional skills (generally 10 to 20) assessed in a typical program can be accounted for by just a few underlying factors. This is likely due in part to the difficulty and complexity of raters' making more refined judgments but also reflects the fact that there have been few attempts to build measures of individual cross-functional skills; that is, the traditionally used procedures have generally attempted to simultaneously assess a variety of such skills, thus exacerbating an already difficult information-processing task (Gaugler and Thornton, 1989).

   In addition, and related to this last point, the content validity of nonsimulation-based measures of cross-functional skills is often suspect. Motowidlo et al. (1990) somewhat euphemistically referred to their situational judgment test of various cross-functional skills as a low-fidelity simulation, in that the stimulus materials were written (rather than "performed") representations of authentic situations derived from the skill content domain of interest, and the required examinee responses (answering test questions about how one would respond to the given problem or situation) did not represent actual performance of the skill. Similar tools are being pilot tested in educational research (O'Neill et al., 1992) and nonprofit (American College Testing, 1991) domains, and an increasing number of such instruments are being marketed commercially. Many purport to measure such cross-functional skills as teamwork, customer service, and decision making. Sometimes these are administered in video form (wherein a scene presenting, say, a customer service problem is acted out), sometimes in oral form (as in situational interviews), and sometimes in written form (as in situational judgment tests). In each case, examinees must indicate what they would do or how they would handle the situation, by selecting from among multiple given alternatives, responding orally, writing a brief answer, or writing a longer response or essay. Despite the labels ascribed to these measures and the claims of some of their developers, there is, to my knowledge, not a shred of evidence that any such measures tap the target skill content domains to any significant degree. Particularly for interpersonally or performance-oriented skills (teamwork, leadership, customer service, communication, etc.), responding cognitively (as in multiple-choice situational judgment tests), orally (as in situational interviews), or in writing (as in free-response or essay situational tests) to hypothetical situations or scenarios, however realistic and skill appropriate they may be, is not the same as "performance." The often legitimate, empirically based claims of predictive validity for such instruments should not be confused with attributions of content (or construct) validity, conclusions about which are not appropriate until such time as relationships between responses to such instruments and "true" performance on the target skills may be established through the appropriate research.

The above discussion suggests that, while some of the available measures of cross-functional skills are likely to have utility in systems designed to predict future performance, their diagnostic value—and hence their value for national skill development initiatives—is limited by the lack of both construct-related and content-related evidence. While "developmental" assessment centers (which are used only to provide developmental feedback to participants but not as a basis for making personnel decisions) have been commonplace in industry for many years, they universally have been almost based on, or designed in terms of, the work content and work context structure of particular occupational areas (e.g., first-line supervisors) or occupational levels (e.g., midlevel managers). They can thus have high developmental value to participants in those occupational areas or contexts but do not lend themselves to programmatic use across the occupational spectrum, nor is there any straightforward way to equate similarly targeted assessment center programs because of the absence of any "marker variables" for cross-functional skills in the sense that these exist, for example, within the realm of cognitive ability measurement.

Cross-Functional Skills and Evaluation Systems

The evaluation function of cross-functional skill assessment is a critical component of several of the federal skills-related initiatives described earlier (SCANS and Goals 2000). The establishment of skill standards (i.e., proficiency levels) and the development of skill certification (indicating specified degrees of mastery) for cross-functional skills are central to both of these initiatives and are viewed by many as key to reforming school curricula and raising educational standards, strengthening the link between schools and workplaces, and increasing the likelihood that all American young people will have the opportunity to acquire the skills and knowledge necessary to effectively participate in the nation's economy (SCANS, 1992). However, as I have discussed elsewhere (Pearlman, 1993, 1994a), this is easier said than done, as cross-functional skills pose special challenges for such applications.

The basic concept of a skill standard implies a translation or an association between a given skill level of a person and a given performance level on a job. This implies the need for a number of things, such as the following: (1) definition of the target performance (task or task cluster) to which a skill standard will be addressed (with special consideration given to the narrowness or broadness with which such performance is defined), (2) determination of the worker attributes related to performance of the defined task or task cluster, (3) reliable and valid means of measuring performance on the defined task or cluster, (4) reliable and valid means of measuring the performance-related attributes, (5) specification of various levels of performance against which the performance-related attributes will be benchmarked, and (6) specification of the levels of performance-related attributes associated with these performance levels.

When such standards are used for certification purposes, an additional (and very high-stakes) step is required, namely, to establish which level of performance will be required for certification (or qualification, mastery, or whatever delineations are to be used)—in other words, to decide "where to make the cut." Failure to carefully and appropriately set such skill certification levels creates the risk of either of two types of errors, which decision theorists call "false positives" and "false negatives," each having different—but inevitably dysfunctional—consequences for both individuals and organizations. False positives refer to situations in which standards are set too low, resulting in incompetent or insufficiently skilled people being considered qualified, or certified, and consequently assigned to jobs, training, or other activities for which they are not equipped. This is obviously harmful to the receiving organization but can also result in possible psychological and even physical damage to individuals so misclassified. More insidiously, the proliferation of such effects over time will inevitably lower both the perceived and the actual market value of the certification or qualification standard, producing a de facto system of credentialism rather than a truly competence-based system.

False negatives refer to situations in which standards are set too high, resulting in competent or highly skilled people being disqualified or not certified. This results in potentially significant costs in terms of lost opportunities for organizations, especially if the skills in question are rare or in high demand. Such errors are additionally costly in terms of the cynicism and sense of unfairness they are likely to engender among the individuals who are so misclassified.

To the above considerations can be added the even more sobering fact that there are no "objective" procedures for setting skill or performance standards—all such procedures ultimately rely (directly or indirectly) on human judgment. However, one can enhance the developmental rigor of the standards-setting process, and hence the ultimate credibility and utility of the resulting system, by paying careful attention to the numerous methodological and operational issues that affect this judgment process. These issues include such factors as the types and qualifications of judges (job incumbents, supervisors, outside subject matter experts, etc.); the referent population represented by the judges (i.e., the scope or domain of their expertise and the frame of reference implied by this domain—task specific, job specific, job-family-wide—which in turn affects both the breadth or narrowness of the standard and its content); the number of judges to be used; the training provided to judges; and the amount and type of stimulus material and instructional information provided to judges.

The above generic process for deriving and setting skill and certification standards is relatively straightforward, if not necessarily easy. However, when applied to cross-functional skills, it becomes considerably less straightforward because the available evidence suggests that such level setting is much more tractable for highly specific skills or knowledge than for more general skills or attributes. This is because specific skills and knowledge typically have fairly singular and objectively specifiable behavioral (i.e., performance) referents. For example, it is not hard to envision or find examples of definable and differentiable levels for such specific skills as word processing (through such indices as words-per-minute or error-rate levels) or for such specific areas of knowledge as emergency medical procedures (such as through degree of mastery, as measured by a job knowledge test, of the required component area knowledge, such as cardiopulmonary resuscitation or first aid). Nor is it hard to envision the establishment of performance standards for given jobs or tasks that can be meaningfully linked to such levels. In such cases the establishment of meaningful performance standards and associated skill or knowledge levels is possible because of their more or less objectively specifiable performance referents.

However, this sort of endeavor is much more problematic when applied to cross-functional skills, which have no such unitary or easily specifiable behavioral or performance referents. That is, they refer to the ability to perform classes, groupings, or aggregates of more specific tasks, behaviors, or skills. This can be readily seen in Table 6-1, discussed earlier, in which information gathering was operationally defined differently for each of three jobs, depending on the underlying task or occupation-specific skill structure. There is thus no unitary performance referent for this skill that applies across all the jobs. As I have discussed in more detail elsewhere (Pearlman, 1994a), the prospects for our being able to establish meaningful proficiency levels (for people) that are linked to required performance levels (for work or jobs) are at best extremely challenging when cross-functional skills are dealt with. Without the type of rigorous underpinnings of work and job analysis discussed earlier in this paper, assessment standards for cross-functional skills are likely to be either lacking in critical measurement properties (reliability and validity) or not very useful for an integrated national system.

What about the appropriateness and usefulness of a skill certification framework for cross-functional skills? First, it is important to recognize that the certification model has conventionally been used in a criterion-referenced measurement context. In this context, certification represents attainment or mastery of some specifiable—and specific—body of knowledge or some unambiguously definable—and defined—type, amount, or level of skill. Once certified, an individual is expected to have sufficient competence to carry out the basic tasks or functions implied by this certification in a manner that assures consumers or recipients of the associated product or service of a certain basic level of quality and conformance to generally accepted norms or standards of performance.

As noted above, such a model readily lends itself to application with more narrowly defined, occupation-specific skills and knowledge, whereas its application to cross-functional skills, which can connote a multiplicity of performance or behavioral referents, is more problematic. For example, what would it mean to be certified in "decision making" or "problem solving" (two of the SCANS foundation skills) or "works with cultural diversity" or "exercises leadership" (two of the SCANS "workplace competencies")? It would be easy to argue that one can have attained a certain "level" of, or have been "certified" on, such cross-functional skills but still not know how to *do* anything (i.e., in any concrete, job-specific sense).

It is always somewhat artificial and hence problematic to specify a given level of any skill or human attribute that will result in effective versus ineffective performance or similar delineations, such as work ready/not work ready, certified/noncertified, or novice/apprentice/journeyman/master/expert. This is because work or job performance, however it is measured or operationalized, virtually always represents an underlying *continuum* (i.e., from low to high or poor to outstanding), and most human attributes tend to be linearly related to job performance (meaning the more of the attribute possessed, the higher the performance). However, the problem is mitigated in the realm of more specialized skills and knowledge because of their more objective and specifiable behavioral or performance referents.

This point also raises the more general concern that, by falsely implying a discontinuity of the attribute-performance relationship, skill certifications, if not appropriately positioned, or if based on insufficiently rigorous standards, could end up inadvertently promoting a minimum competency rather than a high-performance mindset, by signaling to students and worker trainees that development or acquisition of a certain amount of a skill or attribute is "enough." It could thus have the unintended effect of constraining rather than promoting both upward and lateral occupational mobility and discouraging rather than motivating the lifelong growth and development of valued skills.

Thus, the challenges of operationalizing the measurement of cross-functional skills in terms of both instruments and systems that optimize their diagnostic, predictive, and evaluative utility are indeed formidable. The near-term success of such endeavors is constrained by a number of key limitations in our current research and knowledge base, particularly with respect to the mapping of skills and knowledge to both the content and the context of the emerging twenty-first century world of work.

There are, nevertheless, some reasons for optimism, at least from a technical standpoint, that interim solutions can be developed on the basis of currently available methods, instruments, and technology, while the research needed to support more rigorous, longer-term solutions (some of which is already under way) is being completed. The key elements of such possibilities are outlined below. The bigger obstacles are likely to arise at the social and policy levels, where, as Thurow (1993) suggests, Americans resist the imposition of national standards in general, and local school boards in particular resist the imposition of national educational standards and assessments.

A VISION OF TWENTY-FIRST CENTURY ASSESSMENT

There is little doubt that widely recognized, highly valued, and commonly understood standards of performance excellence are probably the single most important external drivers of individuals' skill and ability development in both our educational institutions and our workplaces. There is also little doubt that assessment can play a crucial role in promoting such standards, provided it is directed to the right kinds of skills and deployed in a way that motivates, rather than disengages, the target populations. What might such a system look like? The hypotheses and conclusions drawn throughout this paper suggest that an optimal approach to assessment for the twenty-first century workplace might consist of the following principles, characteristics, or elements:

1. A sound basis in empirical, systematic, and comprehensive work and job analysis that will have established the following:

• a clear mapping or linkage between worker-oriented attributes (skills-related information categories) and both work content and context across the occupational spectrum.

• well-founded taxonomies of both broader (cross-functional) and narrower (occupation-specific skill and knowledge) types of skills-related information.

• a system of empirically based job families or occupational clusters that indicate occupational interrelationships and career lattices in terms of work content, work context, and skills-related information and that show which skills are transferable and to what degree among occupational areas of subareas.

2. Adoption of a tiered approach to skill and knowledge development, in which:

• the development of broader skill domains (basic workplace skills and cross-functional skills) are targeted for K-12 and vocational-technical institutions, and more advanced or specialized skill and knowledge domains for postsecondary education and specialized training institutions.

• contemporary principles of education reform (e.g., SCANS, 1992) are adopted in K-12 education to incorporate the integration of cross-functional skill development with traditional academics.

• performance-based assessments, in conjunction with locally developed and teacher-made assessments, are used within the K-12 domain as tools for diagnosis, student feedback, and development planning but not for skill certification or program evaluation.

3. Establishment of a network of standardized, national assessment centers to measure important cross-functional skills; widely deployable and practically feasible through the use of video-based technology (e.g., video teleconferencing, videotaping for later evaluation by others), as well as emerging multimedia-PC-based Internet/Web-based technology; with such centers characterized by the following:

• an exclusively individual/developmental focus during grades 9 through 11, with opportunities for multiple "trials," detailed feedback and coaching, and multiple skill remediation mechanisms and support materials (e.g., lists of key experiences and learning activities targeted to particular cross-functional skills).

- an evaluative focus at grade 12, with skill-level results used for high-stakes purposes (high school diploma, employment recommendations, postsecondary referral and placement decisions, institutional evaluation, etc.).

4. The use of standardized measures of relatively occupation-specific skills and knowledge and academic achievement for evaluative purposes (standards setting and certification) in secondary and postsecondary education contexts, with results used for high-stakes purposes (high school diploma, college or university degree, employment recommendations, postsecondary referral and placement decisions, institutional evaluation, etc.).

The above approach suggests some means by which the diagnostic, predictive, and evaluative/incentive functions of assessment might be usefully integrated in a manner that is consistent with our current research and knowledge base. It combines traditional measurement practices (e.g., paper-and-pencil tests) with newer practices and technology in ways that are both technically appropriate and suitable for the various purposes to which the different types of measures would be applied. Although much research is still needed to expand and refine our knowledge base with respect to the effective measurement of cross-functional skills, the approach suggested above could yield significant educational, social, and economic benefits while the needed research continues.

APPENDIX: CONTENT MODEL

To help revitalize the American economy, the Advisory Panel for the *Dictionary of Occupational Titles* (APDOT) is recommending a national electronic database system that collects, produces, and maintains accurate, reliable, and valid information on occupations. The new *Database of Occupational Titles* (DOT) would serve as a national benchmark and provide a common language for all users of occupational information.

The APDOT proposes the following content model as a framework for the new DOT. The model is intended to provide a coherent and integrated system that identifies the most important types of information about jobs and workers that APDOT believes should be considered for inclusion in the new DOT. *APDOT views this content model as an initial point of departure and as being subject to further research and analysis as well as administrative decisions that will be made during implementation.* APDOT expects that specifics of the descriptors will be designed and developed based on future intensive research and that descriptors will be included when supporting data meet professional standards for reliability, validity, and generalizability.

This content model has been drawn from a thorough analysis of user survey results, public comments, and a wide-ranging review of research in such areas as job and skill analysis, human individual differences, and organization analysis. It embodies a view of occupational analysis that reflects the characteristics of both occupations (through the use of "job-oriented" descriptors) and people (through the use of "worker-oriented" descriptors) as well as the broader labor market.

This content model is not intended to imply that information or data regarding all of its components can or should be collected as part of a single job analysis instrument or even as part of the job analysis process. Some information may more appropriately lend itself to determination through other forms of research or data collection. For example, worker aptitude/ability patterns may be developed

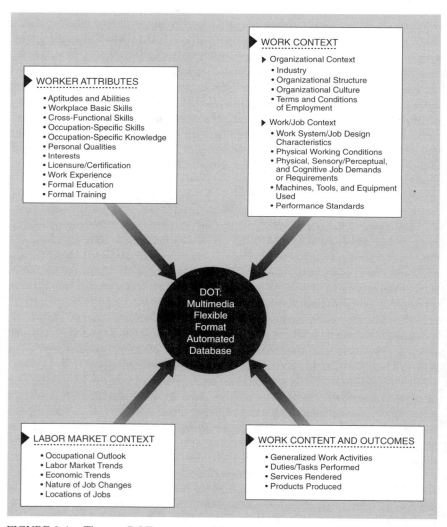

WORK CONTEXT

▶ Organizational Context
  • Industry
  • Organizational Structure
  • Organizational Culture
  • Terms and Conditions
    of Employment
▶ Work/Job Context
  • Work System/Job Design
    Characteristics
  • Physical Working Conditions
  • Physical, Sensory/Perceptual,
    and Cognitive Job Demands
    or Requirements
  • Machines, Tools, and Equipment
    Used
  • Performance Standards

WORKER ATTRIBUTES

• Aptitudes and Abilities
• Workplace Basic Skills
• Cross-Functional Skills
• Occupation-Specific Skills
• Occupation-Specific Knowledge
• Personal Qualities
• Interests
• Licensure/Certification
• Work Experience
• Formal Education
• Formal Training

DOT:
Multimedia
Flexible
Format
Automated
Database

LABOR MARKET CONTEXT

• Occupational Outlook
• Labor Market Trends
• Economic Trends
• Nature of Job Changes
• Locations of Jobs

WORK CONTENT AND OUTCOMES

• Generalized Work Activities
• Duties/Tasks Performed
• Services Rendered
• Products Produced

FIGURE 6-A   The new DOT content model.

through aptitude test validation studies. In addition, some descriptors may be obtained through linkages with other databases and information sources. For example, the development of such descriptors as occupational outlook information, labor market trends and occupational demographics may be completed by linking with appropriate databases developed by sources outside the DOT.

The content model is organized into four sections intended to represent the major elements of a systems model of work: Worker Attributes (Section I), reflecting input variables; Work Context (Section II), reflecting the organizational, social, and physical environment or system in which a job is performed; Work Content and Outcomes (Section III), reflecting output variables; and Labor Market Context (Section IV), reflecting the broader economic system of which all jobs are a part. The Content Model is shown schematically in Figure 6-A, the new DOT content model. Each section defines, provdes examples of, and in some cases lists more specific elements of a set of descriptor categories.

REFERENCES

Ackerman, P.L.
  1987 Individual differences in skill learning: An integration of psychometric and information processing perspectives. *Psychological Bulletin* 102:3-27.
Ackerman, P.L., and L.G. Humphreys
  1990 Individual differences theory in industrial and organizational psychology. Pp. 223-282 in *Handbook of Industrial and Organizational Psychology*, 2d ed., vol. 1, M.D. Dunnette and L.M. Hough, eds. Palo Alto, CA: Consulting Psychologists Press.
Advisory Panel for the Dictionary of Occupational Titles
  1993 *The New DOT: A Database of Occupational Titles for the Twenty-first Century.* Washington, DC: U.S. Department of Labor.
American College Testing
  1991 *Work Keys: National System for Teaching and Assessing Employability Skills.* Iowa City: American College Testing.
  1994 *Performing a National Job Analysis Study: Overview of Methodology and Procedure.* Iowa City: American College Testing.
American Institutes for Research
  1995 *Development of Prototype Occupational Information Network (O*NET) Content Model.* Salt Lake City: Utah Department of Employment Security.
Bailey, T.
  1990 Jobs of the future and skills they will require: New thinking on an old debate. *American Educator* 14(1):10-15,40-44.
Baker, E.L., H.F. O'Neil, Jr., and R.L. Linn
  1993 Policy and validity prospects for performance-based assessments. *American Psychologist* 48:1210-1218.
Bishop, J.H.
  1988 Employment testing and incentives to learn. *Journal of Vocational Behavior* 33:404-423.
Borman, W.C., M.A. Hanson, S.H. Oppler, E.D. Pulakos, and L.A. White
  1993 Role of early supervisory experience in supervisor performance. *Journal of Applied Psychology* 78:443-449.

Borman, W.C., and S.J. Motowidlo
    1993   Contextual aspects of job performance. Pp. 71-98 in *Personnel Selection in Organizations*, N.Schmitt, W.C. Borman, and associates, eds. San Francisco: Jossey-Bass.
Bridges, W.
    1994   *Job Shift: How to Prosper in a World Without Jobs.* Reading, MA: Addison-Wesley.
Burke, M.J., and K. Pearlman
    1988   Recruiting, selecting, and matching people to jobs. Pp. 97-142 in *Productivity in Organizations*, J.P. Campbell, R.J. Campbell, and associates, eds. San Francisco: Jossey-Bass.
Campbell, J.P., J.J. McHenry, and L.L. Wise
    1990   Modeling job performance in a population of jobs. *Personnel Psychology* 43:313-333.
Campbell, J. P., R.A. McCloy, S.H. Oppler, and C.E. Sager
    1993   A theory of job performance. Pp. 35-70 in *Personnel Selection in Organizations*, N. Schmitt, W.C. Borman, and associates, eds. San Francisco: Jossey-Bass.
Cappelli, P.
    1992   *College and the Workplace: How Should We Assess Student Performance?* Philadelphia: National Center for the Educational Quality of the Workforce.
    1995   *Is the "Skills Gap" Really About Attitudes? California Management Review* 37(4):108-124.
Carnevale, A.P., L.J. Gainer, and A.S. Meltzer
    1988   *Workplace Basics: The Skills Employers Want.* Washington, DC: American Society for Training and Development.
Coates, J.F., J. Jarratt, and J.B. Mahaffie
    1990   *Future Work: Seven Critical Forces Reshaping Work and the Work Force in North America.* San Francisco: Jossey-Bass.
Gaugler, B.B., and G.C. Thornton III
    1989   Number of assessment center dimensions as a determinant of assessor accuracy. *Journal of Applied Psychology* 74:611-618.
Gitomer, D.H.
    1992   Cognitive Science Implications for Revising the *DOT*. In the unpublished report, Implications of Cognitive Psychology and Cognitive Task Analysis for the Revision of the Dictionary of Occupational Titles, American Psychological Association, Washington, DC.
Gottfredson, L.S.
    1981   *A Skills Map: The General and Specific Competencies Required by Different Occupations.* Progress report. Baltimore: Center for Social Organization of Schools, Johns Hopkins University.
    1983   *The Validity of an Occupational Classification Based on Job Competencies for Assessing Employability.* EDRS No. ED 246 239. Baltimore: Center for Social Organization of Schools, Johns Hopkins University.
    1986a   Occupational aptitude patterns map: Development and implications for a theory of job aptitude requirements. *Journal of Vocational Behavior* 29:254-291.
    1986b   Societal consequences of the *g* factor in employment. *Journal of Vocational Behavior* 29:340-362.
Grubb, N.W., et al.
    1992   *Betwixt and Between: Education, Skills, and Employment in Sub-baccalaureate Labor Markets.* National Center for Research in Vocational Education Report. Berkeley: University of California.
Hough, L.M.
    1984   Development and evaluation of the "accomplishment record" method of selecting and promoting professionals. *Journal of Applied Psychology* 69:135-146.

Humphreys, L.G.
1989   Intelligence: Three kinds of instability and their consequences for policy. Pp. 193-216 in
        Intelligence: Measurement, Theory, and Public Policy, R.L. Linn, ed. Urbana: Univer-
        sity of Illinois Press.
Hunter, J.E.
1983   A causal analysis of cognitive ability, job knowledge, job performance, and supervisory
        ratings. Pp. 257-266 in *Performance Measurement and Theory*, F. Landy, S. Zedeck,
        and J. Cleveland, eds. Hillsdale, NJ: Lawrence Erlbaum Associates.
1986   Cognitive ability, cognitive aptitudes, job knowledge, and job performance. *Journal of
        Vocational Behavior* 29:340-362.
Janz, T.
1989   The patterned behavior description interview: The best prophet of the future is the
        past. Pp. 158-168 in *The Employment Interview: Theory, Research and Practice*, R.W.
        Eder and G.R. Ferris, eds. Newbury Park, CA: Sage.
Johnston, W.B., and A.E. Packer
1987   *Workforce 2000*. Indianapolis, IN: Hudson Institute.
Kanfer, R., and P.L. Ackerman
1989   Motivation and cognitive abilities: An integrative-aptitude-treatment interaction approach
        to skill acquisition. *Journal of Applied Psychology* 74:657-690.
Latham, G.P., L.M. Saari, E.D. Pursell,and M.A. Campion
1980   The situational interview. *Journal of Applied Psychology* 65:422-427.
Meridian   Corporation
1991   *The Changing World of Work: Implications for the DOT Review Initiative*. Report
        prepared for the Advisory Panel for the Dictionary of Occupational Titles. Washing-
        ton, DC: U.S. Department of Labor.
Michigan Department of Education
1989   *The Michigan Employability Survey*. Ann Arbor: Michigan Department of Education.
Motowidlo, S.J., M.D. Dunnette, and G.W. Carter
1990   An alternative selection procedure: The low-fidelity simulation. *Journal of Applied
        Psychology* 75:640-647.
Motowidlo, S.J., G.W. Carter, M.D. Dunnette, N. Tippins, S. Werner, J.R. Burnett, and M.J.
        Vaughn
1992   Studies of the structured behavioral interview. *Journal of Applied Psychology* 77:571-587.
National Association of Secondary School Principals
1996   *Breaking Ranks: Changing an American Institution*. Reston, VA: National Association
        of Secondary School Principals.
National Center for the Educational Quality of the Workforce
1994   *First Findings: The EQW National Employer Survey*. Philadelphia: University of Penn-
        sylvania.
National Center on Education and the Economy
1990   *America's Choice: High Skills or Low Wages*. Rochester, NY: National Center on
        Education.
National Commission on Excellence in Education
1983   *A Nation at Risk: The Imperative for Educational Reform*. Washington, DC: U.S.
        Government Printing Office.
National Governors' Association
1992   *Enhancing Skills for a Competitive World*. Washington, DC: National Governors' Asso-
        ciation.
Naughton, T.J., and D. Outcalt
1988   Development and test of an occupational taxonomy based on job characteristics
        theory. *Journal of Vocational Behavior* 32:16-36.

Neidig, R.D., and P.J. Neidig
1984   Multiple assessment center exercises and job relatedness. *Journal of Applied Psychology* 69:182-186.
Offerman, L.R., and M.K. Gowing
1993   Personnel selection in the future: The impact of changing demographics and the nature of work. Pp. 385-417 in *Personnel Selection in Organizations*, N. Schmitt, W.C. Borman, and associates, eds. San Francisco: Jossey-Bass.
Olsten Forum on Human Resource Issues and Trends
1994   *Skills for Success.* Westbury, NY: Olsten Corp.
O'Neill, H.F., Jr., K. Allred, and E.L. Baker
1992   *Measurement of Workforce Readiness: Design of Prototype Measures.* CSE Technical Report 344. Los Angeles: Center for the Study of Evaluation and National Center for Research on Evaluation, Standards, and Student Testing, University of California.
Pearlman, K.
1980   Job families: A review and discussion of their implications for personnel selection. *Psychological Bulletin* 87:1-28.
1993   The Skills Standards Project and the Redesign of the Nation's Occupational Classification System. Unpublished paper prepared for the U.S. Department of Labor, contract no. 93-509, by Western Test Development Center, Utah Department of Employment Security, Salt Lake City.
1994a   The Development of Occupational/Skill Clusters for Goals 2000: Suggested Approaches and Key Issues. Unpublished paper prepared for the U.S. Department of Labor under contract to DTI, 2361 Jefferson Davis Highway, Suite 500, Arlington, VA 22202.
1994b   Job Families in the United States Employment Service: Review, Analysis, and Recommendations. Unpublished technical report prepared for the U.S. Department of Labor, contract no. 92-442, by Western Test Development Center, Utah Department of Employment Security, Salt Lake City.
1995   Is "Job" Dead? Implications of Changing Concepts of Work for I/O Science and Practice. Panel discussion conducted at the 10th annual conference of the Society for Industrial and Organizational Psychology, Orlando, FL, May.
Reich, R.B.
1991   *The Work of Nations: Preparing Ourselves for 21st Century Capitalism.* New York: Alfred A. Knopf.
Russell, C.J.
1987   Person characteristic versus role congruency explanations for assessment center ratings. *Academy of Management Journal* 30:817-826.
Sackett, P.R., and G.F. Dreher
1982   Constructs and assessment center dimensions: Some troubling empirical findings. *Journal of Applied Psychology* 67:401-410.
1984   Situation specificity of behavior and assessment center validation strategies: A rejoinder to Neidig & Neidig. *Journal of Applied Psychology* 69:187-190.
Schmidt, F.L., and J.E. Hunter
1992   Development of a causal model: Processes determining job performance. *Current Directions in Psychological Science* 1:89-92.
Schmidt, F.L., J.R. Caplan, S.E. Bemis, R. Decuir, L. Dunn, and L. Antone
1979   *The Behavioral Consistency Method of Unassembled Examining.* Washington, DC: Office of Personnel Management.
Schmidt, F.L., J.E. Hunter, and A.N. Outerbridge
1986   Impact of job experience and ability on job knowledge, work sample performance, and supervisory ratings of job performance. *Journal of Applied Psychology* 71:432-439.

Secretary's Commission on Achieving Necessary Skills
  1991   *What Work Requires of Schools: A SCANS Report for America 2000.* Washington, DC:
           U.S. Department of Labor.
  1992   *Learning a Living: A Blueprint for High Performance: A SCANS Report for America
           2000.* Washington, DC: U.S. Department of Labor.
Thornton, G.C., III, and W.C. Byham
  1982   *Assessment Centers and Managerial Performance.* New York: Academic Press.
Thurow, L.
  1993   Unpublished speech presented at the Business for Social Responsibility Conference,
           Washington, DC, October 21.
Tucker, M.S.
  1993   *Prepared Remarks on Title IV, Goals 2000: Educate America Act before the House
           Subcommittee on Elementary, Secondary, and Vocational Education.* Rochester, NY:
           National Center on Education and the Economy.
U.S. Department of Labor
  1977   *Dictionary of Occupational Titles,* 4th ed. Washington, DC: U.S. Department of Labor.
  1979a   *Guide for Occupational Exploration.* Washington, DC: U.S. Department of Labor.
  1979b   *Manual for the USES General Aptitude Test Battery. Section II: Occupational Aptitude
           Pattern Structure.* Washington, DC: U.S. Department of Labor.
  1979c   *Manual for the USES General Aptitude Test Battery. Section II-A: Development of the
           Occupational Aptitude Pattern Structure.* Washington, DC: U.S Department of Labor.
  1981   *Selected Characteristics of Occupations Defined in the Dictionary of Occupational Titles.*
           Washington, DC: U.S. Department of Labor.
  1991   *Dictionary of Occupational Titles,* 4th ed., rev. Washington, DC: U.S. Department of
           Labor.
Van Horn, C.
  1995   *Enhancing the Connection Between Higher Education and the Workplace: A Survey of
           Employers.* Denver: State Higher Education Executive Officers and the Education Com-
           mission of the States.
Wetrogan, L.I., D.M. Olson, and H.M. Sperling
  1983   A Systemic Model of Work Performance. Unpublished paper presented at the 91st
           annual meeting of the American Psychological Association, Anaheim, CA, August.

7

Postmodern Test Theory

Robert J. Mislevy

Good heavens! For more than forty years I have been speaking prose without knowing it.

Molière, *Le Bourgeois Gentilhomme*

INTRODUCTION

Molière's Monsieur Jourdan was astonished to learn that he had been speaking prose all his life. I know how he felt. For years I have just been doing my job—trying to improve educational assessment by applying ideas from statistics and psychology. Come to find out, I've been advancing "neopragmatic postmodernist test theory" without ever intending to do so. This paper tries to convey some sense of what this rather unwieldy phrase means and offers some thoughts about what it implies for educational assessment, present and future. The goods news is that we can foresee some real improvements: assessments that are more open and flexible, better connected with students' learning, and more educationally useful. The bad news is that we must stop expecting drop-in-from-the-sky assessment to tell us, in 2 hours and for $10, the truth, plus or minus two standard errors.

Gary Minda's (1995) *Postmodern Legal Movements* inspired the structure of what follows. Almost every page of his book evokes parallels between issues and new directions in jurisprudence on the one hand and the debates and new developments in educational assessment on the other. Excerpts from Minda's book frame the sections of this paper. They sketch out central ideas in postmodernism—neopragmatic postmodernism, in particular—and how they are transforming the theory and practice of law. Their counterparts in assessment are discussed in turn.

Modernism and Postmodernism

This section introduces the terms "modernism," "postmodernism," and "neopragmatic postmodernism" as I will use them. It is necessarily incomplete, and adherents of each position will find much to disagree with.

Modernism

> Modern legal theorists believe that they can discover the "right answers" or "correct interpretation" by applying a distinctive legal method based on deduction, analogy, precedent, interpretation, social policy, institutional analysis, history, sociology, economics, and scientific method. . . . Legal moderns . . . express the intellectual and artistic quest for perfection through the process of *uncovering* and *unmasking* the secrets of the world by transcending contexts that limit human understanding. . . . Legal modernism also . . . is based on an understanding of language that assumes that words and conceptual ideas are capable of objectively capturing the meaning of events the law seeks to describe and control. (Minda, 1995:5-6)

To Plato the nature and intelligibility of the world of appearance could be accounted for only by recognizing it as an "image" of the truly intelligible structure of being itself. These "forms" are the essence of being in the world, although we experience only images or imperfect instances of this or that. He likened our condition to that of dwellers in a cave, who see shadows on cave walls but not the objects that cast them. The struggle, by means of logic and the scientific method, to infer the universe's "true" forms and to explicate their invariant relationships to experience characterizes what we may call the modern approach.

Modernism in physics, for example, can be illustrated by the prevailing belief, up through the beginning of the twentieth century, that objects exist in a fixed Euclidean space and interact in strict accordance with Newton's laws. Measurement was a matter of characterizing properties of objects such as their mass and velocity—with uncertainty to be sure but only from the imperfections of our measuring devices. The variables were the universe's; the distance between our knowledge and the truth was quantified by a standard error of measurement and shrank toward zero as we fine-tuned our models and improved our instruments.

In law the essence of modernism is the idea that "there is a 'real' world of legal system 'out there,' perfected, formed, complete and coherent, waiting to be discovered by theory" (Minda, 1995:224). The source was debated, to be sure: Dean Christopher Columbus Langdell (in 1871) maintained that careful study of cases should reveal the underlying axioms of justice, from which "the law" in its entirety follows logically. Oliver Wendell Holmes argued pragmatically that "law and its institutions evolved from views of public policy, social context, history, and experience" (Minda, 1995:18) and that its application always relies on judgments about its role in society.

In educational and psychological testing, modernism corresponds to the pursuit of models and methods that characterize people through common variables, as evidenced by common observations—under the conceit that there are objectively correct ways of doing so. The source of these models and variables has been debated over the years along logical versus pragmatic lines analogous to the Langdell versus Holmes stances. Witness on the one hand, factor analytic research programs that seek to "discover" the nature of intelligence and personality (e.g., Spearman, 1927; Thurstone, 1947) and, on the other, painstaking consensus-building procedures for assembling item pools to "measure achievement" in subject domains (e.g., Lindquist, 1951). These distinct branches within modern test theory correspond to the trait and behaviorist psychological perspectives. Under both perspectives, care is taken (1) to define, from the assessor's point of view, contexts in which to observe students; (2) to specify, from the assessor's perspective, the ways in which students' behavior will be summarized; and (3) to delineate the operations through which the assessor can draw inferences, within the assessor's frame of reference.

Postmodernism

> In jurisprudence, postmodernism signals the movement away from "Rule of Law" thinking based on the belief in one true "Rule of Law," one fixed "pattern," set of "patterns," or generalized theory of jurisprudence. . . . As developed in linguistics, literary theory, art, and architecture, postmodernism is also a style that signals the end of an era, the passing of the modern age . . . describing what happens when one rejects the epistemological foundations of modernity. (Minda, 1995:224)

> Wittgenstein's view of language is that all of our language has meaning only within the language games and "forms of life" in which they are embedded. One must understand the use, the context, the activity, the purpose, the game which is being played. . . . (Minda, 1995:239)

The notion of discourse plays a central role in postmodernism. Language generates our "universe of discourse": the kinds of things we can talk about and the particular things we can say; what we construe as problems, how we attempt to solve them, and how we evaluate our success. But what is the source of words and concepts? Postmoderns claim that the commonsense idea that meanings of words reside "in" language is fundamentally misguided. For them, language constructs, rather than reflects, the meaning of things and events in the world (Minda, 1995:239).

Relativity and the quantum revolution shattered the belief that Newtonian and Euclidean models were the correct ultimate description of the universe. Ironically, improved instrumentation devised to finalize the modern research program revealed that its fundamental models were not in fact the universe's. Mathematical descriptions of observations departed increasingly from such intuitive notions as simultaneity and definitive locations of persistent entities. Just as ironically, while we obtain better accuracy in modeling phenomena and more power to solve applied problems than the "modern" physicists of the nineteenth century dreamed, we feel farther away from ultimate understanding. The universe is not only stranger than we imagine, mused the mathematician J.B.S. Haldane, it is stranger than we *can* imagine!

Just as relativity and quantum mechanics gave rise to postmodern physics, Minda noted several diverse movements that provoked a postmodern era in law in the 1980s: law and economics, critical legal studies, feminist legal theory, law and literature, and critical race theory. Cognitive psychology was the analogous shock to educational assessment—in particular, recognition of the crucial roles of students' perspectives in learning and of the social settings in which learning takes place. Snow and Lohman (1989:317) put it this way:

> Summary test scores, and factors based on them, have often been thought of as "signs" indicating the presence of underlying, latent traits. . . . An alternative interpretation of test scores as samples of cognitive processes and contents, and of correlations as indicating the similarity or overlap of this sampling, is equally justifiable and could be theoretically more useful. . . . Whatever their practical value as summaries, for selection, classification, certification, or program evaluation, the cognitive psychological view is that such interpretations no longer suffice as scientific explanations of aptitude and achievement constructs.

Neopragmatic Postmodernism

> Some postmodernists have adopted a *neopragmatic* outlook as an antidote to the postmodern condition. These postmodern critics are skeptical of the truth claims of modern theory, but they have not given up on theory. On the contrary, they believe that theory can have utility when used as a tool for the empirical investigation of problems. . . . Its practitioners accept the postmodern view that truth and knowledge are culturally and linguistically conditioned. On the other hand, neopragmatist practice is unlike . . . what some theorists call *poststructuralist* criticism because it is less concerned with exposing the contradictions of modern conceptual and normative thought than revealing instrumental, empirical, and epidemiological solutions for the problem at hand. (Minda, 1995:229-230)

Minda distinguishes "neopragmatic" postmodernists from "ironic" postmodernists, the latter of which "embrace the predicaments and paradoxes of the current intellectual condition in order to better understand the world of legal, social, and philosophical thought, and they attempt to bring out the irony of the experience of living in a postmodern world" (1995:4-5). In legal theory "the ironists attempt to facilitate the crisis and fragmentation of modern theory by employing postmodern criticism to 'displace, decenter, and weaken' central concepts of modern legal Western thought" (1995:230). In the fine arts, ironic postmodernism is rather de rigueur. Physics and, by extension, engineering demand a neopragmatic stance. Models and variables may indeed be our creations rather than nature's, and they are ever subject to alternatives and revisions—but we must in some way accommodate the constraints nature imposes upon us as we struggle with the challenges we confront. And if there is a job to do, languages, models, and conceptual frameworks are what we have to work with.

Like law, educational assessment lies somewhere between literature and physics. Cognitive research reveals recurrent patterns in the ways people learn and solve problems, yet what is important to learn and the conditions under which it will be learned are largely socially determined. "Neopragmatic postmodern test theory" explores the potential of using methodological and inferential tools that originated in a modern perspective to support learning in ways conceived in a postmodern perspective.

MODERN TEST THEORY

Technical Considerations

"Legal modernism also . . . is based on an understanding of language that assumes that words and conceptual ideas are capable of objectively capturing the meaning of events the law seeks to describe and control" (Minda, 1995:6).

Most familiar practices of educational assessment can be traced to the first third of the twentieth century. Their forms were shaped by constraints on gathering and handling data in that era and by purposes conceived under then-current beliefs about learning and schooling. A paradigm of mental measurement analogous to classical (read "modern") physical measurement developed, and the tools of test theory evolved to guide applied work within this setting—designing tests, characterizing their evidential value, and evaluating how well they achieved their intended purposes. The targets of inference are aspects of students' learning, characterized as numbers on a continuum, upon which evaluations and decisions would be based if they were known with certainty.

In his 1961 article "Measurement of learning and mental abilities," Harold Gulliksen (1961:9) characterized the central problem of test theory as "the relation between the *ability* of the individual and his *observed score*." Referring explicitly to Plato's cave, he said "the problem is how to make the most effective use of these shadows (the observed test scores) in order to determine the nature of reality (ability) which we can only know through these shadows." The purposes of test theory, in this view, are to guide the construction of assessment elements and events (i.e., domains of test items and test conditions) and to structure inference from students' behavior in the resulting situations. The modernist underpinnings of the enterprise are reflected in a quotation from Gulliksen's (1961:101-102) review of test theory on the occasion of the twenty-fifth anniversary of the Psychometric Society, concerning the search for the "right" item-response-theory models:

> An attempt to develop a consistent theory tying test scores to the abilities measured is typified by Lord's (1952) recent work . . . in which he formulated at least five different theories of the relationship between test scores and abilities, and showed how it was possible to test certain ones of these. It is to be hoped that during the next 10 or 20 years a number of these tests will be carried out so that we will have not five different theories of the relationship between ability and test score and various possible trace lines, but we will be able to say that, for certain

specified tests constructed in this way, here is the relationship between the score and the ability measured, and this is the appropriate trace line to use.

Social Considerations

"Neopragmatists believe that theory merely establishes the rules for playing a particular language game" (Minda, 1995:236).

Although the physical measurement analogue connotes a certain objectivity and detachment, assessment based on the modernist approach nevertheless shapes, and is shaped by, social considerations. It structures conversations about learning in several ways:

• *Communication of expectations.* In and of themselves, domains of tasks and modes of testing convey, to students, teachers, and the public at large, what is important for students to learn and to accomplish.

• *Communication of results.* Once a domain of tasks and conditions of observation have been specified, a score and an accompanying measure of precision give a parsimonious summary of a student's behavior in the prescribed contexts that is easily transmitted across time and place.

• *Credibility of results.* Test scores earn credibility beyond the immediate circumstances of the assessment if the data have been verifiably gathered under prescribed conditions.

That traditional assessment procedures serve these purposes is quite independent of the fact that they evolved under the mental measurement paradigm. Any procedures that might rise in their stead to assess and communicate students' learning would, in some way, need to address the same functions.

PROGENITORS OF CHANGE

The transition from the old to the 'new' jurisprudence began with the breakdown of the core beliefs and theories that served to define modern jurisprudence. The breakdown is partly a manifestation of the proliferation of new jurisprudential discourses and new movements in legal thought. (Minda, 1995:243)

I claimed earlier that developments in the psychology of learning and cognition brought about a postmodern era in assessment, and I shall say more about that later. These developments do indeed lay the groundwork for new developments in assessment, but I do not believe they were sufficient in and of themselves to change the field. Had modern testing seen satisfactory progress in its research agenda, there would have been less impetus for change. But in assessment, as in physics, improved methodology and inferential methods led away from, rather than toward, the anticipated solutions.

Developments in Methodology

"There is a rising sentiment in the legal academy that modern legal theory has failed to sustain the modernists' hopes for social progress" (Minda, 1995:248).

Twenty-five years after Gulliksen's article, Charles Lewis observed that "much of the recent progress in test theory has been made by treating the study of the relationship between responses to a set of test items and a hypothesized trait (or traits) of an individual as a problem of statistical inference" (Lewis, 1986). New modeling and inferential techniques included item response theory, generalizability theory (Cronbach et al., 1972), structural equations modeling (e.g., Jöreskog and Sörbom, 1979), and the application of more powerful estimation methods from the statistical literature (e.g., Bock and Aitkin, 1981). They provided solutions to previously intractable problems such as tailoring tests to individual examinees and sorting out relationships in patterns of achievement test scores in hierarchical schooling systems.

These developments make for more efficient gathering of evidence and more powerful forms of argumentation for addressing questions that could be framed within the universe of discourse of modern test theory. But by requiring analysts to more clearly explicate their targets of inference and how observations provided evidence about them, these advances in modern test theory began to reveal important problems that lie beyond the paradigm's reach. The following two examples illustrate the point:

• How can we measure change, or can we? Through the use of standard test theory, evidence can be characterized and brought to bear on inferences about students' overall proficiency in behavioral domains, for determining students' levels of proficiency, comparing them with others or with a standard, or gauging changes from one point in time to another. Cronbach and Furby (1970:76) cautioned that characterizations about the nature of this proficiency or how it develops fall largely outside the paradigm's universe of discourse:

> Even when [test scores] X and Y are determined by the same operation [e.g., a true-score or item-response-theory model for a specified domain of tasks], they often do not represent the same psychological processes. At different stages of practice or development different processes contribute to the performance of a task. Nor is this merely a matter of increased complexity; some processes drop out, some remain but contribute nothing to individual differences within an age group, some are replaced by qualitatively different processes.

• *Differential item functioning (DIF)*. Classical test theory took test scores at face value, treating all response patterns with the same total score as identical. Item response theory explicated the conditions that would have to hold among patterns of item responses for total scores to capture all nonrandom variations among students. Essentially, the same expectation of success on each given task would have to hold for all students at a given true-score level, regardless of item content or students' background characteristics. Differential-item-functioning techniques devised to check these conditions often found that they failed in achievement tests—most importantly, in ways that related to curriculum (e.g., Miller and Linn, 1988) and solution strategies (e.g., Birenbaum and Tatsuoka, 1983; French, 1965). Because what is hard and what is easy is not universal—they depend, not surprisingly, on what and how students have been studying—summary scores inevitably fail to characterize some aspects of students' knowledge and progress.

Developments in Psychology

Cronbach and Furby's comments on measuring change presaged a growing awareness that domain-referenced assessment methodologies, including item response theory, were simply not rich enough to support discourse about the nature and progress of students' learning. In assessment, as in physics, however, merely recognizing inadequacies in a paradigm is not sufficient for change. Newton and Huygens debated the contradictory wave- and particle-like properties of light as early as the seventeenth century. Paradigms are not displaced by data, the saying goes; paradigms are displaced only by other paradigms. Conceptions of learning that ground a broader universe of discourse for assessment are emerging from cognitive and educational psychology. The following paragraphs review some key insights into the ways people acquire and use knowledge and skills. Each, it will be noted, accents the uniquely personal and socially conditioned nature of learning.

• *Mental models/schema theory.* A "mental model" or "schema" is a pattern of recurring relationships—anything from what happens at birthday parties to how to figure out unit prices to how to carry out conversations—with variables that correspond to particular ways the pattern can occur. Some schemas are informal and intuitive; others we learn in part formally and explicitly. David Rumelhart (1980:55) claims that schemas

> play a central role in all our reasoning processes. . . . Once we can "understand" the situation by encoding it in terms of a relatively rich set of schemata, the conceptual constraints of the schemata can be brought into play and the problem readily solved.

No cognition is purely passive or data driven; we always construct meaning in terms of knowledge structures. Learning sometimes means adding bits to existing structures; sometimes it involves generalizing or connecting schemas; other times it involves abandoning important parts of schemas and replacing them by qualitatively different structures.

• *How expertise develops.* While experts in various fields of learning generally command more facts and concepts than novices, the real distinction lies in their ways of viewing phenomena and representing and approaching problems (e.g., Chi et al., 1981). Experts learn to work from what

Greeno (1989) calls the "generative principles of the domain," and they automatize recurring procedures (they "compile knowledge") so that they can devote their attention to novel aspects of problems. Increasing "metacognitive skills" also mark developing expertise: self-awareness in using models and skill and flexibility in how to construct them, modify them, and adapt them to problems.

• *Situated learning.* Assessment has focused on aspects of learning that are characterized insofar as possible as properties of individual students. Yet the nature of the knowledge we construct is conditioned and constrained by technologies, information resources, and social situations as we learn about tools, physical and conceptual, and how and when to use them. For example, reading comprehension depends on one's competence in recognizing words and parsing syntactic structures, but it also depends as much on am understanding of the context and substance of what the message is about. Students who have similar competences with structural aspects of language can take vastly different meanings away from the same text, depending on their experience with the phenomena in question. These findings, along with those discussed above, argue that learning is more richly characterized in terms of the student's breadth and configurations of connections across social and substantive contexts than by success in a given domain of tasks—even though such success occurs only by virtue of those connections.

These cross-cutting generalizations should not obscure the fact that cognitive psychology is a fractured, often fractious, field. Competing claims of rival researchers differ from one another as much as all differ from the trait and behaviorist perspectives. This is largely because different researchers are exploring different ranges of behavior, acquired and used under different circumstances. Birnbaum (1991:65) suggests:

> Problem-solving depends on the manipulation of relatively fragmented and mutually inconsistent *microtheories*—each perhaps internally consistent, and each constituting a valid way of looking at a problem: "This will allow us to say, for example, that some [set of beliefs] is more appropriate than some [other set of beliefs] when confronted with problems of diagnosing bacterial infections. Scientists are used to having different—even contradictory—theories to explain reality. . . . Each is useful in certain circumstances." (Nilsson, 1991:45)

In assessment, as in law, the neopragmatic postmodernist welcomes all these lines of research as potentially useful tools for solving different practical problems; that is to say:

> For postmodern legal scholars, choosing the "best" answer for legal problems requires "tactical" judgments and questions regarding the values of the decision maker much more than a quest for a so-called "best" argument. One consequence of this has been the realization that there exists a multiplicity of answers for law's many problems. (Minda, 1995:252)

Rapprochement

Good teachers have always relied on a wider array of means to learn about how the students in their classes are doing and to help plan further learning. Alongside the tests and quizzes they design and score under the mental measurement paradigm, they also use evidence from projects, work in class, conversations with and among students, and the like—all combined with additional information about the students, the schooling context, and what the students are working on. Teachers call these "informal" assessments, in contrast with the "formal" assessments typified by large-scale standardized tests.

The stark contrast between formal and informal assessment arises because to understand students' learning and further guide it, teachers need information intimately connected with what their students are working on, and they interpret this evidence in light of everything else they know about their students and their instruction. The power of informal assessment resides in these connections. Good teachers implicitly exploit the principles of cognitive psychology, broadening the universe of discourse to encompass local information and address the local problem at hand. Yet precisely because informal asessments are thus individuated, neither their rationale or their results is easily communicated beyond the classroom. Standardized tests do communicate efficiently across time and place—but by so constraining the universe of discourse that the messages often have little direct utility in the classroom.

The challenge now facing neopragmatic postmodern test theory is to devise assessments that, in various ways, incorporate and balance the strengths of formal and informal assessments by capitalizing on an array of methodological, technological, and conceptual developments.

POSTMODERN TEST THEORY

"Postmodern legal critics employ local, small-scale problem-solving strategies to raise new questions about the relation of law, politics and culture. They offer a new interpretive aesthetic for reconceptualizing the practice of legal interpretation" (Minda, 1995:3).

Cognitive psychology challenges the adequacy of the "one-size-fits-all" presumption of standard assessment, which defines the target of inference in terms of an assessor-specified domain of tasks, to be administered, scored, and interpreted in the same way for all students. The door has been opened to alternative ways to characterize students' proficiency and acquire evidence about it—ways that may involve observing students in different situations, interpreting their actions in light of additional information about them, or triangulating across context and situation, as may be required for one's purpose (Moss, 1996).

Moss (1994) and Delandshere and Petrosky (1994) offer postmodern insights into assessment from a less structural perspective than mine, criticizing test theory as it is conceived from a modernist point of view. I am interested in the utility of model-based inference in assessment, as *re*conceived from a postmodernist point of view. I submit that concepts from psychology and inferential tools from model-based reasoning can support assessment practice as more broadly conceived—just as Newton's laws still guide bridge design, quantum mechanics and relativity theory notwithstanding. The essential elements of the approach are (1) understanding the important concepts and relationships in the learning area in order to know the aspects of students we need to talk about in the universe of discourse our assessment will generate and (2) determining what one needs to observe and how it depends on students' understandings, so as to structure assessment settings and tasks that will provide evidence about the above-mentioned aspects of students' understandings. Here is an example from a project I have been working on recently, concerning advanced placement (AP) studio art portfolios.

Viewed only as measurement, the AP studio art portfolio program would be a disaster. Students spend hundreds of hours creating the portfolios they submit for scoring at the end of the year, and raters who are art educators and teachers spend hundreds of hours evaluating the work—all to produce reliability coefficients about the same as those of 90-minute multiple-choice tests. The situation brightens when the program is viewed as a framework for evidence about skills and knowledge, around which teachers build art courses with wide latitude for topics, media, and projects. A common understanding of what is valued and how it is evaluated in the central scoring emerges through teacher workshops, talked-through examples with actual portfolios, and continual discussions about how to cast and apply rating rubrics to diverse submissions. Meaning emerges through countless conversations across hundreds of classrooms, each individual but with some common concepts and shared examples of their use—each enrichened and individuated locally in a way that grounds instruction and local evaluations but with a common core that grounds more abbreviated program-wide evaluations. This is, at heart, a social phenomenon, not a measurement phenomenon. Carol Myford and I have found an item-response-theory measurement model for ratings valuable, nevertheless, to illuminate how raters use evaluative criteria and to characterize uncertainty about students' scores (Myford and Mislevy, 1995). We do not use the model to "gauge the accuracy of a measuring instrument." We use it to survey patterns of similarity and variation, of agreement and disagreement, among tens of thousands of virtual dialogues among students, raters, and teachers, through their portfolios—to the end of discovering sources of misunderstanding and cross talk that can frustrate the conversations.

Model-based reasoning is useful not so much for characterizing the unique essence of a phenomenon but as a tool of discourse—for organizing our thinking, for marshaling and interpreting evidence, and for communicating our inferences and their grounding to others. The discipline that model-based reasoning demands even benefits us when we don't believe the models are true: it is easier to notice phenomena that don't accord with the patterns we expect to see and, therefore, to revise our thinking. A skeptical attitude about models in assessment makes our uses of them more flexible, more powerful, and, ultimately, more effective at meeting and fulfilling the aims of education than they would be if we believed that they accurately captured the totality of the phenomenon.

From a modernist perspective, Lord Kelvin declared at the turn of the century that "when you can measure what you are speaking about, and express it in numbers, you know something about it; but when you cannot measure it, when you cannot express it in numbers, your knowledge is of a meager and unsatisfactory kind." Measurement, in his eyes, was a one-off representation of truth. From a postmodern perspective, even if you can measure, your knowledge is still meager in a fundamental sense but at least you have a practicable framework for discourse—for structuring action, for communicating your observations and your reasoning, for struggling with practical problems, for surprising yourself in ways that lead to further understanding. Lord Kelvin's quote is a modernist scientific version of Yogi Berra's "it ain't over 'til it's over." The postmodern response is Jesse Jackson's "and even then it ain't over."

SOME IMPLICATIONS OF A POSTMODERN PERSPECTIVE

Neopragmatists thus attempt to explain how one can do theoretical work without rejecting all pretenses of foundational knowledge. Neopragmatists argue that the theorists must take a situated stance in their scholarship and adopt an instrumental approach to theory. Whatever works in context becomes the standard for their theoretical investigation and judgment. . . . When applied to legal studies, neopragmatism forms the academic perspective of scholars who reject all foundational claims of legal theory but remain committed to the view that legal theory can be useful for solving legal problems. . . . Neopragmatists thus believe in and are committed to the Enlightenment idea of progress, even while they resist using the modernist's framework. (Minda, 1995:230)

In the remainder of the main body of the paper, I offer comments from a neopragmatic postmodern perspective on enhancing familiar kinds of assessment, even while moving our interpretational perspective beyond its modernist roots. As an example, I address the question of the degree to which "adult literacy," an essential element of workplace skill, can be defined and gauged across literacy training programs.

Progress Within Modern Test Theory

Familiar forms of assessment were shaped by constraints on how data could be gathered, stored, transmitted, and analyzed. Logistical and economic pressures limited the large-scale use of essays and interviews that required human interpretation, thus favoring objective-response tasks over more constructive and sustained tasks. It was not possible to store or share ephemeral performances in order to develop common standards or to verify that ratings were fair. These constraints are being eased by technological developments—computers, video-taping and audiotaping, electronic communication, mass storage, and access to resources. Some new possibilities appear even within the traditional mental mea-surement paradigm. I will mention some briefly but then argue that technology alone will not break through the essential inferential barriers of the modernist test theory perspective:

- *New kinds of tasks and scoring.* Computers can present students with tasks that are interactive (e.g., simulated experiments), dynamic (e.g., medical treatment problems in which simulated patients' conditions change over time), constructive (e.g., a stimulated construction site onto which elements must be moved to meet client's needs), and less tightly structured (e.g., a word problem that is to be approached in many ways). Some scoring can be also done automati-cally, including for these examples.
- *Distributed testing and scoring.* Students' responses to computerized tasks can now be captured and electronically transmitted. Performances can be videotaped and audiotaped. Constructed paper-and-pencil responses and artwork can be scanned. Students can thus be assessed in remote places and at different times, and raters can evaluate their performances in remote places and at different times. Students in school consortiums can share work on a common project, interacting with, and receiving feedback from, teachers and students across the nation.
- *"Replayability"* (Frederiksen and Sheingold, 1994). Beside easing con-straints on time and location, capturing performances helps address the rater-agreement problems that troubled Horace Mann more than a century ago. Perfor-mances can now be seen, discussed, and evaluated by as many people, in as many times and places, as desired. Now that we are no longer limited to the evaluations of raters present at the original performance, we can have broader and more inter-connected scoring of individual students and use exemplars to establish shared expectations and standards of evaluation, over time and across distance, among raters, teachers, and students.

Despite technology and efficient statistical models, the objective of charac-terizing students' proficiency must remain poorly met if one is constrained to one-size-fits-all data and to ignorance of contextual and educational background factors. The more examinees differ as to relevant contextual and experiential factors, the more likely it is that each task in a complex and context-rich domain will consume considerable time and costs without providing much information about how students would fare on other tasks—the Shavelson et al. (1992) "low generalizability" problem (also see Linn, 1993). Each individual task may pro-vide copious information for some inferences—but not for inferences about the usual target, domain-true score. The same complex task can be invaluable in an assessment linked with instruction and grounded in context yet worthless in a broadly cast survey because it is trivial, unapproachable, or incomprehensible to most students.

Beyond Modern Test Theory

> Postmodernism thus challenges legal thinkers to reconsider their most basic understanding of the nature of law and politics—their belief in an objective and autonomous law. Postmoderns argue that decision making according to rule is not possible, because rules are dependent upon language, and language is socially and culturally constructed and hence incapable of directing decision makers to make consistent and objective choices. Objectivity is possible only if agreement or consensus about different interpretive practices can be reached. (Minda, 1995:245)

Standards of content and performance are a topic of intense current interest. I have argued that limited sets of common assessment tasks, scored and interpreted in common ways that ignore context, cannot by their nature tell us all we would like to know about students' learning. They may tell us something worth knowing, especially if the inferences and actions based on them do take context into account (Messick, 1989). As noted in the preceding section, technology is broadening the span and efficiency of such assessment. And with such assessment it is possible to gauge the levels of performance of individual students and groups of students. The real challenge, it seems, is to extend the notion of standards beyond the confines of the modernist perspective: Is it possible to retain the relevance and connectedness traditionally associated with informal assessment yet simultaneously serve the communicative and credibility-based functions traditionally associated with formal assessment?

The AP studio art experience suggests that the answer is yes. Learning there is individuated, but a shared conception of the nature of intended learning, developed through examples and feedback, makes it possible to interpret work in a common framework. Such a structure appears necessary if assessments with constructive and individuated data, such as portfolios and exhibitions (e.g., Wiggins, 1989), are to span time and distance.

Common meaning is necessary for credibility, but it is not sufficient. Why should anyone trust an interpreted evaluation of a performance from a distant time and place? Standardized test results gain a measure of credibility from their prescribed procedures; these are established "rules of the game," which, if followed, circumscribe the interpretation of the results. Even though the results don't tell about everything that is important, parents and boards of education can ask questions and verify procedures in order to spot invalidating practices. But the more individuated an assessment is, the more difficult it becomes to establish credibility.

For example, in some ways teachers are in the best position to evaluate students' work, by virtue of their knowledge about context and situation. Their contextualized evaluations are unquestionably basic for guiding classroom learning. Can their evaluations be used for high-stakes purposes beyond the classroom, in light of their vested interest in their students' success and the typically wide variation in their interpretations of performance? As noted above, a common framework for interpretation is required first. The validity of mappings of performances into that framework can be addressed by mechanisms such as audits, cross evaluation across schools, and triangulation of types of evidence (Resnick, 1994). Technology can play an enabling role, through replayability, mass storage, and electronic communication. Statistical modeling can play a quality assurance role, through the analysis of ratings of multiply-scored work, as discussed above in connection with AP studio art.

An Example: Adult Literacy Assessment

As defined by the National Literacy Act of 1991, literacy involves "an individual's ability to read, write, and speak in English, compute, and solve problems at levels of proficiency necessary to function on the job and in society, to achieve one's goals, and to develop one's knowledge and potential." The act requires state education agencies to "gather and analyze data—including standardized test data—on the effectiveness of State-administered adult education programs, services, and activities, to determine the extent to which the State's adult education programs are achieving the goals in the state plan" [to enhance levels of adult literacy and improve the quality of adult education services] (*Federal Register,* 1992). These federal evaluation requirements have prompted interest in identifying standardized tests and methodologies that are appropriate for assessing the effectiveness of adult education programs and for determining the feasibility of linking such tests in order to provide national trend data on program effectiveness (Pelavin Associates, 1994).

But the diversity of both the objectives and the participants served by adult education programs reflects a broad and multidimensional definition of literacy. Accordingly, adult education programs vary considerably with respect to the nature and level of skills they emphasize and with respect to the kinds of students with whom they work. Some strongly resemble and largely replace the academic reading experience that high schools supply, in order to help dropouts obtain General Education Development certificates. Others help immigrants and others who are literate in languages other than English to speak, read, and write in English. Still others work with adults who are literate, if not skilled, from the perspective of traditional schooling, in order to develop more specific skills for use in the workplace. Moreover, these diverse programs use tests for a broad variety of diagnostic, instructional, and evaluative purposes. Both the nature of the instruction and the purpose of testing determine the kinds of tests that will be appropriate.

Is it possible to link results from these varied tests, across the diverse programs, to secure a common metric for evaluating program effects and tracking trends over time? Writing on the prospect of calibrating disparate tests to common national standards, Andrew Porter (1991:35) wrote,

> If this practice of separate assessments continues, can the results be somehow equated so that results on one can also be stated in terms of results on the other? There are those who place great faith in the ability of statisticians to equate tests, but that faith is largely unjustified. Equating can be done only when tests measure the same thing.

Professor Porter's skepticism is justified. We are perhaps too familiar with correspondence tables that give exchangeable scores for alternate forms of standardized tests. But they work only because the alternate forms were constructed to meet the same tight specifications; equating studies and statistical formulas merely put into usable form the evidentiary relationships that were built into the tests (see Linn, 1993, and Mislevy, 1993, for definitions, concepts, and approaches that have been developed to link educational tests for various purposes).

Statistical procedures neither create nor determine relationships among test scores. Rather, the way that tests are constructed and administered and the ways that the skills they tap relate to the people to whom they are administered determine the nature of the potential relationships that exist in evidence that scores from the various tests convey. Much progress has been made recently with statistical machinery for this purpose, with power beyond the expectations of educational measurement researchers a generation or two ago. However, we now recognize the objective of building once-and-for-all correspondence tables as a chimera—it is not simply because we lack the tools to answer the question but because the question itself is vacuous. Statistical procedures, properly employed, can be used to explicate the relationships that do exist in various times and places and harness the information they do convey for various purposes. Perhaps more importantly, they help us understand what information different tests do not, indeed cannot, convey for those purposes.

Thus, the first two conclusions listed below, about what can be expected from applying statistical linking procedures to adult literacy tests, are negative. They repudiate a naive modernist goal of rectifying various indicators of a common true variable, when those indicators have evolved to serve different purposes in different contexts, gathering qualitatively different kinds of information.

- *No single score can give a full picture of the range of skills that are important to all the different students in different adult literacy programs.*
- *No statistical machinery can translate the results of any two arbitrarily selected adult literacy tests so that they provide interchangeable information about all relevant questions about student competencies and program effectiveness.*

What *is* possible? Three less ambitious, but more realistic, affirmative contingencies, each employing modernist statistical techniques from a neopragmatic postmodernist perspective. All require the prerequisite realization that no test scores can capture the full range of evidence about students' developing proficiencies within their courses, nor can they convey all that is needed to determine how well students are progressing toward their own objectives. This understood, here are some options for dealing with such information as there is in literacy test scores, when different literacy programs must use different tests in accordance with their differing goals and instruction:

• *Comparing directly the levels of performance across literacy programs in terms of common indicators of performance on a market basket of consensually defined tasks in standard conditions.* Some aspects of competence, and assessment contexts for gathering evidence about them, will be considered useful by a wide range of programs, and components of an assessment system can solicit information about them in much the same way for all. However, these "universal" assessments—and in particular pre-post comparisons with such assessments—provide seriously incomplete information to evaluate the effectiveness of programs, to the extent that their focus does not match the programs' objectives (to say nothing of the *students'* objectives!).

• *Estimating levels of performance of groups or individuals within clusters of literacy programs with similar objectives—possibly in quite different ways in different clusters—at the levels of accuracy demanded by purposes within clusters, with shared assessments focused on those objectives.* These components of programs' assessments might gather evidence for different purposes, types of students, or levels of proficiency, to complement information gathered by "universal" components.

• *Making projections about how students from one program might have performed on the assessment of another.* When students can be administered portions of different clusters' assessments under conditions similar to those in which they are used operationally, the joint distribution of results on those assessments can be estimated. These studies are restricted as to time, place, program, and population, however. The more the assessments differ as to their form, content, and context, the more uncertainty is associated with the projections, the more they can be expected to vary with students' background and educational characteristics, the more they can shift over time, and the more comparisons of program effects become untrustworthy.

CONCLUSION

It is a critical time for jurisprudential studies in America. It is a time for self-reflection and reevaluation of methodological and theoretical legacies in the law. At stake is not only the status of modern jurisprudence, but also the validity of the Rule of Law itself. In the current era of academic diversity and disagreement, the time has come to seriously consider the transformative changes now unfolding in American legal thought. The challenge for the next century will certainly involve new ways of understanding how the legal system can preserve the authority of the Rule of Law while responding to the different perspectives and interests of multicultural communities. It is without a doubt an anxious and exciting time for jurisprudence. . . .

What was once understood as the mainstream of modern view has broken into a diverse body of jurisprudential theories and perspectives. . . . No matter how troubling it may be, the landscape of the postmodern now surrounds us. It simultaneously delimits us and opens our horizons. It's our problem and our hope. (Minda, 1995:256-257)

Ironist critics of educational assessment reject the modernist notion that the "truth" about a student's understanding or a program's effect lies but a simple step away from our ken, to be spanned by observations with standard, context-free measuring instruments and unambiguous statistical analysis of the results. But to further reject any use of these models and information-gathering tools just because they arose under the discarded epistemology is to forgo decades of experience about some ways to structure and communicate observations about students' learning. Educators fear that wholesale abandonment of familiar assessment methodology strips away tools that help them address these facets of their task. Believing these ways of structuring discourse hold *no* value is as wrong as believing that they *alone* hold value. I hear parents and teachers say that we "should not throw the baby out with the bath water." But how to tell which is which?

My answer (a neopragmatic postmodernist answer, as it turns out) is this: Models, principles, and conceptual frameworks are practicable tools—not for discovering a singular truth but for structuring our discourse about students, so that we may better support their learning, and for learning about expected and unexpected outcomes of our efforts, so that we may continually improve them. Understandings of students' learning and programs' effects are enriched by multiple perspectives and diverse sources of evidence, some new or previously neglected but others with familiar (albeit reconceived) forms. Postmodern architects play with ironies in design, advancing alternative sensibilities and forgotten voices—but they had better design buildings that are livable and safe. Fundamental constraints and fundamental responsibilities persist. And as long as we in education purport to help other people's children learn, at other people's expense, we bear the duty of gaining and using as broad an understanding as we can to guide our actions and of conveying our reasoning and results as clearly as we can to those to whom we are responsible.

ACKNOWLEDGMENTS

I am indebted to Bob Linn and Barbara Storms for their thoughtful comments on an earlier version.

REFERENCES

Birenbaum, M., and K.K. Tatsuoka
 1983   The effect of a scoring system based on the algorithm underlying the students'
         response patterns on the dimensionality of achievement test data of the problem
         solving type. *Journal of Educational Measurement* 20:17-26.

Birnbaum, L.
 1991   Rigor mortis: A response to Nilsson's "Logic and artificial intelligence." *Artificial Intelligence* 47:57-77.

Bock, R.D., and M. Aitkin
 1981   Marginal maximum likelihood estimation of item parameters: An application of an EM-algorithm. *Psychometrika* 46:443-459.

Chi, M.T.H., P. Feltovich, and R. Glaser
 1981   Categorization and representation of physics problems by experts and novices. *Cognitive Science* 5:121-152.

Cronbach, L.J., and L. Furby
 1970   How should we measure "change"—Or should we? *Psychological Bulletin* 74:68-80.

Cronbach, L.J., G.C. Gleser, H. Nanda, and N. Rajaratnam
 1972   *The Dependability of Behavioral Measurements: Theory of Generalizability for Scores and Profiles.* New York: Wiley.

Delandshere, G., and A.R. Petrosky
 1994   Capturing teachers' knowledge: Performance assessment (a) and poststructural epistemology, (b) from a post-structuralist perspective, (c) and post-structuralism, (d) one of the above. *Educational Researcher* 23(5):11-18.

Frederiksen, J.R., and K. Sheingold
 1994   *Linking Assessment with Reform: Technologies that Support Conversations About Student Work* Princeton, NJ: Center for Performance Assessment, Educational Testing Service.

French, J.W.
 1965   The relationship of problem-solving styles to the factor composition of tests. *Educational and Psychological Measurement* 25:9-28.

Greeno, J.G.
 1989   A perspective on thinking. *American Psychologist* 44:134-141.

Gulliksen, H.
 1961   Measurement of learning and mental abilities. *Psychometrika* 26:93-107.

Jöreskog, K.G., and D. Sörbom
 1979   *Advances in Factor Analysis and Structural Equation Models.* Cambridge, MA: Abt Books.

Lewis, C.
 1986   Test theory and *Psychometrika*: The past twenty-five years. *Psychometrika* 51:11-22.

Lindquist, E.F.
 1951   Preliminary considerations in objective test construction. Pp. 119-185 in *Educational Measurement*, E.F. Lindquist, ed. Washington, DC: American Council on Education.

Linn, R.L.
 1993   Educational assessment: Expanded expectations and challenges. *Educational Evaluation and Policy Analysis* 15:1-16.

Lord, F.M.
 1952   A theory of test scores. *Psychometrika Monograph* 17(4, Part 2):1-80.

Messick, S.
 1989   Validity. Pp. 13-103 in *Educational Measurement*, 3rd ed, R.L. Linn, ed. New York: American Council on Education/Macmillan.

Miller, M.D., and R.L. Linn
  1988   Invariance of item characteristic functions with variations in instructional coverage. *Journal of Educational Measurement* 25:205-219.
Minda, G.
  1995   *Postmodern Legal Movements.* New York: New York University Press.
Mislevy, R.J.
  1993   *Linking Educational Assessments: Concepts, Issues, Methods, and Prospects.* Princeton, NJ: Educational Testing Service.
Myford, C.M., and R.J. Mislevy
  1995   *Monitoring and Improving a Portfolio Assessment System.* Princeton, NJ: Center for Performance Assessment, Educational Testing Service.
Moss, P.
  1994   Can there be validity without reliability? *Educational Researcher* 23(2):5-12.
  1996   Enlarging the dialogue in educational measurement: Voices from interpretive research traditions. *Educational Researcher* 25(1):20-28.
Nilsson, N.J.
  1991   Logic and artificial intelligence. *Artificial Intelligence* 47:31-56.
Pelavin Associates
  1994   *Comparing Adult Education Tests: A Meeting of Experts.* Washington, DC: Pelavin Associates.
Porter, A.C.
  1991   Assessing national goals: Some measurement dilemmas. Pp. 21-42 in *The Assessment of National Goals. Proceedings of the 1990 ETS Invitational Conference,* T. Wardell, ed. Princeton, NJ: Educational Testing Service.
Resnick, L.
  1994   Performance puzzles. *American Journal of Education* 102(4):511-526.
Rumelhart, D.A.
  1980   Schemata: The building blocks of cognition. Pp. 33-58 in *Theoretical Issues in Reading Comprehension,* R. Spiro, B. Bruce, and W. Brewer, eds. Hillsdale, NJ: Lawrence Erlbaum Associates.
Shavelson, R.J., G.P. Baxter, and J. Pine
  1992   Performance assessments: Political rhetoric and measurement reality. *Educational Researcher* 21(4):22-27.
Snow, R.E., and D.F. Lohman
  1989   Implications of cognitive psychology for educational measurement. Pp. 263-331 in *Educational Measurement,* 3rd ed, R.L. Linn, ed. New York: American Council on Education/Macmillan.
Spearman, C.
  1927   *The Abilities of Man: Their Nature and Measurement.* New York: Macmillan.
Thurstone, L.L.
  1947   *Multiple-Factor Analysis.* Chicago: University of Chicago Press.
Wiggins, G.
  1989   A true test: Toward more authentic and equitable assessment. *Phi Delta Kappan* 70:703-713.

8

Legal Restrictions on Assessments

Dennis Parker

INTRODUCTION

The School-to-Work Opportunities Act (20 U.S.C.A. §6101 *et seq.* West Supp, 1995), creates a framework for cooperation among federal, state, and local governments and agencies, educational institutions, students, labor unions, employers, and other organizations committed to economic and community development in order to raise educational standards. The act is broad in scope and is designed to provide meaningful benefits to all parties involved.

At one level, the impetus for congressional action was the growing fear that the United States was falling further behind in the global marketplace at least in part because of a failure to properly educate its students: congressional findings included in the act stress the need for the development of a "comprehensive and coherent system" of education that would enable the nation to meet the challenge of increasing global competition and technological advances that seem to increase exponentially.[1]

At a less global level, state and local governments, educational and civic organizations, employers, and labor organizations would benefit by receiving the advantages of better-trained and more productive workers (20 U.S.C.A., §6102 (3), (5)).[2] The primary beneficiaries under the act, of course, are students who

---

[1]The congressional findings noted, with some concern, that 3,400,000 individuals in the United States have entered the work force who have not completed high school, are not enrolled in school, and are particularly unprepared to meet the specialized technical demands of the work force of the twenty-first century (20 U.S.C.A. §6101 (1)-(9)).

[2]Moreover, the act would provide seed funding for underwriting the initial costs of planning School-to-Work Opportunities systems to be maintained with other federal, state, and local resources (20 U.S.C.A. §6102 (4)).

would be offered the opportunity "to participate in a performance-based education and training program that will . . . (i) enable [them] to earn portable credentials; (ii) prepare [them] for first jobs in high-skill, high-wage careers; and (iii)
increase their opportunities for further education, including education in a 4-year
college or university" (20 U.S.C.A. §6102 (1)).

The act's intended consequences for the future of American students go beyond preparing them for entry-level positions or facilitating postsecondary education. Congress clearly intended long-term results to facilitate opportunity for
students throughout their working lives:

> The purposes of this Chapter are to facilitate the creation of a universal, high quality
> school-to-work transition system that enables youths in the United States to iden-
> tify and navigate paths to productive and progressively more rewarding roles in the
> workplace. . . . (20 U.S.C.A. §6102 (2))

For purposes of this paper, the most significant aspect of the breadth of the
act's scope is that it envisions having an impact on students who have thus far not
been reached by existing job training or education reform legislation; it would do
this by providing the means for including in its proposed vision people who had
historically been excluded from educational and economic opportunities. This
would be done by reaching out to school dropouts and low-achieving and dis-
abled youths (those who have traditionally been prime candidates for dropping
out). The act also seeks to include those whose lack of access to equal employment opportunity is due to discrimination in employment: "The purposes of this
chapter are . . . to increase opportunities for minorities, women, and individuals
with disabilities, by enabling individuals to prepare for careers that are not traditional for their race, gender, or disability (20 U.S.C.A. §6102 (13)).

Given the broad scope of the act's goals and its mandate to those seeking to
participate in the program it establishes, the success of the act will be judged in
large part by the degree to which the work force of the twenty-first century more
closely resembles the nation's population. Because the focus of the act is on
changing the content of American education and facilitating the transition from
schoolyard to workplace, assessment of student performance will assume even
greater importance. Although academic success has always had an impact on
later opportunities in life, the greater link between schools and the working world
that the act seeks to accomplish raises the stakes for all involved. Given the
potential impact of programs spawned by the act, it is particularly important that
very careful consideration be given to the way that programs are implemented.

Implicit in the discussion of raised educational standards and increased employment opportunities are questions about the methods by which students will
be evaluated and the effects that this evaluation process will have on determining
which students receive the opportunities envisioned in the act. Also implicit is
the issue of who will be responsible for shaping the curriculum that students
receive. The legislation is significant in that it redefines to some extent the role
of schools and the educational structure that supports them in determining what it

means to be educated. Whereas before the act, to use a commercial analogy that may be particularly appropriate under the circumstances, if it were asked who the primary "customer" for educational services is, the most common answer would undoubtedly have been "students." This is not to say that there was no concern for the ability of graduates to find meaningful employment. An unemployable graduate would certainly not be a satisfied customer. But the primary focus was the development of a well-rounded individual prepared for all aspects of life.[3]

The act, in essence, broadens the concept of "customer." By involving business more directly at the front end, the act essentially acknowledges that it, too, is a "customer" with an interest in the "product" of a graduate who is adequately prepared to meet the employment needs of businesses.

This paper will not address questions of the appropriateness of business involvement in the setting of educational agendas. However, it is important to recognize that one of the challenges presented by implementation of the School-to-Work Opportunities Act will arise from the fact that there is not a complete congruence of interests among all members of the educational partnership that the act creates.

The potential difference in interests, particularly between businesses and schools, will require extreme vigilance in order to assure that the program is implemented in an equitable manner. For the most part, the primary burden of this vigilance will and must fall on the schools, in large part because providing a comprehensive education is their ultimate responsibility but also because the schools would presumably not be driven by profit to the same degree as businesses.

Although educational institutions and schools may have somewhat different interests, both must consider the equity concerns raised by programs in which they are joint partners. It is essential that each partner recognize that each component part of a new program has a potential impact on the question of equal opportunity. This paper will focus on those components that relate to the question of assessment and credentialing.

---

[3]For example, in *Rose v. Council for Better Education, Inc.* (790 S.W. 2d 186, 212 (Ky. 1989)), the Supreme Court defined guidelines for determining if the state had fulfilled its constitutional obligation to provide an adequate education, stating that an educated child must possess "at least the seven following capabilities: (i) sufficient oral and written communication skills to enable students to function in a complex and rapidly changing civilization; (ii) sufficient knowledge of economic, social, and political systems to enable students to make informed choices; (iii) sufficient understanding of governmental processes to enable the student to understand the issues that affect his or her community, state and nation; (iv) sufficient self-knowledge and knowledge of his or her mental and physical wellness; (v) sufficient grounding in the arts to enable each student to appreciate his or her cultural and historical heritage; (vi) sufficient training or preparation for advanced training in either academic or vocational fields so as to enable each child to choose and pursue life work intelligently; and (vii) sufficient level of academic or vocational skills to enable public schools to compete favorably with their counterparts in surrounding states, in academics or in the job market." Although the first and last capabilities include concerns about job readiness, the list of criteria is far more comprehensive.

The chief way in which equal opportunity may be involved in assessment questions deals with the question of access, whether it be to a program in a school or to employment related to a plan created under the act. Potential employee partners under the act as well as the educational institutions involved must be aware of the potential that tests or other selection criteria for student participants may be used in a way that frustrates the goals of the act to increase participation in the work force. This is particularly true when heavy reliance is placed on tests. In an effort to assist those contemplating programs pursuant to the School-to-Work Opportunities Act, this paper outlines some of the relevant law, particularly as it relates to assessment, with an eye toward assisting partners with the development of testing and selection criteria that broaden both the base of knowledge and the experience of students while increasing the pool of students able to participate fully in the American work force in the upcoming century.

LEGAL LIMITATIONS OF SELECTION CRITERIA

The act makes clear that it does nothing to blunt the full force or effect of any law that provides protection against any kind of discrimination:

> Nothing in this chapter shall be construed to modify or affect any Federal or State law prohibiting discrimination on the basis of race, religion, color, ethnicity, national origin, gender, age, or disability, or to modify or affect any right to enforcement of this chapter that may exist under other Federal laws, except as expressly provided by this chapter.

The range of federal laws alone that may limit the uses of tests or other selection criteria is large; these laws frequently overlap in coverage and include prohibitions against discrimination based on race, sex, national origin, and religion (42 U.S.C.A. §2000e *et seq.*(Title VII)) in employment; on the basis of disability (Americans with Disabilities Act) or age (Age Discrimination in Employment Act) in employment; because of race in the entering into or continuing of contracts (42 U.S.C.A. §1981); because of race, color, or national origin in federally assisted programs (U.S.C.A. §2000d *et seq.* (Title VI))[4]; or on the basis of sex in federally funded education programs.[5] In addition, most states and/or localities have separate statutes or regulations that provide similar or more extensive coverage than their federal counterparts. A number of examples can be imagined that would trigger review under one or more of the statutes described above. For example, if employee partners placed onerous conditions on student participa-

---

[4]Title VI provides that "[n]o person in the United States shall, on the ground of race, color, or national origin, be excluded from participation in, be denied benefits of, or be subjected to discrimination under any program or activity receiving Federal financial assistance."

[5]20 U.S.C. §1681 *et seq.* states that "[n]o person in the United States shall, on the basis of sex, be excluded from participation in, be denied the benefits of, or be subjected to discrimination under any education program or activity [receiving] Federal financial assistance except . . ." (the statute then lists exemptions not applicable to this discussion).

tion in training programs that had the effect of unnecessarily limiting access to a protected class, that employer might be liable for violations of various laws. Similarly, schools that made class assignments or set course prerequisites in a manner that had a disparate impact on a protected class might also run afoul of the law.

To understand the limitations imposed on testing and other selection criteria, it is important to understand the ways in which these statutes operate. All of them prohibit intentional discrimination against the classes of people they are designed to protect. Presumably, it is unnecessary to point out to prospective employers that, under the School-to-Work Opportunities Act, that any test or selection criterion that explicitly discriminates on any of the bases listed above can only lead to trouble.

Problems are more likely to arise because of the fact that many of the statutes listed above can be invoked under an "effects" or "impact" theory of discrimination, for example, Titles VI, VII, and IX, the Americans with Disabilities Act, and the Age Discrimination in Employment Act. Under this theory, it is the consequence of an employment criterion used or decision made, rather than the employer's motive, that is significant. Indeed, the employer's bona fides are irrelevant in the analysis of a case under an impact standard. To help the reader understand how specific tests or selection criteria might cause problems for employers under the application of an impact[6] standard, some discussion of how a case is brought and won under such a theory is useful.[7]

PROVING A DISPARATE IMPACT CASE

From the first recognition in 1971 that Title VII violations could be alleged in cases not involving discriminatory intent[8] until the passage of the Civil Rights

---

[6]In *Griggs v. Duke Power* (401 U.S. 424,432 (1971)), the seminal case articulating the impact standard in Title VII litigation, the Supreme Court made clear that an employer is not insulated from a lawsuit by virtue of its good intentions: "Good intent does not redeem employment procedures or testing mechanisms that operate as 'built-in headwinds' for minority groups and are unrelated to measuring job capability."

[7]The following discussion is directed primarily toward employer partners because of the nature of their involvement in the creation of programs. They presumably will have the primary responsibility for defining what they consider to be adequate training and moreover will be instrumental in devising and implementing assessment criteria for purposes of later employment. Title VII is therefore the focus of the discussion here because it deals specifically with employment. At the same time, although the exact contours of Title VI impact analysis have not yet been firmly established, Title VII can be looked at to suggest how courts might approach cases involving differential impacts under Title VI. Certainly, any school that incorporates into its educational program any criterion with a discriminatory impact proposed by a business partner would potentially violate Title VI (see discussion below).

[8]See *Griggs v. Duke Power Company* (401 U.S. 424 (1971)), prohibiting employment practices "that are fair in form, but discriminatory in operation."

Act of 1991, a series of court cases defined the legal requirements of bringing an action under an impact theory. Following a series of Supreme Court decisions in 1989 that cast some doubt on the continuing vitality of much of the earlier case law regarding discriminatory impact cases,*Wards Cove Packing Company v. Atonio* (490 U.S. 642 (1989)) and *Watson v. Fort Worth Bank and Trust* (487 U.S. 977 (1988)), Congress revisited the issue of the scope of Title VII. Although Congress intended for the Civil Rights Act of 1991 to clarify and correct the effect of some later Supreme Court decisions, the language of the legislation raised additional questions about statutory construction and must therefore await further judicial or legislative clarification.

For present purposes, though, the manner in which a Title VII impact case can be proven is sufficiently clear. Proving a case is divided into three stages. A plaintiff wishing to bring a case under the impact standard of Title VII must pass the initial hurdle of making a prima facie case or presenting sufficient factual evidence to create a presumption that the law has been violated. This is done by showing that the employer against whom the charge has been made "uses a particular employment practice that causes a disparate impact on the basis of race, color, religion, sex or national origin" (42 U.S.C.A. §2000e-2(k)(1)(A)(i)). In practice, this means showing "that the tests in question select applicants for hire or promotion in a racial pattern significantly different from that of the pool of applicants" (*Albemarle Paper Company v. Moody*, 422 U.S. 405, 425 (1975)).[9]

Following this demonstration by the plaintiff, the defendant employer has the opportunity, and obligation, to respond. As a preliminary matter, if the employer can show that the challenged practice did not cause the disparity or that no disparity exists, the inquiry ends (42 U.S.C.A. §2000e-2(k)(1)(B)(ii)). Even if the challenged practice is the cause of a real disparity, though, the employer has not necessarily lost the case. In that instance the employer may then introduce evidence that the challenged practice is "job related for the position in question and consistent with business necessity" (42 U.S.C.A. §2000e-2(k)(1)(A)(i)).

Predictably, the precise meanings of "job related" and "business necessity" are unclear, particularly because of the tortured legislative history of the Civil Rights Act of 1991, during which Congress changed the language of the

---

[9]Notwithstanding the apparent clarity of the Supreme Court's pronouncement about making a prima facie case, courts in individual cases have grappled with the application of the standard to particular fact situations in an attempt to interpret the meaning of such terms as "significantly different," "racial pattern," and "pool of applicants." An exegesis of these cases is beyond the scope of this paper; however, in his excellent treatise on employment discrimination, Lex K. Larson (1996) suggests the following guideline for determining if a prima facie case has been adequately presented: "For present purposes, it is sufficient to say that the plaintiff will have succeeded in presenting a strong prima facie case under the disparate impact theory if he or she can convince the fact-finder that: (1) The statistics accurately reflect the actual pool of applicants; (2) The statistics demonstrate that the defendant's selection device results in a work force that has a minority group representation drastically different from that of the applicant pool; and (3) It is highly unlikely that this representation could have occurred by chance."

act from "required by business necessity" to "consistent with business necessity," suggesting a somewhat more relaxed burden on the defendant employer. Despite ambiguities in language, the inclusion of both business necessity and job relatedness indicates that the employer's obligation goes beyond merely articulating a nexus between the selection criteria and the job to be filled and includes a more substantial requirement that the criteria fairly reflect the requirements of the job.

Under the three-step process, the plaintiff is given a further opportunity to prevail by showing either that the selection criteria are not job related or that there exist alternatives that do not have the same discriminatory effect (*Griggs v. Duke Power Company*, 401 U.S. 424 (1971)).

After this outline of the stages of a proceeding brought under a disparate impact theory of discrimination, it is useful to examine how the process played out in some actual Title VII cases. Such an examination is particularly helpful since many of the early cases that helped to define disparate impact jurisprudence arose from challenges of the uses of testing in employment, making them particularly relevant for this paper.

Griggs v. Duke Power Company (401 U.S. 405 (1975)), involved a challenge of the hiring practices of a North Carolina power company. Although the company employed both black and white workers, black employees were limited by policy to jobs in the labor department, the lowest paying of five departments in the company. Before the passage of Title VII, the only other job qualification beyond the overtly discriminatory racial policy was the requirement that all applicants to any department other than labor have a high school diploma. In 1965 the company dropped the explicitly discriminatory policy of assigning blacks only to the labor department and instituted testing procedures for the first time.[10] All applicants were required to take and pass both the Wonderlic Personnel Test and the Bennett Mechanical Comprehension Test, while persons currently in the job were grandfathered into their positions.

The Supreme Court overturned the decision of the district court and the circuit court of appeals, both of which had found in favor of the defendant because of an absence of a showing of intentional discrimination. In ruling for the plaintiff that there had in fact been a violation of Title VII, the Supreme Court noted that only 12 percent of black males in North Carolina were high school graduates while 34 percent of white males had completed high school. Even more dramatic was the difference in the impact of the tests. The court observed that,

---

[10]The implication of the timing of the institution of the testing requirements will not be considered here because the focus of this discussion is on practices that have a disproportionate impact. However, evidence of the initiation of a testing requirement in the context of a case such as these may help give rise to an inference of discriminatory intent. See *Metropolitan Housing Development v. Village of Arlington Heights* (558 F2d 1283 (7th Cir 1977), *cert. denied*, 434 U.S. 1025 (1978)), holding that intentional discrimination may be evidenced by pretextual actions.

while 58 percent of whites had passed the Wonderlic and Bennett tests, only 6 percent of blacks had done so.

On the basis of those statistics, the Supreme Court held that the lower courts had erred in dismissing the case because of an absence of discriminatory intent. Instead, the court faulted the earlier decisions for failing to address the impact of tests that were unrelated to measuring job capability (401 U.S. 432).

Further refinements of the definition of job relatedness came in the case of *Albermarle Paper Company v. Moody* (422 U.S. 405 (1975)). Like the Duke Power Company, the Albermarle Paper Company had a history of discriminatory policies under which black workers were forbidden from working in certain departments. In the 1950s, in the wake of modernization of its facilities, the company required that applicants have completed high school. This requirement remained in effect until enjoined by court order even though there was no dispute that the new high school diploma requirement produced no discernible improvement in the quality of employees or productivity.

Two years after institution of the high school graduation requirement, the company began using standardized tests to screen applicants for skilled positions. These tests, which included the Beta Examination, the Bennett Mechanical Test and later the Wonderlic Test had the same effect as was seen in the Duke Power Company case—very few black workers met the requirements for positions.

Significantly for the purposes of this discussion, the reasons given by both the Duke Power Company and the Albermarle Paper Company would sound familiar to anyone who knew about the goals of the School-to-Work Opportunities Act: both companies based the newly imposed education and test requirements on a belief that the quality of their work force would improve. In *Albermarle* the court held that this justification did not meet the job-relatedness requirement necessary to rebut the plaintiffs' showing that the tests and graduation requirements resulted in the selection of applicants in a racial pattern significantly different from that of the pool of applicants (422 U.S. 408). Applying the standards described in *Griggs*, the court held that the employer failed to show by professionally accepted methods that the tests either could predict or have been significantly correlated with important work behaviors relevant to the particular job the test taker sought. In short, the court found that Albemarle's attempts at test validation fell far short of its legal requirements.[11] In both *Griggs* and *Albemarle*,

---

[11] Specific shortcomings were (1) that there were no attempts to analyze required job skills; (2) that the company failed to conduct validation studies for all of the jobs included in the individual studies; (3) that a test that existed in two forms did not correlate to a sufficient number of job groupings in either form; (4) that although the validation study compared test results with supervisor's ratings, the supervisors were given no guidance on how to make their ratings; (5) that the study focused on higher-level jobs than the tests tested and; (6) that the study focused on whites with substantial job experience while those tested lacked job experience and were not all white.

the fact that not all workers were tested or met educational requirements further undercuts claims of validity.

Despite the challenges to some poorly constructed or validated tests, Title VII should not be seen as prohibiting the use of tests. In fact, Title VII contains a specific endorsement of professionally prepared tests that do not result in discrimination in employment decisions. This endorsement was included partly to allay employer's fears that all employment testing would run afoul of Title VII.[12]

> Notwithstanding any other provision of this [title], it shall not be an unlawful employment practice for an employer . . . to give and to act upon the results of any professionally developed ability test provided that such test, its administration or action upon the results is not designed, intended or used to discriminate because of race, color, religion, sex or national origin (42 U.S.C.A. §2000e-2(h)).

Although this section does permit the use of professionally prepared tests, employers should realize that the section cited above does not create an exemption for all such tests. Particularly misleading is the language describing tests "not designed, intended or used to discriminate," which suggests that tests can be attacked only when their use involves intentional discrimination. Both the courts (see, e.g., *Griggs v. Duke Power Company*, 401 U.S. 424) and the Equal Employment Opportunities Commission (401 U.S. 434) have made clear that this section does not impose an intent requirement in cases regarding professional tests—any test that is not job related and has a disproportionate impact against a protected group will violate Title VII.

Employers must also realize that tests and educational requirements are not the only selection criteria vulnerable to challenge under Title VII and other statutes that rely on an impact analysis. Any requirement that has a disproportionate impact and is not sufficiently job related presents potential problems. With varying degrees of success, cases have been brought challenging the disparate impact and job relatedness of minimum height and weight requirements,[13] experience

---

[12]Larson (1996) describes the effect of civil rights legislation and court decisions on the prevalence of test use in the business community. In 1963, before enactment of Title VII, only 64 percent of companies used any tests, and three-fourths of those said they had reduced their reliance on tests. Another 14 percent stated their intention to halt the use of tests entirely. Larson further quotes a recent upswing in the use of tests, which he attributes to the need to measure increasingly complex skills and a realization that subjective selection criteria have become increasingly susceptible to legal challenge.

[13]See, for example, *Dothard v. Rawlinson* (433 U.S. 321 (1977)), a successful challenge of minimum height and weight requirements for prison employment on grounds that the requirements unfairly discriminate against women; *Officers for Justice v. Civil Service Commission* (395 F Supp 378 (ND Cal 1975)), a successful challenge of the 5'6" height requirement for police officers as discriminatory against Asians, Latinos, and women; *Craig v. County of Los Angeles* (626 F 2d 659 (9th Cir 1980), *cert. denied* 450 U.S. 919 (1981)), which successfully challenged height standards as discriminatory against Mexican-Americans.

requirements,[14] arrests and convictions,[15] wage garnishment,[16] and bankruptcy.[17]

UNIFORM GUIDELINES ON EMPLOYEE-SELECTION PROCEDURES

Because of the difficulty in compiling and keeping track of the myriad court decisions dealing with the use of testing and selection procedures, a practical alternative available to employers is the Equal Employment Opportunity Commission's 1978 *Uniform Guidelines on Employee Selection Procedures*. The *Guidelines* are a comprehensive collection of standards for using and evaluating selection criteria. Although not legally binding on courts, the *Guidelines* are entitled to "great deference" from the judiciary (*Griggs v. Duke Power Company*, 401 U.S. 424, 433-434).[18] They therefore represent a useful, if not final, statement about the use of tests and selection criteria consistent with the demands of Title VII. The following overview touches on some highlights of the *Guidelines* and is not intended as an exhaustive discussion to be used in lieu of reference to the *Guidelines* themselves.

As set forth in its statement of purpose, the *Guidelines* were implemented to fill a need for a uniform set of principles on the question of the use of tests and other selection procedures (29 C.F.R. Ch.. XIV §1607.1). The *Guidelines* were intended to provide "a single set of principles which are designed to assist employers, labor organizations, employment agencies and licensing and certification boards" to comply with requirements of federal law (29 C.F.R. Ch. XIV §1607.1). The *Guidelines* carefully point out that employers or other parties are not required to conduct validation studies of every selection criterion. Although the *Guidelines* urge the use of fair and job-related criteria in all circumstances,

---

[14]*Chrisner v. Complete Auto Transit* (645 F 2d 1251 (6th Cir 1981)) alleged disparate impact on women due to a 2-year experience requirement for truck drivers.

[15]*Gregory v. Litton Systems, Ltd.* (326 F Supp 401 (CD Cal 1970) *aff'd in relevant part*, 472 F.2d 631 (9th Cir 1972)) challenged a disproportionate impact on blacks of a rule barring applicants who had been arrested on "a number of occasions"; *Green v. Missouri Pacific Railroad* (523 F 2d 1290 (8th Cir 1975)), an unsuccessful challenge to a rule barring applicants with records of convictions.

[16]*Johnson v. Pike Corporation* (332 F Supp 490 (CD Cal 1971)); *Wallace v. Debron Corporation* (494 F 2d 674 (8th Cir 1974)).

[17]*Bell v. Citizens Fidelity Bank & Trust Company* (636 F 2d 1119 (6th Cir 1980)).

[18]In a later decision the Supreme Court noted that deference was due the *Guidelines* but also observed that the *Guidelines* were not administrative regulations promulgated pursuant to formal procedures (*Albermarle Paper Company v. Moody*, 422 U.S. 431). For that reason the court declined to fully endorse the *Guidelines* and instead picked and chose among them. Areas about which there is disagreement between courts and the Equal Employment Opportunity Commission are noted in the discussion below.

they do not require the validation of selection procedures that have no adverse impact (29 C.F.R. Ch. XIV §1607.1).

The definition of selection procedures used in the *Guidelines* is broad but does not include recruiting practices for purposes of affirmative action nor do they address the legality of seniority systems "except to the extent that such systems utilize selection procedures to determine qualifications or abilities to perform the job" (29 C.F.R. Ch. XIV §1607.2).

The definition of discrimination in the *Guidelines* is straightforward: if there is a disproportionate impact[19] as a result of a selection procedure in hiring, promotion, or other employment or membership opportunities on a person because of race, sex, or ethnic group and the party using the selection procedure has not followed the process for validation in the *Guidelines*, there is a presumption that the selection criteria were discriminatory (29 C.F.R. Ch. XIV §1607.3). Moreover, the *Guidelines* also oppose certain affirmative obligations on users of selection criteria regarding the consideration of alternative selection procedures. Unlike court decisions that place the burden on plaintiffs to come up with alternative selection criteria that would have less of a disparate impact (*Albermarle Paper Company v. Moody*, 422 U.S. 405, 25, 436), the *Guidelines* place a host of responsibilities on the user. For example, users are expected to investigate alternative procedures as part of a validation study; they should review alternatives after a "reasonable" period of time; and they should actively investigate any alternatives brought to their attention that might have less of a disparate impact (29 C.F.R. Ch. XIV §1607.3).

TYPES OF VALIDATION

The *Guidelines* outline three acceptable types of validation studies. The first, criterion-related validity, examines whether there are data that prove the selection procedure "is predictive or significantly correlated with important elements of job performance (29 C.F.R. Ch. XIV §1607.5). Content-related validation focuses on the test or other selection criterion to decide if the content of the selection criteria represents important aspects of performance on the job for which applicants are to be evaluated (29 C.F.R. Ch. XIV §1607.5). Construct validation examines whether the selection test or procedure measures identifiable characteristics that have been determined to be important in successful performance on the job for which the candidates are to be evaluated.

No matter which of the three validation methods, or which combination thereof is used, the *Guidelines* set forth some general instructions. These include

---

[19]The *Guidelines* employ a "four-fifths" rule for determining if the impact of a selection criterion is disproportionate. Under this rule, if the "selection rate for any race, sex, or ethnic group . . . is less than four-fifths of the rate for the group with the highest rate [the selection policy] will generally be regarded by the Federal enforcement agencies as [an]adverse impact" (29 C.F.R. Ch. XIV §1607.4 (D)).

the need for documentation of validity (29 C.F.R. Ch. XIV §1607.5 (D)); adherence to standards of accuracy and standardization (29 C.F.R. Ch. XIV §1607.5 (E)); a warning against selection based on knowledge or skills normally learned in a brief orientation period and that have an adverse impact (29 C.F.R. Ch. XIV §1607.5 (F)); the need for reasonable and consistent use of cut off scores (29 C.F.R. Ch. XIV §1607.5 (H));[20] and care in the use of selection procedures to determine proficiency for a higher-level job than the one being sought (29 C.F.R. Ch. XIV §1607.5 (I)).[21] Users may also rely on interim selection procedures if there is substantial evidence of validity and the user is in the process of conducting a study to provide the additional information required by the *Guidelines* within a reasonable period of time (29 C.F.R. Ch. XIV §1607.5 (J)). Finally, care should be taken to assure that the validity tests are current (29 C.F.R. Ch. XIV §1607.5 (K)).[22]

The *Guidelines* contain technical standards for each of the three types of validity studies. These standards are too detailed for complete examination here but can be summarized as follows.

For criteria-related studies, users should determine the appropriateness of the study for the particular employment context, should conduct a job analysis to determine what work behaviors or performance are important, should assure that fair measures of these criteria are used, should rely on sample subjects who represent candidates normally available in the relevant job market, should use professionally accepted statistical standards for measuring the degree of relationship between selection procedure scores and criterion measurements, and should carefully examine the fairness of procedures relied on (29 C.F.R. Ch. XIV §1607.14).

Many of the same standards apply to content validity studies. Added to the list is the need for determining if tests or selection criteria closely approximate observable work situations or products and for assuring that, if prior or training experience is part of the content, there is a resemblance between the specific behaviors or skills in the experience or training and those required by the job itself. Similarly, content-validated criteria can depend on success in a training program only when there is a sufficiently strong relationship between the training program and the job (29 C.F.R. Ch. XIV §1607.14).

The *Guidelines* recognize that construct validation studies are the most complex of the three methods and accordingly urge caution in their use. These studies require extensive job analysis indicating the work behaviors needed for success-

---

[20]This consideration directs the user to set cut-off scores that are appropriate and consistent with normal expectations of acceptable proficiency within the work force.

[21]This confusing guideline means simply that, if there is generally job progression within a reasonable period of time, the selection criteria can examine an applicant's qualifications for the higher-level job.

[22]Factors to be considered in determining whether a validity study is outdated include the relationship between the particular validity strategy used and changes in the relevant job market and the particular job in question.

ful performance of the job, the important work behaviors being studied, and an identification of the constructs believed to underlie successful performance of the job (29 C.F.R. Ch. XIV §1607.14 (D)). Having identified the construct, the user must show (1) that the selection procedure is validly related to the construct and (2) that the construct itself is related to job performance (29 C.F.R. Ch. XIV §1607.14 (D)).

Legal Limitations on Educational Institutions

Because programs created under the act rely on the use of federal funds and the program is administered by the U.S. Departments of Education (DOE) and Labor (DOL), participants in the program are protected by a panoply of federal civil rights statutes.[23] Although both departments are required to issue guidelines for each of the federally assisted programs, neither has complied with this requirement.[24] Unfortunately, programs established under the School-to-Work Opportunities Act are among those without specific guidelines.

Despite the failure of the two departments to promulgate specific guidelines under the act, there are specific guidelines in their Title VI regulations to suggest that assessment practices used in schools would be evaluated in a similar manner as described above in relation to Title VII. Under Title VI, educational institutions would be required to be certain that all of their assessment and credentialing practices serve legitimate educational purposes without having undue adverse impacts on classes protected under statute. Also, educational institutions would be required to prohibit any assessment practice, or indeed any other kind of practice, that include:

- denial to an individual of any service, financial aid, or other benefit provided under the program;
- distinctions in the quality, quantity, or manner in which the benefit is provided;
- segregation or separate treatment in any part of the program;
- restriction in the enjoyment of any advantages, privileges, or other benefits provided to others;
- different standards or requirements for participation;
- methods of administration which directly or through contractual relation-

---

[23]In addition to Title VI, DOE and DOL have enforcement responsibility for Title IX (20 U.S.C. §§1681-1688 (1988)); Section 504 of the Rehabilitation Act of 1973 (29 U.S.C. §794 (1988 & Supp. V 1993)); the Age Discrimination Act of 1975 (42 U.S.C. §§6101-6107 (1988)); and Title II of the Americans with Disabilities Act (42 U.S.C. §§12,131-12,134 (Supp. V 1993)).

[24]See pp. 212 and 375-377 in *Federal Title VI Enforcement to Ensure Nondiscrimination in Federally Assisted Programs, A Report of the U.S. Commission on Civil Rights*, U.S. Commission on Civil Rights, Washington, DC, 1996.

ships would defeat or substantially impair the accomplishment of effective non-discrimination;

 • discrimination in any activities conducted in a facility built in whole or in part with Federal funds;

 • discrimination in any employment resulting from a program which has a primary purpose of providing employment.[25]

Although there are no regulations that specifically apply to these prohibitions to the act, educational partners can get some idea of the types of equity considerations that might come into play under a specific proposal by looking at the U. S. Department of Education's treatment of its enforcement responsibilities in another context. One such area relates to ability grouping or tracking. In recognition of the fact that assignment of students to different classes can result in both in-school segregation and the diminution of educational opportunities for African-American students, the Department of Education has applied criteria that were originally part of implementing regulations promulgated under the Emergency School Aid Act[26] in order to assure compliance with Title VI:

 • Grouping must be based on nondiscriminatory objective measures that are educationally relevant for the purpose of the grouping. Such measures (1) treat minority and majority students equally, (2) provide an objective assessment of student ability or achievement level, and (3) pertain to the subject areas in which students are ability-grouped.

 • Grouping must be determined by the nondiscriminatory application of the measures. This means that the measures are used consistently for minority and majority students so that, for example, students with the same test scores are ability grouped at the same level.

 • The grouping must be validated by test scores or other reliable objective evidence indicating the educational benefits of such grouping. Evidence of educational benefit, such as improved academic achievement or mobility to higher-level classes demonstrates whether the ability-grouping practice benefits the students in the lower groups.

Although the School-to-Work Opportunities Act does not deal specifically with student assignment questions, the equity issues outlined above do have some relevance. First, the act, like ability grouping practices, has enormous potential to affect later achievement possibilities, both in terms of education and subsequent employment of students. Moreover, to the extent that a program

---

[25]See p. 5 in *Compliance Officer's Manual: A Handbook of Compliance Procedures Under Title VI of the Civil Rights Act of 1964*, U.S. Commission on Civil Rights, Washington, DC, 1964.

[26]The Emergency School Act of 1976 provided financial assistance to school districts undergoing desegregation. The act and its regulations were repealed by the Education Consolidation and Improvement Act of 1981, which consolidated 28 categorical grant programs into a single block grant known as Chapter 2.

implemented under the act involves discretion in admission or assignment, considerations like those outlined above could be implicated. So, for example, the school partner must be sure that all students are assured equal access both in terms of involvement with particular employers and in training for particular types of positions. Clearly, any program that tended to track students of a particular protected class into lower-prestige or lower-paying jobs would not only violate the intent of the act but also violate the law.

CONCLUSION

The discussion here on the validity of selection criteria is not meant to frighten or confuse but rather to show that the law and fairness demand that any standards developed in the course of the implementation of the School-to-Work Opportunities Act must balance the need for a more highly trained work force with the requirement that the new standards bear some meaningful relationship to the work that students will ultimately perform. Employers and educational institutions must be aware that selection criteria may measure less about an individual's ability to perform or learn a task than they do the person's background and culture. Accordingly, consistent with the goals of the School-to-Work Opportunities Act, employers must devise standards that will enrich the skills of students, particularly those whose access to the work force has been limited, and not serve as another in a series of barriers to a productive career.

REFERENCES

Equal Employment Opportunity Commission
   1978   *Uniform Guidelines on Employee Selection Procedures.* Washington, DC: Equal Opportunity Employment Commission.
Larsen, Lex K.
   1996   *Employment Discrimination.* New York: Matthew Bender.

9

Assessment Without Adverse Impact

Neal Schmitt

The 1964 Civil Rights Act stimulated an examination of employers' decisions in hiring, promotions, and other human resource actions. In the employment arena, the first Supreme Court case that ruled on the provisions of the act established that the court would look first at the hiring rates in different subgroups (*Griggs v. Duke Power Company*, 40 U.S. 424,432 (1971)). If these hiring rates were different, the employment process would be examined to discover whether employment decisions were based on job-related concerns. In the absence of evidence about the validity of the employment procedures, the procedures were considered discriminatory, and the courts typically prescribed some remedial action. Between *Griggs* and the late 1980s, this was the legal status quo in employment discrimination cases. Employers realized that their human resource decisions would not be challenged if the "numbers came out right," and some adapted their procedures in ways that ensured this outcome.

The quandary for employers was that many of the measures they were using that were cognitively based (or related to various academic skills) provided valid predictions of applicants' subsequent job performance but produced large subgroup differences in test scores and subsequent hiring rates. Technically, an employer should be able to use those procedures (i.e., valid procedures that produce adverse impact), but in many instances the employer or the courts or both were unhappy with the resulting composition of the work force. This produced the impetus for within-group scoring and other types of adjustments designed to achieve the desired work-force composition. These actions, in turn, produced an increased concern about reverse discrimination, which still continues. Ultimately, the public demanded change (or so our congressional representatives believed), and one result was the Civil Rights Act of 1991, which explicitly prohibits any kind of score adjustments designed to favor one group over another with regard to employment decisions.

This, then, is a simple version of the quandary faced by organizational decision makers. How do employers use the valid assessment procedures they have been using in a way that will produce a work force that is optimally capable and that is representative of the diverse groups in our society? Or how do we develop equally valid instruments that do not produce adverse impact?

This paper attempts to describe some of the ways in which organizations and assessment specialists have tried to adjust to this quandary, the success of these attempts, and what new legal issues might be raised when these procedures are challenged, as they either have been or almost certainly will be. Specifically, the following five approaches to reducing or eliminating the adverse impact of psychological measures will be discussed: (1) inclusion of additional job-related constructs with low or no adverse impact in a battery that includes cognitive or academically based measures with high adverse impact; (2) changing the format of the questions asked or the type of response requested; (3) using computer or video technology to present test stimuli and collect responses; (4) using portfolios, accomplishment records, or other formalized methods of documenting job-related accomplishments or achievements; and (5) changing the manner in which test scores are used: specifically, by the use of banding.

USE OF ADDITIONAL CONSTRUCTS TO ASSESS COMPETENCE

One criticism of traditional personnel selection procedures is that they often focus on a single set of abilities, usually cognitive. These cognitive abilities are relatively easy and inexpensive to measure in a group context with paper and pencil instruments. Moreover, they tend to exhibit some validity for most jobs in the economy. They also, of course, exhibit large subgroup differences. It should be noted that with unequal subgroup variances, a possibility not often examined, the differences between lower- and higher-scoring subgroups might vary as a function of the part of the test score distribution examined.

If the job requires other capabilities, such as interpersonal or teamwork skills, for example, why are these capabilities not measured? If we did measure these alternative constructs, what would happen to the organization's ability to identify talent and to the size of the subgroup difference when information from multiple sources on multiple constructs is combined to make hiring decisions? Recently, Sackett and Wilk (1994) examined a simple instance of this case in which one predictor with a large subgroup difference (i.e., one standard deviation) was combined with a second predictor on which subgroup scores were equivalent. If the two measures are uncorrelated, the subgroup difference of a simple equally weighted composite is 0.71. In Sackett and Wilk's case the two predictors were equally valid and uncorrelated with each other. In the presence of some correlation between the two predictors, the difference between subgroups on the combined scores would be larger than 0.71. When first examining this case, one might predict that the subgroup difference would be 0.5. This simple example suggests that the combination of predictors with different levels of subgroup difference will not yield nearly the dampening effect on subgroup differences one might hope for. In the actual prediction of academic or job performance criteria, the situation will always be more complex.

Recently, Elaine Pulakos and I (Pulakos and Schmitt, 1996) had the opportunity to examine various possible combinations of assessment scores and their impact on three groups (African Americans, Hispanic Americans, and whites) of applicants for jobs in a federal investigative agency. A traditional multiple-choice measure of verbal ability (analogies, vocabulary, and reading comprehension) was used along with two performance measures of writing skills. One of these measures required examinees to watch a video enactment of a crime scene and then write a description of what had happened. The other performance test required examinees to study a set of documents and reports of interviews and then write a summary of their observations of the case. The two performance measures were rated for writing skills (grammar, spelling, and punctuation), organization, persuasiveness, and the degree to which the examinee attended to and reported details of the case. In addition, the examinees responded to a biographical data questionnaire (a multiple-choice measure of background experiences, interests, and values), a situational judgment test (requesting their choice of one of three or four alternative reactions), and a structured interview designed to measure their actions in past situations that required job-related skills. These measures were relatively uncorrelated (all less than .39), valid against at least one of two performance rating criteria (i.e., observed correlations with the criterion exceeding .14), and varied considerably in the degree to which scores were characterized by subgroup differences.

Of most relevance to the current discussion, the traditional verbal ability measure by itself produced a difference between white and African American examinees equal to 1.03 standard deviations. The white and Hispanic American difference was equal to 0.78 standard deviations. With one exception, the differences on the biographical data measure, the structured interview, and the situational judgment test were less than 0.22. The exception was the situational judgment test comparison for the African American and white groups, which produced a 0.41 standard deviation difference. That test was the most "verbal" and cognitive of these measures. When the four tests were combined, the difference between the African American and white groups was 0.63; that between the Hispanic American and white groups was 0.48. Both represent a drop in the subgroup difference of about 0.30 to 0.40 of a standard deviation, but note that this drop was accomplished by combining one test that had a large subgroup difference with three measures on which there were minimal or no subgroup differences. The use of all four measures added uniquely to the overall multiple *R* relating the criteria to predictors.

It is certainly appropriate to include all four measures (particularly the noncognitive tests) in this battery. The three noncognitive tests are measures on which the Hispanic American and African American groups typically do better, and these measures have often been excluded on the grounds that they were too expensive to develop and implement or added nothing above and beyond more traditional test batteries. Using all four measures is fair as well as optimal in a scientific sense in that a broader sampling of job-relevant constructs results. Combining measures that have relatively no adverse impact with traditional measures that have high adverse impact will not diminish the overall impact as much as one might hope, but they will lessen subgroup differences substantially.

Two other studies of which I am aware address the question of the degree to which adverse impact will be diminished when tests of varying levels of adverse impact are combined. The degree to which adverse impact is lessened appears to be a complex combination of the level of adverse impact each part of the battery displays, the reliability of the individual tests, the intercorrelation of the tests (with increased levels of intercorrelation, such combinations will result in smaller decreases in the level of adverse impact), and the selection ratio. Sackett and Roth (1995) have examined the case in which one alternative predictor with no subgroup difference is combined with a predictor that displays a large subgroup difference (i.e., one standard deviation) for a variety of test use strategies. Schmitt et al. (1997) examined the role some of these factors play in determining levels of adverse impact and predictability. Both papers confirm the complex interaction of these factors in the determination of both predictability of performance and the size of subgroup differences. Obviously, whether any or all of these alternative measures should be used to make employment decisions is always contingent on their validity.

On a legal basis it would be hard to challenge the use of additional tests with less adverse impact if in fact they are valid. What might occur in this situation is a challenge to the use of the traditional test, which, when used singly, produces large adverse impact and, when used in combination with the other predictors, is responsible for a relatively large adverse impact for the composite. In the case of the Pulakos and Schmitt (1996) study described above, the verbal ability test added .02 to the multiple correlation relating the predictors to one of two rating criteria afforded by a combination of the situational judgment test, the biographical data measure, and the interview. So one is comparing an incremental validity of .02 against a rather significant impact on two protected groups. As is so often the case, it seems that the courts and society at large are left with conflicting goals, and the solution will be a function of the decision maker's value system. In one sense this solution to the problem of subgroup differences is another version of the search for equally valid alternatives to tests with high adverse impact. In this particular case, valid alternatives did exist, but each appeared to contribute uniquely to the prediction of the performance construct.

Coincidentally but relevant to the larger purpose of this paper, the findings in this study regarding the three different measures of verbal ability are interesting. The alternative measures of verbal ability had comparable validity (.15, .19, and .22) and reliability (.85, .86, and .92) but displayed radically different levels of subgroup difference in mean scores. As stated above, for the traditional verbal test, African American and white differences were 1.03, and Hispanic American and white differences were 0.78. The performance measure involving written stimulus materials and requiring written output yielded somewhat smaller differences of 0.91 and 0.52, while the same comparisons for the performance measure in which the stimulus material was visual yielded differences of 0.45 and 0.37. Although it would be tempting to attribute the diminution of adverse impact to the change in test format, the intercorrelations between these three measures were only .26, .39, and .31, indicating that there were differences in the abilities or traits measured as well as format differences in these three measures of verbal ability.

DEVELOPING NEW FORMATS

The multiple-choice paper-and-pencil measure of ability has been criticized most frequently and probably remains the most ubiquitous assessment tool. Maintaining that the multiple-choice format is responsible for the magnitude of subgroup differences is tantamount to saying that test variance is partly a function of method variance and that subgroups differ on the method variance component more than they do on the variance components that are construct relevant. That there is something unique about the multiple-choice format has been demonstrated in a number of studies over the years (Cronbach, 1941; Traub and Fisher, 1977; Ward et al., 1980; Ward, 1982; Boyle, 1984). That there are format-by-subgroup interactions that would indicate that method bias differentially affects members of different subgroups has not been frequently studied. When it has, the results have been confusing and contradictory. A paper by Scheuneman (1987) is illustrative. She examined 16 hypotheses regarding differences between African Americans and whites in response to the Graduate Record Examination. Significant interactions were observed for 10 of the 16 hypotheses, but these interactions were so complex (group by item version by item pair) that interpretation was difficult. In addition, the sample sizes were very large; hence, significant effects were associated with small effect sizes. A similar but largely unstudied hypothesis is that minority groups are more likely to omit items than guess.

Recently, Outtz (1994) has pointed out that very few researchers have actively studied the role that such method bias may actually play in producing subgroup differences in measured ability. He also provided a taxonomy of test characteristics that might provide the impetus for some systematic research on this issue. He also cautions, as do others (Ryan and Greguras, 1994; Schmitt et al., 1996), that researchers in this area must be careful not to confound the construct measured with the format in which it is measured. This problem confounds the interpretation of the relatively small body of research on the influence of format differences on measures of ability.

An analysis of the degree to which the stimuli and possible responses in an assessment device are samples of some content domain also points to the problems a researcher encounters when trying to compare different formats. For example, we might ask a potential teacher to answer the following question: What would you do if an angry parent confronted you about the grade a son or daughter received on an examination? We might present this question in multiple-choice format with the following alternatives: (1) try to calm the parent down and then deal with the problem, (2) calm the parent down and then tell him or her to wait until you are finished with the task you are now doing, (3) ignore the parent or walk away because the parent is being rude, (4) inform the parent that you will not tolerate his or her attitude and behavior. This item could also be presented in open-ended format and require an essay response from the prospective teacher. Or it could be an interview question that would require that the respondent give an oral response. We could even provide a role-play situation in which the examinee's response to an angry parent is observed and rated. Or, as is more frequently being done today, a video enactment of the four alternatives could be shown to the examinee, who would then have to indicate which course of action he or she would pursue. Another format might require that the examinee document her or his actual behavior in a similar situation in portfolio fashion. Clearly, these "format" differences vary along various dimensions (e.g., realism, capability of being objectively scored), but perhaps the most significant difference relates to the breadth of content sampling that is possible. In a multiple-choice format we can provide many stimuli (hopefully of a broadly representative nature), but we limit the examinee to a given set of responses to each item. Usually because of time and cost constraints, some other formats are limited in terms of the stimuli sampled but will presumably allow for a wider potential sampling of responses. Whether these differences yield data that decrease or increase the size of subgroup differences on various measures is unknown. One could surmise that if verbal skills are a problem, some of the formats that require extended verbal responses would increase the difference between groups. If groups are differentially motivated by concrete realistic requests for information, we might expect the realism dimension to be related to the size of subgroup differences.

In a similar vein, some authors (e.g., Green et al., 1989; Ryan and Greguras, 1994) have drawn attention to the possible differential subgroup impact of distractors in multiple-choice formats. Whitney and Schmitt (1997) have presented evidence that distractors associated (or not associated) with African American cultural values change the attractiveness of these alternatives in multiple-choice biographical data items. Their hypothesis that options that reflect communal interests and a respect for authority would be more attractive to African Americans than to whites was confirmed, but the overall effects on test scores were very small. Similar efforts to assess differential distractor functioning in the realm of cognitive ability have rarely produced effects beyond chance levels. Even those effects that have been found did not have satisfying substantive interpretations. If these efforts are to be informative, they should be preceded by a careful examination of the cognitive requirements of the items and how they might be associated with subgroup differences. In other words, a priori hypotheses should be presented, as was true of the Scheuneman (1987) and Whitney and Schmitt (1996) work. From a content perspective, it is also important that the response options reflect the domain of possible responses (Guion, 1977).

As was alluded to above, there may also be motivational reasons to be concerned about the content of the item stimuli and response options that are related to subgroup status. There is a small body of research (e.g., Schmidt et al., 1977; Rynes and Connerly, 1993; Smither et al., 1993) indicating examinee preference for job-sample or "realistic" test formats over multiple-choice formats. In the educational arena it will be no surprise to any college professor that students prefer multiple-choice items (e.g., Bridgeman, 1992; Zeidner, 1987). I have used the threat of an essay makeup exam for many years in large college classes to avoid a large group of students demanding that they be given an exam after the scheduled date. Ryan and Greguras (1994), however, reported that minorities in an employment situation were significantly more likely than whites to agree that there was no connection between multiple-choice exams and one's ability to do a job, that multiple-choice exams cannot determine if one is a good employee, and that they would rather take a hands-on test even if it takes a lot more time. Smither et al. (1993) also found significant differences between minority and majority group members and older and younger job applicants on their reactions to various tests. Recently, Chan and co-workers (1997) also found relatively large and statistically significant differences in the perceived fairness and self-reported test-taking motivations of African American and white students who were taking a draft form of a cognitive ability measure to be used in selecting and promoting managerial personnel. It is at least plausible that these differences in motivation and perceived fairness will translate into differences in performance. Chan et al. (1997) provide some evidence that this might be the case.

It is difficult to envision what new legal issues might arise as a function of the use of exams other than multiple choice, *if* those alternative formats and testing methods yield equal reliability and validity. At this time I do not believe that there is any convincing evidence that one group or another performs better as a function of the format of the test items used. The few available comparisons of minority-majority differences on different types of tests completely confound the content or construct measured in the test with the format of the test items. If experimental tests could be devised of item format that do not confound content or construct with format, we will have better answers to these questions. My hypothesis at this point would be that any changes in the size of the difference between majority and minority groups will be moderated or mediated by the motivational impact of these format changes.

USE OF NEW TECHNOLOGIES

A significant stimulus to the question of whether format differences (as well as alternative formats) increase or decrease subgroup differences has been the availability of new video and computer technologies by which test stimuli can be presented and test responses gathered and scored. A large number of paper-and-pencil tests have been computerized: a computer terminal provides a more or less direct translation of the test to an examinee along with the potential responses, and the examinee is required to indicate the response by computer as well. Mead and Drasgow (1993) provide a metaanalysis of the effects of computerization on test scores. They found that the conversion of paper-and-pencil power tests to computerized forms yields scores that correlate highly (.97) and that the computerized version is slightly more difficult ($d = -.04$). Computerized versions of speeded tests do appear to be measuring something different than their paper-and-pencil counterparts ($R = .72$). No mention is made as to whether subgroup differences in scores on these tests increase or decrease when they are computerized.

Computer adaptive testing is being more widely used. In this kind of testing the test items presented to an examinee are matched to the person's ability level, which is estimated on the basis of previous responses. For example, a portion of the national examination used to license nurses is now a computer-adaptive measure, and the Graduate Record Examination can now be taken in computer-adaptive form. To my knowledge there are no data indicating that subgroup differences are smaller or larger on adaptive tests than on traditional tests. Given the possibility that adaptive tests may be uniformly more difficult than standardized tests, which often include easy items, especially at the beginning of the test, one might speculate that a computer-adaptive test would be more demotivating than a paper-and-pencil one. If minority groups are more prone to be negatively motivated by standardized tests of any form, the use of computer-adaptive tests may heighten their demotivation; others (Wainer et al., 1990), however, have used the same arguments to speculate that members of minority groups should do better on adaptive tests.

In addition, it is possible that disadvantaged students will have had little or no past experience with a computer. Some with no experience may actually fear using a computer. Again, there are no data about the effects of such computer phobia and no data of which I am aware showing a differential impact on one subgroup over another. In fact, I was able to find only one mention of this potential problem in books or papers on computer-adaptive testing (Wainer et al.,

1990). If the opportunity to use computers is differentially distributed across members of different subgroups, as well it might be, there may be some negative impact on those who have had less opportunity or experience with computers. As in the case of simple computerization of tests, I am aware of no studies that have examined the nature of subgroup differences on adaptive tests as opposed to full-length tests with varying item difficulties.

In addition to the heightened flexibility and capacity to present stimuli and collect and score responses that are characteristic of computer test administration, computers can also be used to present stimuli and collect responses that are inaccessible through paper-and-pencil tests. On the response side, computers can provide very accurate measurement of time variables such as response latencies. Variables characterizing the process of responding can be measured by tracking the activities of a test taker as he or she makes a decision or solves a problem. On psychomotor tasks, a person's use of a mouse or joystick can be recorded and scored. On the stimulus side, Pellegrino and Hunt (1989) have done research showing that a dynamic spatial ability factor is distinguishable from a static spatial ability factor included in many paper-and-pencil test batteries. This dynamic spatial factor involves the ability to track and project how objects will move in space, something that is clearly impossible with a static two-dimensional display. These technological advances certainly expand the capability to measure human ability, but the impact on subgroup differences is simply speculative at this point. If the use of technology results in more realistic face-valid measures, it is likely that the motivation of test takers will improve. In addition, research on job samples indicates that subgroup differences are likely to be minimized (see, e.g., Schmidt et al., 1977, 1996). On the other hand, if the use of computer technology constitutes an opportunity advantage, subgroup differences may be negatively affected.

In some instances, computer technology has been used to increase the realism of the test stimuli. Drasgow et al. (1993) describe various exercises designed to measure noncognitive managerial skills. In an in-basket exercise, examinees are presented with an interpersonal problem. With the use of CD-ROM technology, two solutions to the problem are presented, and the examinee is asked to pick his or her preferred solution. This solution then produces another problem for the examinee to "resolve." Depending on the particular sequence of examinee responses, different examinees will be presented with different sets of questions. Drasgow et al. (1993) have used item response theory to calibrate the items and score the many different sets of test items that might be presented to the examinee. Several other similar examples are described by McHenry and Schmitt (1994). Ashworth and McHenry (1992) describe a simulation used by Allstate Insurance to select claims adjustors. Dyer et al. (1993) describe a similar test designed to assess examinees' skills in resolving interpersonal problems that confront them in entry-level production jobs at IBM. Wilson Learning (1992) has developed tests of this type for sales, banking, supervisory, and customer service positions, and Schmitt et al. (1993) describe a test to assess the technical skills of applicants for clerical jobs at Ford Motor Company. Only Wilson Learning provides any evidence regarding criterion-related validity (validity equaled .40 for the customer service measure), and none of these investigators mentioned subgroup differences. Given the work-sample nature of these measures, subgroup differences are most likely smaller than they are for paper-and-pencil measures of ability. However, it would again be impossible to determine whether any difference in subgroup differences is a function of the test format or of the constructs measured. Interestingly, with the exception of the Schmitt et al. (1993) study, the focus in most of these efforts has primarily been on interpersonal or noncognitive capabilities.

Some recent efforts to reduce adverse impact of tests have focused on reducing the reading or writing requirements of examinations when those requirements are not essential to the job. This is certainly partly the focus of the multimedia tests described above, but in some cases the only change was from verbal or written to oral or visual test stimuli. That is, a written test of problem-solving skills is presented visually and orally. In some of these tests only the problem is presented visually, and the examinee is asked to select from a number of written options. In other cases both the problem and the situations are presented visually, and the examinee is asked to pick which action he or she would take to resolve the issue (HRStrategies, 1995). Chan and Schmitt (1997) have taken one of the video tests and produced a written paper-and-pencil version of the same test (items were written from the scripts used to produce the videos). They then compared the performance of African American and white examinees on the two versions of the test. They found subgroup differences to be about 0.20 on the video version and 0.90 on the written version. This may be the only comparison of subgroup differences on tests of different formats in which the contents of the test (and hopefully the constructs measured by the tests) were held constant.

While technology presents many alternatives for measuring individual differences in ability, there is an almost total absence of research literature on the validity of these measures as well as their potential impact on subgroup differences. Initial data on test reactions and older data regarding subgroup differences on job samples suggest that some of these changes may reduce subgroup differences. Equally promising is the potential to explore the nature of subgroup differences since the use of this technology allows for a significant expansion in the type of stimuli presented and the responses collected from examinees. The costs associated with the development, scoring, and updating of these measures, however, are certainly substantial. Opportunity differences associated with the previous use of, or exposure to, computers may raise legal concerns. If the test requires responses to different items from different examinees, as is true of computer-adaptive tests or branching tests of the type described by Drasgow et al. (1993), the equating of these tests may be difficult to explain and defend in court.

The major problem with the use of video and computer technology probably remains a simple lack of information on what exactly is being measured, what relationships with performance can be expected, and what differences in subgroup performance can be expected and why.

DOCUMENTATION OF PREVIOUS ACCOMPLISHMENTS

In the past several years a great deal of attention has been directed to a consideration of "authentic assessment" or "portfolio assessment," particularly among educators who are interested in documenting student learning (Schulman, 1988). A portfolio is usually a collection of information about a person's experiences or accomplishments in various relevant areas. If organized around dimensions of importance to a particular job or educational experience, these portfolios may be viewed as indicators of a person's knowledge, skill, or ability in these areas. The contents of a portfolio are carefully selected to illustrate key features of a person's educational or work experiences and include written descriptions of how projects or products were created and accomplished, for what purpose the project was initiated, the examinee's role in the project, with whom he or she worked, and, perhaps most importantly, how the project or product reflects the examinee's competency on various dimensions. Obviously, if a portfolio is to be useful in the selection of individuals for a particular job, it cannot be a random collection and documentation of experiences; it must be targeted to the competencies required in a given job or jobs.

As with all measurement instruments, key concerns with the use of portfolio assessment are reliability and validity issues. Research addressing the reliability of the scoring of portfolios is just beginning to develop, but the results of existing studies suggest that both internal consistency and interscorer reliability are low (Dunbar et al., 1991; Koretz et al., 1992; Nystrand et al., 1993). The validity issue has not been addressed as often, but one might argue that insofar as the portfolio contains evidence of the accomplishment of work tasks or tasks that require similar knowledge, skills, and abilities, no further evidence of validity is necessary. However, low interrater reliability would certainly suggest that validity is low as well.

There is a belief that subgroups who score lower on traditional tests may not score as low in portfolio assessment, but it will be important to document that this is not a function of the lower reliability usually associated with portfolio assessment. While predictive bias studies do not exist, preliminary evidence on subgroup mean scores does not support the view that portfolio assessment will reduce adverse impact or produce equity. Extended-response essays on the National Assessment of Educational Progress, for example, result in mean differences between African American and white students that parallel and, after correction for unreliability, actually exceed those found on multiple-choice reading assessments (Linn et al., 1991). Bond (1995) also reports that in one study

African American students received lower scores than their white counterparts on portfolio evaluations, regardless of the race of the rater.

In the work arena the development and use of accomplishment records is very similar to the use of portfolio assessment (Hough, 1984). However, much greater attention seems to have been placed on the psychometric adequacy of accomplishment records and documentation of the level of examinee involvement in the various items that may appear in a portfolio. Further, the work experiences are usually documented at the time one is applying for a job rather than in an ongoing manner as is the case for many educational portfolios. The development of accomplishment records has followed several well-defined steps that may contribute to their superior psychometric adequacy relative to portfolio assessment. Descriptions of portfolio assessment procedures do not include similar steps. Subject-matter experts meet to define the knowledge, skills, and abilities that best differentiate superior employees from those who are performing at minimally acceptable levels. This information is used to construct an application form that is organized around these job-relevant dimensions, and applicants are asked to describe their achievements on each dimension. This description must include information about the nature of the problem an applicant confronted, what he or she actually did, what outcome resulted, what percentage of the outcome was attributable to the respondent, and the name of someone who could document the respondent's role in producing the achievement described. Data are collected from a pool of applicants, and subject-matter experts are again used to judge the quality of this set of achievements. These achievements are then used as benchmarks against which additional applicants' qualifications are judged.

Schmidt et al. (1979) reported interrater reliabilities averaging .80 when they used this procedure to evaluate accountants for federal civil service jobs. Hough (1984) used the procedure to evaluate attorneys' job-related skills on seven dimensions as well as their overall ability. Interrater reliabilities ranged from .75 to .82 for a three-rater composite. Hough was also able to collect performance data for 307 attorneys, and the correlation between composite performance ratings and accomplishment record scores was .25. Finally, the standardized mean difference between minority and nonminority attorneys was 0.33, which almost exactly matched the difference of these two groups on the performance composite (0.35). In this case the relatively small difference between minority and majority groups was not a function of low reliability. It is also important to note that some of the dimensions rated were cognitive (e.g., researching/investigating, using knowledge, planning and organizing). Hough's minority sample was small ($N = 30$), and very little subsequent research has been published on this method. If Hough's results are replicable, this may be a viable and promising alternative to traditional selection procedures and a significant improvement over the results that seem to be obtained using portfolio assessments.

Completing an accomplishment record or constructing a portfolio can be complex and time consuming; in at least one instance in which this author was involved, the minority group had a significantly lower completion rate than the majority group. The work involved may have a differential motivational impact; the persons involved may have realized that they did not have the required competencies when they read the accomplishment record; or they may have reacted to the organization's climate for minority individuals. In any event the involvement of members of different groups at all phases of an employment process should be monitored in an effort to detect unanticipated outcomes.

The use of an accomplishment record was preceded by the use of training and experience inventories in various civil service jurisdictions. One commonly used method specified the number of points to be awarded for various years of specified training and experience. Points were determined on the basis of some judgment of the relative worth of the various experiences. This approach was essentially credentialistic in that it focused on the amount of experience and education rather than on what was achieved or accomplished during that education or experience. Even this relatively simple approach to assessing competencies appears to have some validity (McDaniel et al., 1988). It should be noted that this extreme attenuation of the portfolio approach is almost certain to be attacked on the grounds that there are large subgroup differences in educational attainment (and almost certainly job experiences) and that direct connections between a high school or college diploma and job performance are difficult to make. This is true in spite of, or perhaps because of, their relatively low level of criterion-related validity (see McDaniel et al., 1988).

Whether or not enthusiasm for the portfolio type of measurement continues and future research suggests practical solutions to some of the measurement inadequacies, there are a number of possible issues that could generate litigation. Explanations of the scoring process and the reliability and qualifications of the scorers are obvious targets. Questions about who actually does the work involved (Gearhart and Herman, 1995) and the extent of the examinee's role in any accomplishment may be questioned. Perhaps the most significant unknown is the degree to which questions about the opportunity to achieve or accomplish along relevant dimensions will arise. As anyone who can remember looking for a first job or for summer employment will verify, one of the easiest ways to dismiss someone is to say the person does not have the requisite experience. But how does one achieve the required experience without that first job? Actually, portfolios and accomplishment records can accommodate this concern if developers and subject-matter experts are sensitive to the fact that relevant experiences can be acquired in nontraditional ways (e.g., through volunteer work or organizations and clubs).

BANDING

The previous sections in this paper discussed various alternative testing methods and their impact on subgroup differences. This section addresses the manner in which test scores are used to make employment decisions. As mentioned at the beginning of the paper, the desire to use valid tests while achieving a diverse work force often led employers to "adjust" scores in a variety of ways to achieve appropriate levels of diversity when the raw scores on those tests displayed subgroup differences. One such method used by the U.S. Employment Service in reporting applicant scores to potential employers in the 1980s was within-group norming. The scores of members of minority and majority groups were determined by reference to members of their demographic group. This adjustment was equal to adding a constant equal to the difference in the scores of these two groups to the scores of members of the lower-scoring group. One provision of the Civil Rights Act of 1991 was to prohibit such adjustments. While adjustments to test scores are now illegal, there are many different ways in which tests scores have been and can be used (e.g., pass-fail, multiple-hurdle, etc.), some of which result in lessened impact in some situations.

Cascio et al. (1995a) describe a banding approach to the use of test scores (see also Sproule, 1984) to increase the likelihood of minority hiring as well as to attain other organizational objectives. This approach to the use of test scores started with the idea that individuals whose scores were not significantly different from the top scorer on the test should be treated as equally capable and that selections from this group of individuals could be made on other bases, including education, racial/ethnic diversity, seniority, job performance, training, experience, or relocation preferences. To determine the size of this band, Cascio et al. (1995a) proposed that the standard error of the difference (which is equal to the standard error of measurement multiplied by the square root of 2) be calculated. This value was then multiplied by 1.65 (if one chose the .05 level of significance) to determine the bandwidth. If the top score on a test was 100 and the bandwidth was 10, then all persons with scores between 90 and 100 would be considered equal, and some other means would be used to determine among this group of people who would be selected.

Minority individuals in this band have greater likelihood of being selected than if only top-down selection based on test scores were used to make selections. This assumes there are subgroup differences on the test and that not all individuals in the top band are selected. It also means that race, or some variable correlated with race, is used to make selections within the band if any reductions in adverse impact are to be realized. As Kriska (1995) has pointed out, this approach to test use is no different than a multiple-hurdle approach in which examinees must achieve some passing test score as the first hurdle in a selection system and are then hired based on other job-relevant bases. The banding method then constitutes a means of setting a pass score on the test and is probably no more or less scientifically or legally defensible than other available means of setting pass scores.

This banding approach is called a fixed band. In the context of this paper, the use of this approach would usually be motivated by a desire to increase minority representation. If all members in this band are selected, the result of this approach will be no different from that of a top-down procedure other than the fact that minority individuals might be selected earlier than would be the case if strict top-down selection occurred. If race is the only consideration used after the establishment of the band, the implication of the Civil Rights Act and a San Francisco case to be discussed below is that it is likely this process will be considered legally inappropriate. When race is combined with other decision factors as was proposed by Cascio et al. (1995a), the impact on the number of minority hires will obviously be minimized. So, whether this fixed banding approach increases minority hiring is a function of the portion of the band hired and the secondary predictors used. In terms of the expected performance of those selected, the use of various banding approaches appears to have little impact (Siskin, 1995). If a fixed-band approach is used, it seems that one could also question why the test is used first in what amounts to a multiple-hurdle system. If test scores of minority and majority individuals are radically different while their standing on the secondary predictors is not, the organization would be using first the predictor on which minority individuals do worst. If I were a plaintiff's attorney, I would challenge this order of events.

A second category of banding approaches proposed by Cascio et al. (1995a) is referred to as a sliding band. In this approach a band is established as above. As the organization makes selections, however, the band changes. As soon as the top-scoring individual or individuals are selected, the band moves down a corresponding number of test score points; thereby, a band of constant width is maintained. If the motivation is to allow consideration of minority (or other) individuals both within the band and just below the original band, a system of top-down selection within a group within a band is recommended (Cascio et al., 1995a). This means that secondary predictors would be used until the supply of individuals possessing those secondary characteristics in the first band is depleted; then the top-scoring person or persons would be selected if this has not already been done. The band would then move down, allowing consideration of additional minority individuals or persons with whatever secondary characteristics are being considered. This sequence of events would be repeated with additional movement of the band until the desired number of people are selected. If only race or sex is considered in isolation of other secondary characteristics when selections are made within the band, the sliding-band approach is equivalent to adding bonus points to the lower-scoring group equal to the size of the band (Sackett and Wilks, 1994). It is important to note that banding advocates do not consider test score differences within a band meaningful; hence, the use of the term "bonus points" is inappropriate. In a 1992 decision from the Ninth Circuit Court of Appeals (*Officers for Justice v. Civil Service Commission of the City and County of San Francisco*, 979 F2d 721), this plan was found acceptable under the Civil Rights Act of 1991 as long as race was only one of several secondary criteria used to make selections within the band. An earlier plan to use race as the sole consideration on which to make selections within the band was not acceptable.

Putting aside the considerable professional debate about the logic and merits of banding, I do not believe this approach represents a workable or highly desirable long-term solution to the problem of subgroup differences in test scores. First, the efficacy of banding in producing increases in minority hiring is a complex function of at least the following variables: the size of subgroup differences on the test and any secondary predictors used, the proportion of minorities in the applicant pool, the selection ratio, the reliability of the test (hence the size of the band relative to the distribution as a whole), the confidence level chosen to set the band, and the intercorrelations among the tests and the other criteria used to make selections. The fact that so many variables determine the outcome means that the manner in which bands are established will almost always be a post hoc consideration of several alternatives and their impact on minority hiring. When, and if, the post hoc manipulation and these variables are explained to a court or jury, they may very likely be interpreted as deliberate tampering with test scores to achieve increases in minority hiring. The same might be said when any alternative test use strategy is explained or used, however. Second, in many situations the use of banding or sliding bands will not produce a large increase in the proportion of minorities hired (Sackett and Roth, 1991). Third, one very undesirable outcome might be a court's (or the public's) perception that this approach represents the means by which psychologists and statisticians are reintroducing within-group norming or something similar. The importance or salience of this latter concern depends on the degree to which demographic characteristics (e.g., race or gender) are used as secondary predictors.

One aspect of the debate on banding that I hope gains greater attention is that industrial and organizational psychologists expand their notion of what constitutes criteria of effectiveness (Cascio et al., 1995b). This would almost certainly expand the domain of variables considered when one appraises the capability of a set of applicants to contribute to organizational effectiveness. As an example, public jurisdictions and private organizations that seek to serve a minority community have recognized the need to employ members of these communities because they are often more effective in providing that service. Use of a traditional paper-and-pencil test of job-related knowledge as a primary selection device in such situations seems almost farcical.

SUMMARY AND CONCLUSIONS

In considering the issues addressed in this paper, I asked myself what I would do at this time if I wanted to maximize the outcomes of a selection process in ways that would reflect societal values (at least as I interpret them) and organizational interests and that would maximize the participation of minority groups in our economy. The following are suggestions for reaching the stated goal:

1. *Consider the performance criteria that one hopes will be maximized.* A very broad consideration of the organization's goals and its role in the community at large should be part of this consideration, as would the varied roles an individual can play in helping the organization accomplish its goals. These considerations may mean that there are multiple nonredundant performance criteria. A candidate's predicted status on one of these criteria may be superior while the predicted status on other criteria may be appalling. The managerial problem then becomes reconciliation of these conflicting predictions, which may very well have implications for minority hiring.

2. *Construct and use measures that reflect the broad range of abilities to engage in accomplishing these organizational objectives.* One should not err by constructing measures that are easy to administer, score, or interpret. An ability's job relevance should be the major concern, not the ease of evaluating or measuring an ability.

3. *Pay attention to face validity as well as scientific validity.* If examinees perceive the process as appropriate in light of what they expect to do when hired, there will be fewer legal problems and it is more likely that the defense of such procedures will prevail in court. Improved perceptions of the fairness of the process may increase examinee motivation (especially for minorities), which may, in turn, affect test performance.

4. *Continue research on alternative testing methods, technologies, and constructs to further our understanding of subgroup differences and to increase the probability that appropriate remedial actions can be taken.* There are many points in this paper at which my conclusion was simply that there was a lack of information to answer a particular question.

5. *Develop job-relevant, psychometrically adequate measures of past achievements and accomplishments.* In doing so, pay special attention to the opportunities various groups have had to engage in activities that would result in these accomplishments.

6. *Admit that there are substantial differences between minority and majority groups that transcend the particular test used to measure ability, primarily in the cognitive domain.* Rather than continuing to focus attention on minimizing these measured differences, focus efforts on developing and supporting programs that will address the social, economic, and educational inequities that have produced these differences. Simultaneously, recognize that some tests, insofar as they constitute the primary gatekeepers, contribute to the perpetuation of these inequities.

REFERENCES

Ashworth, S.D., and J.J. McHenry
   1992   Development of a Computerized In-Basket to Measure Critical Job Skills. Unpub-
          lished paper presented at the fall meeting of the Personnel Testing Council of South-
          ern California, Newport, CA.
Bond, L.
   1995   Unintended consequences of performance assessments: Issues of bias and fairness. *Edu-
          cational Measurement: Issues and Practice* 14:21-24.
Boyle, S.
   1984   The effect of variations in answer-sheet format on aptitude performance. *Journal of
          Occupational Psychology* 57:323-326.
Bridgeman, B.
   1992   A comparison of quantitative questions in open-ended and multiple-choice formats. *Jour-
          nal of Educational Measurement* 29:253-271.
Cascio, W.F., I.L. Goldstein, J. Outtz, and S. Zedeck
   1995a Statistical implications of six methods of test score use in personnel selection. *Human
          Performance* 8(3):133-164
   1995b Twenty issues and answers about sliding bands. *Human Performance* 8(3):227-242.
Chan, D., and N. Schmitt
   1997   Video-based versus paper-and-pencil method of assessment in situational judgment tests:
          Differential adverse impact and examinee attitudes. *Journal of Applied Psychology*
          82:143-159.
Chan, D., N. Schmitt, R.P. DeShon, C.S. Clause, and K. Delbridge
   1997   Reactions to cognitive ability tests: Relationships between race, test performance, face
          validity, and test-taking motivation. *Journal of Applied Psychology* 82:300-310.
Cronbach, L. J.
   1941   An experimental comparison of the multiple true-false and multiple-choice tests. *Journal
          of Educational Psychology* 32:533-543.
Drasgow, F., J.B. Olson, P.A. Keenan, P. Moberg, and A.D. Mead
   1993   Computerized assessment. Pp. 163-206 in *Research in Personnel and Human Resources
          Management*, G.A. Ferris and K.M. Rowland, eds. Greenwich, CT: JAI Press.
Dunbar, S.B., D.M. Koretz, and H.D. Hoover
   1991   Quality control in the development and use of performance assessments. *Applied Mea-
          surement in Education* 4:289-303.
Dyer, P.J., L.B. Desmarais, and K.R. Midkiff
   1993   Multimedia Employment Testing in IBM: Preliminary Results from Employees. Unpub-
          lished paper presented at the annual conference of the Society for Industrial/Organiza-
          tional Psychology, San Francisco.
Gearhart, M., and J.L. Herman
   1995   *Portfolio Assessment: Whose Work Is It? Issues in the Use of Classroom Assignments for
          Accountability.* Technical report. Los Angeles: Center for Research on Evaluation, Stan-
          dards, and Student Testing, University of California.
Green, B.F., C.R. Crone, and V.G. Folk
   1989   A method for studying differential distractor functioning. *Journal of Educational Mea-
          surement* 26:147-160.
Guion, R.M.
   1977   Content validity: The source of my discontent. *Applied Psychological Measurement*
          1:1-10.
Hough, L.M.
   1984   Development and evaluation of the "accomplishment record" method of selecting and
          promoting professionals. *Journal of Applied Psychology* 69:135-146.

HRStrategies
1995   *Design, Validation and Implementation of the 1994 Police Officer Entrance Examination.*
        Technical report. Nassau County, NY: HRStrategies.
Koretz, D., D. McCaffrey, S. Klein, R. Bell, and B. Stecher
1992   *The Reliability of Scores from the 1992 Vermont Portfolio Assessment Program: Interim
        Report.* Los Angeles: RAND Institute on Education and Training.
Kriska, S.D.
1995   Comments on banding. *The Industrial-Organizational Psychologist* 32:93-94.
Linn, R.L., E.L. Baker, and S.B. Dunbar
1991   Complex, performance-based assessment: Expectations and validation criteria. *Educa-
        tional Researcher* 20:15-21.
McDaniel, M.A., F.L. Schmidt, and J.E. Hunter
1988   A meta-analysis of the validity of methods for rating training and experience in personnel
        selection. *Personnel Psychology* 41:282-314.
McHenry, J.J., and N. Schmitt
1994   Multimedia testing. Pp. 193-232 in *Personnel Selection and Classification*, M.G. Rumsey,
        C.B. Walker, and J.H. Harris, eds. Hillsdale, NJ: Lawrence Erlbaum Associates.
Mead, A.D., and F. Drasgow
1993   Equivalence of computerized and paper-and-pencil cognitive ability tests: A meta-analy-
        sis. *Psychological Bulletin* 114:449-458.
Nystrand, M., A.S. Cohen, and N.M. Dowling
1993   Addressing reliability problems in the portfolio assessment of college writing. *Educa-
        tional Assessment* 1:53-70.
Outtz, J.L.
1994   Testing Medium, Validity, and Test Performance. Unpublished paper presented at the
        Conference on Evaluating Alternatives to Traditional Testing for Selection, Bowling
        Green State University, Bowling Green, OH.
Pellegrino, J.W., and E.B. Hunt
1989   Computer-controlled assessment of static and dynamic spatial reasoning. Pp. 174-198 in
        Testing: Theoretical and Applied Perspectives, R.F. Dillon and J. W. Pellegrino, eds.
        New York: Praeger.
Pulakos, E.D., and N. Schmitt
1996   An evaluation of two strategies for reducing adverse impact and their effects on criterion-
        related validity. *Human Performance* 9:241-259.
Ryan, A.M., and G.J. Greguras
1994   Life is Not Multiple Choice: Reactions to the Alternatives. Unpublished paper presented
        at the Conference on Evaluating Alternatives to Traditional Testing for Selection, Bowl-
        ing Green State University, Bowling Green, OH.
Rynes, S.L., and M.L. Connerly
1993   Applicant reactions to alternative selection procedures. *Journal of Business and Psychol-
        ogy* 7:261-277.
Sackett, P.R., and L. Roth
1991   A Monte Carlo examination of banding and rank order methods of test score use in
        selection. *Human Performance* 4:279-295.
1995   Multi-Stage Selection Strategies: A Monte Carlo Investigation of Effects on Performance
        and Minority Hiring. Unpublished manuscript, Industrial Relations Center, University of
        Minnesota, Minneapolis.
Sackett, P.R., and S.L. Wilk
1994   Within-group norming and other forms of score adjustment in preemployment testing.
        American Psychologist 49:929-954.

Scheuneman, J.D.
  1987   An experimental, exploratory study of causes of bias in test items. *Journal of Educational Measurement* 24:97-118.
Schmidt, F.L., A.L. Greenthal, J.G. Berner, J.E. Hunter, and F.W. Seaton
  1977   Job sample vs. paper-and-pencil trades and technical tests: Adverse impact and examinee attitudes. *Personnel Psychology* 30:187-198.
Schmidt, F.L., J.R. Caplan, S.E. Bemis, R. Decuin, L. Dunn, and L. Antone
  1979   *The Behavioral Consistency Method of Unassembled Examining.* Washington, DC: Office of Personnel Management.
Schmitt, N., S.W. Gilliland, R.S. Landis, and D. Devine
  1993   Computer-based testing applied to selection of secretarial applicants. *Personnel Psychology* 46:149-165.
Schmitt, N., C.S. Clause, and E.D. Pulakos
  1996   Subgroup differences associated with different measures of some common job-relevant constructs. Pp. 115-140 in *International Review of Industrial and Organizational Psychology*, Vol. 11, C.L. Cooper and I.T. Robertson, eds. New York: Wiley.
Schmitt, N., W. Rogers, D. Chan, L. Sheppard, and D. Jennings
  1997   Reducing adverse impact of cognitive ability tests by adding measures of other predictor constructs: The effects of number of predictors, predictor intercorrelations, validity, and level of subgroup differences. *Journal of Applied Psychology* (forthcoming).
Schulman, L.S.
  1988   A union of insufficiencies: Strategies for teacher assessment in a period of reform. *Educational Leadership* 46:36-41.
Siskin, B.R.
  1995   Relation between performance and banding. *Human Performance* 8:215-226.
Smither, J.W., R.R. Reilly, R.E. Millsap, K. Pearlman, and R.W. Stoffey
  1993   Applicant reactions to selection procedures. *Personnel Psychology* 46:49-76.
Sproule, C.F.
  1984   Should personnel selection tests be used on a pass-fail, grouping, or ranking basis? *Public Personnel Management* 13:375-394.
Traub, R.E., and C.W. Fisher
  1977   On the equivalence of constructed-response and multiple-choice tests. *Applied Psychological Measurement* 1:355-369.
Wainer, H., N.J. Dorans, B.F. Green, R.J. Mislevy, L. Steinberg, and D. Thissen
  1990   Future challenges. Pp. 233-272 in *Computerized Adaptive Testing: A Primer*. H. Wainer, ed. Hillsdale, NJ: Lawrence Erlbaum Associates.
Ward, W.C.
  1982   A comparison of free-response and multiple-choice forms of verbal aptitude tests. *Applied Psychological Measurement* 6:1-11.
Ward, W.C., N. Fredericksen, and S.B. Carlson
  1980   Construct validity of free-response and machine-scorable forms of a test. *Journal of Educational Measurement* 17:11-29.
Whitney, D.J., and N. Schmitt
  1997   The relationship between culture and responses to biodata and employment items. *Journal of Applied Psychology* 82:113-129.
Wilson Learning
  1992   *Electronic Assessment of First-Line Supervisor: A Criterion-Related Validation Report.* Longwood, FL: Wilson Learning.
Zeidner, M.
  1987   Essay versus multiple-choice type classroom exams: The student's perspective. *Journal of Educational Research* 80:352-358.

10
What Policy Makers and Experts See (and Do Not See) in School-to-Work Transitions

Larry Cuban

INTRODUCTION

Few social scientists would challenge the statement that how public policy problems are framed has a great deal to do with setting the agenda for subsequent debate and which solutions policy makers ultimately adopt. Nor would many social scientists challenge the claim that who defines a situation as a problem has much to do with how the problem is framed. Deaths from auto accidents in this century, for example, have been largely defined by auto manufacturers, national safety coalitions, and public officials as being due to careless and drunken drivers. The problem has been framed in terms of blaming individual drivers, and policy solutions have been laws punishing offenders and public campaigns to educate car owners to drive safely. Not until the 1970s did critics of the definition of the problem of fatal auto accidents pose alternatives for policy makers to consider: unsafe car design and unsafe road engineering. In short, the power, status, expertise, and interests of problem framers have shaped policy makers' deliberations and actions. A problem, then, is socially constructed; it is not an objective rendering of a situation (Gusfield, 1981; Hilgartner and Bosk, 1988).

Nothing new here, yet I raise this issue of how problems are defined and who does the framing because, again, another new federal program—school-to-work transition—has been displayed as a reform (or solution) to a problem defined by policy makers and experts. While the immediate context for the papers in this volume is the matter of how best to assess school-to-work transition, the bulk of the papers' descriptions, analyses of evidence, and arguments are anchored in expert-conceived definitions of problems. Current solutions to these problems, such as the Secretary's Commission on Achieving Necessary Skills (SCANS), Goals 2000 and the School-to-Work Opportunities Act, the establishment of a

National Skills Standard Board, and calls for a new test-driven credential (a certificate of initial mastery) are limited by how narrowly the problems are framed (see Chapter 6, this volume).

Rather than comment on the various positions taken by the writers in this volume, I will take a step back to analyze how problems are framed in these papers and who does the defining. In this analysis what will become obvious is that there are some key perspectives, or "ways of seeing," that have become dominant in framing these youth and labor market problems and that other perspectives, just as important, are absent from this examination of school-to-work issues, sponsored by the Board on Testing and Assessment (BOTA). Finally, I will raise two questions that have been unasked in the other papers and conference discussions: Why is the prevailing architecture of the problem framed as a "youth" problem, and why are solutions to larger economic problems often put forth as school reforms?

WAYS OF SEEING THE SCHOOL-TO-WORK TRANSITION AND ITS ASSESSMENT

Each of the papers in this volume has a "way of seeing" embedded within it. What I mean by a way of seeing is an implicit or explicit explanation of phenomena. For social scientists their ways of seeing are often anchored in disciplinary-based theories drawn from one or more academic disciplines or a combination of concepts stitched together into evidence-based arguments that explain puzzling situations. For policy makers and practitioners, ways of seeing are often implicit explanations drawn from life experiences, values, and prior academic training to make sense of the confusing array of daily signals and events they face, including linkages between school and work. Within each way of seeing, then, are often tacit formulations of the linkages between workplace and school, the problems that exist, and how they should be solved.

In the papers here the ways of seeing are largely macro, top down in policy direction, and heavily influenced by the disciplinary views of economists, psychologists, and lawyers. In short, a dominant way of seeing is that of federal and state policy makers and their expert advisers. None of this, of course, should be surprising at a BOTA-sponsored meeting. Nonetheless, it may help subsequent debate about school-to-work reforms and their assessment to dredge to the surface these unarticulated assumptions about problems and solutions (with their implications for assessment) that so easily go unexamined in the policy-making world.

PREVAILING WAYS OF SEEING

Policy Makers' Perspective on School-to-Work

The world of federal and state policy makers is a political one driven by voters, lobbyists, legislation, polls, and budgets. One thrives in this world by shaping the demands of competing groups into an agenda that secures notice, credit, and, of course, reelection. The policy tools available to elected officials are largely mandates and inducements—the carrot-and-stick cliché captures the limited tools that policy makers have in their repertoire. On occasion, capacity-building tools (e.g., job-training programs) are used (Elmore and McLaughlin, 1988; McDonnell, 1994).

When the issue of work and schooling arises in the policy-making world, the prevailing theory in use is borrowed from economists. Human capital theory holds that investments in education and training will pay off in enhanced economic productivity and individual gains in lifetime wages and salaries. Within such a theory, building skills in current and future workers will yield higher productivity, decrease competition among unskilled workers for low-skill jobs by increasing the pool of higher-skilled employees, and eventually begin smoothing out wage differentials. Anchored in this theory is the mainstay belief that supply and demand in the labor market will take care of imbalances; that is, where shortfalls in the supply of skilled workers exist, wage increases will increase the pool of applicants with the appropriate match of skills. Educational policy makers, of course, have found this theory nicely tailored to their altruistic beliefs in the potency of continued schooling and their vested interest in expanding institutional education. Vocational education, curricula that offered cognitive and social skill development, and programs that retained students until graduation were easily rationalized as both good for society and good for individual students (see Chapter 2, this volume; Kett, 1995).[1]

Given the world of policy makers and the dominant theory in use, two ways of framing problems are clearly evident in the papers and conference discussions. First, workplace changes produce an initial skill deficit in youth seeking entry-level jobs, thereby causing high unemployment and a series of low-wage/low-skill jobs. This skills mismatch, as Holzer (Chapter 2, this volume) frames it, eventually corrects itself as the gaps between the skills that youth bring to employers and the available job pool inch closer together. Thus, the problem is framed as one of supply and demand that is customarily solved as market adjustments, over time, are made. Holzer argues, however, that in the short run this skills mismatch can be alleviated, in part, by upgrading educational opportunities for students to acquire skills and for providing employers with accurate and up-to-date information on applicants for entry-level jobs.

---

[1]During the 1960s and since then, challenges to human capital theory have been made through the segmented market theory, which argued that all jobs can be divided into primary and secondary markets, with the primary market offering on-the-job opportunities for training and advancement and the secondary market being characterized by high turnover and few chances to improve skills and largely dominated by women and teenagers. While some economists advocate this theory, no mention of it occurred at the 2-day BOTA conference, and it was not mentioned by any of the authors. I spoke with two economists during the conference, and both mentioned that human capital theory is mainstream while the theory of segmented markets is "fringe."

Within this supply-and-demand formulation of the problem, Zemsky (Chapter 3, this volume) elaborates the demand side of the equation with his story of an employer saying that what he wanted was a 26 year old with three previous jobs. Employers seek, according to Zemsky's survey data and focus group discussions, what schools cannot produce in an 18 year old who lacks the work experience and maturity that an older seasoned worker can offer. Zemsky argues that, with the problem framed in this manner, employer-crafted solutions include ignoring high school credentials and virtually writing off the 16- to 26-year-old cohort by using trial-and-error hiring; that is, taking a few applicants, getting rid of them if they don't work out, and trying again until the 26 year old with three previous jobs comes along.

A second way of framing the problem of a skills mismatch is to blame the schools. Poor academic preparation and passing students from grade to grade even if they lack basic literacy, computing, and social skills is what schools have done for years, causing the gap between less skilled youth seeking jobs that demand more than what high school graduates have to offer. In a presentation at the BOTA conference, Darvin Winick, a consultant to corporations and public officials, gave example after example of schools failing to prepare their charges for the workplace. The solution to a problem framed in this manner is to fix the schools.

Assessment strategies, popular among state and federal educational policy makers, also draw heavily from the skills mismatch argument embedded in the human capital theory and from the unrelenting press of political accountability. Paper-and-pencil and newly designed performance-based tests have been used (and are being piloted—e.g., the New Standards Project) to achieve multiple (and often conflicting) goals: to diagnose the skills gap among high school youth; to predict how high school students will do in the workplace; to drive instructional practices toward state and national curricular goals; and evaluate individual student, school, district, and state academic performance (Linn, 1994; Chapter 6, this volume).

Such a mixed, if not confused, strategy, forged from both political and technical goals, emerged because policy makers historically respond to critics' calls for political accountability over schooling by demanding that experts create tests that will satisfy these conflicting values. Psychometricians, seeking to respond to public officials' urgent demands for accountability without sacrificing their standards of reliability and validity, developed tests that tried to bridge these differences. A case in point is the California Learning Assessment System (CLAS), a test developed in the early 1990s that swiftly became a national model for appraising student reasoning but that subsequently disappeared.

CLAS's history reveals rival political and technical claims for what the test should do. Governor Pete Wilson wanted a test that would provide individual student scores for parents. Such evidence would offer a basis for moving forward with merit pay plans to reward teachers whose students performed well on CLAS and financially punish those teachers whose students scored low. The state legislature wanted CLAS to produce accurate information on school site performance that would permit high performers to get increased autonomy to forge ahead in further improving their schools. The state superintendent wanted CLAS to measure the new curricular standards in order to influence teachers' routine classroom practices. And the state's education department, charged with developing and administering the test, wanted a reliable and valid instrument that went beyond multiple-choice items and assessed students' knowledge and skills on performance-based tasks (McDonnell, 1994; Kirst et al., 1995).

Such an unwieldy coalition stitched together by conflicting hopes for a better test might have endured except for the aftermath of the first administration of the test. What was revealed were sampling errors in published test scores, the organized opposition of parent and religious groups who were sharply critical of particular book passages (from Alice Walker's novel *The Color Purple*) used in CLAS, and "Sacramento bureaucrats" who were trying to run (and ruin) the schools. The ensuing uproar led Governor Wilson to veto further funding of CLAS. Thus, political and technical tensions disrupted an unlikely coalition (Kirst et al., 1995).

California may be a signal to state and federal policy makers that the inherent conflicts arising from rival political and technical aims for new tests cannot be easily finessed, or it may just be a quirky exception that policy makers can safely ignore. Whatever the case, the data presented in the conference papers and discussions, particularly the two ethnographic studies of different firms (Chapters 4 and 5, this volume), raise stark empirical questions about how the "way of seeing" has framed problems, directed attention toward certain solutions, and advocated particular assessments:

1. Are the cognitive, social, and personal skills employers seek in their employees the ones that workers need in their jobs?
2. Is the skills gap in the workplace as bad as employers say it is?

Both Holzer and Zemsky, relying on cross-sectional survey data enhanced by focus group interviews, answer *yes* to both questions. But the papers by Bonalyn Nelsen on auto repair shops and Glynda Hull on circuit board factories (Chapters 4 and 5, this volume) suggest contrary answers to these questions. Generalizing from firms in two separate industries to the vast and diverse U.S. economy is far too much of a leap. What the two ethnographic studies offer, however, are stunning rebuttals to those that confidently answer *no* to the above questions. At the very least, then, the empirical questions remain open to further investigation by researchers.

It is to these academic experts that I now turn since the second prevailing way of seeing in the papers and conference discussions was that of the specialist.

Experts' Perspective on Assessment of School-to-Work Transition

The authors and conferees who made up this group of specialists were mainly psychologists (industrial, cognitive, and educational) and lawyers. Their way of seeing derives primarily from research-based, disciplinary-driven views of assessment. These experts seek to construct tests that certify and authenticate student performance in skills and knowledge acquisition that are free of bias and can withstand legal challenge. As technical experts, they find themselves in the bind of offering advice to policy makers, even crafting proposals, while simultaneously being skeptical of policy makers' goals, arguments, and specific plans for assessment (see Chapter 7, this volume).

Within this world of expertise, theories in use about assessment come directly from academic disciplines and legal precedents that seek to specify exactly what is being measured and for what purposes and how best to achieve those aims while adhering to exacting technical standards. Lawyers, for example, leaned heavily on previous court decisions banning certain employment tests as discriminatory screening devices resulting in untoward consequences for minorities (see Chapter 8, this volume). For different branches of psychology, theories about generalizability, item responses, measurability, and socially situated cognition compete for attention in determining the direction, scope, and particulars of both traditional and innovative tests (see Chapter 7, this volume).

Yet even with contending disciplinary-based theories, there are prevailing ways of framing problems (and their solutions) in constructing assessments for the school-to-work transition. Many educational and industrial psychologists, for example, will view the problem of assessing school-to-work programs as the absence of rigor and specificity in defining exactly what workplace and school skills are needed. Pearlman (Chapter 6, this volume) points out that even the concept of "skill" lacks precision; it is not an exact measurable unit but embraces numerous cross-cutting categories (workplace basic skills, cross-functional skills, and occupation-specific skills) that make assessment a far more knotty task than policy makers had imagined. He offers the metaphor that plunging ahead with skill-based assessments in SCANS, Goals 2000, and school-to-work programs is like laying out a complex road system before a survey of the land has been done.

Another common way of framing the problem of assessment is whether new tests (e.g., performance-based assessments such as portfolios) meet technical standards of reliability and validity (Linn, 1994). One of the difficulties that California State Department of Education administrators experienced before the demise of CLAS, for example, was wrestling publicly with a critical report from a group of measurement experts on its sampling and statistical procedures (Kirst et al., 1995).

Finally, legal experts often define problems of assessment in terms of what legal hurdles a new test would have to leap, particularly if high stakes for students are attached to their scores. In the 1970s, for example, the introduction of competency tests that students had to pass to receive a high school diploma were challenged in various states because large numbers of racial and ethnic minorities failed the new tests. *Debra P. v. Turlington* established the principle that, if students had not received the appropriate knowledge and skills in their classrooms prior to taking the test and failed it, the diploma could not be withheld (Pullin, 1994). Both Parker (Chapter 8, this volume) and Schmitt (Chapter 9, this volume) frame the problem of assessment-based credentials in the potential challenges to new tests embedded in school-to-work programs.

Solutions to expert-defined problems are consistent with the ways that the problem is framed. Solutions range from devoting more time and money to further research and development in specifying and testing skills to cautious support for particular policy strategies that are consistent with the theories and research findings of these discipline-based specialists (Chapters 6, 8, and 9, this volume).

As I read these expert-defined problems and solutions in the papers and listened to the conference discussions, thorny empirical questions arose in my mind:

1. What exactly is a skill?
2. To what degree are skills transferable within and across occupations?
3. To what extent is training in "cross-functional" skills (communication, teamwork, finding information, problem solving) generalizable?
4. Do high-stakes assessments that certify students for employment disadvantage low-income minorities further?

These questions suggest that policy makers' and experts' ways of seeing overlap but are also distinct enough to generate conflicts over what policy directions should be pursued by those in authority to make decisions on school-to-work programs and assessments. Yet the conflicts I saw between technical and policy perspectives should not obscure the larger fact that these were the dominant ways of seeing represented in the papers, presentations, and conference discussions. As compelling (and traditional) as they are, such perspectives are not the only ways of viewing the school-to-work transition.

What ways of seeing were absent? I offer two missing perspectives; they are far less developed than the ones discussed above. I offer these in shorthand form to suggest that other ways of seeing may begin to fill in empty spaces left by the prevailing perspectives at the conference. These unarticulated perspectives could inform policy making about the school-to-work transition and its assessment by raising different questions than those offered by the authors and conferees.

OTHER WAYS OF SEEING

Historical Precedents for School-to-Work Transition

While there are many versions of the past and no one true rendition of what happened, few informed historians of education would dispute that the transition from school to work has been defined as a problem by national policy makers repeatedly since the closing decades of the nineteenth century. I offer a brief summary of those encounters (Tyack, 1974; Cremin, 1961; Lazerson and Grubb, 1974).

In the 1880s critics began attacking public schools for failing to teach students the necessary skills to work in a factory-dominated industrial economy. Businessmen, searching for skilled, efficient, and loyal workers, turned to the schools and asked why they were preparing students for college and not the workplace. These criticisms emerged at the same time that national policy makers and corporate leaders began defining an economic crisis for this new industrial order. Already competing economically in world markets with their rival, Great Britain, manufacturers and industrial leaders spoke and wrote fearfully about the rapid growth of Germany as an economic power fully capable of besting the United States in foreign trade. American opinion setters in the 1890s attributed Germany's economic success to its vocational education programs, in which employers and schools cooperated in training youth for industrial jobs (Grubb and Lazerson, 1975).

Spurred by these reports of German vocational education, American educators and public officials campaigned initially for separate vocational schools before World War I and then, ultimately, for a vocational track within the comprehensive high school. Coalitions of manufacturers, businesspeople, federal officials (including presidents of the United States), progressive reformers, and heads of labor unions convinced the U.S. Congress to pass the Smith-Hughes Act in 1917, which provided federal funds for programs to train youth for industrial occupations, agriculture, and "domestic sciences" (e.g., home economics, cooking, sewing). Vocational education became a permanent, federally subsidized part of the high school curriculum for the next three-quarters of a century. A virtual industry of vocational teachers, firms in which graduates were placed, and lobbying groups emerged in the decades that followed (Lazerson and Grubb, 1974; Kantor, 1986; Cuban, 1982; Tyack, 1974; Spring, 1986).

The talk of economic crisis in the 1880s was not an isolated instance. Repeatedly the nation turned public attention to the juncture between school and work. In the 1950s, for example, national reports about the sad state of affairs in American high schools and accelerating public concern over burgeoning crime rates among youth led public officials and renowned experts (such as former Harvard University President James B. Conant) to warn about dropouts and unemployed minority youth who could become "social dynamite" in American cities. The Vocational Education Act of 1963 (with later amendments in 1968) specifically provided for grants to high schools and employers to train "disadvantaged" youth to reduce the effects of technological unemployment and to integrate these groups into a changing labor market. New programs drafted teachers into a war against youth unemployment. Vocational teachers were the frontline soldiers who had to equip students with the marketable skills that would get employers to hire them (Grubb and Lazerson, 1975; Cuban, 1982; Kett, 1995).

By the 1970s, increasing automation in manufacturing and rising rates of unemployment had stirred national policy makers to again turn to the schools with visions of "career education"; that is, all students—not just those enrolled in vocational education—should be exposed to the world of work. Federally funded programs created career centers, business-school coalitions, and partnerships between community colleges and high schools. Both elementary and secondary teachers (not only high school vocational teachers but academic ones also) were drafted in this latest reform to help young people get ready for the labor market (Grubb and Lazerson, 1975; Kett, 1995).

With publication of the report *A Nation at Risk* in 1983, another wave of reform swept across public schools, this time, directly linking faltering public schools with a faltering economy (Commission on Excellence in Education, 1983). Falling scores on standardized achievement tests were explicitly linked to declining economic productivity and a shrinking share of world trade. The globalization of the American economy meant heavy job losses in manufacturing, shifts to a service economy with lower-paid, less skilled jobs while high-skill, high-wage technological occupations simultaneously posted strong gains. With such economic and social churning, again, national political leaders turned to the nation's public schools to help youth gain a foothold in a rapidly changing workplace.

This time there was little talk about preparing students with job-specific skills. Instead, the recipe for school reform in the late 1980s and 1990s called for schools to raise their academic standards through higher graduation requirements. Teachers were to train students to think critically, cultivate social skills in teamwork, encourage flexibility in learning new tasks, and guide them in finding information and using it appropriately. A strengthened high school course of study of 4 years of English; 3 years of math, science, social studies each; and even a foreign language—the agenda of many policy makers—had, in effect, vocationalized the academic curriculum. Every teacher was now a vocational teacher. Within less than a century, after repeated waves of reform generated by national economic and social crises, policy makers and educators had converted American secondary schools into generic vocational schools (Kett, 1995; Pullin, 1994; Johnston, 1993).

This abbreviated account of previous times when policy makers, anxious over national changes in the economy, defined these workplace changes as youth and school problems can certainly be challenged for the interpretation that I offer of the vocationalizing of American secondary education. This rendering of previous intersections between policy makers and practitioners with school-to-work transition raises in my mind two very different questions:

1. Why do federal and state policy makers (and related reformers) repeatedly turn to schools to help solve national economic problems?

2. With these vocationally driven reforms most often coming from the top of the American policy system, to what degree did practitioners, located at the bottom of the system, change what they customarily do in their classrooms?

While I will return to the first question in the final section of this paper, it is the second question that suggests another way of seeing that was absent from the conference: the perspective of the practitioner.[2] After all, the target of all the policy talk, legislation, new programs, and tests is to get teachers to help students become more knowledgeable, more skilled, and more marketable than they currently are. As targets for improvement, reformers simultaneously define teachers as the problem blocking student acquisition of appropriate workplace skills and the solution, that is, the agents who will remedy the situation by ending the mismatch between high school graduates and entry-level jobs. This conundrum frustrates policy makers, especially if they lack familiarity with how practitioners view their world.

Practitioner's Perspective

To the teacher, it is not the school, district, or state that is their universe; it is the classroom of 25 or more students. That universe is essentially unpredictable since individual students respond differently to teacher requests and demands. Uncertainty, ambiguity, and improvisation go with the territory of the self-contained classroom. It is a world of action and instant decision making where pragmatic theories in action are tested and tempered daily (Smith and Geoffrey, 1968; Doyle, 1986; Clark and Petersen, 1986).

What drives teachers to work hard in these classrooms are not electoral and budget cycles, reelection, fame, or money. What drives teachers are the psychic rewards of seeing individual students learn to master content and skills and mature socially. A teacher's daily concerns are not standardized test scores but deciding what content to cover and how to teach it, managing scarce time, maintaining classroom order, protecting their time from administrative intrusions, developing personal relationships with their students, and figuring out what their students have learned. These particularistic concerns are light years away from teachers' doing as policy makers bid (Lortie, 1975; Jackson, 1968; Elmore and McLaughlin, 1988).

In such a practitioner-enclosed world, self-reliance and autonomy are virtues. What matters most is that teachers can tailor mandates and new programs to

---

[2]During the conference, two of 23 presenters were from schools. Sandra Black, associate superintendent of curriculum and instruction in Chattanooga, Tennessee (a former principal and teacher), and Vivian Woods, a principal in Chattanooga (and former teacher), were discussants and made brief presentations about assessment in school-to-work programs. While both said they were advocates of teachers and pointed out the complexities of introducing new programs, not one question was directly asked of either of them after their presentations.

fit their students and the daily routines shaped by the topography of the classroom in age-graded schools. To survive, teachers tinker, incrementally adapting that which fits the tasks of maintaining classroom order and helping individual students master content and skills. For new performance-based assessments that expect teachers to teach differently, the degree to which the new tools will be incorporated into classroom routines depends entirely on the help teachers get from experts, the fit between the assessments and the time available to teach as they customarily do and their judgment that the new instruments will benefit their students. More often than not, teachers will ignore, reject, or even sabotage externally designed reforms they are expected to implement yet for which they receive little help in understanding the changes (Doyle and Ponder, 1978; Cuban, 1993; Fullan, 1991; Darling-Hammond, 1994; Tyack and Cuban, 1995).

The practitioner's way of seeing, then, is largely micro rather than macro; it is the view from the bottom looking up, rather than top down; it is heavily influenced by beliefs, pragmatic theories in action, and values grounded in the classroom and individual student relationships rather than the disciplinary views of economists, psychologists, and lawyers. In short, it is a way of seeing that is foreign to federal and state policy makers and their expert advisers.

Both a brief look backward at past instances of school-to-work "crises" and the perspective of the practitioner were missing from the papers and conference discussions. So what? Was anything lost by the absence of these perspectives?

SO WHAT?

The dominant ways of seeing that so characterized the papers and conference discussions left the distinct impression on me that these implicit perspectives were not the only ways of framing school-to-work problems and solutions but were probably the best ones. As a historian and practitioner, I know better, but I felt the press of expert advice to be the best way of viewing school-to-work transition and assessment. Unintentionally, even with the variation among policy makers and experts, the mindset of authors and conference participants gets frozen into the dominant policy maker and expert ways of seeing. Unavoidably, these views, varied as they are among specialists, get narrowed into becoming accepted as accurate perceptions of the issues. Thus, the missing perspectives become important in stretching the mindset and generating different ways of framing problems of the transition from school to work. Imagining other definitions of the problem enlarges the inventory of solutions available to both policy makers and their advisers.

This is particularly so for the practitioner perspective since it is crucial for reformers to understand this way of seeing and to recognize that teachers have been (and are) the implementers of new programs, new assessments, and new ventures in school to work. After all, the world of policy makers and their advisers is a world of policy talk and legislation, of words and newly funded programs. It is not the world of the implementer, the teacher who converts talk into practice. Historically, it has been practitioners who spelled the difference between anticipated and unanticipated consequences of well-intentioned, carefully designed programs. The debris of school reform after reform stands as mute evidence of the huge discrepancy between policy talk and what happens in classrooms (Elmore and McLaughlin, 1988; Tyack and Cuban, 1995). Hence, for policy makers and their expert advisers to ignore or pay only passing, even token, attention to how practitioners see the world from their perch is to put a down payment on failure.

There is another reason why including other perspectives becomes important. The framing of problems is not an objective process where factual accuracy and truth overcome bias; it is a socially constructed act that is closely related to who does the defining of the problem and therefore sets the agenda for which solutions get chosen. Those, for example, whom federal and state policy makers accept as experts on school-to-work transition (generally economists when it comes to national policies, psychologists when it comes to assessment, and lawyers when it comes to legal challenges to new assessments) determine which ways of seeing get access over others and ultimately shape the problem-solving agenda. This is as much a matter of power and status as it is an objective process of sorting through available data and defining the problem. Including other perspectives, then, becomes essential to the process of policy making for schools in a democracy.

Finally, there are the puzzling questions of why policy makers and their advisers have so often framed the problem of a changing labor market as a skills gap of youth and have consequently turned to schools when economic crises beckon. Because policy makers and experts drawn from the academic disciplines have framed problems as a relationship between the economy and youth, schools have become the locus for reformers and teachers, the target for major change. Need it be said that it is easier to fix the schools than the economy? It is also easier to point the finger at unprepared youth as the problem to be solved than it is to blame corporate executives for shortsighted decisions or changes in an economy driven by market forces that are dimly understood. A number of historians and nonmainstream economists have pointed out that the fixation on reform has been damaging to schools, which are impotent to alleviate economic conditions, and that far more effort ought to be expended on nonschool sectors to help youth and older workers adjust to economic changes (Grubb and Lazerson, 1975; Balanz, 1991; Johnston, 1993; Kerr, 1994; Kett, 1995).

This meta-analysis of the taken-for-granted perspectives that dominated the papers and subsequent conference discussions on school-to-work transition suggests that much more can be considered and even done about youth, schools, and the economy if a broader net were thrown out to capture different ways of seeing beyond the dominant policy-making and expert ones. Because problems and solutions are socially constructed and because such social constructions have social and political consequences, especially for schools and high-stakes assessment, it is no trivial matter to examine who defines problems and how they see the world.

REFERENCES

Balanz, R.
  1991   Local knowledge, academic skills, and individual productivity: An alternative view. *Educational Policy* 5(4):343-370.
Clark, C., and P. Petersen
  1986   Teachers' thought processes. Pp. 255-296 in *Third Handbook of Research on Teaching*, M. Wittrock, ed. New York: Macmillan.
Commission on Excellence in Education
  1983   *A Nation at Risk.* Washington, DC: U.S. Government Printing Office.
Cremin, L.
  1961   *The Transformation of the School.* New York: Vintage.
Cuban, L.
  1982   Enduring resiliency: Enacting and implementing federal vocational legislation. Pp. 45-48 in *Work, Youth, and Schooling*, H. Kantor and D. Tyack, eds. Stanford, CA: Stanford University Press.
  1993   *How Teachers Taught*, 2d ed. New York: Teachers College Press.
Darling-Hammond, L.
  1994   National standards and assessments: Will they improve education? *American Journal of Education* 102(3):478-510.
Doyle, W.
  1986   Classroom organization and management. Pp. 392-431 in *Third Handbook of Research on Teaching*, M. Wittrock, ed. New York: Macmillan.
Doyle, W., and G. Ponder
  1978   The practicality ethic in teacher decision-making. *Interchange* 8(3):1-12.
Elmore, R., and M. McLaughlin
  1988   *Steady Work.* Santa Monica, CA: RAND Corporation.
Fullan, M.
  1991   *The New Meaning of Educational Change.* New York: Teachers College Press.
Grubb, N., and M. Lazerson
  1975   Rally 'round the workplace: Continuities and fallacies in career education. *Harvard Educational Review* 45(4):451-474.
Gusfield, J.
  1981   *The Culture of Public Problems: Drinking-Driving and the Symbolic Order.* Chicago: University of Chicago Press.
Hilgartner, S., and C. Bosk
  1988   The rise and fall of social problems: A public arenas model. *American Journal of Sociology* 94(1):53-78.
Jackson, P.
  1968   *Life in Classrooms.* New York: Holt, Rinehart & Winston.
Johnston, B.
  1993   The transformation of work and educational reform policy. *American Educational Research Journal* 30(1):39-65.
Kantor, H.
  1986   Work, education, and vocational reform: The ideological origins of vocational education, 1890-1920. *American Journal of Education* 94(3):401-426.

Kerr C.
    1994   *Troubled Times for American Higher Education.* Albany, NY: SUNY Press.
Kett, J.
    1995   School leaving: Dead end or detour? Pp. 265-294 in *Learning from the Past,* D. Ravtich
            ad M. Vinovskis, eds. Baltimore: Johns Hopkins Press.
Kirst, M., G. Hayward, J. Koppich, N. Finkelstein, L. Birky, and J. Guthrie
    1995   *Conditions of Education in California.* Report no. PP95-4-1. Berkeley, CA: Policy
            Anlaysis for California Education.
Lazerson, M., and N. Grubb
    1974   *American Education and Vocationalism: A Documentary History, 1870-1970.* New York:
            Teachers College Press.
Linn, R.
    1994   Evaluating the technical quality of proposed national examination systems. *American
            Journal of Education* 102(3):565-579.
Lortie, D.
    1975   *Schoolteacher.* Chicago: University of Chicago Press.
McDonnell, L.
    1994   Assessment policy as persuasion and regulation. *American Journal of Education*
            102(3):394-420.
Pullin, D.
    1994   Learning to work: The impact of curriculum and assessment standards on educational
            opportunity. *Harvard Educational Review* 64(1):31-54.
Smith, L., and W. Geoffrey
    1968   *The Complexities of an Urban Classroom.* New York: Holt, Rinehart & Winston.
Spring, J.
    1986   *The American School, 1492-1985.* New York: Longman.
Tyack, D.
    1974   *One Best System.* Cambridge, MA: Harvard University Press.
Tyack, D., and L. Cuban
    1995   *Tinkering Toward Utopia.* Cambridge, MA: Harvard University Press.

11

Getting to Work: Thoughts on the Function and Form of the School-to-Work Transition

Lauren B. Resnick

The question of articulation between the formal schooling system and young people's early work experience is as old as schooling itself. Once it became normal for most young people to be educated in schools rather than in apprenticeships, or even less formal on-the-job settings, the transition between school and work took on broad social import. Over the years public discussions in this country have mostly concerned issues of *selection* and *preparation* for the work force. For the most part there has been only peripheral attention to how the nature of the transition between schoolhouse and workplace might affect the broad *social fabric* of the nation: the kinds of responsibilities people feel toward one another, their sense of belonging to a polity, their sense of personal and civic purpose. In the course of this essay I will discuss all three of these functions of a school-to-work system, considering the kinds of institutional arrangements and technical resources each calls for and how a system might be designed that meets all three sets of needs. To set the stage, I begin with a brief consideration of the three functions.

SELECTION AND SIGNALING

Economists have long been concerned with the ways in which school performance and educational attainment can play a role in allocating young people to job opportunities (e.g., Arrow, 1973; Spence, 1974; Wolpin, 1977). More recently, John Bishop (1996), has argued that a more efficient system of signaling high school students' competencies to employers would be economically beneficial to employers by helping them to select the candidates most likely to perform well in their companies. Such a system, he claims, would also motivate individual students to greater effort. Similar arguments are made in this volume.

Advocates of more efficient signaling systems note that employers today are not, for the most part, attending to evidence of the quality of high school performance. Such evidence is not easily available to employers, to be sure, but it is also true that employers rarely ask for it. When queried about why, many express distrust of high school records, claiming that grade inflation and the irrelevance of much that is taught in high school render the high school diploma of little value as a signal of a young person's competence in the workplace.

Some employers see little value in the high school record because they are looking for very little in the way of academic or technical preparation. They seek instead little more than regularity of attendance at work and willingness to carry out routine chores reliably and personably. These are mostly employers who offer little in the way of career prospects to young people. They are the kinds of jobs through which, according to Zemsky (Chapter 3, this volume), many young people *churn* between their late teens and mid-to-late twenties.

IMPROVING THE SKILL AND TALENT POOL

Another growing group of employers, however, complain that they need better prepared, more highly skilled workers and that there are good jobs with career prospects going unfilled because of a lack of adequately prepared young people (see also Chapter 2, this volume). They want some skills that have traditionally been the purview of the high schools and postsecondary vocational training system: knowledge of mathematics, science, communication, some specific technical skills. But they also want what Murnane and Levy (1996) call the *new basics:* the "soft skills" of teamwork, resource management, and problem solving (see also Secretary's Commission on Achieving Necessary Skills, 1991 and New Standards, 1997).

The importance of these skills today derives from basic changes in the economy. The dramatic growth of communication and transportation capabilities over the past two or three decades has brought an end to isolated national and regional economies. All goods and many services can now be shipped anywhere in the world. At the same time, the productive capacities of Europe and Japan have recovered from their postwar incapacity and many formerly underdeveloped countries have become able to produce goods and services of a quality interesting to buyers in the more developed parts of the world (see also Baumol et al, 1991). The resulting international competition has increased the demand for highly reliable goods and services and for customization.

Not only can goods and services be shipped all over the world but so too can most jobs. There is far less advantage today than there used to be in producing goods close to buyers. Even many services can be provided long distance. For example, with the availability of reliable and speedy electronic networks, data-handling services can be carried out anywhere. The "back room" of a New York bank can be in Ireland or Singapore. Economic theory predicts that over time jobs will migrate to wherever in the world the balance between wage demands and the productive capacity of the work force works out most favorably for companies.

Only highly skilled work forces—people with the capacity and the will to use their minds as well as their hands in work that is varied and challenging—will be able to command the kind of wages that many Americans thought was their birthright until 10 or 20 years ago. That is one reason the high-wage/low-skill factories, the backbone of American prosperity until the 1970s, have been closing and why real wages have declined dramatically for all but the top, college-educated population. That is also why a critical long-term investment the country can make in its economic future is an investment in skills.

MENDING A FRAYING SOCIAL FABRIC

An organized program of school-to-work transition is not, however, just about the economics of jobs and incomes. It is also about policies and technical tools for a radically revised way of welcoming American young people into the responsibilities and rewards of productive adulthood. The data reported by Zemsky (Chapter 3, this volume) confirm what people familiar with the hiring practices of American companies have been saying for some years: most companies are afraid of young people, viewing them as unreliable workers. They would rather hire more mature individuals, those in their upper twenties and, when possible, those who come with some prior history of work. *But there exists in this country no systematic way for most young people to gain the experience that would make them attractive to employers.* So they drift from one short-term minimum-wage job to another, with frequent periods of unemployment in between.

This kind of churning seems to be the experience of a substantial majority of our young people in the 18- to 28-year-old range. This is not a marginal under-class. It is not ethnically or racially limited. With the exception of a small number of technical associate degrees offered by community colleges and sometimes by proprietary trade schools, the 75 percent or so in this country who do not earn a bachelors degree have nothing serious to show for their effort, training, study, and even work experience. They have no credentials that are honored by employers and no way of building a resume of evidence that shows how a young potential employee can benefit a potential employer.

As they drift from one short-term job to another, the experience of churning develops and reinforces among young adults the lack of responsibility about which many older people complain. A commitment to work and self-improvement is not available to or expected of them. (I believe that this experience has much to do with why many young fathers walk away from their family responsibilities. Unable to meet traditional family financial responsibilities even if they want to, multiple social pressures drive young men away from situations in which the most likely outcome of their efforts will be failure.) For all who experience it, this kind of early adulthood carries the message that society does not need or want them as responsible adults. For society as a whole, a critical opportunity to welcome young people into full citizenship and social responsibility is lost. For many young people, drifting and a lack of commitment become a way of life.

The extent of the problem, in social terms, is underlined in Katherine Newman's (1988) study of the declining fortunes of the American middle class. According to Newman, many children of people who achieved middle class status in the heady years of economic growth following World War II have been unable to follow in their parents' footsteps. Unable to establish a secure economic foothold for themselves, they are losing both their economic hopes for the future and a sense that their efforts will pay off.

America has now experienced more than 20 years of declining real wages for all except the top two or three deciles of wage earners (see, e.g., Murnane and Levy, 1996), a decline related to a general slowing of economic growth since the early 1970s. As Jeffrey Madrick (1995) has suggested, there is no guarantee that we can return to the high growth rates of the postwar decades. In friendlier economic times we could largely rely on tossing young people into the economy as a way of socializing them and welcoming them into adulthood and responsibility. That option has now ended. Frontier and economic boom thinking cannot substitute for thinking institutionally and socially about our young people. Other countries have known this for some time and have been developing more structured patterns of absorbing young people into adulthood. We need to do the same, or we face a very uncertain social future, even if measured unemployment continues at its present low rates.

AN EFFORT-BASED SCHOOL-TO-WORK SYSTEM

A school-to-work system that could reasonably meet the triple goals of signaling, improving the skill pool, and providing a smooth transition to adult responsibility must be designed, above all, to evoke and reward directed effort by young people at each stage of their careers. Such an *effort-based* system would not only motivate learning and thus enhance the overall skill levels among our young people but also restore to the young a sense that they can make positive and productive contributions to society. Creating such a system will require overcoming long traditions in both education and job selection of privileging judgments about aptitude over expenditure of effort. Our present system of education and its accompanying modes of entry into the work force were designed primarily around a belief that talent and ability are largely inherited and fixed. Educational practices are designed to select the talented, to educate them in high-demand curricula (e.g., programs for the gifted and talented, Advanced Placement causes), and to provide the others with either a general education or a vocational preparation—often of a kind ill suited to the demands of today's high-performance workplaces. IQ tests or their surrogates are used to determine who will have access to enriched programs. This curriculum is denied to other students who are judged less capable.

Our typical standardized tests are normed to compare students with one another rather than with a standard of excellence. We expect teachers to grade on a curve. If most students receive As or Bs, we often assume that standards are too low, discounting the possibility that they may all have worked hard and succeeded in learning what was taught. These practices make learning invisible to students and everyone else: one can learn a lot in the course of a year and yet remain in the same relative ranking compared with others. Effort is suppressed for all but the best students.

College entrance, the ultimate prize for many students, also is heavily dependent on tests that have little to do with the curriculum studied and that are designed—like IQ tests—to spread students out on a scale rather than to define what one is supposed to work at learning. The same is true of most tests used for employment selection. From the students' point of view, there is no apparent way to prepare for these tests, nothing specific they can do to ready themselves for high-demand, interesting work.

Our current tests are designed with *prediction*, not skill and knowledge certification, as their primary goal. The technology of predictive test design calls for a focus on discriminating among applicants rather than describing what specific skills or knowledge an applicant has mastered. Our most frequently used "high-stakes" tests—those used for selection into colleges (e.g., ACT and SAT) and the military (ASVAB)—are deliberately designed not to reflect any specific curriculum. This practice grew up in an era when it was widely believed that certain kinds of tests (usually called aptitude or ability tests) could detect raw talent, without regard to how that talent had been developed through education. Tests divorced from established courses of study, it was believed, would permit students from institutions with different curricula and different quality of instruction to compete on a level playing field (for a historical review of testing in the U.S., see, e.g., W. Garner and A. Wigdor, 1982; D. Resnick, 1982; R. E. Fancher, 1985; OTA, 1992). The practice continues, although now it is generally acknowledged that aptitude tests reflect the overall quality and quantity of a person's education (so that, for example, distributions of SAT scores are routinely used to assess how well schools are performing).

These testing and tracking practices are institutionalized expressions of a belief in the importance of aptitude (Resnick, 1995). Their routine and largely unquestioned use continues to create evidence that confirms aptitude-based thinking. Students who have not been taught a demanding, challenging curriculum do not do well on tests of reasoning or problem solving, confirming our original suspicions that they did not have the talent for that kind of thinking. Students do not try to break through the barrier of low expectations because they, like their teachers and parents, accept the judgment that aptitude matters most and that they do not have the right kinds of aptitude. Not surprisingly, their performance remains low. The system is a self-sustaining one in which hidden assumptions are continually reinforced by the inevitable results of practices based on those assumptions.

It is not necessary to continue this way. Teaching and even selection practices could be built around the alternative assumption that effort actually *creates* ability, that patterns of who tries hard can directly influence ultimate patterns of competence in individuals and in society at large (see Howard, 1995). Effort-oriented education and training emphatically do not mean awarding students As for effort when the quality of their work only warrants a D or an F grade. Rather it means carefully linking effort and achievement in ways that are likely to improve not only specific knowledge but also an overall ability to learn effectively.

Focus on Learning Goals

A long-term program of research on *achievement goal orientation* by social and developmental psychologists provides a theoretical grounding for such an approach (e.g., Ames, 1984; Dweck and Leggett, 1988; Nicholls, 1979, 1984; Resnick and Nelson-Le Gall, 1997). This research shows that the kinds of achievement goals that people have can affect not only how much effort they put into learning tasks but also the *kinds* of effort. Two broad classes of goals have been identified: *performance-oriented* and *learning-oriented*.

People with performance goals strive to obtain positive evaluations of their ability and to avoid giving evidence of inadequate ability relative to others. Performance goals are associated with a view of ability as an unchangeable global entity that is *displayed* in task performance, revealing that the individual either has or lacks ability. This view of ability or aptitude has sometimes been termed an *entity theory of intelligence*. In contrast, people with learning goals generally strive to develop their ability with respect to particular tasks. Learning goals are associated with a view of aptitude as something that is mutable through effort and is *developed* by taking an active stance toward learning and mastery opportunities. Learning goals are associated with a view of ability as a repertoire of skills continuously expandable through one's efforts. Accordingly, this view of aptitude has been labeled an *incremental theory of intelligence* (Dweck and Leggett, 1988).

People who hold incremental views of intelligence tend to invest energy to learn something new or to increase their understanding and mastery of tasks. But brute energy alone does not distinguish them from people with entity theories. Incremental theorists are particularly likely to apply self-regulatory metacognitive skills when they encounter task difficulties and to focus on analyzing the task and trying to generate and execute alternative strategies. In general, they try to garner resources for problem solving wherever they can: from their own store of cognitive learning strategies and from others from whom they strategically seek help (Dweck, 1988; Nelson-Le Gall, 1990; Nelson-Le Gall and Jones, 1990). In general, these individuals display continued high levels of task-related effort in response to difficulty.

The achievement goals that individuals pursue also appear to influence the inferences they make about effort and ability. Performance goals place the greater effort necessary for mastering challenging tasks in conflict with the need to be regarded as already competent, whereas learning goals lead to adaptive motivational patterns that can produce a quality of task engagement and commitment to learning that fosters high levels of achievement over time. An effort-oriented system of the kind I am advocating would be designed to create a learning orientation in our students by teaching them both strategies for learning and broad disposition for applying them (see Resnick and Nelson-Le Gall, 1997).

There are several essential features of an effort-oriented education system (see Resnick, 1995): first, very clear (absolute rather than comparative) expectations—that is, standards for achievement; second, fair and credible evaluations of achievement that are geared to the standards; third, celebration and payoff for success in meeting learning expectations; fourth, access to training and work opportunities based on demonstrated accomplishment and willingness to meet work expectations; and, finally, as much time and expert instruction as necessary to meet the standards.

Clear Achievement Standards

Achievement standards—publicly announced and meant for everyone—are the essential foundation of an equitable, effort-oriented school-to-work system. If young people are to work hard, they need to know what they are aiming for. They need not only to try hard but also to organize their efforts. A school-to-work achievement standards system would begin with a clear set of accomplishment expectations for high school students. These could be defined as standards-referenced assessments that must be passed or as courses that must be taken or credits to be earned. In the latter case, unless the course and credit list specifies the content that must be learned and the quality of work that will count as meeting the expectation, it is not truly an achievement standard. At this foundation stage of a school-to-work system, it is important to set the same high expectations for all students. That will provide a solid foundation for effort by students and teachers alike. This is the idea behind the proposal of a "Certificate of Initial Mastery" (Commission on the Skills of the American Workforce, 1990; Tucker, 1994), an accomplishment-based certificate from which students could go on to more specialized academic or work-oriented learning opportunities.

Assessments for Which Students Can Prepare

The next key component of an effort-based school-to-work system is to give students the opportunity to prepare, in a direct and unambiguous way, for the assessments that will certify their accomplishments and open doors of opportunity for them. As I noted earlier, most tests used today are not designed to be studied for. They are not geared to a particular curriculum, and they become invalid when students are directly trained to take them. The same is true of most selection tests for jobs and higher education. They are geared to assumptions of aptitude in which hard work and direct preparation are not rewarded.

Our new effort-oriented school-to-work system needs to change that by using exams and other forms of assessments (e.g., externally graded portfolios of their work) for which students can study. To make them worth studying for, these new assessments are likely to include a substantial representation of *performance tasks*: open-ended questions requiring exam takers to perform a relatively complex task and, often, explain how and why their solution to a problem is appropriate. After a period of skepticism about the possibilities of creating performance assessments that would meet criteria of valid and reliable measurement, it is now becoming clear that appropriate mixes of extended tasks and short items, along with careful training of graders, can yield accurate and reliable test scores (New Standards Technical Studies Unit, 1997). Furthermore, with adequate structuring, it now seems possible to include portfolios as part of a formal measurement system (Myford and Mislevy, 1994), although issues of cost are not trivial (see, e.g., Klein, 1997).

Payoff for Successful Learning

A school-to-work system that actively tries to promote effort must make it clear to participants that effort and accomplishment will be rewarded. In-school and community recognition for accomplishment in learning is important in much the way that fans at a game are important to the athletes. Recognition sustains effort. For adolescents and young adults, however, fans and cheers are not enough. These young people have to see the relationship between the work they are asked to do in a preparatory setting—whether in school or a workplace internship—and their opportunities for further schooling and satisfying work. This is why it is essential that a reformed school-to-work system be built around *credentials honored by employers and institutions of further learning.*

First steps toward this desirable state of affairs are now being taken in the form of revised high school transcript systems and employer pledges to require evidence of high school accomplishment when considering students. Systems such as "Work Keys" (American College Testing, 1995) go a step further, providing a profile of students' performance on various academic and aptitude tests that can be matched to the general requirements of particular jobs. But none of these, as currently constituted, fully meets the criteria for an effort-oriented system—for the tests on which they are based are not referenced to specific performance standards.

WHAT KINDS OF SKILLS AND KNOWLEDGE ARE NEEDED?

A standards-based education plan brings into high relief the question of what kinds of education standards we want to set and for whom. How closely should school programs be linked to the demands of jobs? What kinds of jobs should drive our thinking about curriculum and assessment? Should our outcome standards—and thus assessments and curricula—be focused on the kinds of skills employers seek now and thus would reward immediately, or should they focus on the future, high-performance workplace? The choice between the skill sets of the present and those of a desired future could drive our standards and education systems in radically different ways.

Our present aptitude-based education and selection system was built on an assumption—reasonable in the 1920s but not now—that we needed only a minority of really well-educated people in the adult population. The others would work at low-demand jobs, many of which would nevertheless pay well by virtue of the way in which work and workers were organized. This view is no longer tenable both because of international competition and because machines have become smart enough to do many of the tasks that only people used to be able to do. Machines can not only fabricate but also monitor the fabrication process within broad limits. Intelligent machines can keep track of masses of data and can signal deviations from standard expectations. They can answer telephones and handle routine inquiries. The list of machine capabilities grows yearly. The inexorable logic of intelligent machines is that the work left for humans to do will increasingly be the nonprogrammable tasks. These are the tasks that are not routinized, where surprise and variability must be accommodated, where only adaptive human intelligence can make the evaluations and decisions needed to assure the fine tuning that makes the difference between high quality that is delivered promptly and shoddy goods and services with unreliable delivery.

The demand for thinking in the high performance workplace creates an opportunity for a truly new kind of school-to-work system, one in which the call for a humanizing education and preparation for work are—perhaps for the first time in history and certainly for the first time since the industrial revolution—in harmony rather than in conflict. At the end of the eighteenth century, Thomas Jefferson promoted the ideal of a universally educated yeoman citizenry, free farmers with the will and the background to debate the public issues of the day and reach reasoned conclusions. Before his vision could be realized, however, new demands born of industrialization and the movement from farms to cities set economic and democratic aspirations at war.

From the earliest years of public education in America, leading educators—

Horace Mann in the nineteenth century, John Dewey in the twentieth, for example—aimed for schools that would cultivate the questioning and reasoning processes and skills of democratic social interaction that were needed by all citizens in a properly functioning democracy. Others joined with the democratic theorists to promote education for full personal lives: lifelong learning and the capacity to engage with enthusiasm and competence in multiple pursuits, ranging from parenting to leisure activities, that would fill people's longer and longer lives. But the demands of the growing industrial economy were different. Industrialists called for a large supply of literate but docile factory workers who would accept the boring and sometimes dangerous conditions of industrial production. Their view of education was locked into place early in this century by a series of policy and educational management decisions that modeled American school systems on the efficient Taylorized factory.

Given this history it is not surprising that many educators and social commentators resist turning our schools into "vocational machines." Such commentators, like several of the authors in this volume, are worried that overly tight linking of schooling to specific workplace demands can lead to constriction of what is taught and to pressures for early tracking and streaming that could restrict individual opportunity. The high-performance workplace, however, is producing a very different set of educational demands than did traditional forms of work. For the first time since the industrial revolution, the demands being made on the education system from the perspectives of economic productivity, democratic citizenship, and personal fulfillment are convergent.

Today's high-performance workplace calls for the same kind of person that Horace Mann and John Dewey sought: someone able to analyze a situation, make reasoned judgments, communicate well, engage with others to reason through differences of opinion, and intelligently employ the complex tools and technologies that can liberate or enslave, according to use. What is more, the new workplace calls for people who can learn new skills and knowledge as conditions change—lifelong learners, in short. As a result, this is a moment of extraordinary opportunity in which business, labor, and education leaders can set a new common course in which preparation for work and preparation for civic and personal life no longer need be in competition. The only way to achieve this higher level of skill and ability in the population at large is to make sure that all students, not just a privileged and selected fraction, learn the high-level embedded symbolic thinking skills of the future.

Throughout the industrialized world, business, labor, and education leaders have been coming together to articulate education goals that reflect this convergence. In this country the SCANS commission (Secretary's Commission on Achieving Necessary Skills, 1991) laid out a set of foundation and work readiness skills. New Standards (1997) has extended the SCANS skills in a framework that identifies three categories of problem-solving skills (design a product, service, or system; improve a system; plan and organize an event or activity), plus communication tools and techniques, information tools and techniques, learning and self-management tools and techniques, tools and techniques for working with others. The SCANS/New Standards competencies are in good accord with the standards and framework documents of other countries.

The competencies outlined by SCANS and New Standards Applied Learning are generic in nature. They are not targeted to any particular job or even group of occupations. Applied learning competencies are not "job skills" for students who are judged incapable of or indifferent to the challenges and opportunities of academic learning. They are the kinds of abilities all Americans will need, both in the workplace and in their roles as citizens. They are the thinking and reasoning abilities demanded by colleges and by the growing number of high-performance workplaces, those that expect employees at every level of the organization to take responsibility for the quality of products and services.

SIGNALING, LEARNING, AND SOCIAL RESPONSIBILITY: A CREDENTIALING SYSTEM FOR ALL AMERICANS

How can all of this be merged into a coherent system that can play all three of the functions outlined at the beginning of this essay—signaling and selection, improving the skill and talent pool, and providing a welcoming route into responsible adulthood? Much depends, I think, on developing a system of skill and knowledge credentialing that provides clear targets at which students and educators can aim while also providing some help to employers in selecting promising employees. Absent the latter, employers will be disinterested in the system, and the motivational impact of credentials will be minimal.

The need for a credentialing system based on accomplishments extends well beyond passage from high school to initial work entry. Our current lack of such credentials effectively traps workers, young and older, in their current jobs with little opportunity for mobility. To illustrate, I describe two young workers whose "learning biographies" have been studied. Chris works for a small heating and air-conditioning installation company, installing ducts and equipment at construction sites ranging from private homes to public housing projects. Teddy works in a midsize manufacturing plant that designs and builds honing and polishing machinery. Both men have stories of drift and churning in their backgrounds, but both now represent success stories, including being recognized by their supervisors as stars in the making. Although both hold reasonably well-paid jobs that call for and recognize considerable skill, both know they are tracked, that their chances for job mobility and promotion are severely limited. As Teddy explained, "I don't know where I could go. I am tied down here because all of my learning has been on the job." Because there is no way in our system to demonstrate what he knows, his skills are not recognizable and his practical chances are limited.

Teddy and Chris are two very productive workers in small American businesses who cannot move to other jobs. If those businesses should not be able to sustain themselves, these men are vulnerable, expressing some of the same worries as Katherine Newman's informants. They recognize the current trend toward contingent workers, although without using economists' fancy words. They say, in effect, "My only capital is what I know, but nobody can see it, and so I am vulnerable." A performance-based credentialing system would be a bulwark against that vulnerability. At the same time, such a system would provide motivation for learning. It would, thereby, help to *create* learning and work opportunities and not just allocate people to the limited opportunities that now exist.

Assessments for a Credentialing System

An effort-oriented credentialing system will require a different system of testing and assessment than is traditional in the United States. To see why, consider three broad functions of work-related assessment: selection of workers, guidance of instruction and learning, and certification of competence with respect to specific standards and guidance.

Selection of Workers

This is the most common function of work-related assessment, and sophisticated technologies for selection testing have been developed over many decades (see Chapter 9, this volume). These tests usually measure the traits (e.g., cognitive, social, attitudinal) of individuals and are not based on analyses of the kinds of jobs workers will need to do. An initially presumed match between measurable traits and job needs is verified by studies of how well the tests *predict* job performance (as measured by supervisors' ratings, promotion records, and the like). Because a test's predictive capabilities are its primary criterion of validity, there is no need for the items on the test to match directly any aspect of actual job performance. This makes it possible to use a number of item formats and testing techniques that are cost efficient and reliable. However, these predictively validated tests are virtually impossible to use in *developing* a generally more competent work force. Training individuals to do better on the items of a predictive test will often raise test scores but lower the predictive validity of the test. For this reason I argue against the use of predictive test methodology as the primary basis for a credentialing system.

Instructional Assessment

It is common to build assessment into instructional programs. Such assessments can range from simple end-of-chapter quizzes to sophisticated assessments embedded in electronically delivered instruction. These assessments are primarily diagnostic in function, suggesting to students or teachers exactly what they should focus on next. To work well, they need to be tied directly to the instructional program being used. For exactly that reason, however, instructionally oriented assessments are probably not an appropriate focus for credentialing. They would require a choice among instructional delivery programs and even among teaching methods, rather than providing the framework for a system in which multiple providers with different ideas about how to teach successfully could all compete.

Certification of Competence

Assessments aimed at certifying competence take direct aim at the kinds of activities in which workers are likely to engage. They start with a standard that specifies both a unit of work for which a worker might be responsible and the output or performance criteria for successful completion of that work. With the standard as a point of reference, assessment developers then organize one or more situations (usually called *tasks* or *prompts*) in which candidates can engage in the kinds of performance called for in the standard. Validity of such assessments lies in the extent to which the task or prompt actually evokes the kind of performance the standard demands, as well as in the extent to which judges can agree on the quality of the performance and to which there is adequate sampling of the range of performances considered important.

Because of this direct match to standards, competence certification assessments can be used as targets for training and education, although usually not as diagnostic instruments. They can thus contribute materially to the production of an increased pool of skilled and knowledgeable applicants for jobs. Prediction is not, at the outset, a primary concern of certification assessment, although the match to actual job performances will yield a high measure of face validity for employers. In addition, certification assessments can be used to predict competence on the job by adding to the development process studies of the relationship between scores on a cluster of certification assessments and supervisor ratings or other measures of an employed person's eventual success on the job.

In sum, disconnected from curricula and not specific about what has been mastered or what is to be learned, most of today's tests are poor vehicles for certification and credentialing. They cannot evoke directed effort toward specific learning goals, so they do not support creation of an effort-oriented education system. They are not, therefore, tools for raising the overall pool of skills and knowledge in our society. Furthermore, because they do not specify for employers the skills and knowledge that students have acquired, they cannot easily play the role of more efficient signaling that is called for by economists concerned with tighter school-employment linkages.

By focusing on certification of competence, in contrast, we could meet all three major goals of a school-to-work system. Certifications can organize and motivate learning, thus improving the overall level of work-relevant skill and knowledge in our population. They can assist employers in selecting workers, which will also maintain the motivational power of the system. And, finally, a system of certification beginning with very general competencies and proceeding toward increasing specialization (such as that envisaged in the new program of the National Skill Standards Board) can provide young people with pathways into the kinds of work opportunity that will allow them to take their places in society as responsible contributing adults.

REFERENCES

American College Testing
 1995   *Work Keys USA* 2(1).
Ames, C.
 1984   Competitive, cooperative, and individualistic goal structures: A motivational analysis. Pp. 177-207 in *Research on Motivation*, Vol. 1, R. Ames and C. Ames, eds. San Diego: Academic Press.
Arrow, Kenneth
 1973   Higher Education as a Filter. *Journal of Public Economics* 2:193-216.
Baumol, William J., Sue Anne Batey Blackman, and Edward N. Wolff
 1991   *Productivity and American Leadership: The Long View*. Cambridge, MA: The MIT Press.
Bishop, J.
 1996   Signaling the competencies of high school students to employers. Pp. 79-124 in *Linking School and Work: Roles for Standards and Assessment*, L.B. Resnick and J.G. Wirt, eds. San Francisco: Jossey-Bass.
Commission on the Skills of the American Workforce
 1990   *America's Choice: High Skills or Low Wages!* Washington, DC: National Center on Education and the Economy.
Dweck, C.S.
 1988   Motivation. Pp. 187-239 in *Handbook of Psychology and Education*, R. Glaser and A. Lesgold, eds. Hillsdale, NJ: Lawrence Erlbaum Associates.
Dweck, C.S., and E.L Leggett
 1988   A social-cognitive approach to motivation and personality. *Psychological Review* 95:256-273.
Fancher, Raymond E.
 1985   *The Intelligence Men: Makers of the IQ Controversy*. New York, NY: W.W. Norton and Co.
Garner, Wendall R., and Alexandra K. Wigdor, eds.
 1982   *Ability Testing: Uses, Consequences, and Controversies*. Committee on Ability Testing, National Research Council. Washington, DC: National Academy Press.
Howard, J.
 1995   You can't get there from here: The need for a new logic in education reform. *Daedalus* 124:85-92.
Klein, Stephen
 1997   The Lost Effectiveness of Performance Measures. Unpublished remarks at the conference, "Science Educational Standards: The Assessment of Science Meets the Science of Assessment," Board on Testing and Assessment, National Research Council, Washington, DC, February 22-23.
Madrick, J.
 1995   *The End of Affluence: The Causes and Consequences of America's Economic Dilemma*. New York: Random House.

Murnane, R., and F. Levy
  1996   *Teaching the New Basic Skills: Principles for Educating Children to Think in a Changing Economy.* New York: Free Press.

Myford, C.M., and, R. J. Mislevy
  1994   Monitoring and Improving a Portfolio Assessment System. Unpublished manuscript, Educational Testing Service, Princeton, NJ.

Nelson-Le Gall, S.
  1990   Academic achievement orientation and help-seeking behavior in early adolescent girls. *Journal of Early Adolescence* 10:176-190.

Nelson-Le Gall, S., and E. Jones
  1990   Cognitive-motivational influences on children's help-seeking. *Child Development* 61:581-589.

New Standards
  1997   *Performance Standards for Applied Learning,* 3 vols. Washington, DC/Pittsburgh, PA: National Center on Education and the Economy/University of Pittsburgh, Learning Research and Development Center.

New Standards Technical Studies Unit
  1997   *1996 New Standards Reference Examination Technical Summary.* University of Pittsburgh, Learning Research and Development Center.

Newman, K.
  1988   *Falling from Grace: The Experience of Downward Mobility in the American Middle Class.* New York: Basic Books.

Nicholls, J.
  1979   Quality and equality in intellectual development: The role of motivation in education. *American Psychologist* 34:10071-1084.

Nicholls, J.
  1984   Achievement motivation: Conceptions of ability, subjective experience, task choice and performance. *Psychological Review* 91:328-346.

Resnick, D.
  1982   The History of Educational Testing. In *Ability Testing: Uses, Consequences, and Controversies,* part 2, A. Wigdor and W. Garner, eds. Washington, DC: National Academy Press.

Resnick, L.B.
  1995   From aptitude to effort: A new foundation for our schools. *Daedalus* 124:55-62.

Resnick, L.B., and S. Nelson-Le Gall
  1997   Socializing intelligence. In *Piaget, Vygotsky and Beyond,* L. Smith and P. Tomlinson, eds. London: Routledge, forthcoming.

Secretary's Commission on Achieving Necessary Skills
  1991   *What Work Requires of Schools: A SCANS Report for America 2000.* Washington, DC: U.S. Department of Labor.

Spence, A.M.
  1974   *Market Signaling: Information Transfer In Hiring and Related Screening Processes.* Cambridge, Mass: Harvard University Press

Tucker, M.
  1994   *The Certification of Initial Mastery: A Primer.* Washington, DC: National Center on Education and the Economy.

U.S. Congress, Office of Technology Assessment
  1992   *Testing in American Schools: Asking the Right Questions,* OTA-SET-519. Washington, DC: U.S. Government Printing Office.

Wolpin, K.
  1977   Education and screening. *American Economic Review* 67:949-958.

12

Transitions in Work and Learning

Alan Lesgold

INTRODUCTION

The schools that we have today were heavily shaped by the great industrial expansion in the early part of this century. Simultaneously, we asked of our public schools that they teach all children, including a large cadre of newly arrived immigrants, and that they prepare a large proportion of the students for work in our rapidly expanding manufacturing economy. The rise of the assembly line and the emergence of scientific management placed specific requirements on this educational mandate. Students were expected to emerge from the public school system ready to work in jobs carefully designed to minimize further training requirements. A smaller proportion of students were expected to be capable of absorbing a large body of specific factual knowledge and also knowledge of specific procedures. These would become the skilled practitioners of trades in our society: electricians, plumbers, carpenters. Many of the literacy demands on them originated in their social responsibilities to produce safe outcomes from their work, to abide by governmentally established codes. A very small proportion of students were to become generally smart and able to take on positions of leadership and decision making.

OUR SCHOOLS

Schools evolved to provide capable assembly line workers and other needed talent for industrial society, such as craftspeople and management trainees. Further, because the schooling demands of work remained rather stable and populations did, too, it was easy for information about school successes and failures to filter back to the schools. Also, students often had part-time or summer jobs that reflected the industrial workplace, so some level of speedy feedback from workplaces to schools was possible. And everyone understood the basic work situation.

If, as a society, we all know that jobs are designed to be learned quickly and then executed in an environment of close supervision, the needs for schooling for this can be quite clear. Students need to be able to stick to a task; work efficiently; read, write, speak, and listen well enough to receive directions and report outcomes and problems; and do arithmetic well enough to receive and produce basic quality and process management data. Teachers needed to work during the summer to make ends meet, so they experienced the workplace firsthand, and parents also knew what work was about and what it would be about when their children entered the work force. Or so everyone thought.

As we gained national resolve to be a fairer and more open society, schools faced new demands, and some of our beliefs about the content of schooling and about where learning happens were called into question. We began to wonder how much of the successful performance of a worker was due to what was learned in school and how much to what was learned in everyday life, especially life in families that were already part of the so-called American dream. We also began to wonder whether we had confused necessary content and necessary teaching process with culture-specific practices that might be barriers to some students' educations.

As the workplace evolved away from the form in which most people, including school people, understood it, and as school populations became more culturally diverse, informal relationships between schooling and the workplace needed to be codified into explicit standards. In the short run this led to a variety of degree requirements for jobs, requirements that were not always defensible when challenged. However, in the early stages of the period of diversification of both work and the population, these standards were accepted, and a variety of mechanisms arose to help children "pass" through the ranks of schooling. Especially on the education side of the school-to-work system, either standards that were indefensible were eliminated or else mechanisms arose to assure they were no longer significant barriers to disadvantaged and minority workers. This worked as long as the output of the schools was generally good enough for the adult roles to which we aspired for ourselves or our children. The emergence of the standards movement in recent years is an indication that schooling's output may not have kept up with workplace needs.

OUR WORKPLACES

Work evolved while schooling was evolving, initially at a relatively slow pace. So the first demands for "smarter" workers were met by establishing more stringent schooling requirements for employment and perhaps adding more focused technical testing as well. This worked for a while, though never all that well. As the gap[1] between knowledge and skills transmitted universally by our culture through schooling and the knowledge and skills transmitted by economically productive communal experiences grew, the business world responded by developing more elaborate screening mechanisms for worker selection. Employers came to believe that certain less tangible capabilities were also important: showing up on time, respecting authority, being a team player, and so forth.

Basic Work Skills

My own sense is that there are four components that trade off with each other in determining worker competence:

1. *Specific job skills—the routines tied directly to a specific job.* These are not likely to be central targets of schooling. However, schooling must prepare students to learn these specific skills quickly during job-specific training.

2. *The broader "new basic skills."* A reasonable list was provided by Murnane and Levy (1996): reading, mathematics, problem solving, working in groups, communications, and simple computer use.

3. *Basic skills and strategies for learning.* The fundamental source of value in human work has become adaptability. The ability to provide exactly what someone needs quickly is worth a lot. As a function becomes stereotyped, it can be performed either completely or partly by machines, and these machines become commodities. Consequently, a special characteristic of the high-performance job world is that jobs and new job components continually emerge. This gives special value to the ability to quickly learn new processes, heuristics, and ways of viewing the world.

4. *Knowledge of the core schemata for the processes of a general line of work.* While high-performance jobs require adaptation, one platform for adaptation is the underlying productive culture and basic methodology of a line of work. For example, the materials and tools used by plumbers may change from time to time, but a certain basic understanding of fluid sources, fluid distribution, and waste disposal remains part of the plumbing business, and those with experience in even older ways of plumbing will have some advantage over the newcomer who has never threaded a pipe or cleaned a drain.

Significant trade-offs are possible among these categories of competence, especially in the beginning of a new job.[2] This has a variety of implications,

---

[1]Drops in test scores have multiple explanations, including changes in the universality of testing. What is important to the discussion is what society believed was happening.

[2]Years ago Perfetti and I (Lesgold and Perfetti, 1978) suggested that reading facility comes from various mixtures of facility in word recognition, domain knowledge, and discourse structure knowledge. The argument was basically the same as I make now: that competence is characteristically overdetermined and that having high levels of one of the core ingredients can compensate for some lack of other ingredients.

including the possibility that job incumbents may focus more attention on the first and fourth categories above and may misinterpret the uses they themselves once made of the second and third categories. We at the Learning Research and Development Center of the University of Pittsburgh have seen a few examples of this in our own workplace efforts. For example, metalworkers will claim that they learned certain mathematics they use in their work from trigonometry courses, even though we have demonstrated that those who teach these courses cannot do the mathematics to which the workers refer (shop teachers can; see Lesgold, 1996).

A more important implication is that it is difficult to demonstrate the importance of some of the above components of work readiness. The primary means for demonstrating that some piece of knowledge is necessary to some performance is to show a correlation between the extent to which the knowledge is present in different people and the extent to which they are successful in their work. A stronger test is to show that no one who is successful lacks the knowledge in question. If trade-offs are possible, these demonstrations will fail, since some workers will manage without high levels of the specific piece of knowledge, even if having it is the easiest and most reliable way to become job ready.

This leads me to suggest two research problems that need to be addressed in this area of school-to-work transition:

1. How does reusable knowledge accumulate from experience in a progression of work situations, and how can this knowledge be enhanced or facilitated?

2. How do various components of being ready for a job trade off, and what are the implications of this trade-off for worker retraining, equity in worker selection, and the relative roles of classroom and on-the-job training?

Work Complexity and Equity

Almost simultaneous with changes in the nature of work was a societal decision to make education and employment selection less discriminatory against those outside the culture that dominated higher-status and higher-paying work. This social decision evolved a body of statutes and case law that restricted testing procedures to those with (1) a demonstrated relationship to specific jobs in the case of employment selection and (2) quantitatively indexed nondiscrimination in the case of educational credentialing and selection.

So on the one hand, the valuable jobs in our society were rapidly changing, demanding more complex competencies, demanding social skills not yet enculturated into either the classroom or the educational test, and demanding new kinds of "basic skills." On the other hand, we found ourselves in need of mechanisms for allocating learning and job opportunities that did not discriminate against people who might have different cultural backgrounds and different initial learning opportunities. In the absence of a strong base of trust and a widely shared knowledge of what makes someone a good worker or a good learner, it was natural to rely on "objective" tests to make the unbiased decisions that were demanded.

OUR TESTING TECHNOLOGY

The basic idea was that a well-developed arsenal of test instruments could be tuned to be unbiased. Measures with stable long-term existence could be validated as important predictors of successful functioning in courses and jobs, we believed. Further, with a clearly established process of selection testing, disadvantaged students or workers could be selectively taught to do better on the tests.

Classical test theory evolved throughout the post-World War II period in which the social changes discussed above were occurring. Impressive mathematical development yielded a technology of testing that was extremely powerful. Students could take different tests with different items at different times in different places, and results could still be reported for them all on a single scale. Item response theory (Lord, 1980), among other technologies, allowed for great refinement of testing procedures. Soon, student performances could be compared across national boundaries as well as across time and space, or so it seemed.

From the beginning, test developers were concerned with the validity of tests as well as with their reliability. (For a good treatment of validity, see Wainer and Braun, 1988.) Initially, validity was seen as a mathematical matter, concerning the correlation of test measures with indices of real competence. However, limitations on feasibility tended to result in rather shallow demonstrations of validity in many cases. For example, many college selection tests were validated against the grades of students in their first year of college, when classes were often large and tests were similar to the selection tests characteristically used. As a result, special abilities related to test taking could, in principle, have been an important part of what the tests measured, rather than general readiness for further learning.

The diversification of cultures and curricula further interfered with validity. A common test for students from schools with different curricula must necessarily be grounded in content common to them all, and such content is either the most basic or the most abstract parts of the curriculum, at least when the test consists of short items requiring quick multiple-choice responses. As time passed, discussions of validity began to challenge the very basis of test theory, namely that a test score consists of a person's actual standing on some universal scale of achievement plus some error that has been kept small by the testing technology.

In this respect, as Mislevy (in this volume) has pointed out, the technology of testing, while impressive in its development in recent decades, was not really up to the new challenge. In a stable culture it is possible to develop reliable and valid test items. Often, however, these test items do not purely measure the desired worker or learner characteristic. Rather, they measure something that can be measured readily and that strongly predicts a less-well-understood capability. When a job is stable, the appropriate criterion for this prediction can be measured quite directly. For example, if a job involves sorting small cards with names and addresses on them, and if this kind of sorting is relatively common in the culture, it is easy to do a task analysis of that job and to develop efficient, reliable, and valid test items that predict this card-sorting skill.

However, a number of factors have pushed the criterial capabilities for which we need to test outside the envelope in which extant test theory and testing practice can be counted on to function. A major problem is that much of what we want to assess is the ability to adapt to new situations. Consider the logic of fair testing. I identify some component of a job that needs to be selected for. I publicly validate an instrument that measures that component. Because the necessary job performances are clearly established, it is easy to have a sufficiently public process of validation and it is easy to "teach to the test" in all cultures. Now, when the very skill to be predicted is the ability to adapt to new situations, we no longer have this wonderful stability of criterion and predictor measures. Indeed, it could well be that the best test of suitability for a number of modern jobs is the ability to perform in novel situations.

We could, in principle, stay fair by developing tests in which people had to apply their knowledge to situations so novel that they were distant from every possible cultural background from which a testee might come. There is one validity problem with this. The ability to perform in purely abstract situations is different from the ability to adapt "a little bit" to known procedures. So solving the cultural embeddedness problem through excessive abstraction is potentially unfair, since real jobs do not need such extreme adaptability, and it could even be that adaptability grounded in concrete knowledge is more useful than a level of abstraction removed from the real world.

But the real world is a pretty big place, parts of which are more real to you and other parts of which are more real to me. This creates a whole new testing problem and may call for an entirely new logic of testing. To assess your ability to handle problem situations that depart modestly from what you have already mastered, I need to know more about you. To handle adaptability in context, I may even need to know more about the environment in which you learned basic skills or in which you live. Except on a high level of abstraction, it is fundamentally impossible to assess adaptability without having some person-specific knowledge. But the whole logic of fair testing has been that we can find some one test that is fair for everyone and remove personal background from the process as much as possible.

One "solution" is to set a very high threshold and measure adaptability in very abstract contexts. However, this has two problems. First, there is no guarantee that the ability to think abstractly about adapting is the same as the ability to actually behave adaptively in the real world. Indeed, many humorous reactions to us professors are grounded in societal rejection of this premise.

Second, there is evidence that overly abstract test items discriminate against minority and disadvantaged groups—indeed, this is the basis of many, if not most, court challenges of selection tests. So we need to find new approaches to testing that are demonstrably fair and that, as part of being fair, measure knowledge and skills actually useful for modern productive work and civic participation.

THE PATH FROM SCHOOL TO WORK

A central means for specifying what should be taught in school is to examine what capabilities are required to pass valid selection tests for valued adult roles, such as paid jobs. However, as we have seen, there are reasons to doubt whether current criteria for employment selection are fully valid, and there is considerable disagreement about what is needed to succeed in the workplace. Accordingly, while the standards movement—a U.S. effort to reform education by increasing the standards for being deemed educated—rests on the sensible premise that standards can drive the educational process, we do face some hard questions about just what the standards should be.

Fundamentally, the problem involves counterevidence for each of the primary contenders for necessary workplace selection standards. These contenders include the following:

- basic literacy and numeracy skills;
- strong collaborative skills, including both the social skills of collaboration and the communication skills needed to sustain communication;
- basic character factors such as diligence, promptness, responsibility, and trustworthiness;
- the ability to learn quickly under self-direction;
- the ability to deal with abstractions and formalisms; and
- the ability to solve a wide range of problems easily.

However, when we probe hard, we find evidence that none of these characteristics is always necessary. For example, Lia DiBello (Laboratory for Comparative Human Cognition, University of California at San Diego, personal communication, 1996) trains bus mechanics in the use of modern just-in-time inventory systems. These systems are an aspect of high-performance work that characteristically proves difficult for traditional workers. Hence, we would think that ability to do this kind of work would depend on the special schooling that we seek in response to changes in work. DiBello reports, though, that her group has been able to train the janitors in bus garages just as easily as the mechanics and that there seem to be no special prior requirements for being trained. However, no training group has consisted exclusively or even primarily of nonmechanics, as far as I know, so it could well be that, as a group, trainees with the full range of useful preparation help the less well prepared to learn useful new roles. Even without a universal requirement, though, it is still important to understand the knowledge and skill demands of modern work and to focus research on learning and assessment, especially on competencies that have recently become more critical. I return to this issue of universality of prerequisite knowledge below.

THE DEEP DILEMMA: EDUCATION IS NECESSARY BUT NO SPECIFIC KNOWLEDGE IS NEEDED

In the present economy it appears that there is a shortage of people able to fill the high-productivity, high-paying jobs, while people with inadequate skills continue to be laid off (see Levy and Murnane, 1992). The effects of these changes in the demand for cognitive competence often fall hardest on minorities, women, and the poor. Taking the path of preparing more people for the high end of the work world would alleviate the shortage—and thus enable more wealth to be produced for more people—and would also facilitate a fairer approach to selection in many cases. It is easier to diversify a work force when many members of every targeted group are adequately trained for the work.

Achieving this higher level of readiness for high-performance work will require that we better understand just what competencies are exercised in high-performance jobs and that we have both a learning path that will get people taught those competencies and some measurement schemes that will provide guidance in navigating that path.

What implications can we draw from reflection on the nature of work in the information age? My own thinking is shaped by the following view of modern work:

• You can't see it. Much of modern work involves thinking about systems that do not exhibit any physical manifestation of their functions. For example, automobile engines are regulated dynamically by computer programs, and credit card transactions are approved by expert systems.

• It changes fast. The high-value part of modern work is a timely, tailored response to an emergent need. Ubiquitous communications allow companies to sell higher levels of customer-specific adaptations. The trend toward making communications and shipping costs independent of distance allows more competition, more markets, more rapidly emergent markets, and more rapid learning by competitors.

• Part of the work is figuring out what the work is and how it should be evaluated. When a customer presents a problem, an enterprise must often find an interpretation of the problem that it can address, find a way of solving the problem, and find a way to help the customer decide whether the solution is appropriate.

• Anything simple or well understood gets done by machines. If I can write a traditional step-by-step training procedure for a process, I may well be able to write a computer program to do it for me. To the extent that I cannot write the program, the job must involve some thinking that a worker will need to do without complete algorithmic guidance from prior training.

The volatility of knowledge value and the extent to which workers construct the knowledge they need when they confront a modern piece of work lead to a serious dilemma. On the one hand, education and experience seem more valuable than ever. The person with a good combination of rich schooling and diverse work experience is likely to do better in most jobs than someone with limited education and a limited range of experience. On the other hand, almost all jobs require some specific job training, and often there is no specific piece of knowledge that is absolutely necessary for success in that training or later on the job. This is simply a second view of the universality issue addressed above.

WHAT'S LIKELY TO BE NEW?

While much work still needs to be done, it is certainly possible to predict some of the kinds of skills that have emerged as particularly important to modern productive life. I will mention three, commenting briefly on their implications for assessment as well as schooling.

"Everything I Do at Work Is Called Cheating in School"— Collaboration as the Basis of Modern Work

Teamwork and quick thinking are often cited as critical parts of modern work. In the modern workplace, great value is placed on being able to quickly put together a team to figure out the solution to a problem and implement that solution. For example, while the steel industry in my hometown died in the 1960s and 1970s, small-batch specialty steel companies thrived and continue to do pretty well today. These companies make the exact kind of steel a customer needs for a specific project, and they do it quickly and efficiently. In fact, the steel industry is about as large in the United States today as it was 20 years ago, but with far fewer employees (Rifkin, 1995). In other manufacturing areas, each item coming down the assembly line requires different assembly activity. In Helsinki last year I visited a plant in which consecutive items reaching a workstation ranged from the size of a breadbox to the size of a small garage. The assembly instructions arrived at the workstation with the item in question, by computer, and training in the details of assembly were also available "just in time."

More often than not, it is teams of people that need to quickly learn, quickly solve a problem, and quickly configure to make something happen. A worker told me one day, "Everything I do at work used to be called cheating at school." This highlights a major difference in the demands on schooling in the age of the assembly line versus today. Instead of policing to be sure students never collaborate in their schoolwork, teachers today are struggling to find ways to let students work together and develop their collaborative work skills.

Numerous problems are raised by this change. If I insist that each student do his or her own work, and I evaluate the products of that work, there is clear accountability on both the teaching side and the learning side. If the products to be evaluated are produced by a group, there is always some lack of clarity about who did what and who knows what. Finding new assessment schemes that handle this problem is critical to making the new collaborative skills part of the school-to-work pipeline. One emerging answer is the use of broader scoring rubrics for bigger projects, perhaps combined with self-appraisals and diary accounts of how a job was done. Mislevy (Chapter 7, this volume) mentions this kind of approach when discussing the Advanced Placement art exam, but it might well stretch to group work, too.

More broadly, we need to do more research on the role of collaborative skills in modern work. In recent years, projects have been started that look specifically at the workplace and ask both how the social structure of work supports workers who may lack an important competence (see Hull, 1993; Chapter 5, this volume) and how the possession of certain social and communications skills can support informal on-the-job learning (see Nelson, Chapter 4, this volume). More such work is needed.

Dialectical Skills: Mediating Between Worlds That Are Logical Internally but Difficult to Interconnect Logically

A second area of change in productive life is that things are just plainly more complicated than they once were. Any thinking job that can be clearly described and taught as an algorithm or even as a set of reliable heuristics can also be embodied in a program and done by a computer. People are valuable because they bridge the gap between one systematic world and another and because they can handle a variety of inconsistencies that remain significant challenges to everyday software tools. This dialectical capability—understanding a complex situation from multiple viewpoints and using divergent schemes to untangle it— is much more valuable today, in both commerce and civic life. A good auto mechanic can not only fix cars but also explain the problem to a customer and get useful diagnostic information from a customer. The customer's view of the car differs from the auto designer's view, and the technician must reconcile these on the fly when talking with a customer.

Notice, however, that complexity, multiple viewpoints, and idiosyncratic approaches to bridging between systems are all problems to the traditional designer of fair, objective tests. I am reminded of the problem Escalante, from the film "Stand and Deliver," had when his students took the Advanced Placement calculus test. They all performed in a different manner than most students but all more or less alike. To the seasoned professor, if you take a weird solution path and the person next to you does the same, and it works but doesn't seem to make sense, it looks as if you cheated. Again, though, tying new problems to things you already understand and doing so quickly and powerfully is exactly the skill that is valued today. We just need to learn to measure this ability accurately and fairly.

Public Versus Private Argumentation

A related competency that is becoming more valued is the ability to jointly handle several coordinated cognitive activities. Recent work that Vimla Patel and I have undertaken (with colleagues A. Kushniruk, S. Katz, J. Arocha, and C. Pierre) with the World Bank have led me to realize that many modern jobs involve a combination of extensive work done privately, by one or a few people, with public accounts of that work that are only loosely coupled to the private argumentation structure. In many "due diligence" situations[3] there is a distinction between public, and private work. Some conclusions cannot be stated directly in public and some of the information that supports those conclusions cannot be publicly stated. There has been some indication that part of the problem in training new task managers is getting them to do a sufficient private analysis and to represent the results of that analysis in a form that is both publicly tolerable and fundamentally sound.[4]

Appraisal and management of projects are ongoing activities in many organizations like the World Bank, though they have great political and social complexity. It is not necessarily easy to either know that there is a problem that must be raised in a report or to know whether the arguments in the report are sufficient. On the one hand, there is complexity of problem formulation or problem finding. On the other hand, a part of the task is to know whether one has done an adequate appraisal. This is especially a problem when one is trying to decide whether to

---

[3]Under U.S. law, there are certain situations in which a person is required to exercise due diligence before obligating someone he or she represents or spending that person's money. For example, if a broker recommends to me that I buy shares in a new business, he or she is, of course, not responsible if the business fails. However, if I can show that the broker did not exercise reasonable diligence in checking out the new company before recommending it, he or she might be liable to make good my losses. The public statements behind a due diligence investigation are usually very short because brokers cannot directly state suspicions they had that proved groundless, for example. However, there must be a reasonable connection between what a broker reasoned and what he or she found out in investigations and what he or she tells me about the company.

[4]For the moment I assume that an argument is fundamentally sound if its public conclusions are, for all practical purposes, consistent with the full conclusions of an adequate private analysis. That is, the actions that a prudent person would take after being given the public conclusions match the actions supported in the more complete private analysis.

use materials from prior analyses or to gather new information and produce a new analysis.[5]

A project appraisal involves a set of issues, each representing a viewpoint from which the soundness of the project must be considered. There is a large set of generic issues, and therefore one component of the task is to identify which of the generic potential problem areas merit development as analysis problems. The second component of the task is to actually solve each of the identified subproblems, that is, to speak to each of the relevant issues. A third task component is the decision structure for determining that an issue has been adequately addressed, that is, that a subproblem has been solved. Finally, the fourth component is to express the results of the appraisal in a form suitable for public distribution.

Any argument involves making some claims and then offering support for those claims. Even this simple activity can be demanding, especially if the task includes careful searching for counterclaims and evidence that might support them. Arguments that must be presented in a socially or politically charged context are especially hard to develop. In essence, there are two arguments, one public and one private, that have a complex and implicit connection between them. The analyst first does the best analysis he or she can do, ignoring political realities. The results of this might be an argument for a politically difficult outcome or an argument that rests on premises that cannot be explicitly stated.

In such a case, the analyst, to adequately serve the World Bank, must find a way to state a public conclusion that captures the problem without actually claiming that the project is at risk because the ruler might die. Figure 12-1 provides a schematic example of this complexity. The top half shows a private argument, in which two pieces of evidence support one conclusion and one of them, plus some additional evidence, supports a second conclusion. Related to this private argument is the public argument diagrammed in the bottom half of the figure, which contains a set of public conclusions that, as a group, capture the practically relevant aspects of the private conclusions. In principle, the mapping between public and private conclusions may or may not be one to one.

It is possible that the public-versus-private nature of modern work is a fundamental property. It is also possible, though, that the general phenomenon of modern work is the need to loosely coordinate various clusters of problem solving and reasoning. In either case, it is readily apparent that psychology has not really addressed this area of competency and that it is likely to be productive to do so now.

---

[5]I understand, of course, that totally unconsidered use of prior report contents is not common. However, it seems quite possible that substantial expertise is involved in deciding the extent to which a project should be analyzed and reported de novo as opposed to building partly on past reports.

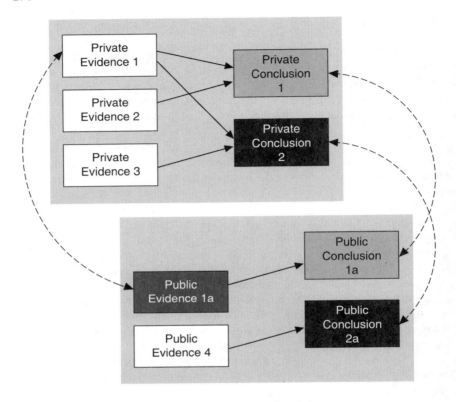

FIGURE 12-1   Public and private arguments and their relations.

Systems Understanding: A Goal for Mathematics and Science

One last candidate on my list of the new work skills is the ability to understand systems—the physical and information systems of modern work and especially the work organization's social systems. Part of the complexity of modern productive life comes from the many systems that interact with each other and with ourselves. Consider, for example, the public decisions being made about freon compounds. Certain of these compounds have been implicated in the destruction of the ozone layer. To make a good decision about whether, for example, cars with old air conditioners that use the "bad" freon should be eliminated, we need to understand the hypothesized systemic mechanisms whereby freon has this bad effect, the level of evidence to support the hypotheses defining that system, the costs and benefits to our economy, and a variety of ethical issues having to do with what sorts of costs should be paid by whom to benefit whom— a lot of complexity to deal with.

Traditional instructional design has handled complexity by breaking complex things down into simple things and then teaching each simple tidbit separately. This can be a useful learning strategy, but sometimes systems need to be broken down in different ways to reveal different aspects of their function. For example, the lungs are part of the circulatory system when one is trying to understand general cardiovascular function but closer to the pleural sac than the aorta when one is trying to understand an infection like pleurisy. Teaching by giving students different views for different purposes seems like a strong way to proceed, and some work is starting to be done in this direction (see Spiro et al., 1989). In addition, work on computer-generated explanations is starting to provide a systematic basis for developing different decompositions of a complex system to explain its aspects (see Liu, 1991). Like teaching, testing will need to be adapted to handle assessment of understanding of complexity. For purposes of guiding students toward career goals, testing systems may need to engage the student in conversations that include extensive self-analysis and self-report. This idea, that the student is an integral part of assessment of his or her own knowledge, is likely to become more important for assessments that steer the course of learning (Lesgold, 1988).

Estimation: Quickly Getting to the Right Ballpark

A known characteristic of experts is that when confronted with a problem they spend more of their time representing the problem adequately and proportionately less on the mechanics of solution. While expertise is domain specific (Chi et al., 1988), certain aspects of this expert disposition seem to be widely prevalent, and I advance the hypothesis that multiple experiences in a situation with which one has expertise may have effects that go outside the specific domain of expertise. Specifically, the ability to quickly categorize a situation as fitting approximately to a rough model may come with practice in exercising expertise. Given enough practice in quickly applying expertise in various settings, people may become able to approximate a good response very quickly even if identifying the perfect response takes quite a while.

The ability to estimate is usually considered only a practice capability with numbers. However, the world of mathematics education (see National Council of Teachers of Mathematics, 1989) is becoming more convinced that estimation requires a mixture of number sense (presumably derived from extensive experience using numbers in various ways (as counts, measurements, proportions, etc.), practice in representing situations using mathematics, and perhaps practice in computation as well. An example may help clarify this. Consider two people discussing how fast they would have to travel around the earth (presumably at the equator) to track the sun exactly. One person says he would have to go 5,000 miles per hour to match the sun. The other says that this might be about five times too fast. The second person's thinking has probably gone like this. First, we know that to match the sun we have to circle the earth once a day. Second, we know that the circumference of the earth is about 25,000 miles. There are 24 hours in a day, so that means one would have to cover a bit over 1,000 miles per hour, since 25/24 is about 1. To do such an estimation this way requires knowing how to think about the problem (covering the circumference of the earth in one 24-hour period). Some facts (the circumference of the earth and the length of a day) are needed. The arithmetic fact $25/24 \approx 1$ is only a tiny piece of the process.

So the special human capability of estimation involves system modeling, approximations, and number sense, among other capabilities. I suggest that we need to better understand which components of estimation performances are critical and how those components are acquired by ordinary folk in school, in other life experiences, and at work.

KNOWLEDGE DISTRIBUTION AND REDUNDANCY AS A FUNDAMENTAL CHARACTERISTIC OF MODERN WORK

I conclude by returning to the DiBello work discussed earlier. DiBello was able to train even janitors to do complex high-performance management of just-in-time inventory. But, as I noted, no one has tried to operate such a work system using *only* workers who had no prior domain knowledge and minimal basic communications and problem-solving preparation. In fact, a central feature of a learning organization is that it has distributed and redundant knowledge. It is not necessary for any one worker to have every useful competency, and most critical knowledge is shared by multiple people and partly embodied in the socially shared knowledge of the workplace culture.

This state of affairs is important to organizational success, since it limits the cost of losing any one team member. However, it conflicts with the basic logic that psychology often brings to job analysis. We want to be able to make broad, general statements, like "every bus garage worker needs to understand enough arithmetic to be able to quickly master the operation of just-in-time inventory management." The problem is that the standard empirical test of such a statement is to seek counterexamples. $X \supset Y$ cannot be true if we find any cases of $X \& \neg Y$. The input requirements for adaptive, distributed, redundant systems need to be stated differently and confirmed differently. We might, for example, say that "in any bus garage using just-in-time inventory systems, almost all workers need to understand enough arithmetic to be able to master the operations quickly." The empirical test of such a claim would be that when the proportion of workers without the identified arithmetic skills exceeds some threshold, the work is not done very well. We would expect a pattern something like that shown in Figure 12-2.

On the school side of preparation for work, such a relationship is pretty easy to handle. Clearly, one's usefulness for work will rise as one has more of the skills that show this kind of relationship to workplace success. Further, over time

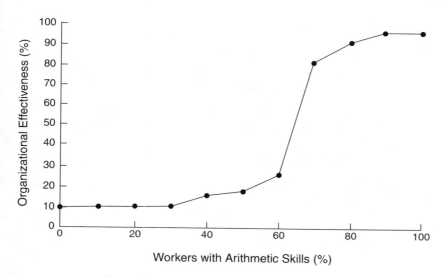

FIGURE 12-2   Example relation of job skill to group work performance.

the value of various of these skills may become more evident, with employers bidding for whichever knowledge/skill clusters are not yet being acquired almost universally. Schools, in turn, can adjust to these market signals—once the critical capabilities are better defined and measured.

On the employee-selection side, we will need to develop new standards of fairness. If I lack a skill that is needed by 75 percent of the workers in a company, the company could well afford to hire me so long as it does not make a similar concession in each hire that it makes. This creates a new view of how fairness might be assessed. Instead of asking whether jobs are distributed proportionally to the representation of different minority groups in the work-seeking population, we can start to ask whether the concessions—the hiring of an employee who lacks important skills but who can be accommodated if other workers have those skills—are distributed reasonably. A simple rule would be that minority workers not be denied their proportionate share of these concessions. An "affirmative-action" view might be that the concessionary positions should be reserved for minority applicants whenever these applicants are underrepresented in the overall workplace. Which approach to choose is not a scientific decision.

REFERENCES

Chi, M.T.H., R. Glaser, and M.J. Farr, eds.
   1988   *The Nature of Expertise*. Hillsdale, NJ: Lawrence Erlbaum Associates.

Hull, G.
  1993   Hearing other voices: A critical assessment of popular views on literacy and work. *Harvard Education Review* 63(1):20-49.
Lesgold, A.
  1988   The integration of instruction and assessment in business/military settings. In *Proceedings of the 1987 ETS Invitational Conference.* Princeton, NJ: Educational Testing Service.
  1996   Quality control for educating a smart work force. Pp. 147-191 in *Linking School and Work: Roles for Standards and Assessment*, L.B. Resnick and J. Wirt, eds. San Francisco: Jossey-Bass.
Lesgold, A., and C.A. Perfetti
  1978   Interactive process in reading comprehension. *Discourse Processes* 1:323-336.
Levy, F., and R. Murnane
  1992   U.S. earnings levels and earnings inequality: A review of recent trends and proposed explanations. *Journal of Economic Literature* 30:1333-1381.
Liu, Z-Y
  1991   Tailoring tutorial explanations via model switching. Pp. 383-403 in *Proceedings of the Contributed Sessions, 1991 Conference on Intelligent Computer-Aided Training.* NASA Conference Publication 10100, vol. II. Houston, TX: National Aeronautics and Space Administration.
Lord, F.M.
  1980   *Application of Item Response Theory to Practical Testing Problems.* Hillsdale, NJ: Lawrence Erlbaum Associates.
Murname, R.J., and F. Levy
  1996   *Teaching the New Basic Skills: Principles for Educating Children to Thrive in a Changing Economy.* New York: Free Press.
National Council of Teachers of Mathematics
  1989   *Curriculum and Evaluation Standards for School Mathematics.* Washington, DC: National Council of Teachers of Mathematics Commission on Standards for School Mathematics.
Rifkin, J.
  1995   *The End of Work: The Decline of the Global Labor Force and the Dawn of the Post-Market Era.* New York: Jeremy P. Tarcher/Putnam.
Spiro, R.J., P.J. Feltovich, R.L. Coulson, and D. Anderson
  1989   Multiple analogies for complex concepts: Antidotes for analogy-induced misconception in advanced knowledge acquisition. Pp. 498-531 in *Similarity and Analogical Reasoning*, S. Vosniadou and A. Ortony, eds. New York: Cambridge University Press.
Wainer, H., and H.I. Braun, eds.
  1988   *Test Validity.* Hillsdale, NJ: Lawrence Erlbaum Associates.

Appendix

NATIONAL ACADEMY OF SCIENCES/NATIONAL RESEARCH COUNCIL

BOARD ON TESTING AND ASSESSMENT

Transitions in Work and Learning: Implications for Assessment

March 22-23, 1996
Lecture Room, National Academy of Sciences

FRIDAY, MARCH 22

8:30 a.m. **Coffee/Pastries**

9:00 **Welcoming Remarks:**
Richard Shavelson (Stanford University and Chair, Board on Testing and Assessment)
Alan Lesgold (University of Pittsburgh, Board member, and Conference Chair)
J.D. Hoye (Executive Director, National School-to-Work Office)
Timothy Barnicle (Asst. Secretary, Employment & Training Administration, U.S. Department of Labor)

9:15 **SESSION 1: The Knowledge Gap: Rhetoric and Evidence**

Moderator: *David Grissmer* (RAND Corporation)

Papers: *Harry Holzer* (Michigan State University)
Is There a Gap Between Employer Skill Needs and the Skills of the Workforce?
Robert Zemsky (University of Pennsylvania)
Skills and the Economy: A Context for Understanding the School-to-Work Transition

Discussants: *Darvin Winick* (Advisor to Texas Governor George W. Bush)
Seth Zimmer (Southwestern Bell Corporation)

FRIDAY, MARCH 22 (cont'd.)

10:45   **Break**

11:00   **SESSION 2: What is Work? Rhetoric and Ethnographic Evidence**

Moderator: *James Outtz* (Outtz and Associates and Board member)

Papers: *Bonalyn Nelsen* (Cornell and Stanford Universities)
              Should Social Skills be in the Vocational Curriculum?
              —Evidence from the Field of Automotive Repair
              Glynda Hull (University of California, Berkeley)
              Manufacturing the New Worker: Literate Activities
              and Working Identities in a "High Performance" vs. a
              Traditionally Organized Workplace

Discussants: *Stephen Barley* (Stanford University)
             Brigitte Jordan (Institute for Research on Learning)
             Vivian Woods (Soddy Elementary School, Soddy-Daisy,
             Tennessee)

12:30 p.m.   **Lunch/Discussion Sessions** (Box lunches available)

2:15 p.m.   **SESSION 3: Assessing Assessment: What We Know
                  How to Measure, What We Need to Know**

Moderator: *Vicki Vandaveer* (The Vandaveer Group, Inc.)

Papers: *Kenneth Pearlman* (Lucent Technologies)
              21st Century Measures for 21st Century Work
              Robert Mislevy (Educational Testing Service)
              Postmodern Test Theory

Discussants: *Sandra Black* (Hamilton County Department of Education, Chattanooga, TN)
             Robert Linn (University of Colorado and Vice Chair,
             Board on Testing and Assessment)

4:30   **Reception—Members' Room**

SATURDAY, MARCH 23

8:30 a.m.   **Coffee/Pastries**

9:00   **SESSION 4: Caution Flags**

Moderator: *Iraline Barnes* (Vice President for Corporate Relations,
                    PEPCO and Board member)

Papers: *Dennis Parker* (NAACP Legal Defense and Education Fund)
                    Legal Restrictions on Assessments
                    Neal Schmitt (Michigan State University)
                    Assessment Without Adverse Impact

Discussants: *Henry Braun* (Educational Testing Service)
                    David Finkelman (St. Mary's College)
                    Lawrence Lorber (Verner, Liipfert, Bernhard, McPherson
                    and Hand)

10:30   **Break**

10:45   **SESSION 5: Visions of the School-to-Work Transition**

Moderator: *Laurie Bassi* (American Society for Training and Devel-
                    opment and Vice Chair, Board on Testing and Assess-
                    ment)

Speakers: *Lauren Resnick* (University of Pittsburgh and New Stan-
                    dards Project)
                    Larry Cuban (Stanford University)

Discussant: *Nevzer Stacey* (Special Assistant for Research and Develop-
                    ment, National Office of School-to-Work Opportunities)

1:00 p.m.   **Lunch/Discussion Sessions** (Box lunches available)

2:30   **Closing Synthesis**
                    Alan Lesgold
                    Lisa Lynch (Chief Economist, U.S. Department of Labor)

3:30   **Adjourn**

*Conference sponsored by the National School-to-Work Office,
under a grant administered by the U.S. Department of Labor*